Securing Remote Access in Palo Alto Networks

Practical techniques to enable and protect remote users, improve your security posture, and troubleshoot next-generation firewalls

Tom Piens

BIRMINGHAM—MUMBAI

Securing Remote Access in Palo Alto Networks

Group Product Manager: Wilson D'souza
Publishing Product Manager: Vijin Boricha
Senior Editor: Shazeen Iqbal
Content Development Editor: Rafiaa Khan
Technical Editor: Shruthi Shetty
Copy Editor: Safis Editing
Project Coordinator: Shagun Saini
Proofreader: Safis Editing
Indexer: Rekha Nair
Production Designer: Jyoti Chauhan

First published: June 2021

Production reference: 1030621

Published by Packt Publishing Ltd.
Livery Place
35 Livery Street
Birmingham
B3 2PB, UK.

ISBN 978-1-80107-744-6

www.packt.com

I want to dedicate this book to my son, godson, and newborn nephew: life starts at 40, so don't grow up too fast.

Contributors

About the author

Tom Piens, PCNSE, CISSP, and founder of PANgurus, has over 10 years of experience working with Palo Alto Networks customers. Tom has been on the forefront of engaging with customers, responding to questions, and analysing unique needs to apply the best possible solutions or workarounds. He has authored a great many articles on the Palo Alto Networks knowledge base and discussion forum solutions, and a book, *Mastering Palo Alto Networks*. Also known as `reaper` on the PANgurus and LIVEcommunity forums, and `PANWreaper` on Twitter, Tom has been recognized by Palo Alto Networks user groups and community members, and by countless thankful customers.

I want to extend a special thanks to Nick "Ndx" for helping to review and fact-check this book, Aref Alsouqi for being a technical sounding board, and Rutger Truyers for his much-appreciated insights.

In these trying times I have very much enjoyed their friendship above all.

About the reviewer

Kris Znamierowski is an IT professional with over 18 years of experience in securing and supporting multiple operating systems, including PAN-OS, Microsoft, Linux, and BSD UNIX. An OpenBSD user since forever. He holds many credentials from industry leaders.

Table of Contents

2

Configuring Advanced GlobalProtect Features

3

Setting up Site-to-Site VPNs and Large-Scale VPNs

4

Configuring Prisma Access

Section 2: Tools, Troubleshooting, and Best Practices

5 Enabling Features to Improve Your Security Posture

6 Anti-Phishing with User Credential Detection

7 Practical Troubleshooting and Best Practices Tools

Preface

In this book, we will review remote connectivity in depth and learn about the different ways to deploy GlobalProtect and site-to-site VPN. Besides traditional methods, we will also learn about Large Scale VPN and Prisma Access SASE. Other topics that will be covered include anti-phishing and credential detection, hardening the management interface, and getting the most out of your logs.

Who this book is for

This book is for anyone who wants to learn more about remote access for users and remote locations leveraging GlobalProtect, Prisma Access, and Large Scale VPN. You will learn about the added value that log forwarding can bring and how to improve the security posture of your management interface. Anti-phishing and credential detection are covered in depth to help those who want to protect their organization from credential theft and data leaks.

What this book covers

Chapter 1, *Centralizing logs*, is all about how to get more out of logging.

Chapter 2, *Configuring Advanced GlobalProtect Features*, looks at best practices, troubleshooting, and advanced configuration.

Chapter 3, *Setting up site-to-site VPNs and Large Scale VPNs*, covers the ins and outs of traditional IPSec and GlobalProtect as a LargeScale VPN solution.

Chapter 4, *Configuring Prisma Access*, explores the complete configuration of a Prisma Access deployment.

Chapter 5, *Enabling features to improve your security posture*, talks about configuring advanced security measures to reach compliance.

Chapter 6, *Anti Phishing with User Credential Detection*, gets into how to prevent the leaking of user credentials due to phishing or misuse.

Chapter 7, *Practical troubleshooting and Best Practice Tools*, explains troubleshooting for User-ID and NAT and some best practices.

To get the most out of this book

To get the most out of this book, it is highly recommended that you have a small lab at your disposal with two firewalls, Windows 10, and Windows Server 2016. Access to a Panorama management server would be helpful to follow the covered material but not required. Familiarity with IPSec, syslog, and accessing systems through CLI is recommended, as well as working experience with PAN-OS. Basic knowledge of Palo Alto Networks, network protocols, and network design would be helpful, so reading Mastering Palo Alto Networks first is recommended.

Software/hardware covered in the book	Requirements
PAN-OS 10.0	A hardware chassis. A local hypervisor such as ESXi. A cloud service subscription with a provider such as Azure, AWS, or GCP.
Prisma Access	No requirements, but there is no free trial of this product available at the time of writing. Chapter 4, Prisma Access, is intended as preparation and reference material for if your company intends to deploy Prisma Access.
GlobalProtect	Windows 10 or macOS. Windows Server 2016.
MineMeld	Any Docker-capable system.

If you are using the digital version of this book, we advise you to type the code yourself or access the code via the GitHub repository (link available in the next section). Doing so will help you avoid any potential errors related to the copying and pasting of code.

Code in Action

Code in Action videos for this book can be viewed at `https://bit.ly/3votQBS`.

Download the colour images

We also provide a PDF file that has colour images of the screenshots/diagrams used in this book. You can download it here: `https://www.packtpub.com/sites/default/files/downloads/9781801077446_ColorImages.pdf`.

Conventions used

There are a number of text conventions used throughout this book.

`Code in text`: Indicates code words in text, database table names, folder names, filenames, file extensions, pathnames, dummy URLs, user input, and Twitter handles. Here is an example: "Mount the downloaded `WebStorm-10*.dmg` disk image file as another disk in your system."

A block of code is set as follows:

```
html, body, #map {
 height: 100%;
 margin: 0;
 padding: 0
}
```

When we wish to draw your attention to a particular part of a code block, the relevant lines or items are set in bold:

```
[default]
exten => s,1,Dial(Zap/1|30)
exten => s,2,Voicemail(u100)
exten => s,102,Voicemail(b100)
exten => i,1,Voicemail(s0)
```

Any command-line input or output is written as follows:

```
$ mkdir css
$ cd css
```

Bold: Indicates a new term, an important word, or words that you see onscreen. For example, words in menus or dialog boxes appear in the text like this. Here is an example: "Select **System info** from the **Administration** panel."

> **Tips or important notes**
>
> Appear like this.

Get in touch

Feedback from our readers is always welcome.

General feedback: If you have questions about any aspect of this book, mention the book title in the subject of your message and email us at `customercare@packtpub.com`.

Errata: Although we have taken every care to ensure the accuracy of our content, mistakes do happen. If you have found a mistake in this book, we would be grateful if you would report this to us. Please visit `www.packtpub.com/support/errata`, selecting your book, clicking on the Errata Submission Form link, and entering the details.

Piracy: If you come across any illegal copies of our works in any form on the Internet, we would be grateful if you would provide us with the location address or website name. Please contact us at `copyright@packt.com` with a link to the material.

If you are interested in becoming an author: If there is a topic that you have expertise in and you are interested in either writing or contributing to a book, please visit `authors.packtpub.com`.

Reviews

Please leave a review. Once you have read and used this book, why not leave a review on the site that you purchased it from? Potential readers can then see and use your unbiased opinion to make purchase decisions, we at Packt can understand what you think about our products, and our authors can see your feedback on their book. Thank you!

For more information about Packt, please visit `packt.com`.

Section 1: Leveraging the Cloud and Enabling Remote Access

In this section, we will configure and troubleshoot remote connectivity through direct access and the cloud.

The following chapters will be covered in this section:

- *Chapter 1, Centralizing logs*
- *Chapter 2, Configuring Advanced GlobalProtect Features*
- *Chapter 3, Setting up site-to-site VPNs and Large Scale VPNs*
- *Chapter 4, Configuring Prisma Access*

1
Centralizing Logs

In this chapter, we will take a closer look at how to forward firewall logs to an external system and discuss some of the benefits. Logs can be forwarded to an external **Security Incident and Event Management System** (**SIEM**) and can be used to create a range of alerts whenever an interesting event occurs. You will learn how to set up the configuration and apply best practices when dealing with log forwarding. We will then review how logs can be forwarded to **Panorama and log collectors**, as well as how to leverage alternative log protocols such as **syslog**. We will also cover how to troubleshoot forwarding issues and how to apply filters to forwarding profiles to specify which log events are forwarded.

In this chapter, we are going to cover the following main topics:

- Understanding log forwarding profiles and best practices
- Learning about Panorama and log collectors
- Forwarding logs to syslog, SMTP, and other options
- Exploring log forwarding profiles
- Troubleshooting logs and log forwarding

Technical requirements

For this chapter, you will need to have a **Palo Alto Networks** firewall set up and connected to a management network. It will be helpful if you are able to spin up a syslog server and email relay to reproduce the log forwarding settings we are about to configure. If you can set up or repurpose a **Panorama instance**, you will be able to follow along with some of the threat correlation examples.

Check out the following link to see the Code in Action video:
`https://bit.ly/3oTeYZW`

Understanding log forwarding profiles and best practices

In this section, you will learn the steps required to ensure logs are forwarded to an external system. You will also learn how to apply filters so that only specific types of events are forwarded, as well as how to ensure **Log forwarding** configuration is applied automatically. First, we will look at where and how logs are stored.

Allocating log storage

All **NGFW firewalls** and **Panorama Systems** are built from a Linux operating system running proprietary *PAN-OS* on top. Log files for the system daemons reside in the root partition. They are only accessible via the *command line* and are included in a `Tech Support` file for troubleshooting. All logs related to PAN-OS live in the `/opt/panlogs` partition. Use the following command to review filesystem usage statistics:

```
reaper@PA-VM> show system disk-space

Filesystem      Size  Used Avail Use% Mounted on
/dev/root       7.0G  4.2G  2.5G  64% /
none            3.5G   92K  3.5G   1% /dev
/dev/sda5        16G  2.9G   13G  20% /opt/pancfg
/dev/sda6       8.0G  1.4G  6.3G  18% /opt/panrepo
tmpfs           2.8G  2.4G  420M  86% /dev/shm
cgroup_root     3.5G     0  3.5G   0% /cgroup
/dev/sda8        21G  598M   20G   3% /opt/panlogs
```

In this example, `/dev/sda8` is a partition on the local disk that's used to store logs. Some of the larger hardware platforms may have a secondary hard disk for logging, and on VM firewalls, an additional disk can be installed post-deployment.

The available disk space needs to be shared by all the different log databases, so it is worth reviewing how much space is allocated to each database and tweaking the quotas and expiration periods to optimize them for retention. You can review the current quotas with the following command:

```
reaper@PA-VM> show system logdb-quota

Quotas:
      system: 4.00%,  0.629 GB Expiration-period: 0 days
      config: 4.00%,  0.629 GB Expiration-period: 0 days
       alarm: 3.00%,  0.472 GB Expiration-period: 0 days
     traffic: 29.00%, 4.559 GB Expiration-period: 0 days
      threat: 15.00%, 2.358 GB Expiration-period: 0 days
...snipped for brevity...
Disk usage:
traffic: Logs and Indexes: 211M Current Retention: 46 days
threat: Logs and Indexes: 24K Current Retention: 0 days
system: Logs and Indexes: 11M Current Retention: 46 days
config: Logs and Indexes: 21M Current Retention: 46 days
...snipped for brevity...
```

As you can see, the traffic logs are only assigned 29% of the totally available log space on this particular firewall.

These quotas can be adjusted via the web interface by going to **Device** > **Setup** > **Management** > **Logging and Reporting Settings**, as shown in the following screenshot. The log databases on the left represent logs that are the direct result of *sessions* or *system events* taking place; the column on the right contains the *summary databases* that are used to compile larger datasets containing statistical data that can be used in reporting:

Logging and Reporting Settings

Log Storage | Log Export and Reporting | Pre-Defined Reports | Log Collector Status

Log Storage Quota

	Quota(%)	Quota(GB/MB)	Max Days
Traffic	29	4.56 GB	[1 - 2000]
Threat	15	2.36 GB	[1 - 2000]
Config	4	643.88 MB	[1 - 2000]
System	4	643.88 MB	[1 - 2000]
Alarm	3	482.91 MB	[1 - 2000]
App Stats	4	643.88 MB	[1 - 2000]
HIP Match	3	482.91 MB	[1 - 2000]
GlobalProtect	1	160.97 MB	[1 - 2000]
App Pcaps	1	160.97 MB	[1 - 2000]
Extended Threat Pcaps	1	160.97 MB	[1 - 2000]
Debug Filter Pcaps	1	160.97 MB	[1 - 2000]
IP-Tag	1	160.97 MB	[1 - 2000]
User-ID	1	160.97 MB	[1 - 2000]
HIP Reports	1	160.97 MB	[1 - 2000]
Data Filtering Captures	1	160.97 MB	[1 - 2000]
GTP and Tunnel	2	321.94 MB	[1 - 2000]
SCTP	0	0.00 MB	[1 - 2000]
Authentication	1	160.97 MB	[1 - 2000]
Decryption	1	160.97 MB	[1 - 2000]

Traffic Summary	7	1.10 GB	[1 - 2000]
Threat Summary	2	321.94 MB	[1 - 2000]
GTP and Tunnel Summary	1	160.97 MB	[1 - 2000]
SCTP Summary	0	0.00 MB	[1 - 2000]
URL Summary	2	321.94 MB	[1 - 2000]
Decryption Summary	1	160.97 MB	[1 - 2000]
Hourly Traffic Summary	3	482.91 MB	[1 - 2000]
Hourly Threat Summary	1	160.97 MB	[1 - 2000]
Hourly GTP and Tunnel Summary	0.75	120.73 MB	[1 - 2000]
Hourly SCTP Summary	0	0.00 MB	[1 - 2000]
Hourly URL Summary	1	160.97 MB	[1 - 2000]
Hourly Decryption Summary	0	0.00 MB	[1 - 2000]
Daily Traffic Summary	1	160.97 MB	[1 - 2000]
Daily Threat Summary	1	160.97 MB	[1 - 2000]
Daily GTP and Tunnel Summary	0.75	120.73 MB	[1 - 2000]
Daily SCTP Summary	0	0.00 MB	[1 - 2000]
Daily URL Summary	1	160.97 MB	[1 - 2000]
Daily Decryption Summary	0	0.00 MB	[1 - 2000]
Weekly Traffic Summary	1	160.97 MB	[1 - 2000]
Weekly Threat Summary	1	160.97 MB	[1 - 2000]
Weekly GTP and Tunnel Summary	0.75	120.73 MB	[1 - 2000]
Weekly SCTP Summary	0	0.00 MB	[1 - 2000]
Weekly URL Summary	0.75	120.73 MB	[1 - 2000]

Figure 1.1 – Logging and reporting settings

As hardware platforms are somewhat limited in terms of their capacity for storing logs, the need to export logs for a longer log retention period may arise quite quickly. A production firewall may see up to 40 GB or more of logs being created daily, thus decreasing log retention to less than a day on smaller platforms. Virtual machines, on the other hand, support having an additional disk added to them, which we will review in the next section.

Adding disk space to a VM firewall

Virtual appliances, both firewalls and Panorama, support local storage expansion by having additional virtual disks added to enlarge their log capacity.

> **Important note**
>
> The primary disk that's assigned to a virtual system cannot be enlarged to accommodate more logs. The partitions are predefined and additional disk space will be left unused.

As shown in the following screenshot, an additional disk can be added that's between 60 GB and 2 TB in size to a firewall VM. Panorama VM can support from 1 to 14 2-TB disks, or one single 24-TB disk in **Panorama mode**. Panorama systems that are deployed in **Legacy mode**, which means they were installed in an older version and have since been upgraded, can have a single disk added that's up to 8 TB in size:

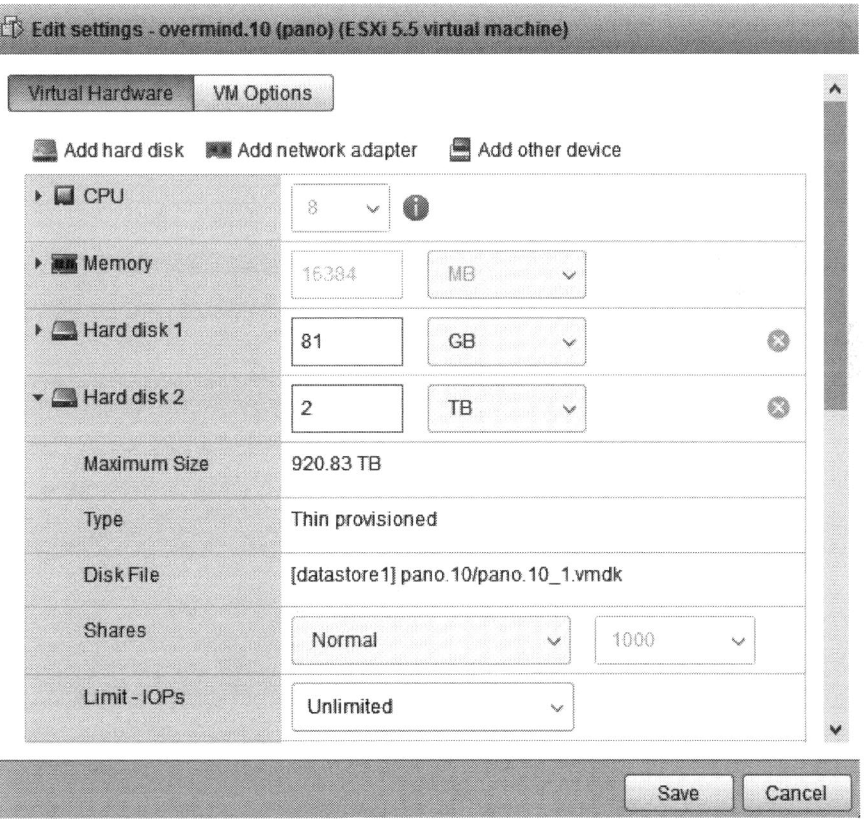

Figure 1.2 – Adding disks to a VM

Disks need to be **thick provisioned**, and the controller must be set to **SCSI**. Make sure that you shut down the system before adding the new disk. During bootup, the disk will be discovered and mounted as the new `/opt/panlogs` partition.

The next stage is to enable log forwarding to an *external system*.

Learning about Panorama and log collectors

To enable log forwarding to Panorama, the firewall must be connected to a **Panorama server**. This can be achieved by adding the Panorama IP via **Device** > **Setup** > **Panorama Settings**, as shown in the following screenshot:

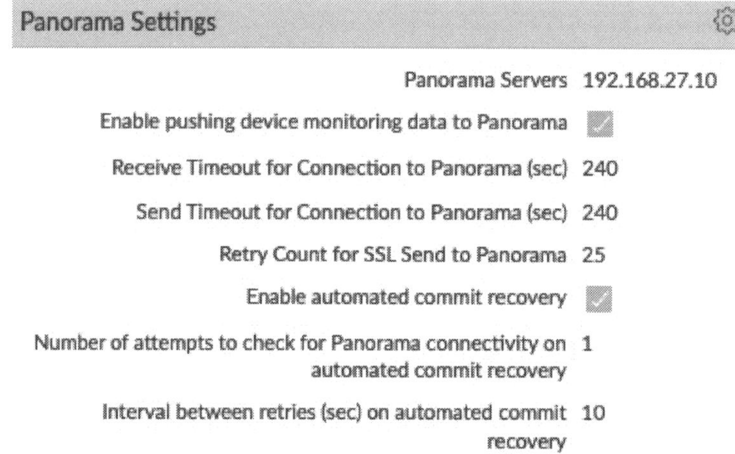

Figure 1.3 – Panorama settings on the firewall

Once the firewall has established a connection with Panorama, Panorama sets its external logging destinations to what you specify in the collector group configuration.

As shown in the following screenshot, enabling **Enable log redundancy across collectors** will ensure each log entry has a copy on a different log collector in the same group. Enabling **Forward to all collectors in the preference list** will let *PA-5200* and *PA-7000* devices forward to all collectors in a preference list, managed by Panorama in a *round-robin* fashion. Otherwise, the default behavior is to send logs to the first available collector in the list:

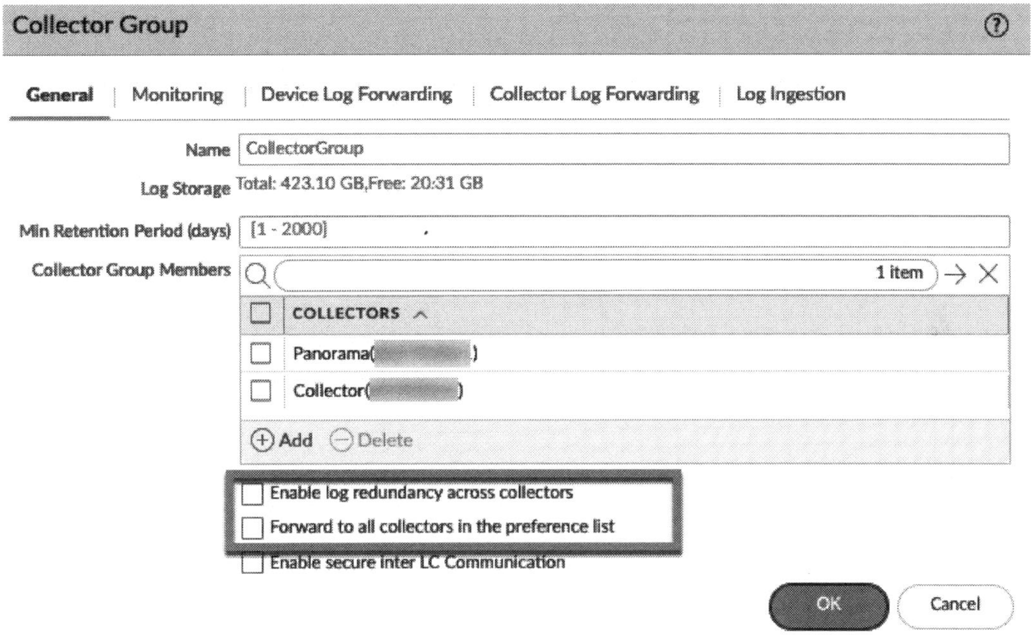

Figure 1.4 – Collector Group general settings

In the **Device Log Forwarding** tab, you can select firewall devices and assign a list of collectors that they may send logs to. The first member of a collector group is the primary collector; firewalls will send their logs to this collector for as long as it is available, using the next collector down the list as a fallback collector for redundancy. In the following screenshot, we have two firewalls that have different preferences assigned for the two available collectors. The firewall called **PANgurus** will send logs to **Panorama** itself, while the **RemoteLAB** firewall will send logs to **Collector**. If one of the log destinations becomes unavailable, the firewalls will fall back to the second collector in the list:

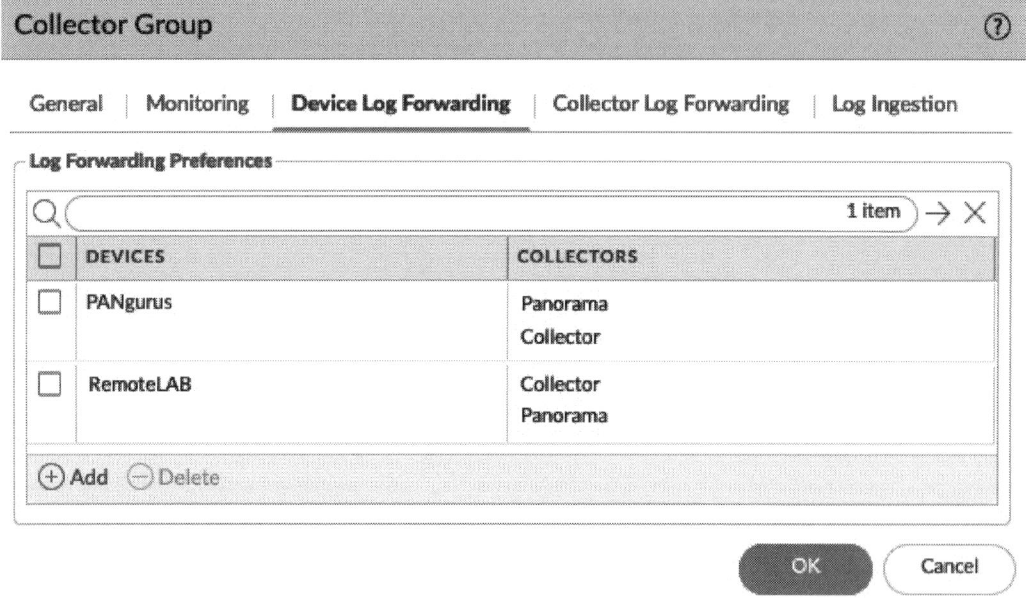

Figure 1.5 – Device log forwarding

In the next section, we will review other useful log forwarding options.

Forwarding logs to syslog, SMTP, and other options

In addition to forwarding logs to Panorama, other **server profiles** can be set up so that logs can be sent to a third-party log management or **SIEM** via **Simple Network Management Protocol** (**SNMP**). All profiles can be created in the **Device** > **Server Profiles** menu.

SNMP trap server profile

As shown in the following screenshot, there are two variations of the **SNMP trap profile**. **SNMP protocol version V2c** is very simple and requires only a server IP or FQDN, as well as a community string. This is insecure and should not be deployed in an untrusted network and should only be used if the receiving server is legacy. The **V3** protocol version uses both an authentication password and a privacy password. SNMP traps and the privacy password are encrypted using `AES 128`; the authentication password is sent hashed with `SHA1-160`. Both passwords need to be between 8 and 256 characters in length. `engineID` is used as an identification number by the SNMP server and must consist of a hexadecimal format, prefixed by `0x` and another 10 to 128 characters. If this is left empty, the firewall will use its serial number as the ID:

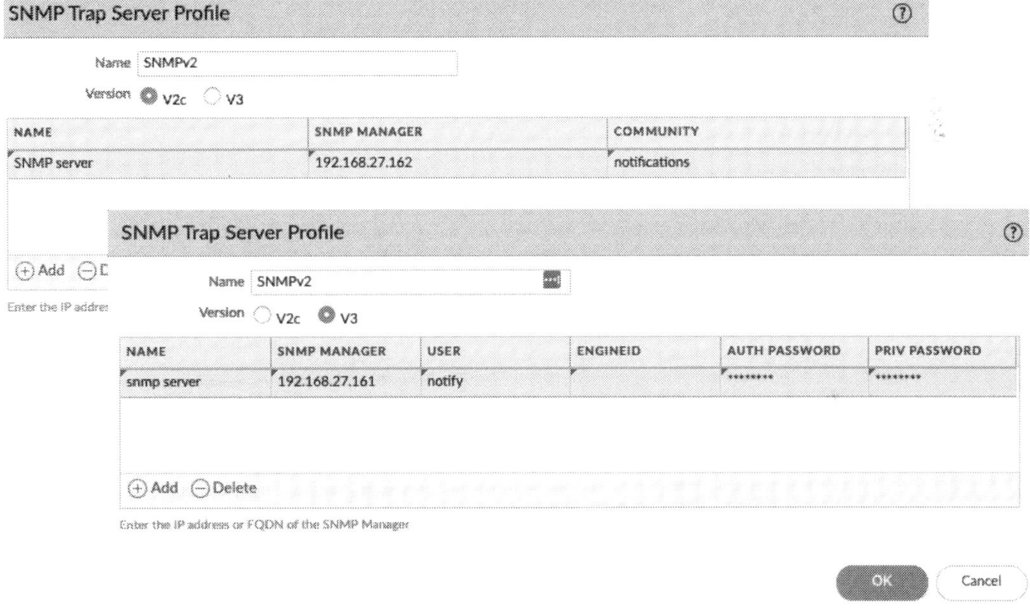

Figure 1.6 – SNMP trap profile

Syslog server profile

As you can see in the following screenshot, for **syslog**, you can select traditional **UDP** or **TCP** connections over port `514` or enable **ssl** encryption via port `6514`. These ports can be changed if needed. The format can be changed to either **BSD** or RFC5424 **IETF**, and the facility field can be adjusted to accommodate how the receiving server manages incoming messages:

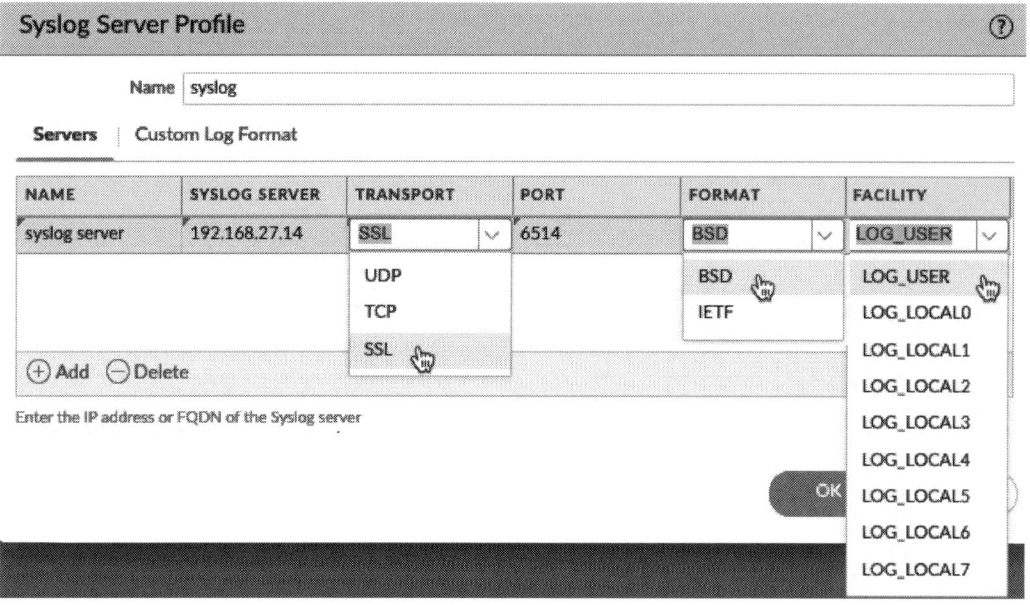

Figure 1.7 – Syslog server settings

An additional feature in the syslog profile is the ability to select the fields to include in forwarded logs for each log database. As shown in the following screenshot, this allows you to choose which fields and in which order they will appear in the forwarded log. This can come in handy if only a limited number of fields are supported, or to weed out unneeded log data. If the syslog server requires some characters to be escaped, you can list them here and define the escape character.

For example, a semicolon (;) may need to be escaped by encapsulating it with single quotes (') for compatibility reasons. Enable escaping and add the required characters, as shown here:

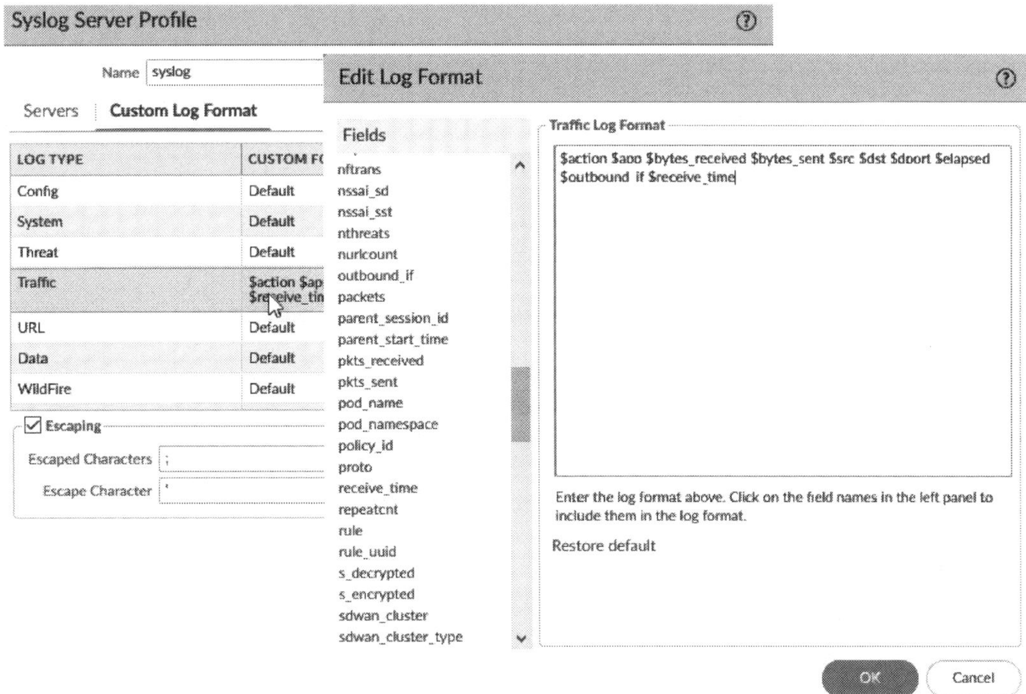

Figure 1.8 – Syslog custom log format

By default, the forwarded syslog message will include the source firewall's FQDN hostname. If the syslog server prefers an IP address or simple hostname, this default value can be changed in **Device** > **Setup** > **Logging and Reporting Settings** > **Log Export and Reporting** > **Syslog HOSTNAME Format.**

Email server profile

The **Simple Mail Transfer Protocol** (**SMTP**) profile can be configured with a friendly **Email Display Name** (this display name is injected in the **From** field in `smtp` DATA) so that the recipient can easily identify the firewall as the sender, the source email address (so that the relay will accept the sender), and the recipient. Only one email can be added in the **To** field, so an additional sender field is available to add a second email address. As shown in the following screenshot, since PAN-OS 10.0, the connection can be set to use **SMTP over TLS 1.1** or **1.2** for added security. The authentication method can be set to **Auto**, **Login**, or **Plain: Login** with a `base64` encoded username and password but send them separately or **Plain** with a `Base64` encoded username and password but send them together. `Auto` will let the client and server sort out the preferred method of sending the username and password.

Logs can also be customized so that only the relevant fields are forwarded via email:

Figure 1.9 – SMTP profile

Important consideration

Emails can be a great notification method for critical events as most people will have immediate access to incoming emails, but over-abundant use of email notifications may lead to alert fatigue and important messages may go ignored or filtered. Use email notifications sparingly and only for the most critical notifications.

HTTP server profile

The **HTTP profile** can be used in two separate ways; first, you can add server details, choose a HTTP or HTTPS protocol, set the destination port and TLS version. Second, a certificate profile can be added, and a username and password can also be added.

This profile can be used to simply forward logs via HTTP or the payload can be edited to integrate with third-party API- or HTTP-based services. Several pre-defined payloads are available, so, as illustrated in the following screenshot, ServiceNow tickets can be created as the result of a log file being generated:

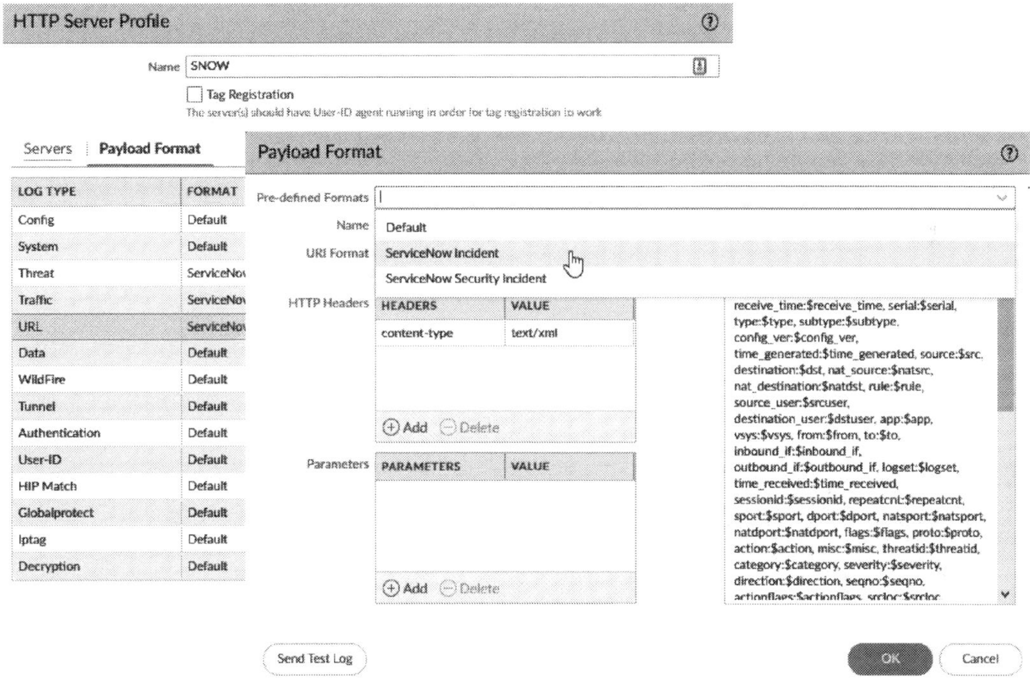

Figure 1.10 – Predefined formatting

As shown in the following screenshot, you can also enable **Tag Registration**. This changes the profile from regular log forwarding to a dynamic tagging role. This type of profile can be used to send dynamic tag registration or deregistration to a remote **User-ID Agent** (both a firewall and server installed agent) that has XML enabled. See the *Log forwarding profile* section later in this chapter for more details:

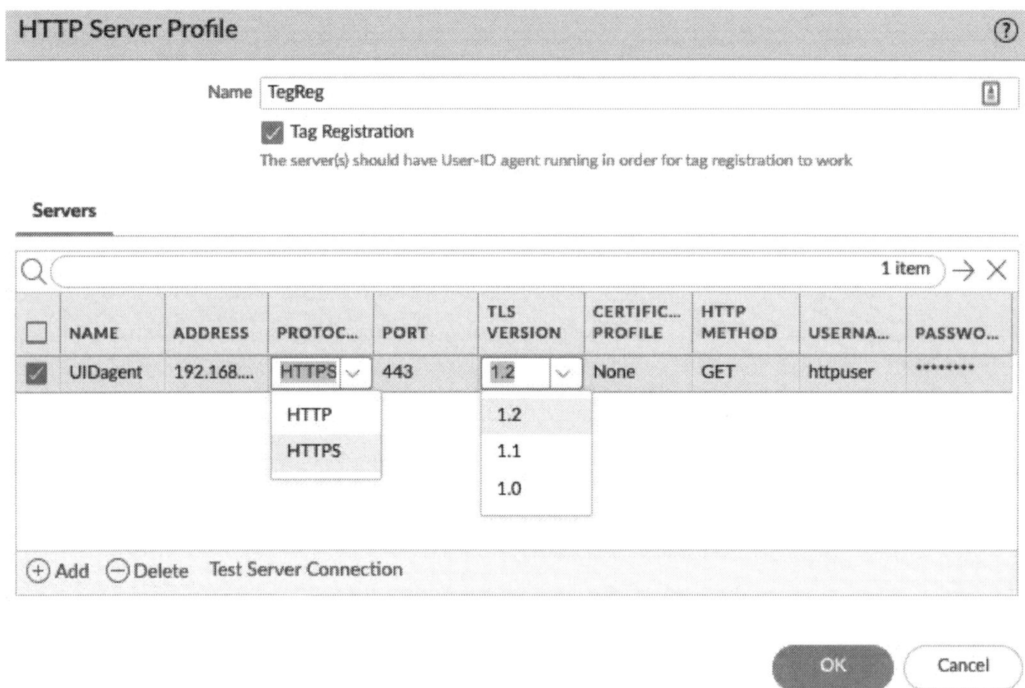

Figure 1.11 – HTTP server profile

For a regular **HTTP Server Profile**, the GET, PUT, POST, and DELETE methods are available, while for **Tag Registration**, only **GET** is supported as a HTTP method currently.

Netflow Profile

The **Netflow Profile** is the only profile that is assigned directly to an interface, as shown in the following screenshot. Unlike other log forwarding server profiles, no filter can be added to selectively forward certain logs; instead, all session information on an interface is directly streamed to the Netflow server:

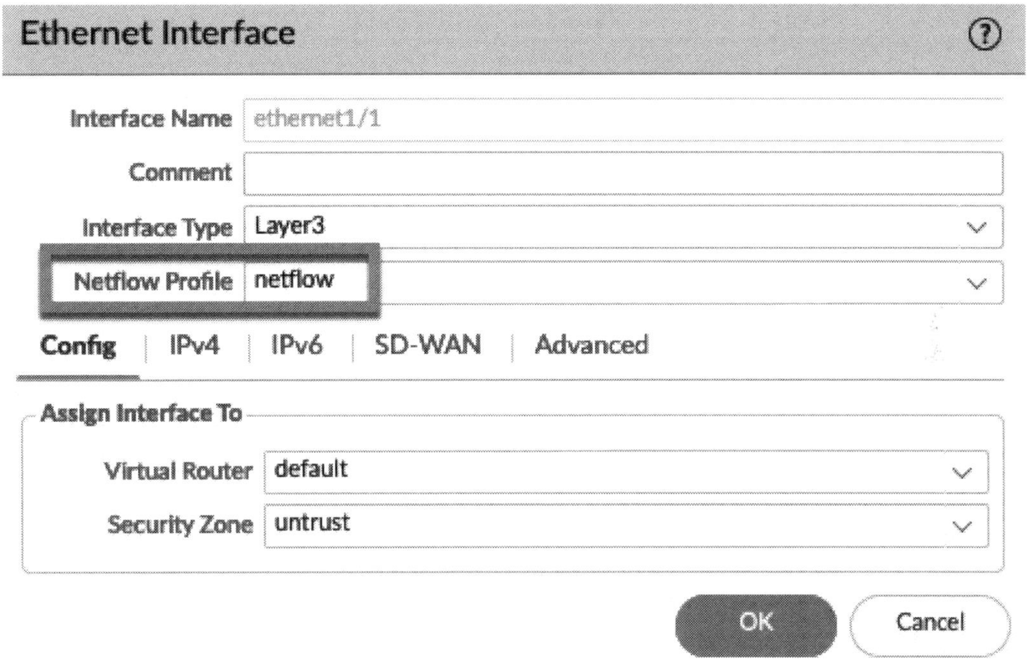

Ethernet Interface	
Interface Name	ethernet1/1
Comment	
Interface Type	Layer3
Netflow Profile	netflow

Config | IPv4 | IPv6 | SD-WAN | Advanced

Assign Interface To

Virtual Router	default
Security Zone	untrust

OK Cancel

Figure 1.12 – Adding a Netflow profile to an interface

Now that we have reviewed the available log forwarding profiles, we'll learn how to use them to forward *logs*.

Configuring system log forwarding on the firewall

Logs on the firewall fall roughly into two main categories: **system logs** and **session-based logs**. Each is made up of several more specific logs. Log forwarding must be configured for each log type individually. The system logs can be configured via **Device** > **Log Settings**. As shown in the following screenshot, the available logs are **System**, **Configuration**, **User-ID**, **HIP Match**, **GlobalProtect**, and **IP Tag**:

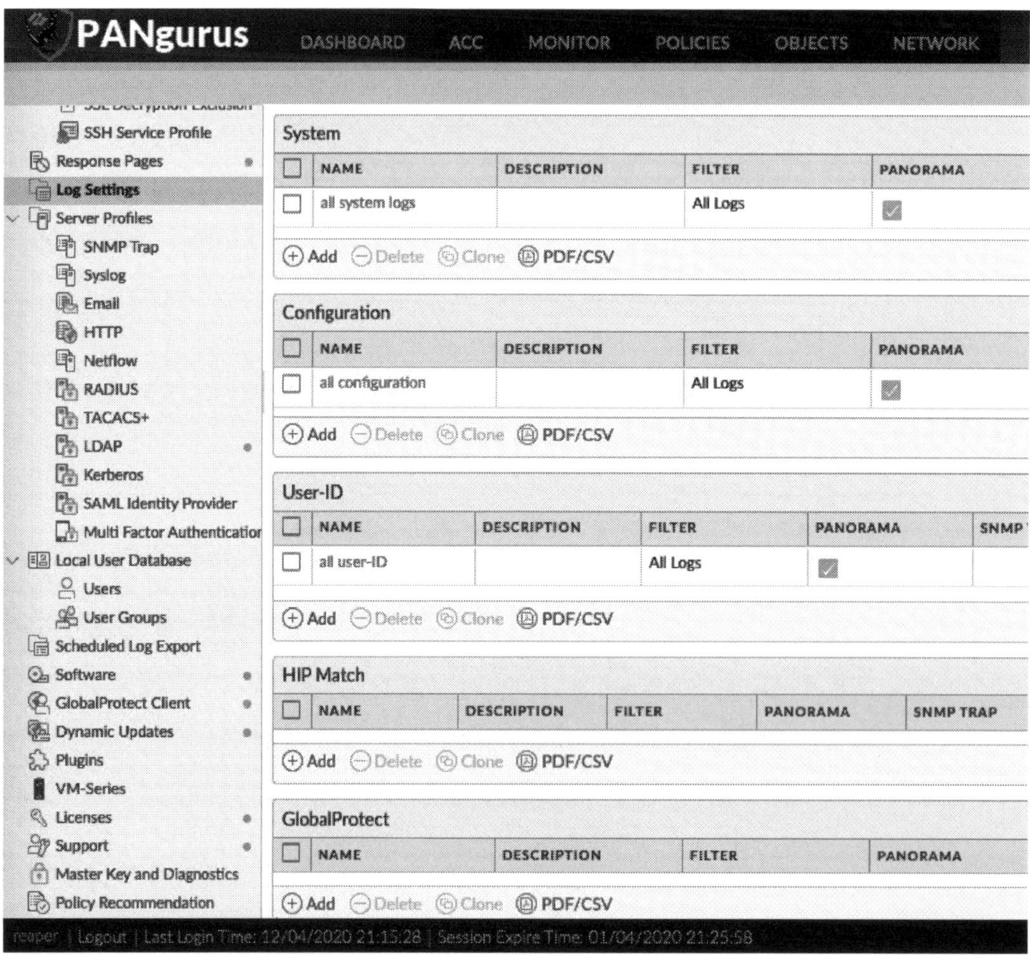

Figure 1.13 – System log forwarding configuration

Each log type can have multiple profiles associated with it, thus allowing filters and filter-specific actions to be applied. All the profiles are applied, so if a profile exists that sends all the logs of a certain type to Panorama, for example, a second profile for the same log type with a filter does not need to have Panorama checked.

In the preceding screenshot, you can see that we have already set up log forwarding for **System log**, **Configuration logs**, and **User-ID logs** to be sent to Panorama. Additional log forwarding **Server Profiles** can be added in the same profile, or in different profiles with different filters assigned. The following screenshot shows how to add an additional profile with a **Filter** set to critical events and one or more log forwarding profiles.

When this profile is added to the system logs, both profiles will be applied at the same time for each log. Log forwarding actions will be applied, depending on the filters that have been set in the profiles: the **all system logs** profile will always forward all logs to Panorama, while critical system events will match both profiles. The syslog server listed in the second profile will also receive the log:

Figure 1.14 – Adding additional server profiles to the System log forwarding profile

To determine a **Filter**, if any, you can click the little arrow to the right of the **Filter** field. **Severity filters** are preloaded and can simply be clicked. Alternatively, you can open the filter builder to review all the available attributes and values that can be added to the filter:

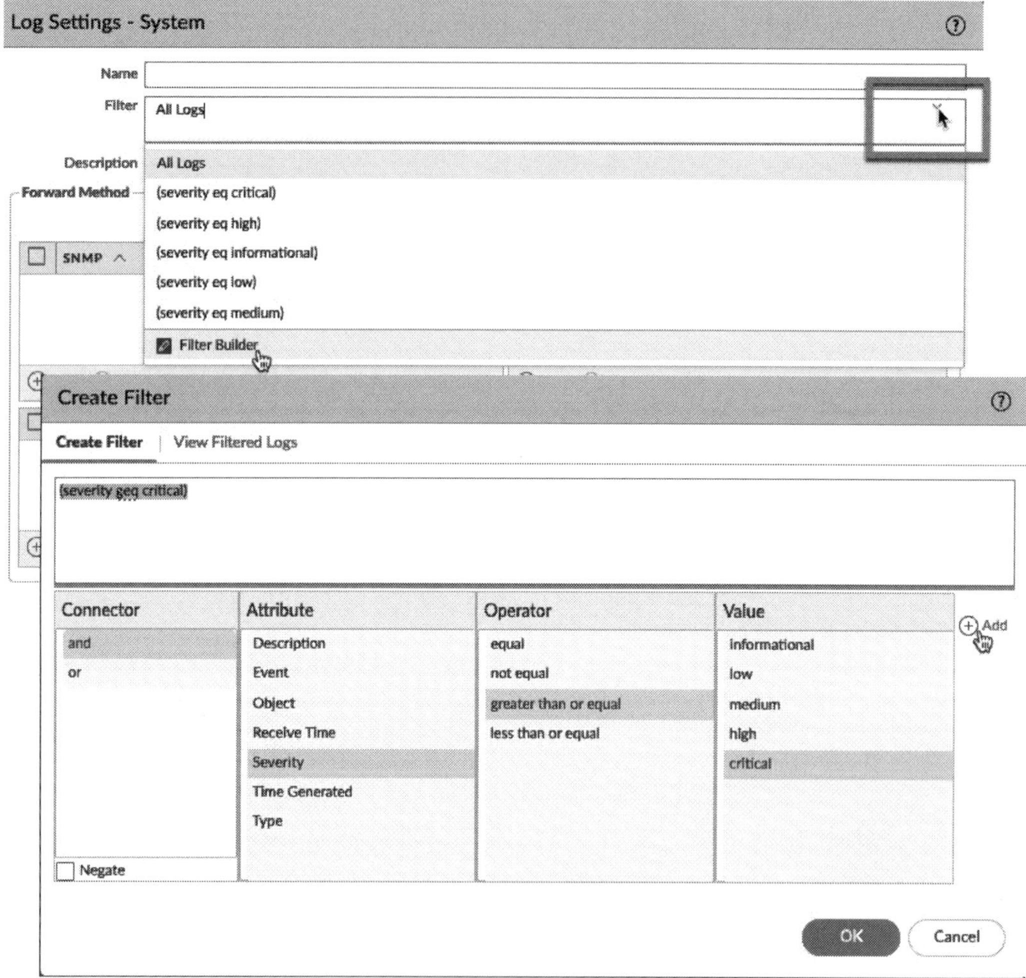

Figure 1.15 – Filter builder

Now that we've seen how to forward system logs, we will take a closer look at how to forward *session-based logs*.

Exploring log forwarding profiles

Security rules determine how the firewall processes sessions traversing its interfaces. Not only are ports and applications determined by the security rules, but also which security profiles and even which log forwarding profile is applied. This means that you need to attach a **Log Forwarding profile** to every security rule so that matching sessions are logged to an external system. First, you will need to create a Log Forwarding profile.

> **Important Note**
>
> Creating a Log Forwarding profile named `default` will automatically add it to every new security rule that is created afterward.

In **Objects** > **Log Forwarding**, create a new profile and name it `default`. This will ensure that this profile will be added to each new security policy moving forward. Additional profiles can be added as needed. Only one Log Forwarding profile can be added per security rule.

The default profile should look somewhat like the profile depicted in the following screenshot:

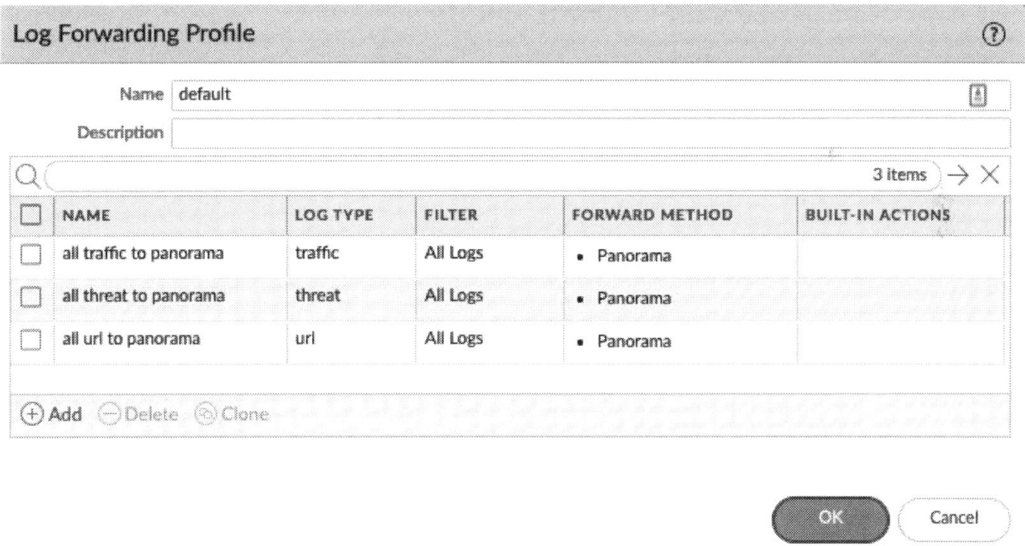

Figure 1.16 – Default log forwarding profile

A log forwarding profile consists of a set of match lists. Each match list contains the log type that needs to be forwarded, the destination server profiles the logs will be sent to, and optional filters to limit which logs will be forwarded. A typical log forwarding profile will contain all the common logs, such as **traffic**, **threat**, and **url** filtering logs. More specific **Match** lists can be added and tailored to take a specific action when an event is registered. For example, the following **Match List** will send out an email and forward the log to a syslog server when a critical threat is detected. This can be leveraged to alert the IT security team of an event and forward the information to an **Security Operations Centre (SOC)**:

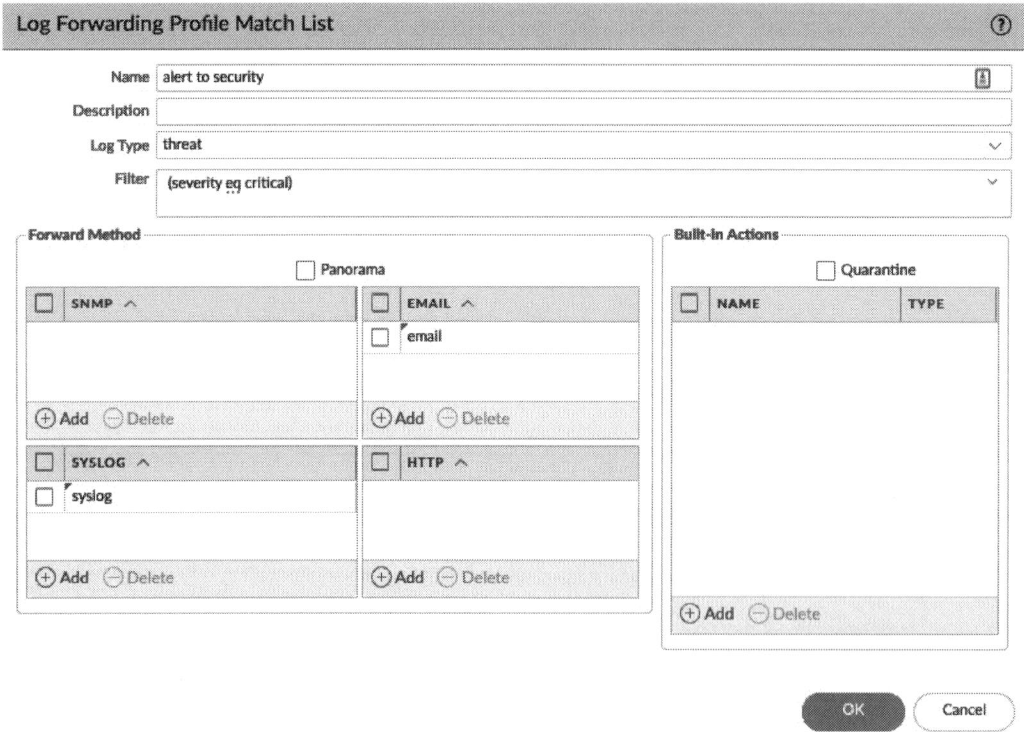

Figure 1.17 – Email and syslog log forwarding

Built-In Actions take log forwarding one step further by dynamically taking action on log events that can help protect critical systems from attacks, as we will see in the next section.

Dynamic tagging

The **Built-In Actions** section of **Match List** can be used to act dynamically when an event is seen that matches the filter.

The **Quarantine** checkbox can be used to add a source host to the device's quarantine list (the list can be found via **Device** > **Device Quarantine**). These devices can then be matched against the **Quarantine** attribute in a security policy, as shown in the following screenshot. The default behavior is to block the session that triggered a signature without interfering with other sessions initiated by a potentially malicious client. The advantage of adding this capability to **Quarantine** is that hosts are placed in a controlled group that can be cordoned off from sensitive resources, and even prevented from establishing a GlobalConnect VPN connection, until an unregister action is triggered or manually removed by an administrator:

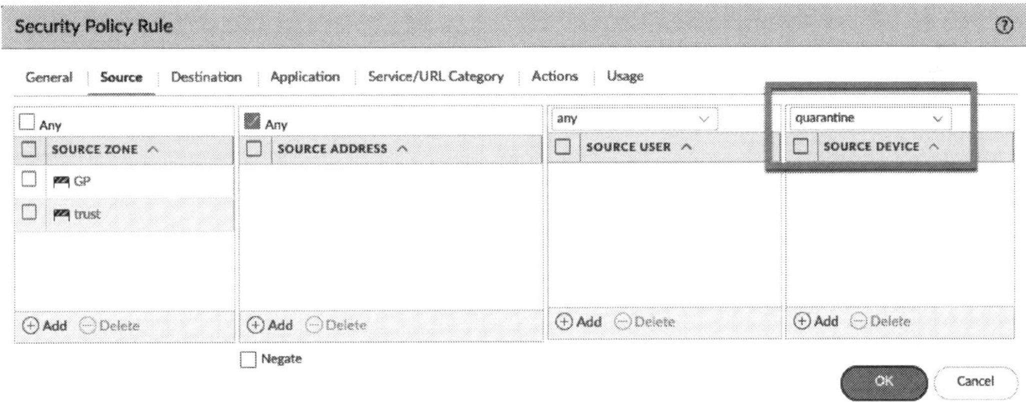

Figure 1.18 – Quarantine match on a security policy rule

As shown in the following screenshot, additional actions can be taken that will add a tag (these can be created in **Objects** > **Tags**) to a **Target**:

1. **Destination Address**
2. **Source Address**

3. **User**

   X-Forwarded-For-Address: The address contained in the x-forwarded for header added by a proxy server, indicating the original client IP:

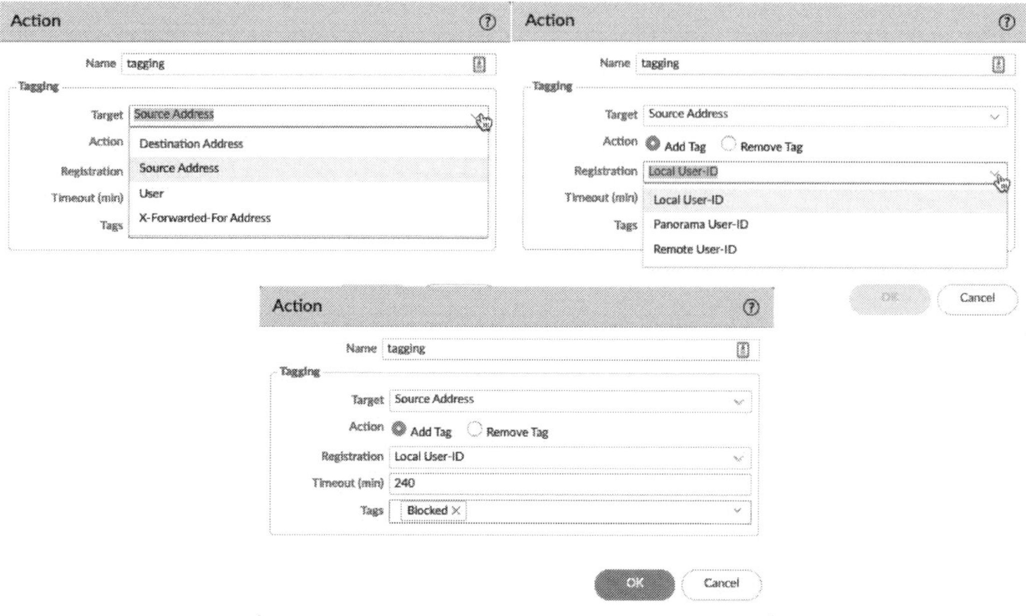

Figure 1.19 – Dynamic tag action

Tags can be added or removed by our **Action**. The tag can currently be registered to three different systems:

1. **Local User-ID**: This is the local firewall.
2. **Panorama User-ID**: This is a Panorama management server that can redistribute the tags via User-ID redistribution.
3. **Remote User-ID**: This is the User-ID agent that's been installed on a Windows server.

For Panorama and the Remote User-ID, an XML API needs to be enabled in the configuration of the User-ID agents. A timeout can be added so that a tag is removed after a certain amount of time.

As shown in the following screenshot, once tagging has been set up, a **Dynamic User Group** can be created for tagged users, or an **Address Group** can be used for tagged addresses. These groups can then be added to security rules so that they can be granted or **blocked** access to resources:

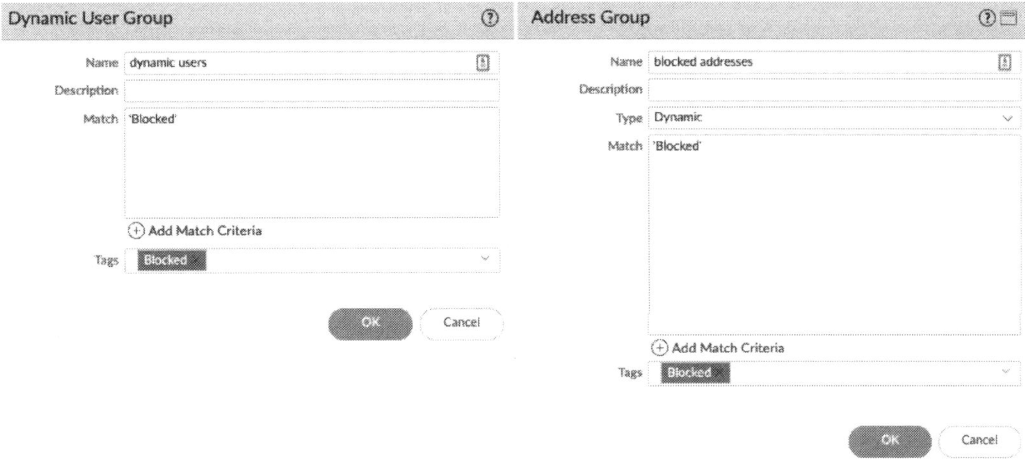

Figure 1.20 – Dynamic user group and address group

Once the dynamic tags are active and IPs start getting tagged, you can follow their progress in the **Monitor** > **IP-Tag** log, as you can see in the following screenshot:

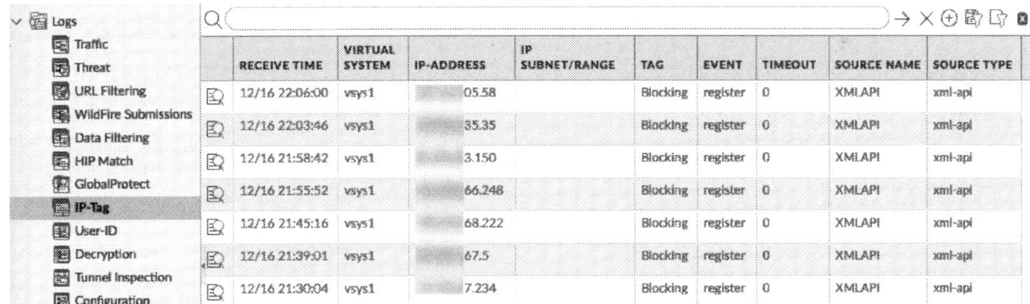

Logs
Traffic
Threat
URL Filtering
WildFire Submissions
Data Filtering
HIP Match
GlobalProtect
IP-Tag
User-ID
Decryption
Tunnel Inspection
Configuration
RECEIVE TIME
VIRTUAL SYSTEM
IP-ADDRESS
IP SUBNET/RANGE
TAG
EVENT
TIMEOUT
SOURCE NAME
SOURCE TYPE
12/16 22:06:00 vsys1 05.58 Blocking register 0 XMLAPI xml-api
12/16 22:03:46 vsys1 35.35 Blocking register 0 XMLAPI xml-api
12/16 21:58:42 vsys1 3.150 Blocking register 0 XMLAPI xml-api
12/16 21:55:52 vsys1 66.248 Blocking register 0 XMLAPI xml-api
12/16 21:45:16 vsys1 68.222 Blocking register 0 XMLAPI xml-api
12/16 21:39:01 vsys1 67.5 Blocking register 0 XMLAPI xml-api
12/16 21:30:04 vsys1 7.234 Blocking register 0 XMLAPI xml-api

Figure 1.21 – IP-Tag logs

The IP addresses or users that were tagged can be viewed by clicking the **more...** link next to the dynamic profile. If needed, addresses can be unregistered from this pop up as well:

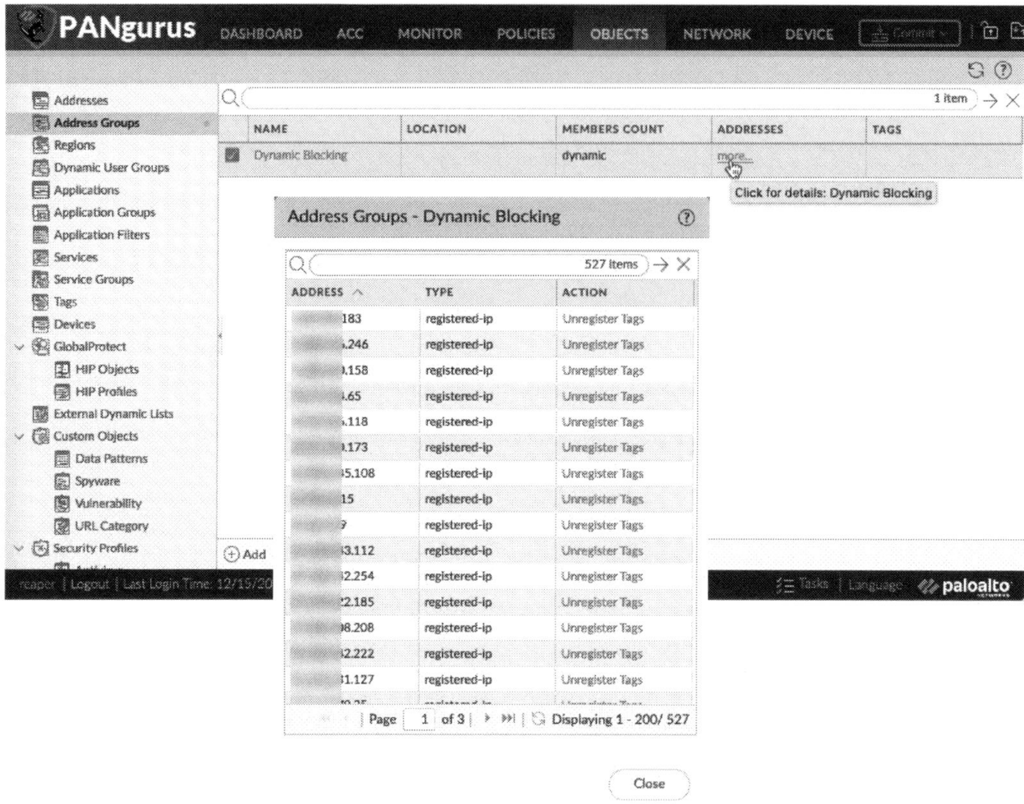

Figure 1.22 – List of tagged addresses in the dynamic profile

Before the Log Forwarding profiles can effectively start sending logs out and taking dynamic actions, they need to be assigned. We will learn about assigning log forwarding actions in the next section.

Assigning log forwarding actions

The last thing we need to do, before logs can be sent out to external systems, is add the log forwarding profile to all **Security Policy** rules that process sessions of interest. Log actions are determined by the Security Policy rule a session is handled by, so a log forwarding profile should be added to all security rules.

> **Important Note**
>
> Even rules that have no logging action enabled in the Security Policy Rule Log Settings may still generate logs: any threat event or URL filtering event with an action that is not **allowed** (that is, alert, block, and so on) will generate a log in the threat or URL filtering log database. The WildFire, Data Filtering, and File Blocking events will also still generate logs.

As shown in the following screenshot, the most common setting is set so that our **Security Policy Rule Log Setting** is **Log at Session End**, accompanied by a **log forwarding** profile.

Log at session end is the default setting that generates a log at the end of a session. This means that all the relevant data pertaining to the session can be recorded in one entry (for example, the number of transmitted bytes and packets, APP-ID, NAT actions, and so on).

Log at session start will create a log entry at every stage of a session, which includes when the SYN packet is received but also every mutation the App-ID may go through, which could be several stages for a child application. This log setting may be useful for troubleshooting but can be very chatty and storage-intensive when applied to regular traffic:

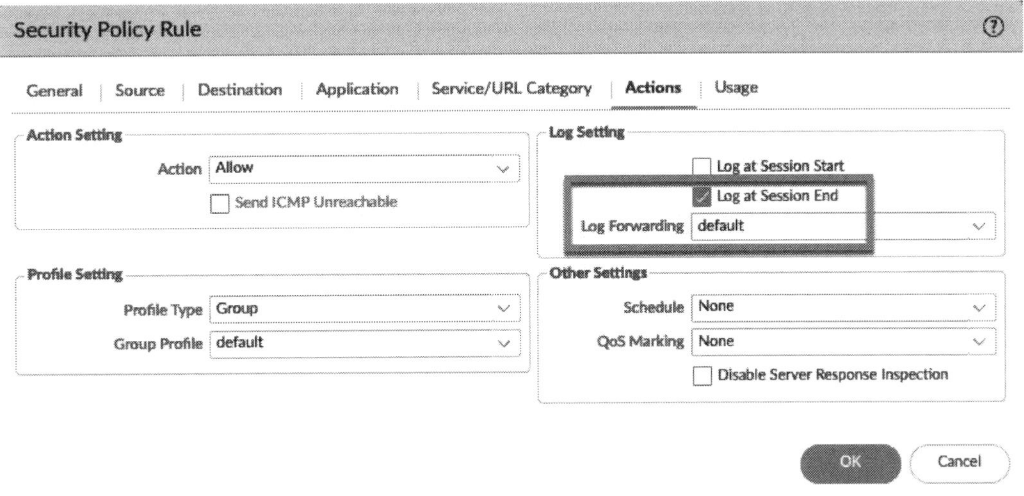

Figure 1.23 – Log forwarding profile in a security policy rule

Now that we have seen what we can do with logs, we will learn how to troubleshoot issues that could arise while forwarding logs.

Troubleshooting logs and log forwarding

Each log entry has multiple time indications that not only track when a session started and how long it lasted, but also when it was processed by the log receiver:

- **Start Time** is the timestamp when the session was accepted by the firewall.
- **Generate Time**: This is the timestamp for when the log file was generated. A log is generated based on the log action that was set in the security rule:

  Log at session start will **Generate Time** for each "start" event, such as the session being accepted, but also every time the App-ID changes. In this case, multiple logs will be generated for the same session, all with the same start time, but having a progressively later **Generate Time**.

  Log at session end will **Generate Time** when the session has ended.

Receive Time is when the log is received and written to a log database by the `logreceiver` daemon; this happens when the data plane hands the log over to the management plane to be written into the log database, or in the case of Panorama, when it is received from the firewall on Panorama.

As shown in the following screenshot, the **Receive Time** property of Panorama is several hours after **Generate Time**, which could be an indication of several possible issues. There could be a time mismatch between the firewall and Panorama, so make sure both systems are set to the proper time zone and have NTP enabled so that the system's time is kept synchronized. The firewall could have been disconnected from Panorama, so check the *System logs* to see if the firewall was disconnected at one point:

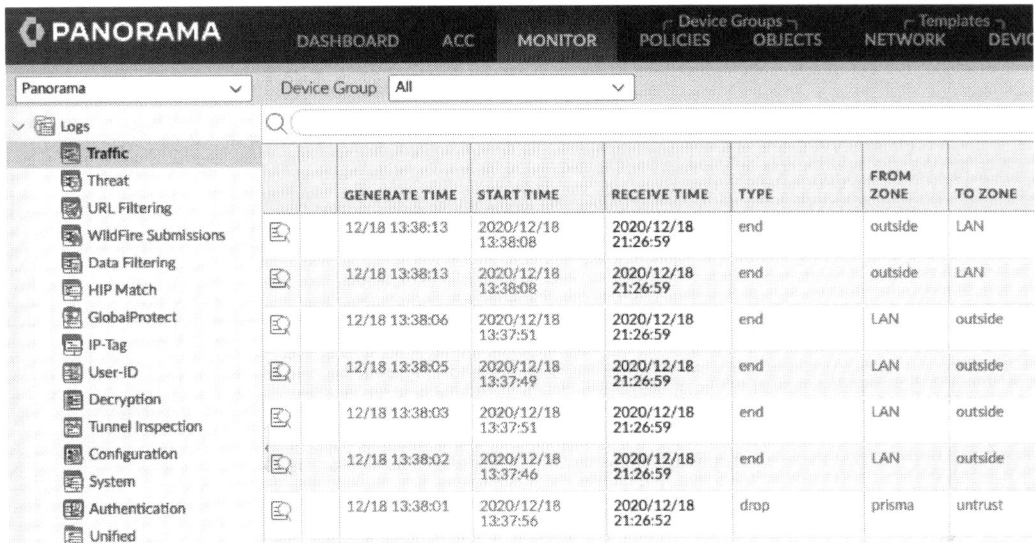

Figure 1.24 – Time indications in log entries

Debugging log-receiver

To find out if there is an issue on the firewall, run the `debug log-receiver statistics` command to review the overall health of the `log-receiver` daemon. If it is receiving an extremely large volume of logs, it may have difficulty writing all of them in a timely manner. It will start queueing logs and if the queue is filled to the limit, logs will be discarded. Take note of `Log incoming rate` versus `Log written rate` and keep the `Logs discarded (queue full)` counters in mind to determine if log generation is too high on the firewall.

For log forwarding issues, review `Log Forward discarded (queue full) count` and `Log Forward discarded (send error) count`.

If the data plane is somehow sending corrupted log entries, those will be recorded here as well. If there is an issue with the log partition, you will see the count of `Logs not written since disk became unavailable` increase:

```
reaper@PANgurus> debug log-receiver statistics

Logging statistics
------------------------------ -----------
Log incoming rate:             1/sec
Log written rate:              1/sec
Corrupted packets:             0
Corrupted URL packets:         0
Corrupted HTTP HDR packets:    0
Corrupted HTTP HDR Insert packets: 0
Corrupted EMAIL HDR packets:   0
Logs discarded (queue full):   0
Traffic logs written:          382902
Tunnel logs written:           186
Auth logs written:             0
Userid logs written:           0
GlobalProtect logs written:    5
DECRYPTION logs written:       79
URL logs written:              232716
Wildfire logs written:         2
Anti-virus logs written:       0
Wildfire Anti-virus logs written: 0
Spyware logs written:          0
Spyware-DNS logs written:      0
Attack logs written:           0
Vulnerability logs written:    380
Data logs written:             0
URL cache age out count:       0
URL cache full count:          0
URL cache key exist count:     4049
URL cache wrt incomplete http hdrs count: 0
URL cache rcv http hdr before url count: 0
URL cache full drop count(url log not received): 0
```

```
URL cache age out drop count(url log not received): 0
Traffic alarms dropped due to sysd write failures: 0
Traffic alarms dropped due to global rate limiting: 0
Traffic alarms dropped due to each source rate limiting: 0
Traffic alarms generated count:  0
Log Forward count:              249
Log Forward discarded (queue full) count: 0
Log Forward discarded (send error) count: 0
Total logs not written due to disk unavailability: 0
Logs not written since disk became unavailable: 0
```

The following are some indications of the *maximum* supported log rates per device. New PAN-OS upgrades may come with new supported log rates, so please check the release notes to ensure there are no changes:

PA-220	1,200 logs/second
PA-800	10,000 logs/second
PA-3220	7,000 logs/second
PA-3250	15,000 logs/second
PA-3260	24,000 logs/second
PA-5220	30,000 logs/second
PA-5250	55,000 logs/second
PA-5260	120,000 logs/second
PA-7000	70,000 logs/second
VM-100	2,250 logs/second
VM-300/500	8,000 logs/second

If the total volume of logs is too high, you can review the queue statistics with the `debug log-receiver queue_stats` command. This ensures that this conclusion is accurate:

```
reaper@PANgurus> debug log-receiver queue_stats

Logging statistics
------------------------------ ----------
Log incoming rate:             6/sec
Log written rate:              6/sec
Logs discarded (queue full):   0
```

```
Ring buffer entries:                  0/16383

Traffic taskqs:
     comp_taskq:                      0/64
     disk_flush_taskq:                0/64
     summary_calc_taskq:              0/64
     summary_flush_taskq:             0/1
     bdx_taskqs[ 0]:                  0/128
     bdx_taskqs[ 1]:                  0/128
     bdx_taskqs[ 2]:                  0/128
     bdx_taskqs[ 3]:                  0/128

Threat taskqs:
     comp_taskq:                      0/64
     disk_flush_taskq:                0/64
     summary_calc_taskq:              0/64
     summary_flush_taskq:             0/1
     bdx_taskqs[ 0]:                  0/128
     bdx_taskqs[ 1]:                  0/128
     bdx_taskqs[ 2]:                  0/128
     bdx_taskqs[ 3]:                  0/128
```

Next, we will learn about reading system resources.

Reading system resources

To verify whether the system is having I/O issues reading and writing to the disk, you can review some parameters in `show system resources`. To see the output *live*, add `follow` to the command and press *1* to see all CPU cores.

The output is similar to the output of `top` in Linux and will return the load and memory usage of the system, as well as a list of all the running processes and their resource demands.

As shown in the following screenshot, cores 1 and 2 are 100% loaded, and there are two processes taking up 100% of CPU capacity. In this case, this is due to the chassis being a PA-220, which shares a single quad-core CPU between the data plane and the management plane. `pan_task` processes are packet processing daemons that are *pre-spun up*, so it is expected that they take up about 100% of the CPU cycles:

```
top - 01:35:49 up 1 day, 22:20,  1 user,  load average: 2.30, 2.62, 2.74
Tasks: 146 total,   4 running, 141 sleeping,   0 stopped,   1 zombie
%Cpu0  :  6.3 us,  5.9 sy,  6.6 ni, 81.2 id,  0.0 wa,  0.0 hi,  0.0 si,  0.0 st
%Cpu1  :100.0 us,  0.0 sy,  0.0 ni,  0.0 id,  0.0 wa,  0.0 hi,  0.0 si,  0.0 st
%Cpu2  :100.0 us,  0.0 sy,  0.0 ni,  0.0 id,  0.0 wa,  0.0 hi,  0.0 si,  0.0 st
%Cpu3  :  8.9 us,  4.0 sy,  3.0 ni, 82.8 id,  0.0 wa,  0.0 hi,  1.3 si,  0.0 st
KiB Mem :  4119684 total,   374860 free,  1890600 used,  1854224 buff/cache
KiB Swap:  4097968 total,  4087960 free,    10008 used.  1687028 avail Mem

  PID USER      PR  NI    VIRT    RES    SHR S  %CPU %MEM     TIME+ COMMAND
 4959 root      20   0   91288  37828   9968 R 100.0  0.9   2772:43 pan_task
 4961 root      20   0   66608  12856   9776 R  99.7  0.3   2773:05 pan_task
 3096 root       0 -20  202292  38024   6672 S   5.9  0.9  17:35.09 masterd_apps
 3116 root      15  -5  121516   9704   3808 S   5.9  0.2  36:01.46 sysd
 5404 root      20   0  528236  59904   7608 S   0.7  1.5  20:33.87 dnsproxyd
 3285 root      20   0 1022616  12800   5684 S   0.3  0.3   1:25.75 sysdagent
 3290 root      30  10  198380  18704   6356 S   0.3  0.5  15:47.09 python
 3591 nobody    20   0   44244   5364   1344 S   0.3  0.1   7:28.24 redis-server
 3596 nobody    20   0   41684   2032   1172 S   0.3  0.0   7:19.29 redis-server
 4943 root      20   0   71380  10000   7196 S   0.3  0.2   1:53.10 sdwand
 4945 root      20   0   58160   9416   6756 S   0.3  0.2   7:17.89 pan_dha
 5383 root      20   0  130836  26568   3308 S   0.3  0.6  19:15.40 identityclient
 8155 reaper    20   0    4228   1636   1128 R   0.3  0.0   0:00.13 top
```

Figure 1.25 – Show system resources

For logging issues, ensure the `logrcvr` process does not appear to be stuck or taking up more resources than expected. The value under the `VIRT` column represents memory usage in KB and should not run into the GB range.

The `wa` value next to the CPU readings represents the time spent waiting on disk I/O and should be as close to 0 as possible. A high value, such as over 10%, could indicate a disk problem.

Ideally, there should be a little memory left in both `free` values, but if you run out of volatile memory, the system will start to swap. Requiring a swap may introduce latency, but when the swap space is depleted, the system will start to degrade severely. If the swap is depleted, look down the list for the process that is taking up all this memory under the `VIRT` column and consider restarting it using the `debug software restart process` command, followed by the process name. If these issues present themselves regularly, check if your current PAN-OS requires an upgrade or consider upgrading the firewall to a larger platform that can process more logs.

Using tcpdump

If the system resources and `logrcvr` stats look healthy, you may be facing an external issue. The connection to the external system may be unreliable or have a lower-than-expected MTU, which could cause logs to be queued up, discarded along the way, or fragmented.

Capturing packets on both ends is usually the best way to find out if something is happening on the network connecting both systems to each other. On the management plane, you can use the `tcpdump` command followed by a filter. Older PAN-OS limited the default size per packet to 64 bytes, so take note of the *capture size* and add `snaplen 0` to capture whole packets if the capture size is limited.

Unlike `tcpdump` in Linux systems, there is no need to add an interface as only the management interface (`eth0`) can be captured. Filters are added between double quotes:

```
reaper@PANgurus> tcpdump filter "tcp port 514"
Press Ctrl-C to stop capturing

tcpdump: listening on eth0, link-type EN10MB (Ethernet),
capture size 65535 bytes
^C
10 packets captured
10 packets received by filter
0 packets dropped by kernel
reaper@PANgurus>
```

The available filters are similar to their Linux `tcpdump` counterparts; that is, `host 10.0.0.1`, `src net 10.0.0.0/24/24`, and `tcp port 22`. You can add *operators* to include or exclude attributes, but not port `22`.

You can then view `packetcapture` via CLI using the `view-pcap mgmt-pcap mgmt.pcap` command. You can add some parameters, such as the following:

- `no-dns-lookup yes`, to not resolve IP addresses to hostnames
- `no-port-lookup yes`, to display the actual port number instead of a name
- `verbose++ yes`, to add more details
- `no-timestamp yes`, to leave out the timestamp:

```
reaper@PANgurus> view-pcap no-dns-lookup yes no-port-lookup yes
no-timestamp  yes mgmt-pcap mgmt.pcap

IP 192.168.27.115.47055 > 192.168.27.7.514: Flags [P.], seq
3534228492:3534228807, ack 3260149837, win 115, length 315
IP 192.168.27.7.514 > 192.168.27.115.47055: Flags [.], ack 315,
win 8211, length 0
IP 192.168.27.115.47055 > 192.168.27.7.514: Flags [P.], seq
```

```
315:632, ack 1, win 115, length 317
IP 192.168.27.7.514 > 192.168.27.115.47055: Flags [.], ack 632,
win 8210, length 0
IP 192.168.27.115.47055 > 192.168.27.7.514: Flags [P.], seq
632:949, ack 1, win 115, length 317
IP 192.168.27.7.514 > 192.168.27.115.47055: Flags [.], ack 949,
win 8208, length 0
IP 192.168.27.115.47055 > 192.168.27.7.514: Flags [P.], seq
949:1269, ack 1, win 115, length 320
IP 192.168.27.7.514 > 192.168.27.115.47055: Flags [.], ack
1269, win 8207, length 0
IP 192.168.27.115.47055 > 192.168.27.7.514: Flags [P.], seq
1269:1828, ack 1, win 115, length 559
IP 192.168.27.7.514 > 192.168.27.115.47055: Flags [.], ack
1828, win 8212, length 0
```

The `pcap` file can also be exported to an SCP or TFTP server so that it can be inspected using a tool such as Wireshark using the `tftp export mgmt-pcap from mgmt.pcap to <host>` or `scp export mgmt-pcap from mgmt.pcap to user@host/path/` commands:

```
reaper@PANgurus> tftp export mgmt-pcap from mgmt.pcap to
192.168.27.7
mode set to octet
Connected to 192.168.27.7 (192.168.27.7), port 69
putting /opt/pan/.debug/mgmtpcap/mgmt.pcap to
192.168.27.7:mgmt.pcap [octet]
Sent 2582 bytes in 0.0 seconds [805931 bit/s]
```

In the next section, we will take a closer look at troubleshooting log forwarding issues to a Panorama log collector.

Troubleshooting forwarding to a log collector

To verify that the firewall is connected to Panorama, you can run the following command to check the status of the log collector agent:

```
debug management-server log-collector-agent-status
```

The output will clearly state which log collectors are known and if the firewall is currently connected to them:

```
reaper@PANgurus> debug management-server log-collector-agent-status

Logcollector agent status
-------------------------
Serial  IP Address   Connected  Last Disconn Time  Failed conns
-------------------------
0007001 192.168.27.10    no                                  0
```

> **Important Note**
>
> The firewall will always initiate the connection toward Panorama and additional log collectors. Any commands, updates, or configuration originating from Panorama or a log collector will be backhauled over the connection established by the firewall.

You can then check additional information by running `request log-collector-forwarding status`. As shown in the following screenshot, it will show timestamps for certain events, such as when it last registered and connected to the log collector, but also the timestamp when the last log was forwarded. A large gap between the current time and the last time a log (most commonly, traffic and a threat) was forwarded, or a very short time between when the last connection was established and the current time, could be an indication of connectivity issues. Take note of `Last Seq Num Fwded` and `Last Seq Num Acked` as you will need to compare these log sequence numbers on the log collector:

```
reaper@PANgurus> request log-collector-forwarding status

Log Collector Preference List
Forward to all: No
Serial Number: 0007        IP Address: 192.168.27.10 IPV6 Address: unknown

---------------------------------------------------------------------------------------------------------------------
     Type      Last Log Created          Last Log Fwded          Last Seq Num Fwded  Last Seq Num Acked         Total Logs Fwded
---------------------------------------------------------------------------------------------------------------------
> CMS 0
        Not Sending to CMS 0
> CMS 1
        Not Sending to CMS 1

>Log Collector
'Log Collection log forwarding agent' is active and connected to 192.168.27.10


DNS :
    Successfully resolved FQDN (), IP (192.168.27.10)
                               success
              2020/12/21 00:36:42

Registration :
         registration request sent
                               success
              2020/12/21 00:36:45

SSL :
    ssl channel established to (192.168.27.10)
                               success
              2020/12/21 00:36:44

Status :
             Connection successful
                               success
              2020/12/21 00:36:45

TCP :
        tcp connection established
                               success
              2020/12/21 00:36:42

Connect-Agent-Status :
    DNS resolution success for  (IP: 192.168.27.10)
                               success
              2020/12/21 00:36:32

    config   2020/12/21 00:17:41   2020/12/21 00:37:55                     3241               3241                  4
    system   2020/12/21 22:10:53   2020/12/21 22:11:11                 24693947           24693947              13383
    threat   2020/12/21 22:11:47   2020/12/21 22:11:52                  7335620            7335606             293082
   traffic   2020/12/21 22:11:47   2020/12/21 22:11:52                 83644996           83644987             499747
```

Figure 1.26 – Log collector forwarding status

On Panorama, you can verify if the log collector is connected and whether it received the latest configuration, in case something changed, using the `show log-collector connected` command:

```
reaper@Panorama> show log-collector connected
Serial   CID Hostname  Connected Config Status SW Version
IPv4 - IPv6
-------------------------------------------------------------
0007001 2   Panorama  yes        In Sync       10.0.3
192.168.27.10 - unknown

Redistribution status:       none
Last commit-all: commit succeeded, current ring version 1
SearchEngine status:     Active
md5sum  updated at ?
```

```
Certificate Status:
Certificate subject Name:
Certificate expiry at: none
Connected at: none
Custom certificate Used: no
Last masterkey push status: Unknown
Last masterkey push timestamp:  none
```

Once you've verified that the collector is connected and in sync, you can check the statuses of the firewalls sending logs to Panorama using `show logging-status device <serial of firewall>`. You will see the timestamp of the last logs that were received and which `sequence number` was received:

```
reaper@Panorama> show logging-status device 012000001


    Type              Last Log Rcvd     Last Seq Num Rcvd
Last Log Generated


Source IP         : Default
Destination IP    : Default
Source Daemon     : unknown
Connection Id      : 012000001-log-collection
Log rate: 1
    config       2020/12/21 00:37:55                3241
2020/12/21 00:17:41
    system       2020/12/21 22:34:55            24693983
2020/12/21 22:34:49
    threat       2020/12/21 22:35:15             7336943
2020/12/21 22:35:10
   traffic       2020/12/21 22:35:15            83646677
2020/12/21 22:35:10
    userid                      N/A                  N/A
N/A
     iptag       2020/12/21 22:35:15               14127
2020/12/21 22:35:07
```

You can check the current flow rate of incoming logs by running the `debug log-collector log-collection-stats show incoming-logs` command.

At the bottom, it will also indicate if there are logs being discarded from devices, which can be an indication that the log rate is too high:

```
reaper@Panorama> debug log-collector log-collection-stats show
incoming-logs

Last time logs received Mon Dec 21 23:00:20 2020

Incoming log rate =   1.10

Detail counts by logtype:
traffic:60936
config:16
system:2650
threat:32723
...
Inbound logger stats:
traffic generation logcount:60936 blkcount:926 addition-
rate:0(per sec)
config generation logcount:16 blkcount:2 addition-rate:0(per
sec)
system generation logcount:2650 blkcount:638 addition-
rate:0(per sec)
threat generation logcount:32723 blkcount:922 addition-
rate:0(per sec)
...
Num of discarded log messages from devices: 0
```

If there has been a connectivity outage between the firewall and Panorama, the firewall will try to send all its logs starting from the last `acked` (acknowledged by Panorama that it was received) sequence number. If the disconnection was lengthy, the firewall may need to send a vast volume of logs across, which could lead to more congestion or a long wait time for old logs to catch up and fresh logs to become visible on Panorama. There are a few commands available to control how the firewall will forward its backlog, all of which you can initiate from Panorama.

This command will tell the firewall to stop sending logs:

```
request log-fwd-ctrl device <FW serial> action stop
scheduled a job with jobid 0.
0
```

The following command will tell the firewall to start forwarding logs again, from the last `acked` log, and buffer any future logs if a disconnect were to happen again. This is the default setting for log forwarding:

```
request log-fwd-ctrl device <FW serial> action start
scheduled a job with jobid 0. Converted log-fwd-ctrl action to
'start-from-lastack'
0
```

The following command will instruct the firewall to start sending logs, starting from the latest sequence number, working its way back. This can help you get newer logs faster while allowing yourself some time to catch up on old logs:

```
request log-fwd-ctrl device <FW serial> action latest
scheduled a job with jobid 0.
0
```

The following command will tell the firewall to start forwarding *live* logs only. It will not attempt to forward the buffered logs. If a disconnect happens again, the firewall will not buffer logs during this outage and will simply continue from the latest log once connectivity is re-established:

```
request log-fwd-ctrl device <FW serial> action live
scheduled a job with jobid 0.
0
```

This will tell the firewall to start regular log forwarding again, starting from the last `acked` log file. This command can be executed after the `action live` command to pick up logging, but with buffering enabled:

```
request log-fwd-ctrl device <FW serial> action start-from-
lastack
scheduled a job with jobid 0.
0
```

Let's look at a few examples of how these commands could be leveraged during troubleshooting.

If there is an issue with catching up on the buffered logs, due to bandwidth constraints or because the load on Panorama is too high due to a high log ingestion rate, it may be necessary to abandon the buffered logs. The sequence to achieve this is to `stop` logging and then start logging `live`. Then after a few minutes, when you've verified that *fresh* logs are coming in, execute `start-from-lastack` so that the buffer is active in case there is another short disconnect.

If the log rate is too high at a peak moment, logging could be stopped for a less critical firewall to reduce the load on the log collector and restarted once the peak has faded away. Buffering will ensure no logs are lost.

In some cases, the log rate on the firewall may be so high, or the outage may be so long, that the firewall was unable to keep the oldest logs and the `last ack` log was purged. In this case, `start` and `start-from-lastack` could have trouble restarting as the sequence numbers no longer match up. Here, try `latest` or run `live` for a few minutes, followed by `start-from-lastack`.

Check if your commands are causing the expected log action by executing `show logging-status device <FW serial>`.

Summary

In this chapter, you learned about all the elements that come into play before logs are sent to a third-party logging device or email relay. You learned some troubleshooting steps and how to review whether Panorama and the firewall are in a healthy state. This knowledge will help you set up proper forwarding profiles and leverage these capabilities to aggregate logs on a **SIEM** solution, or even notify security teams when certain events occur.

In the next chapter, we will take a deeper look at setting up and troubleshooting *GlobalProtect*.

2
Configuring Advanced GlobalProtect Features

In this chapter, you will learn about the advanced features in **GlobalProtect** that will allow for more versatility and security in remote user deployments. We will learn about authentication methods and configuration methods that can dynamically change the user experience, depending on the user's needs and the security of the corporate network.

These features will allow you to gain more control over the endpoints while integrating the user experience into the latest generation of **Single Sign-On** (**SSO**) authentication and the *always-on* way of working. By the end of this chapter, you will be able to configure SAML-based SSO and ensure endpoints are always protected in an optimal fashion. In this chapter, we are going to cover the following main topics:

- Learning about advanced configuration features
- Leveraging quarantine to isolate agents
- Practical troubleshooting for GlobalProtect issues

Technical requirements

This chapter will assume you have some experience setting up `user-vpn`. You will need a *Windows 10* or *macOS 10.15* to deploy the configuration we will be discussing in this chapter. This chapter is based on the capabilities of PAN-OS 10. Some features may not be fully available in lower versions of PAN-OS.

Check out the following link to see the Code in Action video:
`https://bit.ly/2SuThmN`

Learning about advanced configuration features

In this section, we will take a look at the less common and more advanced features that can be set in GlobalProtect to provide more flexibility or increase security, or both. First, we will look at integrating authentication with **Security Assertion Markup Language** (**SAML**).

Integrating SAML into authentication methods

With more and more services moving to the cloud, it makes sense for organizations to also move (part of) their **Active Directory** into the cloud. This makes setting up authentication for GlobalProtect a little more challenging as there may no longer be an option, or a need, to use older protocols such as **LDAP** or **RADIUS** in favour of newer authentication standards such as SAML.

Configuring Microsoft Azure for SAML SSO

Microsoft Azure provides a user-friendly experience and has a free option with limited features but sufficient capabilities for you to experiment with, so I will start from Azure as a template for other implementations. Any other SAML provider will require similar settings, but the exact approach may differ.

Before we start, we need to make sure we have at least one Active Directory group we will use for users that are allowed to authenticate. Groups can be created by accessing the main menu in Azure, by navigating to **Azure Active Directory** and going into the **Groups** menu. As shown in the following screenshot, you can create a **security group** by clicking on **New group**. We'll use this group for the authentication profile. You can add users to the group as needed later, but we'll start with at least one test user account:

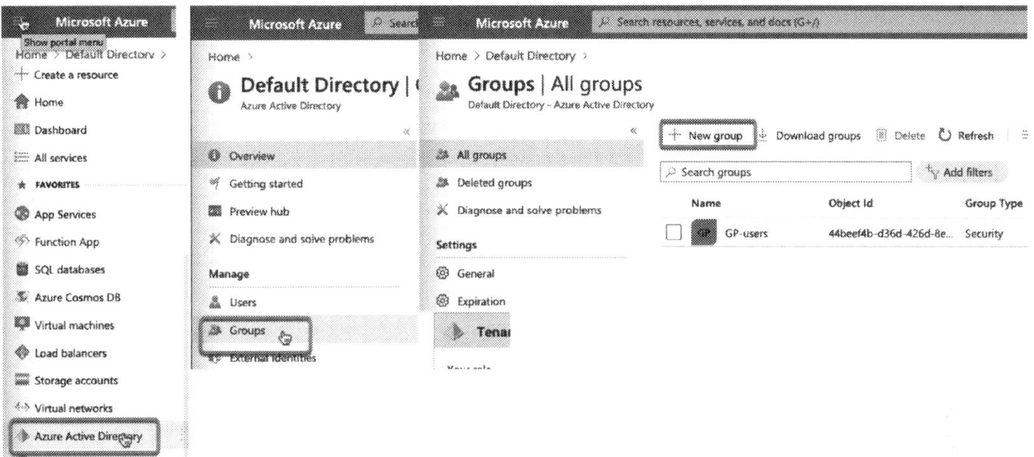

Figure 2.1 – Azure Active Directory group

The next part is easy as there are already a few **applications** available: from the home page, click **Enterprise Applications** and then select **New application**. Search for `Palo Alto Networks` and select the **GlobalProtect** application, and then click **Create**. If you head back to the **Enterprise applications window**, the newly created GlobalProtect Enterprise application is now available for further configuration, as shown in the following screenshot:

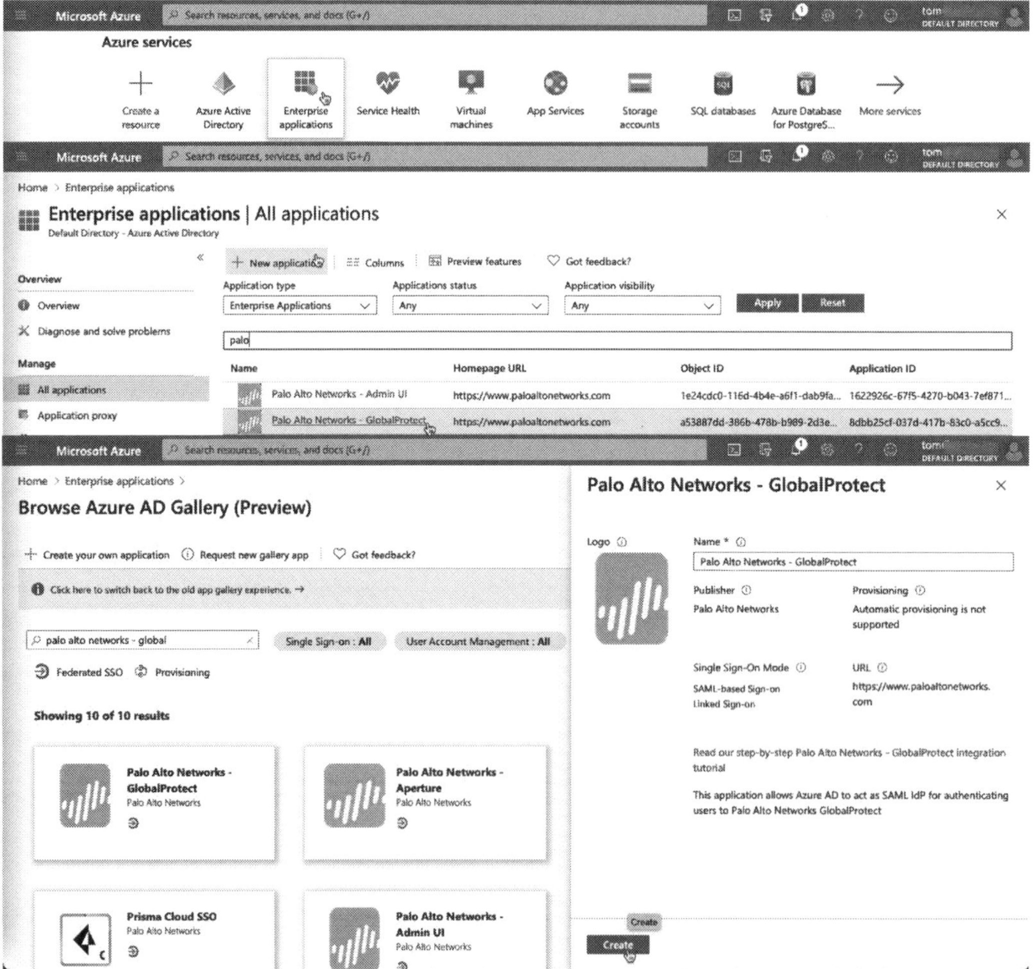

Figure 2.2 – Creating a new Enterprise application

Open the newly created Enterprise application and navigate to **Manage** > **Users and groups**. Here, you can add the group you created earlier or a handful of test users, as shown here:

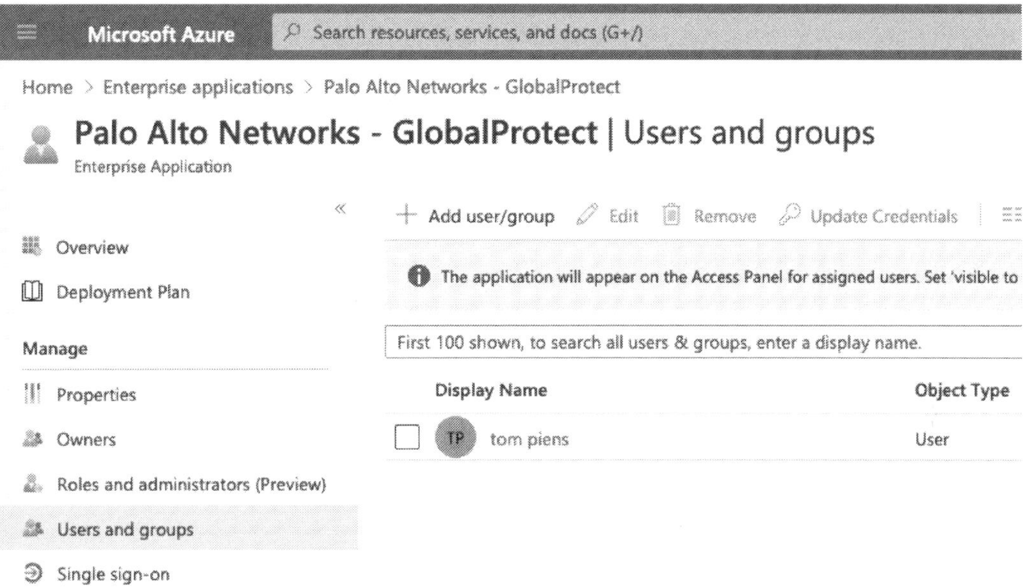

Figure 2.3 – Adding users or groups to the GlobalProtect Enterprise application

Next, as shown in the following screenshot, open **Manage** > **Single sign-on**. Here, you will need to select **SAML** as the **SSO** method:

Figure 2.4 – Configuring SSO for the Enterprise application

Once you've selected SAML as the SSO method, we need to set up our **Basic SAML Configuration**. Proceed by clicking the **Edit** button and filling out the following fields:

- **Identifier (Entity ID)**: `https://<yourURL>:443/SAML20/SP`.
- **Reply URL (Assertion Consumer Service URL)**: `https://<yourURL>/SAML20/SP/ACS`.
- **Sign on URL**: `https://<yourURL>`.
- **Relay State**: This field can be left blank.
- **Logout Url**: A logout option won't be used on GlobalProtect, so this option can be left blank as well.

Make sure to add the port indicator, `:443`, to **Identifier** as Azure requires this port for the identifier during authentication.

The Set Up **Single Sign-On with SAML** configuration should look similar to what's shown in the following screenshot. Now, you can download the **Federation Metadata XML** file, which contains all the URL information and the Azure self-signed certificate. If you have a fully integrated Azure deployment, you may have certificates associated with your Azure environment for your own domain name. Make sure that you install the **Certificate Authority** (CA) issued certificate on the firewall if it hasn't been imported through the XML import:

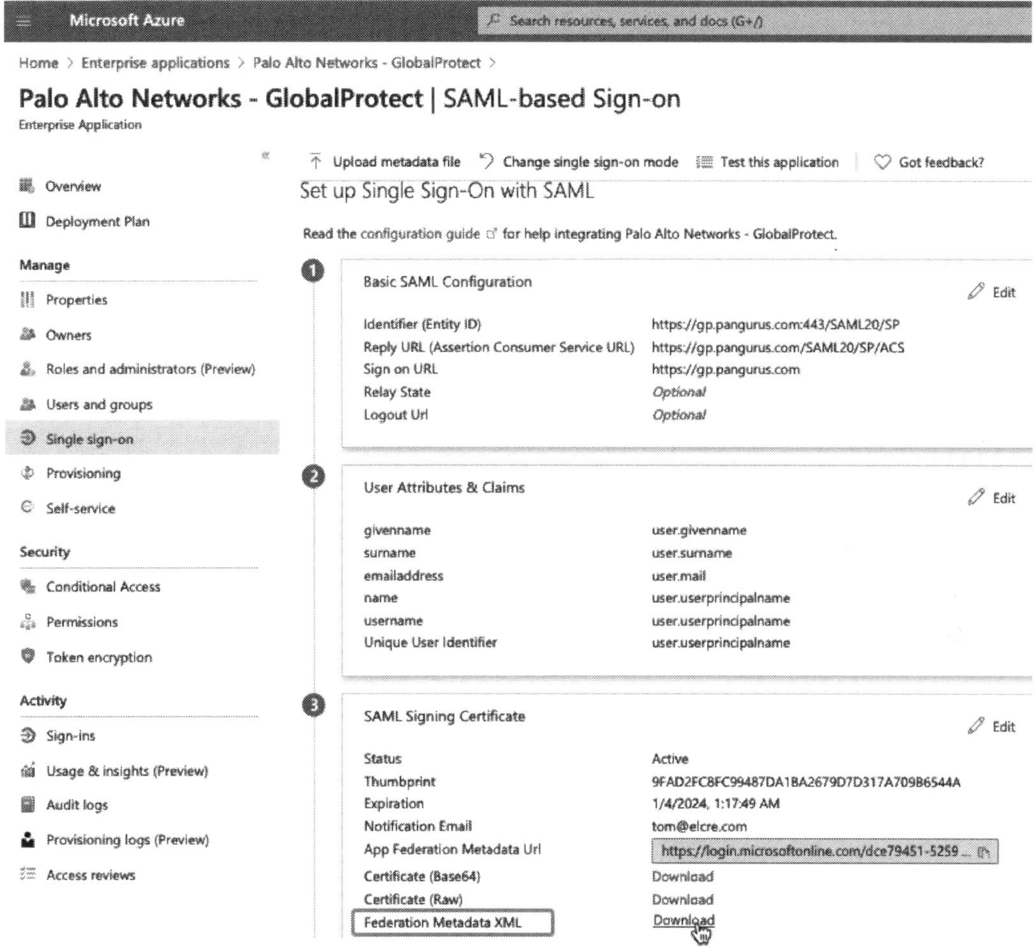

Figure 2.5 - SAML=based SSO configuration

Alternatively, and for SSO providers that do not provide an exportable metadata XML file, you can also take note of the URL information, as shown in the following screenshot, and export the certificate you will need to add to the firewall to configure the SAML profile:

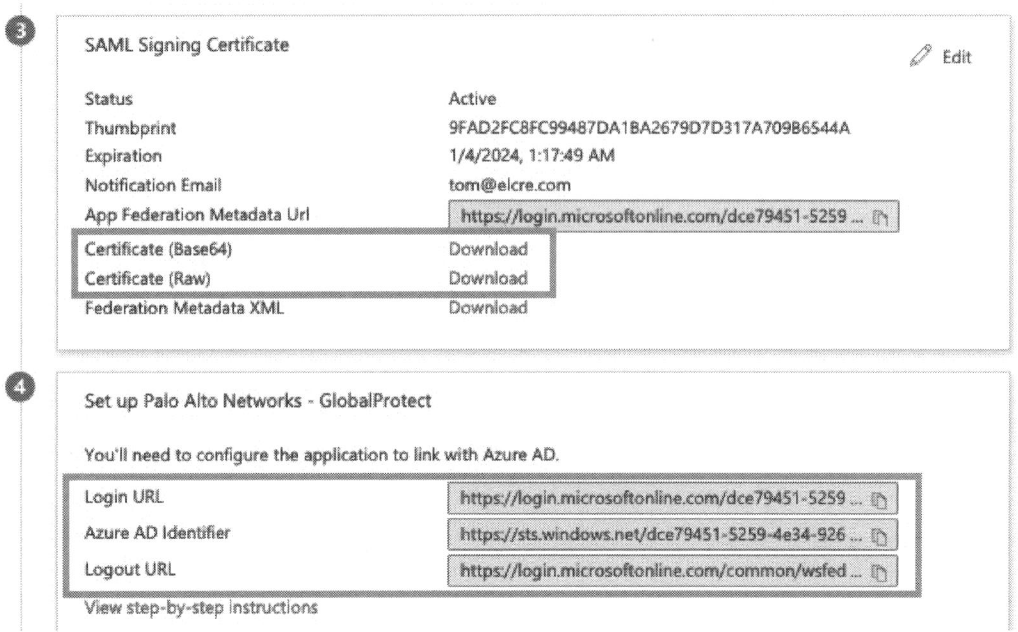

Figure 2.6 – Manual configuration URLs

The next step is to configure the firewall so that it can start using the SAML configuration.

Configuring the firewall for SAML authentication

Many cloud-based SSO services provide a downloadable XML configuration file once you've set up the basic parameters for SAML. This file can be imported directly into the firewall but is not required to set up a SAML profile. On the firewall where the profile will be created, navigate to **Device** > **Server Profiles** > **SAML Identity Provider** and select the **Import** button if you have an XML config file available. The import pop up will look similar to the following. If you are using the free version of any SSO SAML **identity Provider (IDP)**, the provided certificate will most likely be self-signed, which means it can't be validated. Disable **Validate Identity Provider Certificate** to prevent the possibility of running into errors. If your environment has proper certificates, leave this option enabled:

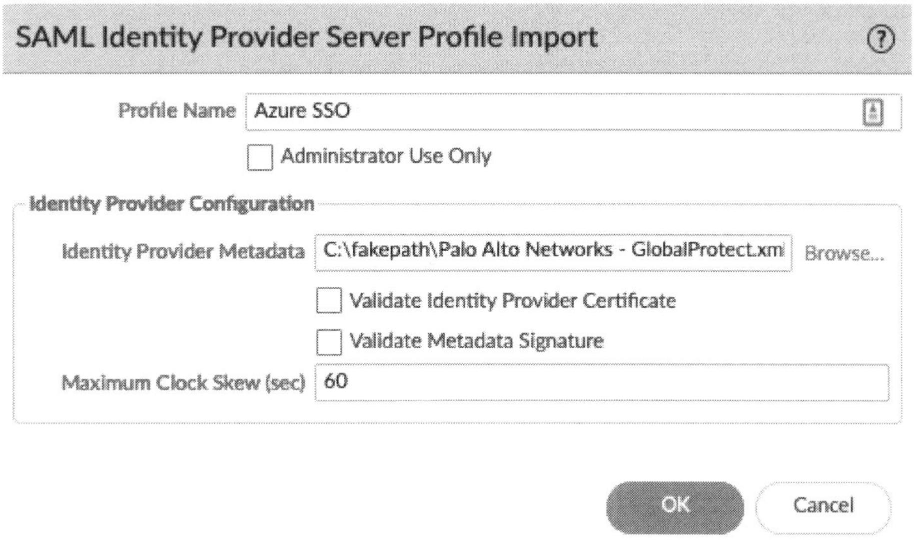

Figure 2.7 – Importing the SSO SAML configuration XML

Once the profile has been created, click its name to open its properties or click **Add** if you need to input the parameters manually. The **SAML Identity Provider Profile** should look similar to what's shown in the following screenshot:

- **Identity Provider ID** will contain a URL that identifies your tenant ID with the IDP.
- **Identity Provider Certificate** contains the certificate that was downloaded from the IDP.
- **Identity Provider SSO URL** is the URL that's used to log on a user.
- **Identity Provider SLO URL** can be used to log off a user. For GlobalProtect, this URL is not used, but for administrators using the profile, this URL is needed to log off.
- **SAML HTTP Binding for SSO/SLO Requests to IDP** is used to control if the aforementioned two URLs will use the **Post** method, where the firewall sends a `base64 encoded HTML form` to the IDP, or the **Redirect** method, where the firewall sends `base64` encoded messages within URL parameters.
- If a self-signed certificate was downloaded from the IDP, disable **Validate Identity Provider Certificate**.
- Similarly, the firewall can be set to **Sign SAML Message to IDP** to provide more integrity to outbound authentication messages. However, this will only work if a certificate is used that the IDP can verify. Disable this option if the firewall uses self-signed certificates.

- A maximum clock skew of `60` seconds should be more than sufficient to account for latency. Make sure that the firewall is set to the correct time zone in **Device** > **Setup** and has NTP servers set up in **Device** > **Setup** > **Services**:

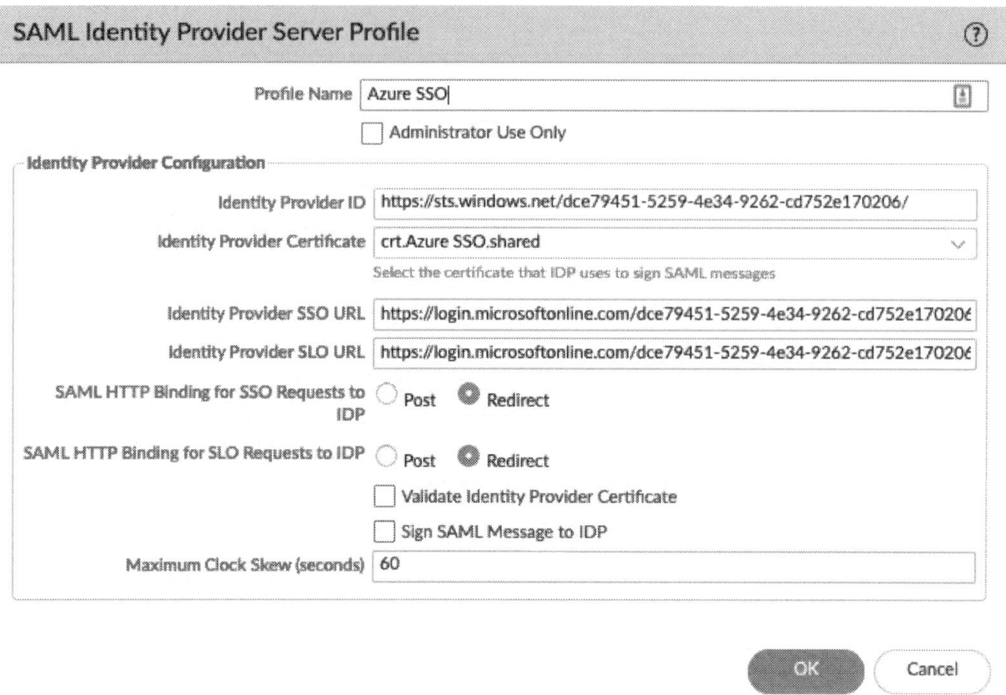

Figure 2.8 – SAML Identity Provider Server Profile

Once the server profile has been created, create a new authentication profile in **Device** > **Authentication Profile**. As shown in the following screenshot, set the authentication **Type** to SAML and select the newly created server profile as **IdP Server Profile**. **Certificate for Signing Requests** can be added if a commercial CA certificate is available and installed on the firewall that was signed by a public root CA. This allows the IDP to identify its authenticity. **Enable Single Logout** can be enabled if the profile will also be used to authenticate administrators on the firewall. In **Certificate Profile**, you should set a profile containing the Intermediary CA certificate information that was used to sign the IDP certificate. This will allow the firewall to verify the authenticity of messages originating from the IDP. If the IDP is using a self-signed certificate, leave this as **None**.

In **User Attributes in SAML Messages from IDP**, set the same username attribute to how it's set in the Azure Enterprise application:

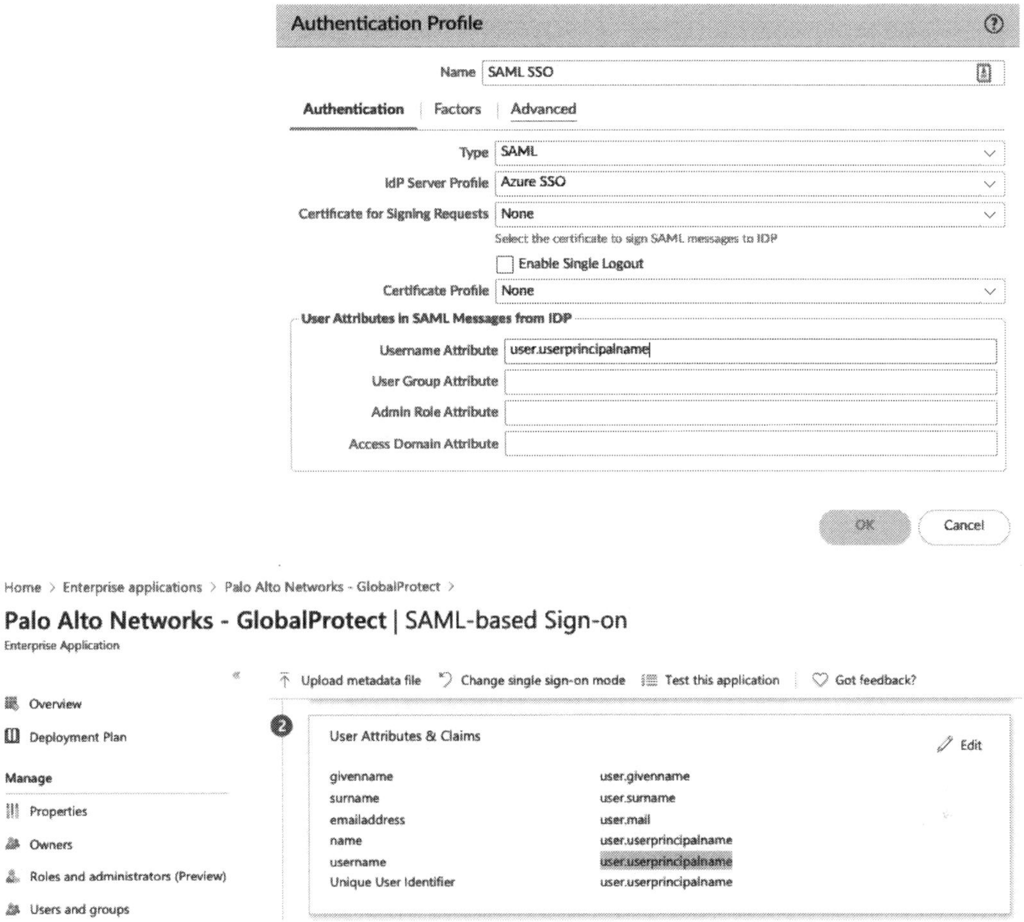

Figure 2.9 – SAML authentication profile and Azure user attributes

In the **Advanced** tab, set **Allow List** to `all` for now, as shown in the following screenshot. If you have User-ID group mapping enabled, you can add an appropriate user group here:

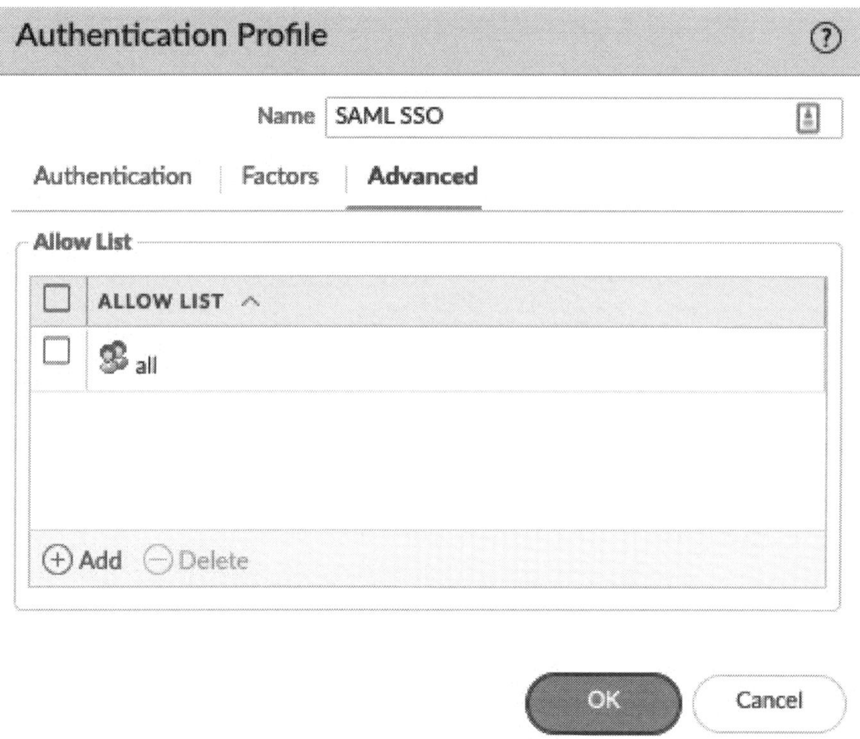

Figure 2.10 – Authentication Profile advanced options

The next step is to add the new authentication profile to GlobalProtect to apply SAML SSO to the new connection. If there is already an existing GlobalProtect deployment and you are aiming to replace LDAP but want to test your new profile a bit first, you can set an **OS** parameter to limit when a specific authentication profile is invoked. From the GlobalProtect portal, open **Network** > **GlobalProtect** > **Portals** > **<portal-name>** and add a new **Client Authentication**. As shown in the following screenshot, there are many operating system options, but there is also a **browser** option. This will only trigger a Client Authentication profile if the portal is opened via a **web browser**, which makes this a good option for testing the new SAML profile.

This also means you could set up a specific Client Authentication profile for anyone that needs to be able to download the GlobalProtect agent, which can be accomplished via a web browser, and one or multiple other Client Authentication profiles for anyone already using the GlobalProtect agent and reaching out to the GlobalProtect Portal for configuration information:

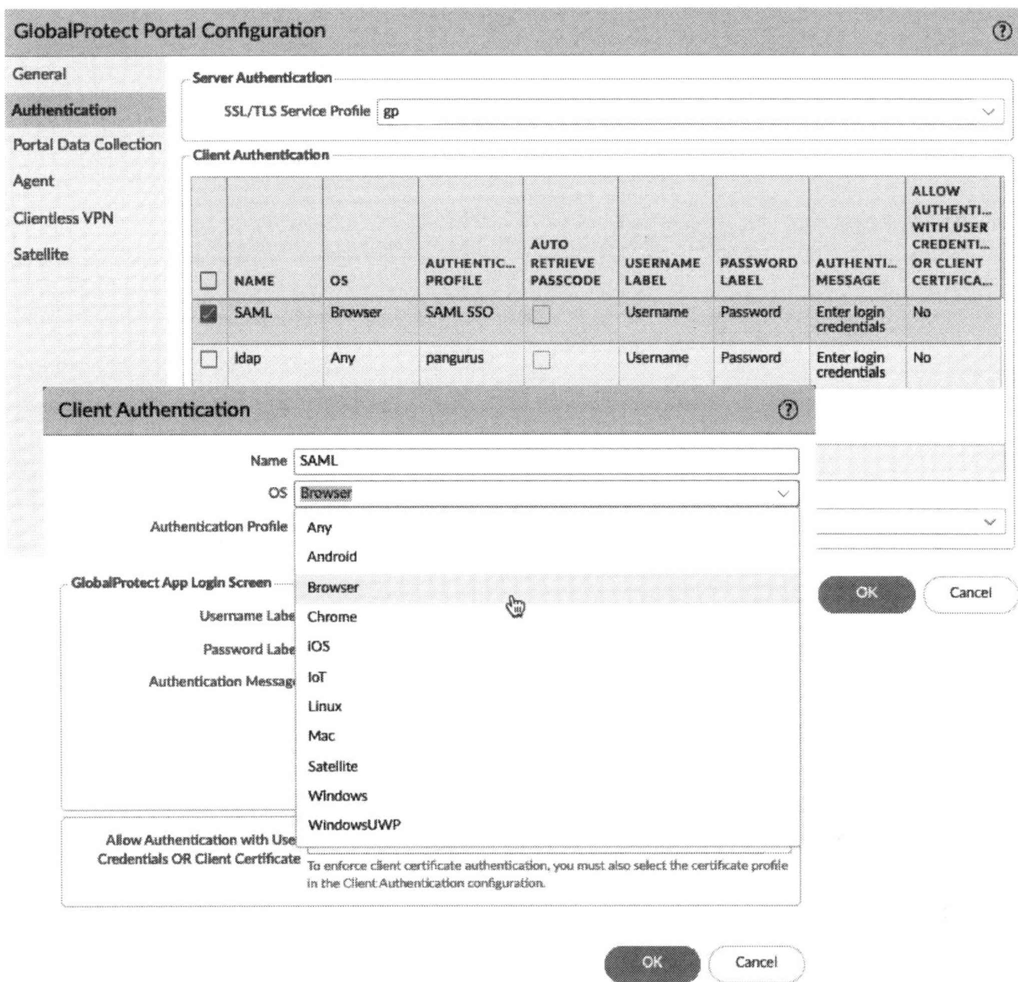

Figure 2.11 – GlobalProtect Client Authentication OS settings

> **Important Note**
>
> The Client Authentication profiles are parsed top to bottom, so if an **Any** profile is at the top, subsequent profiles will not be considered.

Once this new setting has been committed to the firewall, the regular login page will redirect you to Identity Provider SSO URL instead, since it was entered in the SAML Identity Provider Server Profile. As shown in the following screenshot, the regular login page should now return the IDP page instead:

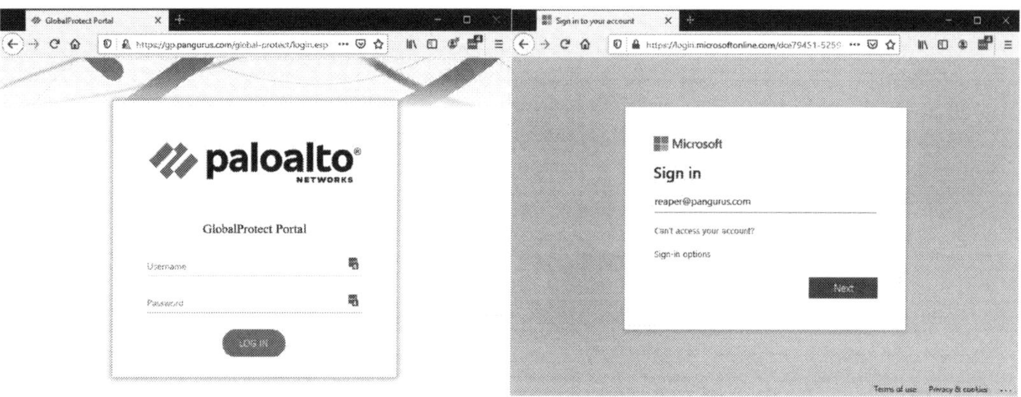

Figure 2.12 – Regular and SAML portal login page

After logging onto the IDP, the portal should redirect you back to the regular GlobalProtect portal and produce a list of downloadable GlobalProtect agents. If you encounter an error message instead, carefully review what might be wrong since in most cases, there will simply be an error in the identifier or redirect URL since it was configured on the IDP. One example is Azure requiring port `443` to be in the identifier URL, as we mentioned earlier. The error message shown in the following screenshot will appear if the port was not added:

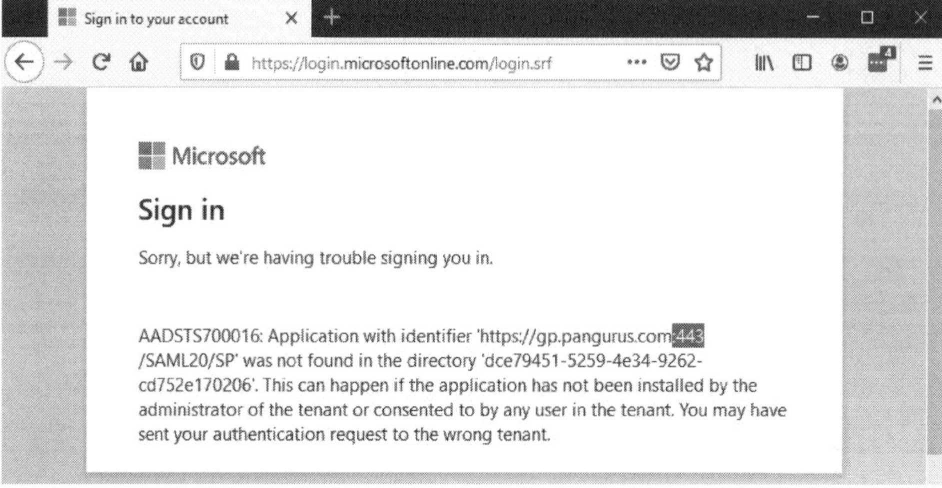

Figure 2.13 – Error in the identifier URL

Once the portal configuration is working as expected, the authentication profile can be applied to all OS types and also added to the gateway configuration, as shown in the following screenshot:

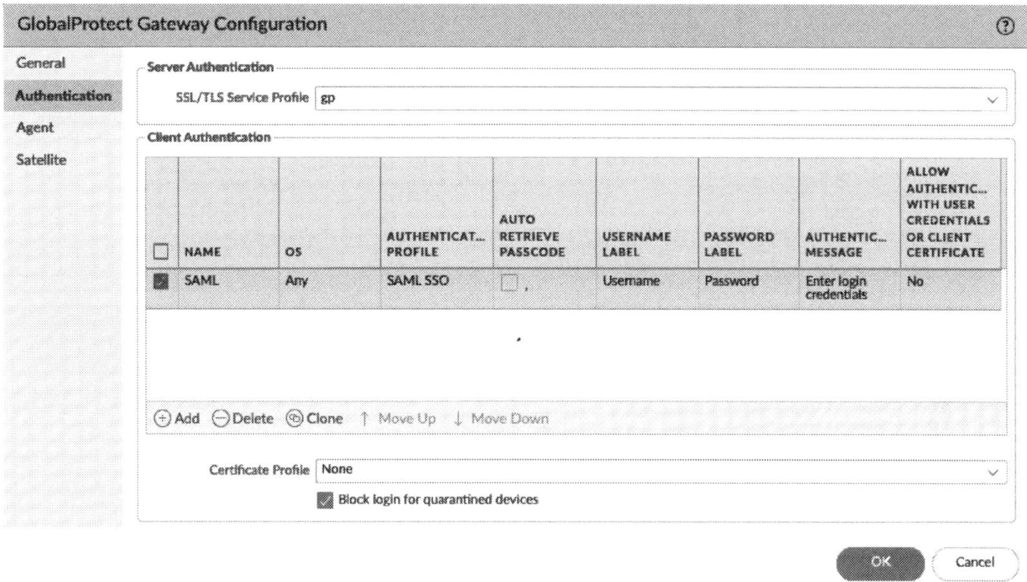

Figure 2.14 – The SAML SSO in GlobalProtect Gateway Configuration

With this configuration, the users will now be able to log into GlobalProtect using Azure AD credentials. In the next section, we'll learn about enabling **pre-logon**, which enables a VPN connection before the user has actually logged onto Windows.

Setting up a VPN connection before the user has logged on

For network drives to be mapped properly and logon scripts to be executed when a user logs onto their desktop, you may need to have a VPN connection established before the user logs on. This is because there may be timing issues between the user passing their credentials to the operating system, scripts being called to be run, and the desktop variant of GlobalProtect coming on and setting up a connection. Pre-logon is a feature that allows such connections to be set up. Starting from **GlobalProtect 5.0.3**, there are two variants of pre-logon that can be deployed: *user initiated pre-logon* and *de facto pre-logon*.

Configuring user-initiated pre-logon

The user-initiated flavour of pre-logon does exactly what it advertises by letting a user decide for themselves when they want to establish a pre-logon connection. This can be useful if the user does not always need to have a connection, and only requires one if they need to boot into a preloaded environment that depends on mapped drives or pre-established connections to the data centre, or maybe for their laptop to run updates from a central update server without them being logged onto their desktop environment.

Configuring the portal

To enable pre-logon, first, access the agent configuration via **Network** > **GlobalProtect** > **Portal** > **<portal-name>** > **Agent** > **Agent Configs** > **App.**

As shown in the following screenshot, set **Connect Method** to Pre-logon or **Pre-logon then On-demand** so that the feature is enabled. Also, make sure **Use Single Sign-on** is enabled:

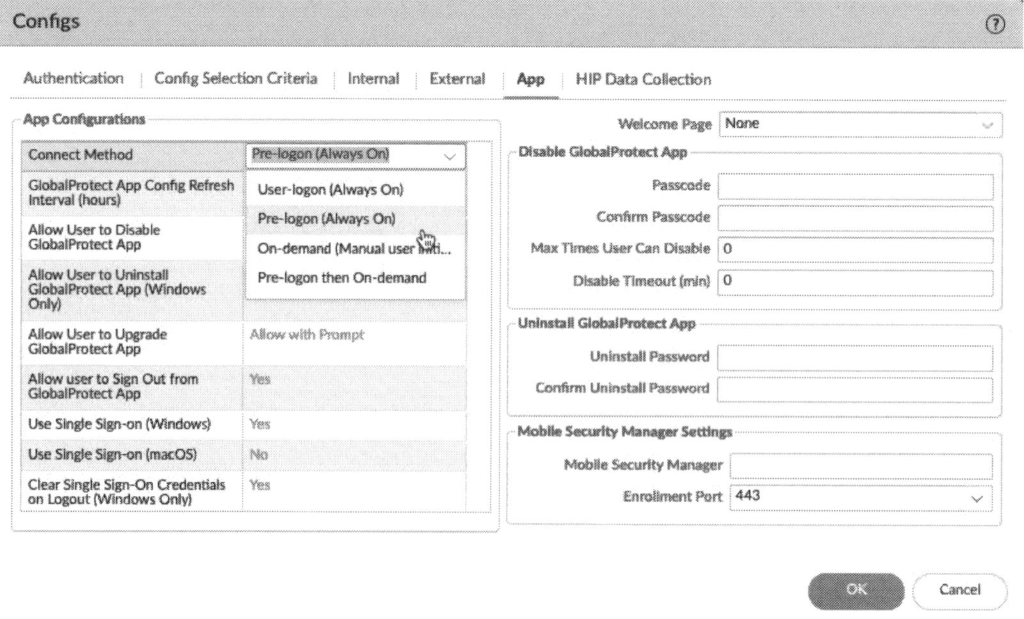

Figure 2.15 – Pre-logon configuration

Next, activate **Authentication Override Cookies**.

As shown in the following screenshot, the authentication override cookies can be enabled in both the agent configuration for the portal and gateway individually. The override cookies for the portal connection allow an agent to collect configuration updates, while the override cookie on the gateway allows the agent to establish an `ssl` or `IPsec` connection to the gateway. Both the portal and gateway use the same cookie, so they can be generated on one or the other or both, with the portal and gateway each having a different lifetime. When the cookie expires, GlobalProtect will prompt the user to re-authenticate, creating a new cookie with a refreshed lifetime. The portal can have a longer lifetime, so users need to authenticate less frequently to collect configuration data while the gateway grants access to the corporate network. This should prompt the user for credentials more frequently.

In **Network** > **GlobalProtect** > **Portal** > *<portal-name>* > **Agent** > *<agent configuration>* > **Authentication**, enable **Generate cookie for authentication override** and **Accept cookie for authentication override**.

Set a cookie lifetime that is representative of the expected time between logon events.

A certificate is required to sign the cookies. The GlobalProtect portal certificate can be used, or a self-signed certificate.

Configuring the gateway

In **Network** > **GlobalProtect** > **Gateway** > *<gateway-name>* > **Agent** > **Client Settings** > *<Client Settings configuration>* > **Authentication Override**, enable **Generate cookie for authentication override** and **Accept cookie for authentication override**.

Use the same certificate as the one you set in the GlobalProtect portal:

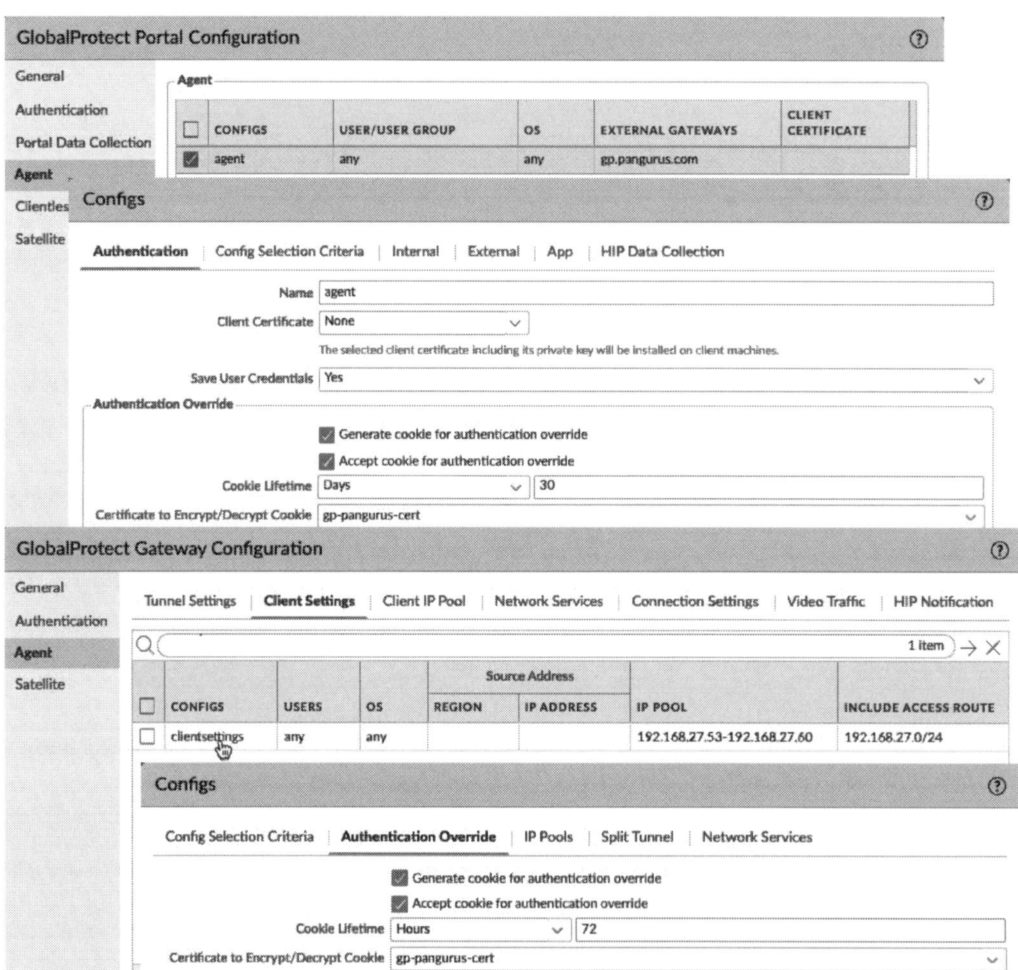

Figure 2.16 – Client settings configuration for pre-logon users

In addition, add a second **Client Settings** configuration specifically for the pre-logon users. This will allow more granularity while users are connected in pre-logon mode as their actual username will be unknown (they will register as `pre-logon` on the firewall), so a different IP pool is applied to these users. Specific security rules can be created that allow this subnet or IP range to only access specific servers. As shown in the following screenshot, create a new **Client Settings** configuration. This can be achieved by selecting the existing configuration and clicking **clone**.

You can then open the configuration and rename and edit its parameters. In the **Config Selection Criteria** section, make sure to change the user dropdown from any to **pre-logon**. In **the IP POOL column for client**, set a different subnet to distinguish logged-in users from pre-logon users:

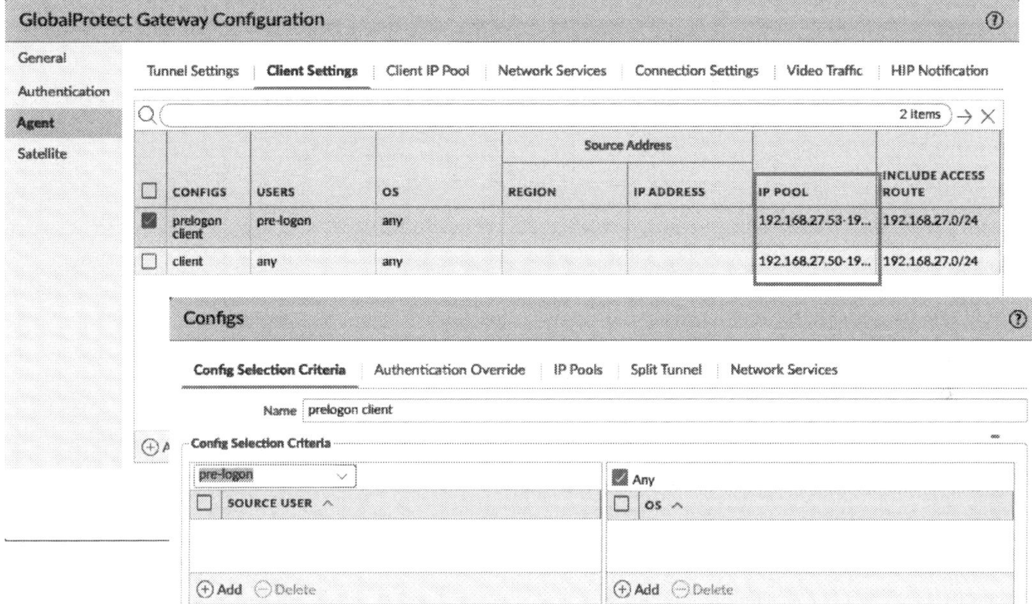

Figure 2.17 – Client settings configuration for pre-logon users

Preparing the endpoint

For user-initiated pre-logon to work, a few registry settings need to be added to the endpoint in **HKEY_LOCAL_MACHINE\SOFTWARE\Palo Alto Networks\GlobalProtect\PanSetup**.

As shown in the following screenshot, ensure that your **Prelogon** value data is set to **1**. This configuration should be passed down from the GlobalProtect portal.

Create two new string values by clicking **Edit** > **New** > **String Value**:

- **use-sso**: Set the value data to `yes` .
- **ShowPreLogonButton**: Set the value data to `yes`:

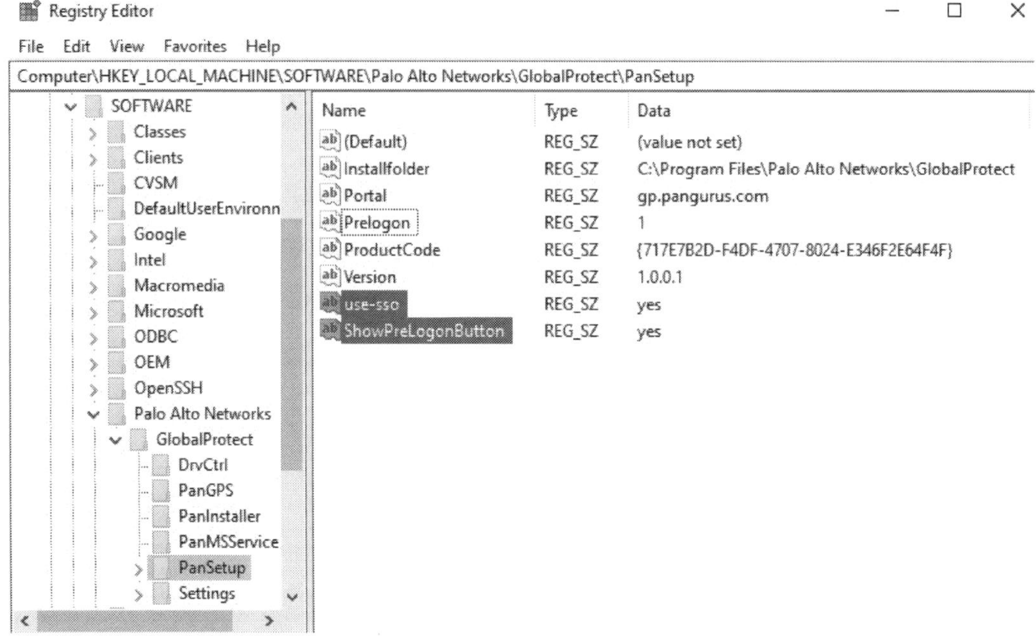

Figure 2.18 – Registry entries for user-initiated pre-logon

To activate these changes, reboot your Windows machine. Once the endpoint has been restarted, click **Sign in options** to expose the GlobalProtect tile, which, in turn, displays the user-initiated pre-logon option.

As shown in the following screenshot, with cookies enabled and a valid cookie still residing on the system, the user can click **Start GlobalProtect Connection** without entering a password and the connection will be established:

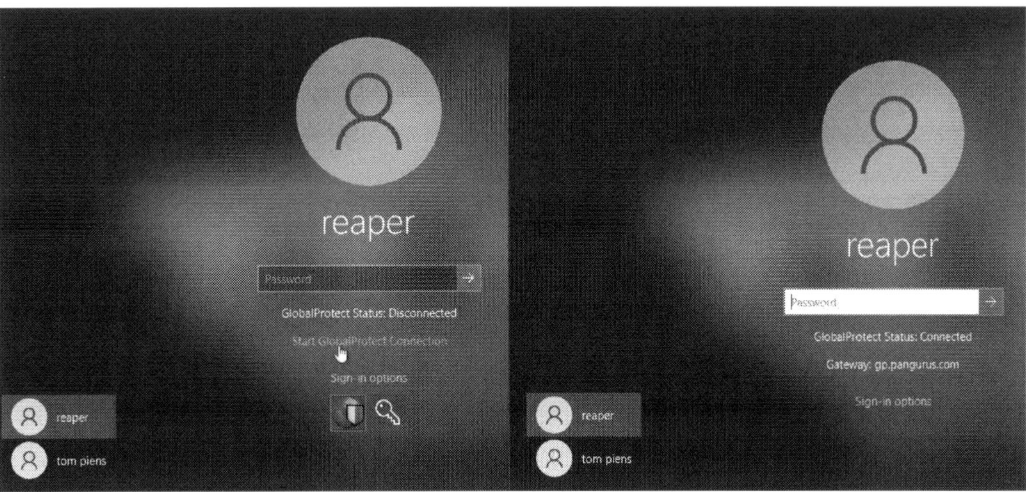

Figure 2.19 – User initiated pre-logon

When corporate assets need an always-on connection, pre-logon can also be enabled so that it always connects, not just when a user manually connects.

Configuring always-on pre-logon

Opposed to occasionally needing to create an IPsec connection while the user is not logged on yet, a permanent pre-logon is also available that consistently starts a tunnel connection whenever an endpoint is booted up. This helps us establish mapped drives, run start-up scripts, and deploy software, and even allows IT staff to access devices if a user is not logged on. It also enables full control of all the outgoing connections the operating system makes without a user's interaction. GPO policies can be updated even while a user is logged off.

> **Important Note**
>
> Always-on pre-logon can't be used at the same time as user-initiated pre-logon. If a mixture is needed, a different portal and gateway set need to be used.

Similar to user-initiated login, the portal connection (configuration) can be established using cookies from a previously established full connection. The gateway connection will be established using a machine certificate so that it can always be established, even if the user has never logged on, an existing cookie has expired, or user credentials were not saved. The machine certificate should ideally be generated on the internal **Public Key Infrastructure** (**PKI**) but can also be provided through a self-signed certificate on the firewall.

Preparing pre-logon certificates

First, the Enterprise CA root certificate needs to be imported via **Device** > **Certificate Management** > **Certificates**. Click the certificate to open its properties and enable **Trusted Root CA**, as shown in the following screenshot. If an OCSP certificate is available from the Enterprise CA, import that certificate next. It should appear slightly indented below the root certificate to indicate that it was signed by said root certificate:

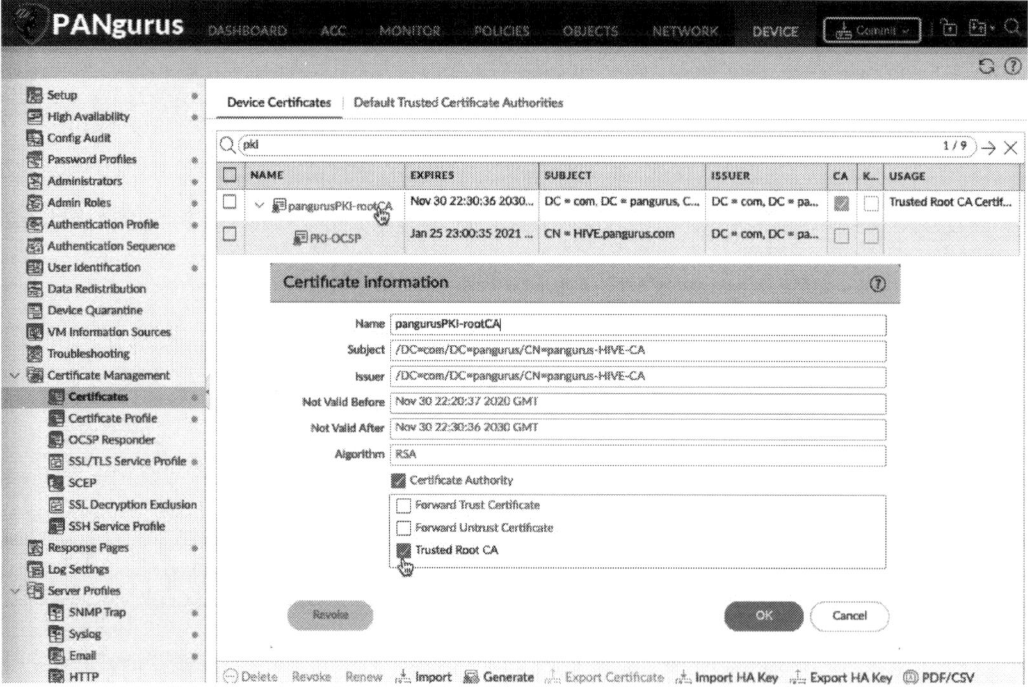

Figure 2.20 – Importing the CA root certificate

If no Certificate Authority is available, generate a self-signed certificate that resembles the one shown in the following screenshot. Make sure that the **Certificate Authority** box is checked and add the appropriate AAN information to the **Certificate Attributes** fields at the bottom:

Figure 2.21 – Self-signed certificate authority

Next, create a **Certificate Profile** via **Device** > **Certificate Management** > **Certificate Profile**. As shown in the following screenshot, provide an easily identifiable name and leave the username field as `None`. Add your CA certificate and, if available, fill in the **Default OCSP URL** and the **OCSP Verify Certificate fields** (optional). Check the **Use OCSP** checkbox if OCSP is available. If the firewall will use a self-signed certificate, leave the OCSP information blank:

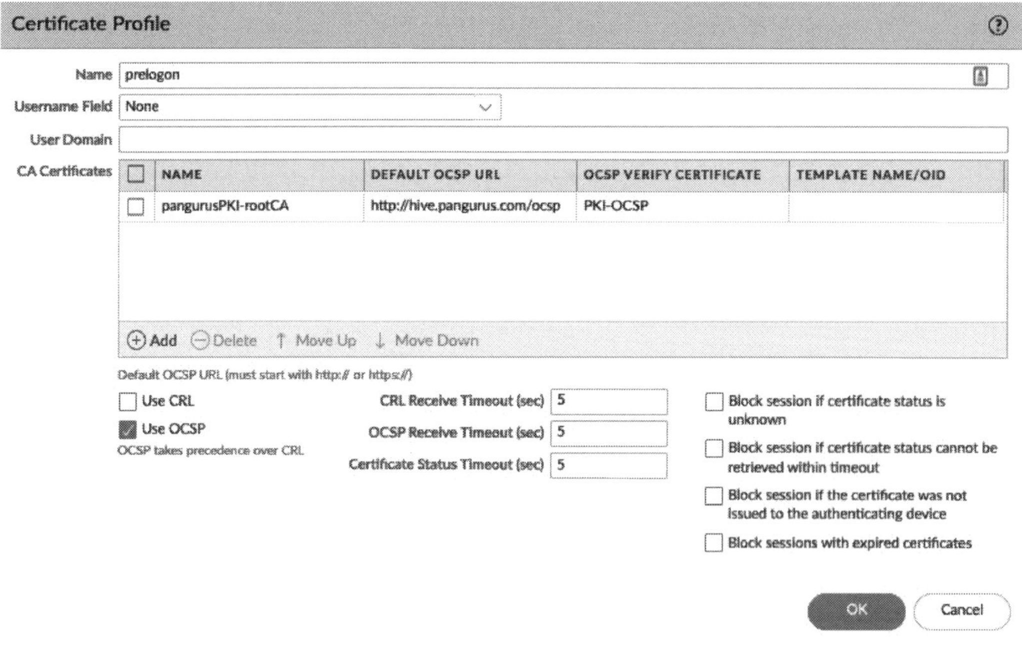

Figure 2.22 – Adding a certificate profile for pre-logon

> **Important Note**
>
> This same certificate profile can also be used for client certificates that are used during authentication. If the client certificates are issued by a different CA, you can add the second CA certificate to this profile.

The next step is to add the certificate profile to the gateway.

Configuring the GlobalProtect gateway for pre-logon

Open the GlobalProtect gateway **Authentication** tab via **Network** > **GlobalProtect** > **Gateways** > *<gateway name>* > **Authentication** and add the **prelogon** certificate profile, as shown in the following screenshot.

Because the pre-logon certificate profile does not have an association in **Username Field** such as **Subject** or **Subject Alt**, which are values it would normally take from a client certificate that's assigned to a specific user, any authentication profile in the gateway object must have **Allow Authentication with User Credential OR Client Certificate** set to **No**:

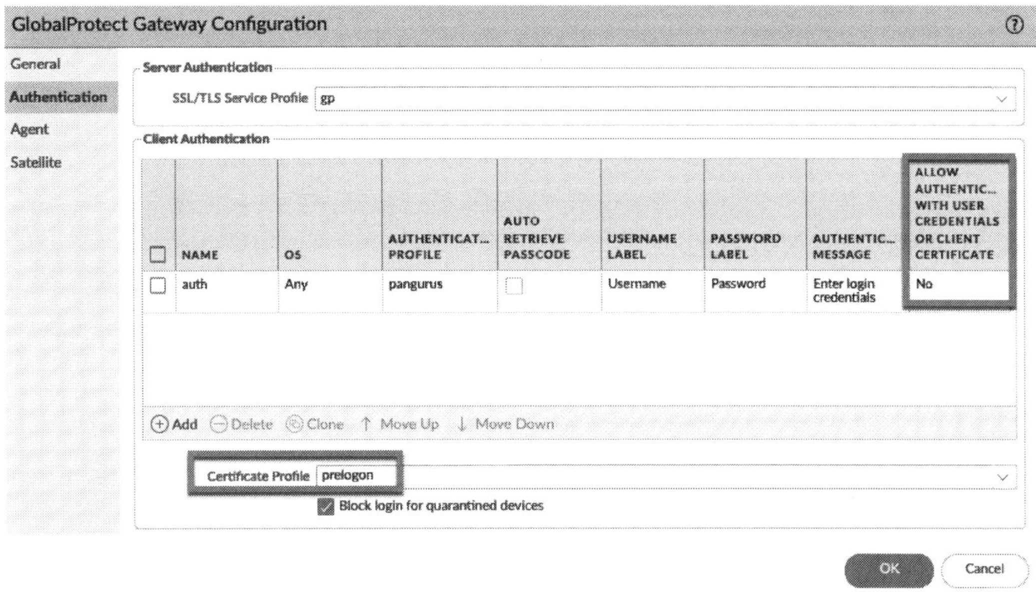

Figure 2.23 – Adding the certificate profile to the GlobalProtect gateway

> **Important Note**
>
> If this setting were to be set to Yes, a client would be able to set up a full VPN tunnel while logged into their desktop using only the pre-logon certificate, which does not contain a username. A commit error will appear if this setting is forgotten; that is, **GlobalProtect gateway(gateway) auth setting is invalid: no username field is configured in certificate profile**.

Then, the pre-logon agent configuration needs to be added to the **Agent** tab. As shown in the following screenshot, both a pre-logon and normally logged-on user configuration can be created on the same gateway. Both configurations can have all the same settings, including DNS servers and split tunnelling, except for the IP pools, which need to be different.

For the pre-logon config, set **Config Selection Criteria** to **pre-logon**.

For all **regular** users, either use **any** or **select** and then add group information:

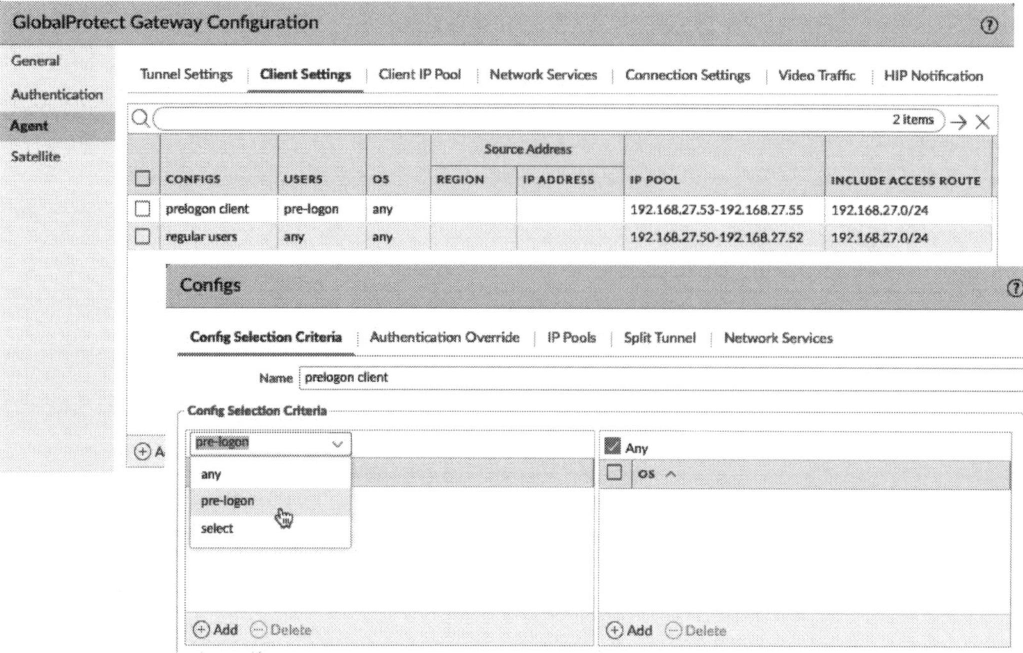

Figure 2.24 – Pre-logon and logged on user configuration on the GlobalProtect gateway

If needed, pre-logon and regular users can also be set up to use separate gateways. This will allow pre-logon users to be placed in a completely different network segment with a unique zone to identify them in security rules, in addition to the IP pool and pre-logon username. After creating a duplicate gateway object, access the portal configuration.

Configuring the GlobalProtect portal for pre-logon

Open the GlobalProtect portal agent configuration via **Network** > **GlobalProtect** > **Portals** > *<portal name>* > the **Authentication** tab and add the **prelogon** certificate profile, making sure **Allow Authentication with User Credential OR Client Certificate** is set to **No** for all the authentication profiles that are configured on this page, as shown in the following screenshot:

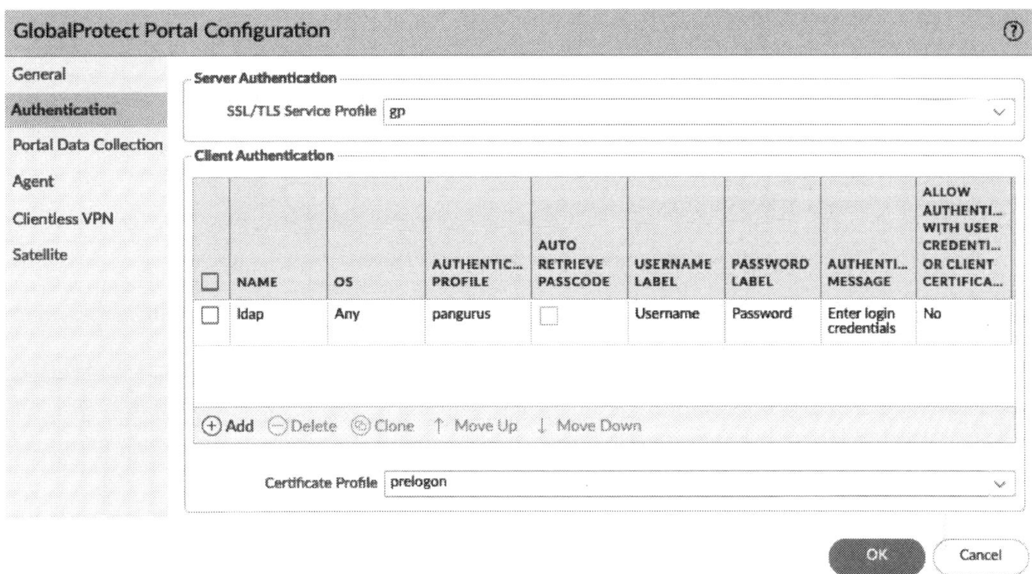

Figure 2.25 – GlobalProtect portal authentication configuration

Next, access the **Agent** tab. If a single gateway is used for pre-logon and regular users, *only one agent config is needed* and must be set to **any** as the user/user group.

If different gateways need to be used, create a new agent configuration and set the user/user group to pre-logon. *Make sure the pre-logon agent configuration is at the top*; otherwise, pre-logon users will use the any config instead.

This new agent config can now be set to different gateways, as shown in the following screenshot. In the **App** tab, set **Connection Method** to **Pre-logon (Always On)** or to **Pre-logon then On-demand**:

- **Always On** will make the endpoint set up the pre-logon connection as soon as it is booted up and then immediately connect once the user logs on.

- **Pre-logon then On-demand** will immediately set up the pre-logon connection once it's booted up, but then disconnect once the user logs on, waiting for the user to manually set up the connection:

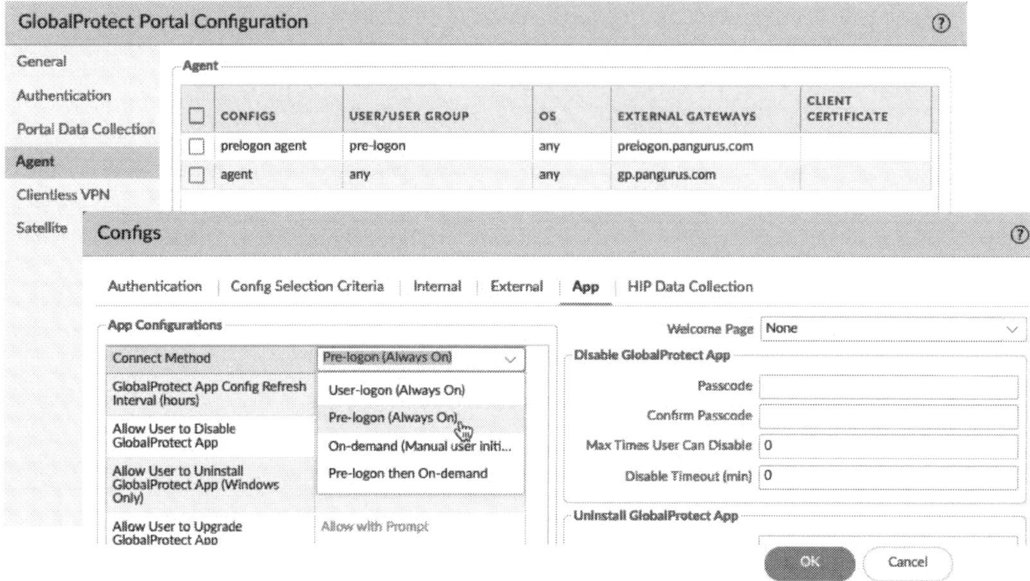

Figure 2.26 – Separate agent configuration on the GlobalProtect portal

In the **Authentication** tab for each Agent Config, you can *optionally* enable an authentication override so that portal authentication can also be established via the override cookie that was generated the last time the user logged on.

> **Important Note**
>
> Since there are two different IP pools between pre-logon and logged on users and the username switches from pre-logon to the proper username, the tunnel needs to be renamed during the logon process. To ensure this happens and that the logged-in user receives an IP address in the new IP pool, set the **Pre-Logon Tunnel Rename Timeout (sec) (Windows Only)** to 0 in **Portal** > **Agent** > **App** > **App Configuration**.

The last part is making sure the endpoint can connect via pre-logon.

Preparing the endpoint for pre-logon

If a self-signed CA certificate was generated to be used in the certificate profile, a new machine certificate will need to be generated that was signed by the CA. This ensures that trust can be established when the pre-logon GlobalProtect agent tries to authenticate itself using the certificate.

If the internal Enterprise CA is going to be used, a machine certificate may already have been issued to all the endpoints. Double check if a certificate has been loaded in **Certificate**s - **Local Computer** > **Personal**. You can access the certificate store by running `certlm.msc` on a Windows machine.

If an Enterprise CA exists but machines have not been issued a certificate yet, we can generate a **Certificate Signing Request** (**CSR**), which can then be exported and manually installed on endpoints. The following screenshot shows the difference in generating a **self-signed subordinate certificate** and a CSR:

Figure 2.27 – Generating machine certificates

The self-signed certificate can immediately be exported and installed on the endpoint, but the CSR will need to be signed by the Enterprise CA before it can be used. As an example, the following screenshot shows how I access my CA via `http://hive.pangurus.com/certsrv` and initiate a certificate request, input the CSR signature, and download a freshly created certificate:

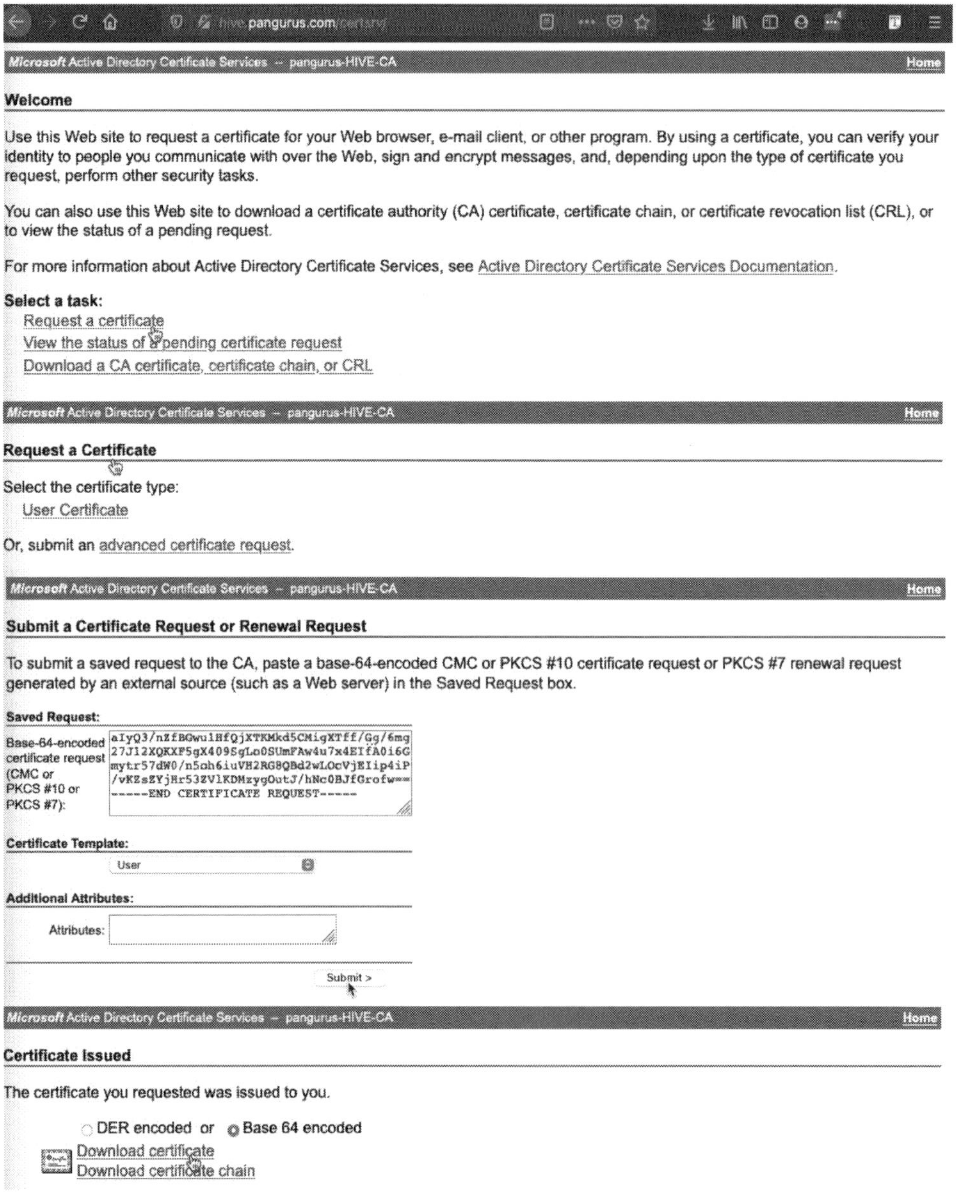

Figure 2.28 – Generating a certificate from a certificate signing request

The newly generated certificate can then be imported into the firewall, as shown in the following screenshot. Make sure that the certificate name is set to the same name as the CSR. This way, the CSR will be replaced by the actual certificate and will also be linked to the certificate chain if a CA certificate was imported:

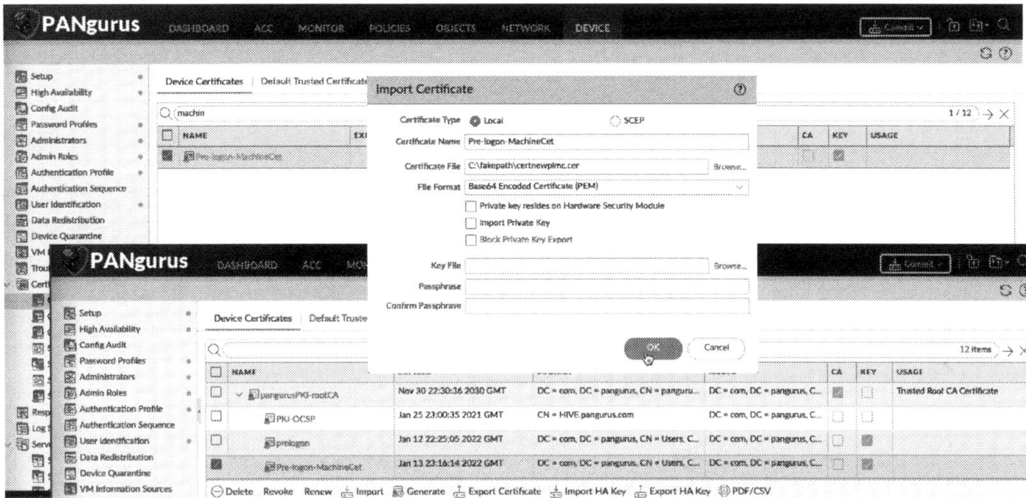

Figure 2.29 – Importing the CSR output

The very last step is to import the self-signed or CA-issued certificate into the endpoint. As demonstrated in the following screenshot, export the certificate from the firewall in `pkcs12` format certificate and copy it to the endpoint:

Figure 2.30 – Exporting the machine certificate

Once the certificate has been copied to the endpoint or available from a share, you can double-click the certificate file and follow the steps shown in the following screenshot:

1. Select **Local Machine**.
2. Enter the required **Password** information so that the private key can be imported.

3. Enter `Personal` in the **Certificate store** field to save the certificate:

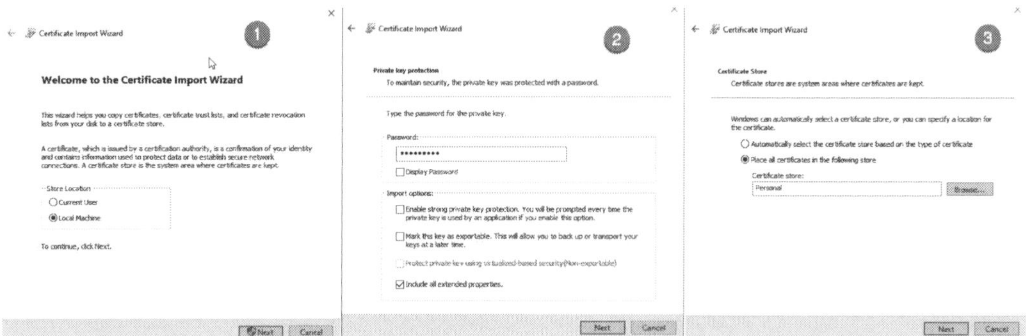

Figure 2.31 – Installing a machine certificate

Once the certificate has been loaded, refresh the GlobalProtect agent and restart or log out of the endpoint. A GlobalProtect dialog window will now appear in a connected or disconnected state on the logon screen, as shown in the following screenshot:

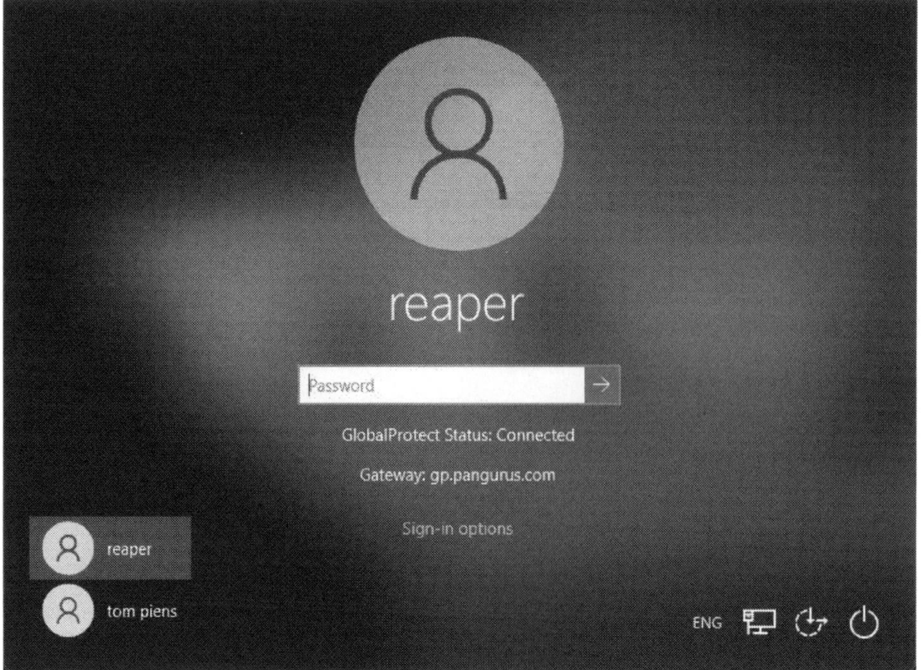

Figure 2.32 – Windows logon screen with GlobalProtect pre-logon connected

With users connecting remotely, there's always the risk of an endpoint displaying suspicious behaviour, so what can we do to mitigate a threat to the network?

Leveraging quarantine to isolate agents

In *Chapter 1*, *Centralizing Logs*, we learned about *built-in actions* in log forwarding profiles and we saw that there is a quarantine option. So, how can this option be leveraged to protect the core network?

If suspected devices are not allowed to connect under any circumstance, access can be declined by checking the **Block login for quarantined devices** checkbox as shown in the following screenshot, which will make it impossible for devices that were placed in quarantine to connect. This could make remediation more difficult as IT will not be able to simply connect to the device over a secured connection. This could cause some frustration with a quarantined user as they may be confused about why they are unable to connect, and they won't be able to do anything until staff have resolved the situation:

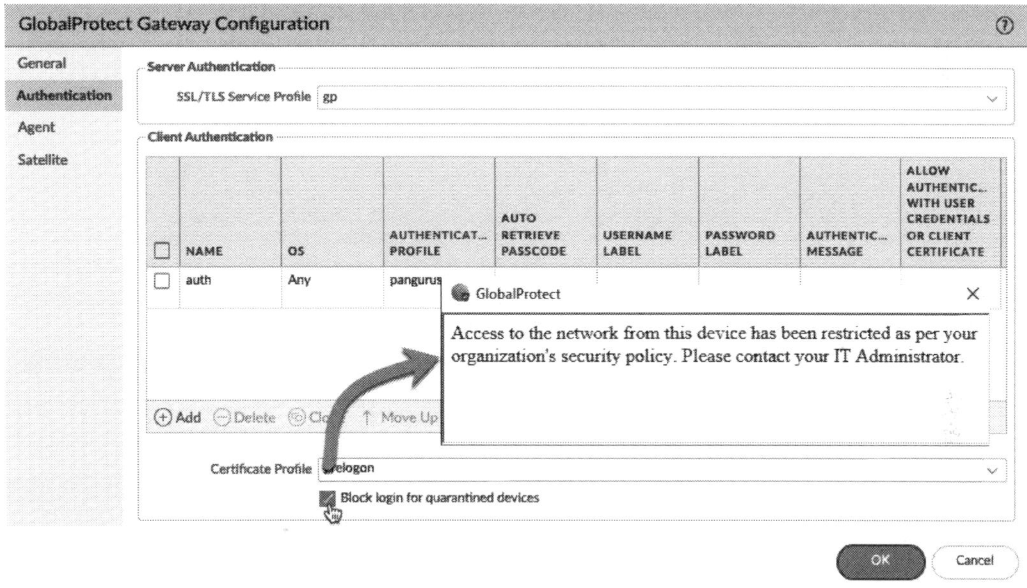

Figure 2.33 – Blocking access completely for quarantined devices

The quarantine message can be customized via the **Portal** > **Agent** > **App** menu.

A more user-friendly and practical approach is to leverage the quarantine isolation capabilities of the security rule base. As shown in the following screenshot, there are two rules – 25 and 26 – that will intercept any quarantined endpoints and only allow access to certain applications while blocking everything else. Rule 27 controls all pre-logon connections, while rule 28 allows regular users to access all the resources they need. Since the user can create a connection, IT staff will be able to set up a secure remote desktop connection to the affected user if needed:

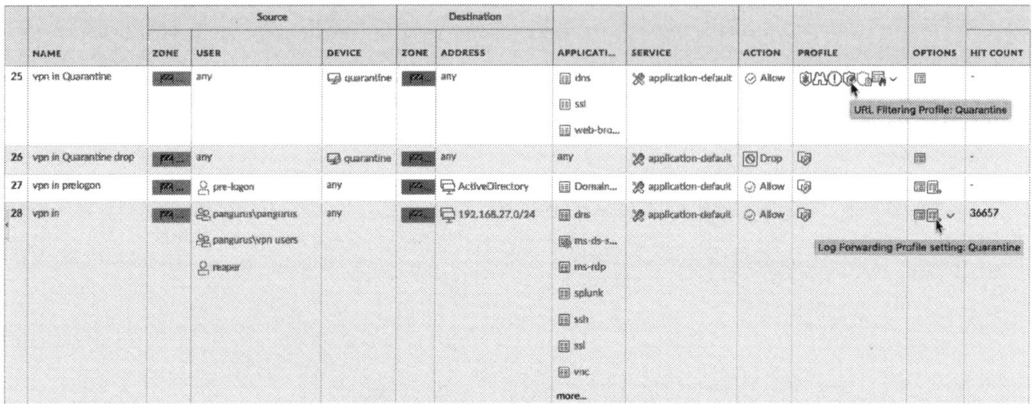

Figure 2.34 – Quarantined sources in the security policy

Important Note

For the preceding setup to function properly, the **Block login for quarantined devices** option shown in *Figure 2.33* needs to be unchecked so that endpoints can create a VPN connection to the gateway.

Rules 27 and 28 contain a log forwarding profile set to quarantine any host that generates a threat log with a severity of **high** or **critical**, as shown in the following screenshot. Rule 25, which allows quarantined hosts access to DNS, SSL, and web browsing, has a URL filtering profile that has all its categories set to **override**:

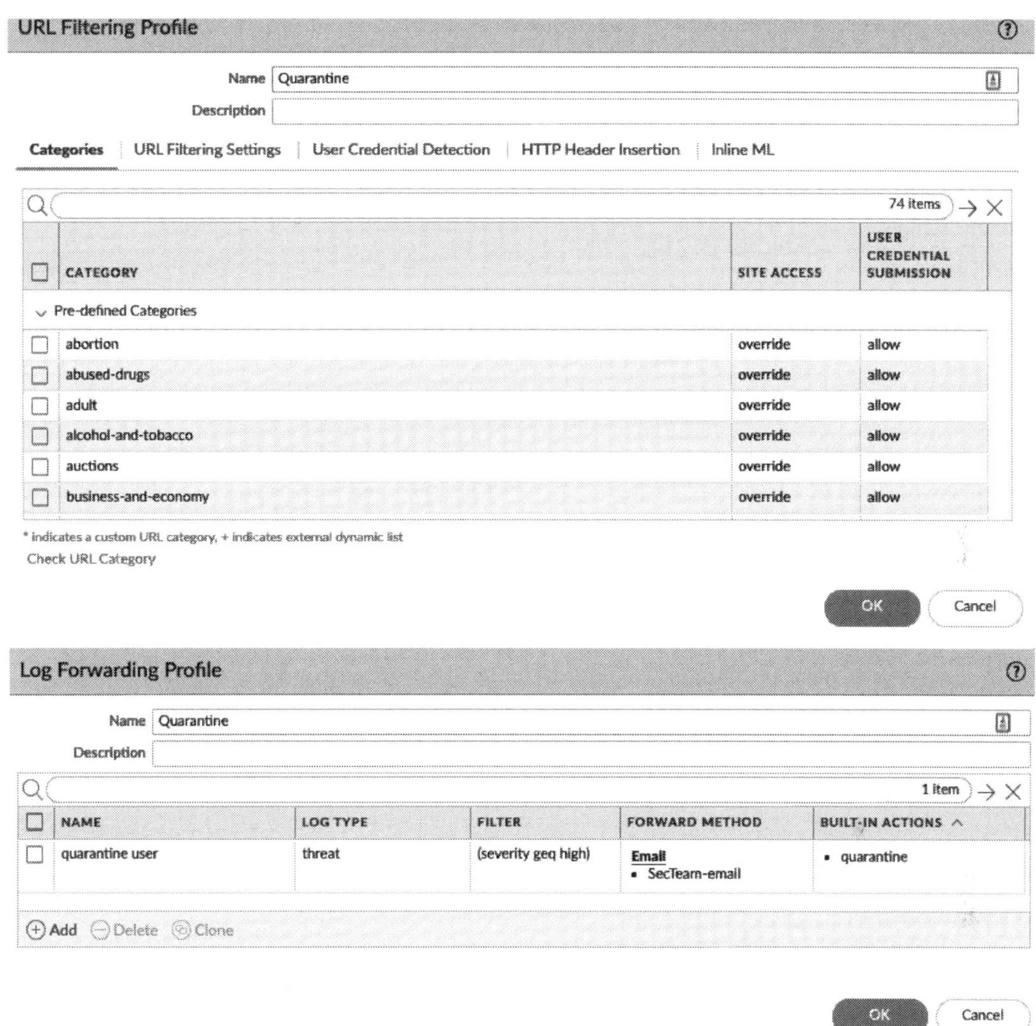

Figure 2.35 – URL Filtering Profile and Log Forwarding Profile pages

The URL filtering profile, which has all its categories set to override, will provide two functionalities:

1. An override response page can be customized to display a friendly message to the user, showing steps they need to take to get the issue resolved as quickly as possible, including remediation steps they can take and numbers to call to reach IT, for example.

2. The override page offers a password field that allows a remotely connected IT person to grant access to any URL category, in case a remediation file needs to be downloaded. The password can be set via **Device** > **Setup** > **Content-ID** > **URL Admin Override**.

The response pages can be found in **Device** > **Setup** > **Response Pages** > **URL Filtering Continue and Override Page**.

The currently predefined page can be downloaded for easy editing and then uploaded as a shared page in **Device** > **Response pages**, as shown in the following screenshot. An example page can be found at `https://github.com/PacktPublishing/Mastering-Palo-Alto-Networks/blob/master/override%20example`:

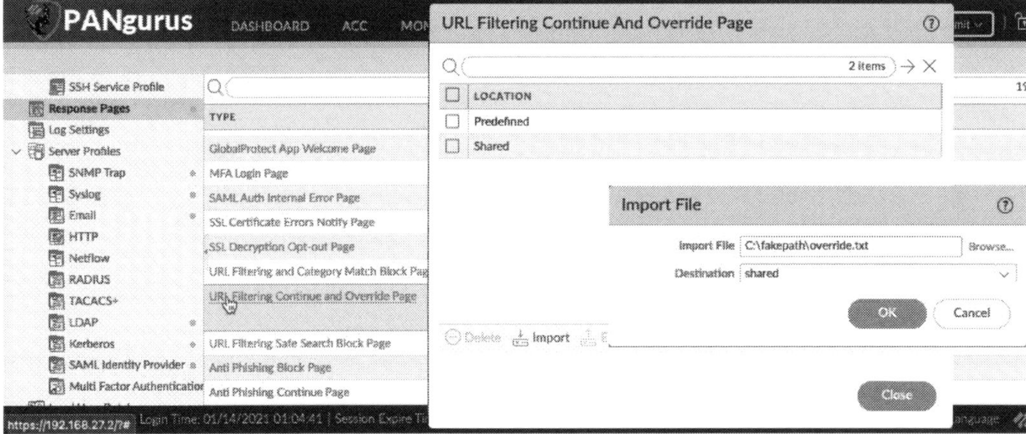

Figure 2.36 – Uploading a customized response page

Once a device has been placed in quarantine, an administrator must remove it from quarantine via **Device** > **Device Quarantine** > (select the device) and click **Delete**, as shown in the following screenshot:

Figure 2.37 – Device quarantine

While configuring and using GlobalProtect, some users may run into some issues or some features may not appear to work. Next, we'll learn how to troubleshoot some common issues.

Practical troubleshooting for GlobalProtect issues

When you're troubleshooting connectivity issues, there are several places where information can be gathered to try and determine the cause of a user not being able to connect. Starting from **PAN-OS 9.1**, most of the useful GlobalProtect logs can be found in **Monitor** > **Logs** > **GlobalProtect**, while the authentication logs can still be found in **Monitor** > **Logs** > **System**, as shown in the following screenshot. Before PAN-OS 9.1, all these logs were contained in the system log. Common issues such as a missing client certificate, a wrongly entered username or password, or an agent that tries to authenticate with an expired cookie can be found here so that the user can be directed accordingly:

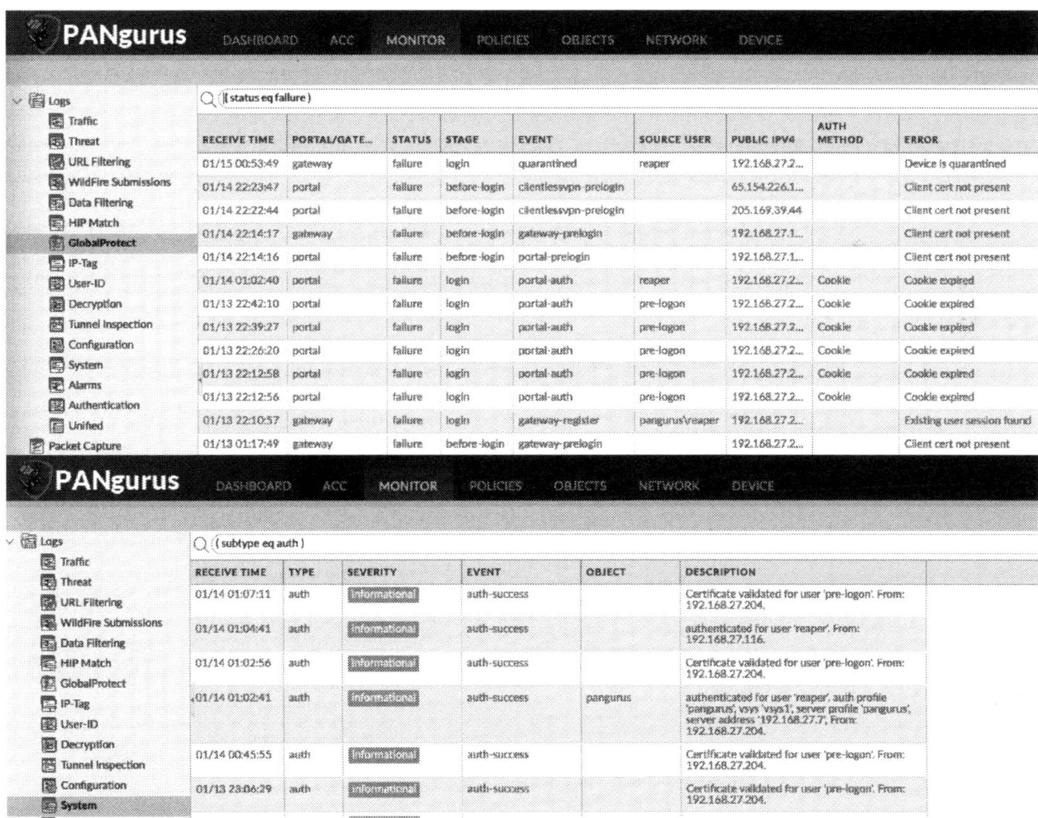

Figure 2.38 – GlobalProtect and system logs

The currently connected users can be accessed from the portal and gateway pages via **Network** > **GlobalProtect**. The **Current User** section of the portal will show which users are currently connected to the web portal, which, in most cases, will only reflect users trying to download the agent or using clientless apps. As shown in the following screenshot, the **Remote Users** area of the gateway section reflects users that currently have a tunnel. Previously connected users are also listed in the **Previous User** tab so that you can easily verify is a user has recently made a successful connection:

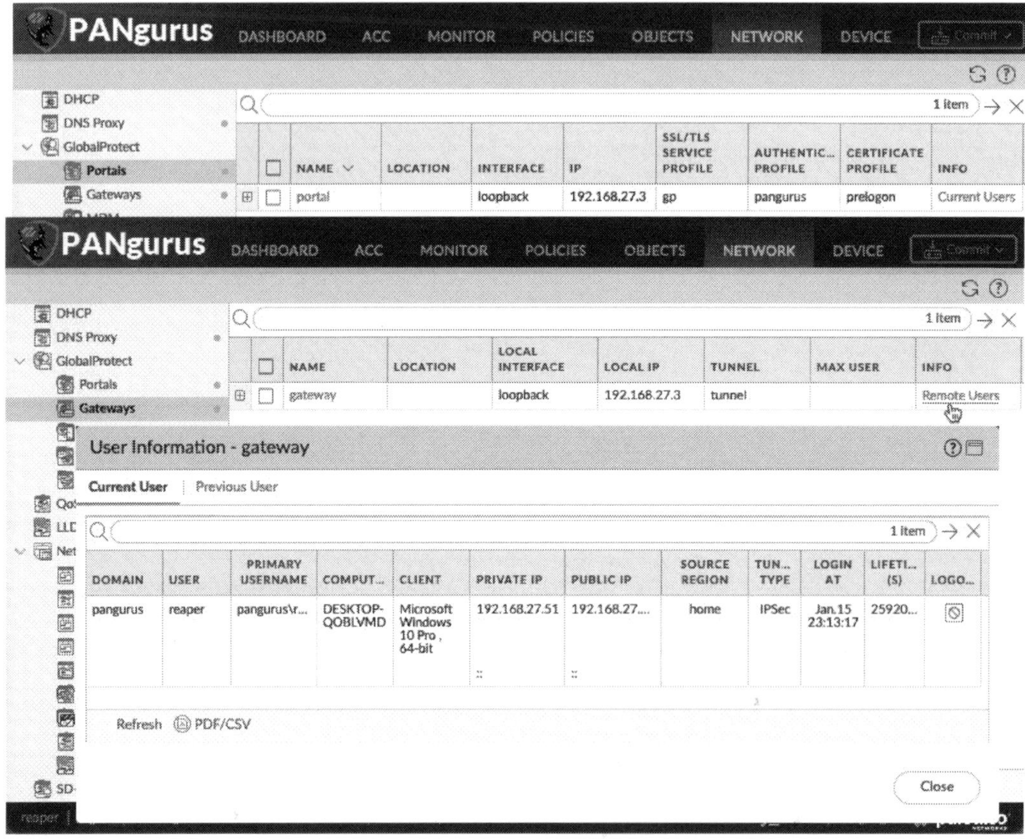

Figure 2.39 – Current and remote users in the GlobalProtect portal and gateway

If you can't find the information needed to troubleshoot an issue, there are still more options available via the **command-line interface** (**CLI**).

The preceding information can also be acquired in the CLI using the following commands:

- `show global-protect-gateway current-user` will display the current users and can also be set to filter for a domain, part of a username, or only for a specific gateway if multiple have been configured on the system. You can also look at previous users using `show global-protect-gateway previous-user`:

```
reaper@PANgurus> show global-protect-gateway current-user
+ domain     Show users which domain name start with the
string
+ gateway    Show for given GlobalProtect gateway
+ user       Show users which user name start with the
string
  |          Pipe through a command
  <Enter>    Finish input

reaper@PANgurus> show global-protect-gateway current-user
user reaper

GlobalProtect Gateway: gateway (1 users)
Tunnel Name            : gateway-N
        Domain-User Name              : pangurus\reaper
        Computer                      : DESKTOP-QOBLVMD
        Primary Username              : pangurus\reaper
        Region for Config             : home
        Source Region                 : home
        Client                        : Microsoft Windows 10
Pro , 64-bit
        VPN Type                      : Device Level VPN
        Mobile ID                     :
        Client OS                     : Windows
        Private IP                    : 192.168.27.51
        Private IPv6                  : ::
        Public IP (connected)         : 198.51.100.2
        Public IPv6                   : ::
        Client IP                     : 198.51.100.2
        ESP                           : exist
```

```
        SSL                               : none
        Login Time                        : Jan.15 23:13:17
        Logout/Expiration                 : Feb.14 23:13:17
        TTL                               : 2589248
        Inactivity TTL                    : 8064
        Request - Login                   : 2021-01-15
23:13:17.737 (1610748797737), 192.168.27.204
        Request - GetConfig               : 2021-01-15
23:13:18.038 (1610748798038), 192.168.27.204
        Request - SSLVPNCONNECT           :  (0), ::
```

- Basic information about the configured gateways on the system can be retrieved using the `show global-protect-gateway flow` command:

```
reaper@PANgurus> show global-protect-gateway flow

total tunnels configured:
1
filter - type GlobalProtect-Gateway, state any

total GlobalProtect-Gateway tunnel shown:
1

id   name                local-i/f         local-ip
tunnel-i/f
--   ----                    ---------          --------
----------
3    gateway-N               loopback
192.168.27.3                   tunnel

```

- It is also important to understand the difference between GlobalProtect and traditional IPsec VPNs. Even though the GlobalProtect agents also connect via IPsec, there is a different software process (a daemon) that handles agent connections instead of a site-to-site VPN.

- GlobalProtect is built to leverage SSL and has the portal as its starting point. This means it uses a web service for most of its operations, which is also reflected in the software processes that can be debugged. Interestingly, this process goes by a few different names, so it could be confusing when troubleshooting. If, for some reason, the service needs to be restarted, it should be addressed as `sslvpn-web-server`:

```
reaper@PANgurus> debug software restart process sslvpn-web-server

Process sslvpn was restarted by user reaper
```

- To debug the process itself, it is referred to as `ssl-vpn`:

```
reaper@PANgurus> debug ssl-vpn
> global                    global
> global-protect-gateway    global-protect-gateway
> global-protect-portal     global-protect-portal
> socket                    socket
```

- To start debugging, you can increase the overall debug level of the `ssl-vpn` process:

```
reaper@PANgurus> debug ssl-vpn global show

sw.sslvpn.debug.global: info

reaper@PANgurus> debug ssl-vpn global on debug

sw.sslvpn.debug.global: debug
```

- There is also a `global-protect` process that can be debugged, but this will only apply to HIP profile debugging and can also be used to change the interval at which HIP reports are sent:

```
reaper@PANgurus> debug global-protect portal show

cfg.global-protect.portal.debug: True
cfg.global-protect.portal.hip-report-interval: 86400

reaper@PANgurus> debug global-protect portal interval
  <value>  <60-86400> interval to send hip report
```

- Finally, the debug logs are stored as `appweb3-sslvpn.log`, with `appweb3` being the actual service that serves all portal pages, including the **Management** web interface and GlobalProtect portal:

```
reaper@PANgurus> less mp-log appweb3-sslvpn.log
```

- If no interesting logs appear in the GlobalProtect log or debug log, there might be an issue on the client itself. The GlobalProtect Agent also has some debugging capabilities that can be accessed from the settings in the **Troubleshooting** tab, as shown in the following screenshot. There are two options available for debugging:

  PanGP Agent is the graphical interface for GlobalProtect. Debugging should be turned on if the user can't refresh the configuration or is having trouble with certain buttons or options in the agent itself.

  PanGP Service is the actual service running on the endpoint that establishes a connection and authenticates against the portal and gateway. Start debug logging on this process for connectivity issues.

- Once the issue has been reproduced, click **Collect Logs** to receive a zipped collection of logs that can be reviewed for issues the client may encounter:

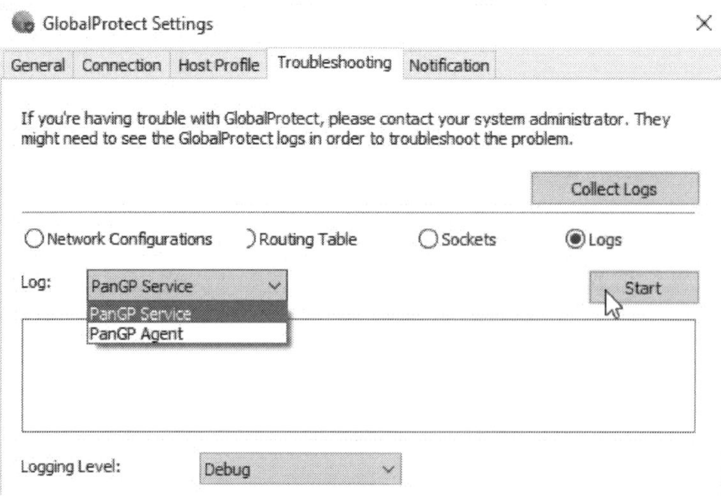

Figure 2.40 – GlobalProtect agent troubleshooting

With the preceding commands, you should be able to collect enough information to find and fix most common issues. Don't forget to check the traffic log to see if connections are being allowed in, as well as the client network to make sure connections are allowed to connect out. This is because some networks may not allow outbound VPN connections or require a user to authenticate against a local captive portal (hotels) first.

Summary

In this chapter, we learned how SAML authentication can be leveraged to replace more traditional authentication methods. We learned how user-initiated pre-logon and always-on pre-logon can be set in GlobalProtect so that endpoints are connected before the user is logged onto the desktop environment. This knowledge will help provide your users with a more integrated and smoother environment, while also ensuring the endpoints are secured the moment they are booted up until they are shut down.

In the next chapter, we will investigate different ways of establishing a site-to-site VPN and how to troubleshoot problems connecting to sites, as well as an alternative means of connecting to remote sites using a hybrid GlobalProtect solution called satellites or **Large-Scale VPN (LSVPN)**.

3
Setting up Site-to-Site VPNs and Large-Scale VPNs

In this chapter, we're going to learn about various ways to configure a **site-to-site Virtual Private Network** (**VPN**) connection. There are many different situations where exceptions need to be made to the *standard* way of setting up an **Internet Protocol Security** (**IPSec**) VPN connection. Every vendor seems to use different defaults, and every company has its own way of implementing VPN connections. During the process of establishing a secure tunnel between two sites, there may be a lot of negotiation required before you can come to a consensus about which parameters to use.

In this chapter, we're going to cover the following main topics:

- Configuring a site-to-site VPN connection
- Configuring the **Large Scale VPN** (**LSVPN**)
- Troubleshooting VPN issues

Technical requirements

In this chapter, we will cover different aspects of VPNs; basic knowledge of this topic is required in order for you to optimally benefit from the material we will cover in this book. Having at least two devices, of which at least one is a **Palo Alto Next-Generation Firewall (NGFW)**, that are capable of IPSec VPN connectivity will prove valuable to reproduce the examples covered in this chapter.

Check out the following link to see the Code in Action video:
`https://bit.ly/3oOF5B8`

Configuring a site-to-site VPN connection

IPSec with **Internet Security Association and Key Management Protocol** (**ISAKMP**) has been around for quite some time and has seen many upgrades in the form of improved algorithms and standards. Because so many legacy systems remain online far beyond their capability of adopting newer and stronger cryptography, many vendors, including *Palo Alto Networks*, keep including older algorithms in the available *Crypto suite*. This is so connections can still be maintained with those legacy systems or, simply, to provide extremely rudimentary and computationally cheap protection against network sniffing. This provides a wide range of available options; however, you might still encounter mismatching options, most commonly in the available **Diffie-Hellman** (**DH**) groups.

Establishing a site-to-site tunnel happens in two stages. In the first stage, which is also called **Phase-1** or **Internet Key Exchange** (**IKE**), all the information that is needed to arrive at a mutual trust, such as local and remote identification, a shared secret or certificate, and the *cryptographic* suite, are exchanged and need to be matched before we can set up the actual tunnel. **Phase-2**, or IPSec, is the next and final stage where the encryption keys or **Security Associations** (**SAs**) are negotiated, which will be used to encrypt the packets. Once `phase-2` has been established, the tunnel is considered *up* and any packets transmitted will be encrypted using the negotiated SA for the duration of its lifetime.

Each individual site-to-site connection has its own set of cryptographic parameters for each phase, which can be configured in **Network** > **Network Profiles** > **IKE Crypto** for `phase-1` and in **Network** > **Network Profiles** > **IPSec Crypto** for `phase-2`.

To keep things as simple as possible, ideally, you should use a single profile for all connections. However, in practice, there will be several different profiles that suit the needs of each remote site. Therefore, rather than loading all possible permutations of standards, algorithms, and protocols into a single profile, it is better to split differing configurations to prevent weaker ciphers from inadvertently being used in a high-security connection.

As you can see, in *Figure 3.1*, the IKE Crypto Profile has the following options available:

- **DH GROUP**: `1`, `2`, `5`, `14`, `19`, and `20`.
- **ENCRYPTION**: This includes algorithms with **Cipher Block Chaining** (**CBC**) and **Galois/Counter Mode** (**GCM**) such as `aes-128-cbc`, `aes-192-cbc`, `aes-256-cbc`, `aes-128-gcm`, and `aes-256-gcm`. `DES` and `3DES` should be avoided.
- **AUTHENTICATION**: This supports disabling authentication entirely by setting `non-auth` or one of the following algorithms: `sha256`, `sha384`, or `sha512`. `Sha1` and `md5` should be avoided.
- **Key Lifetime**: This can be seconds, minutes, hours, or days.

- **IKEv2 Authentication Multiple**: This determines how many times the gateway is allowed to rekey before being forced to reauthenticate IKEv2. Leaving this value at `0` disables the forced reauthentication:

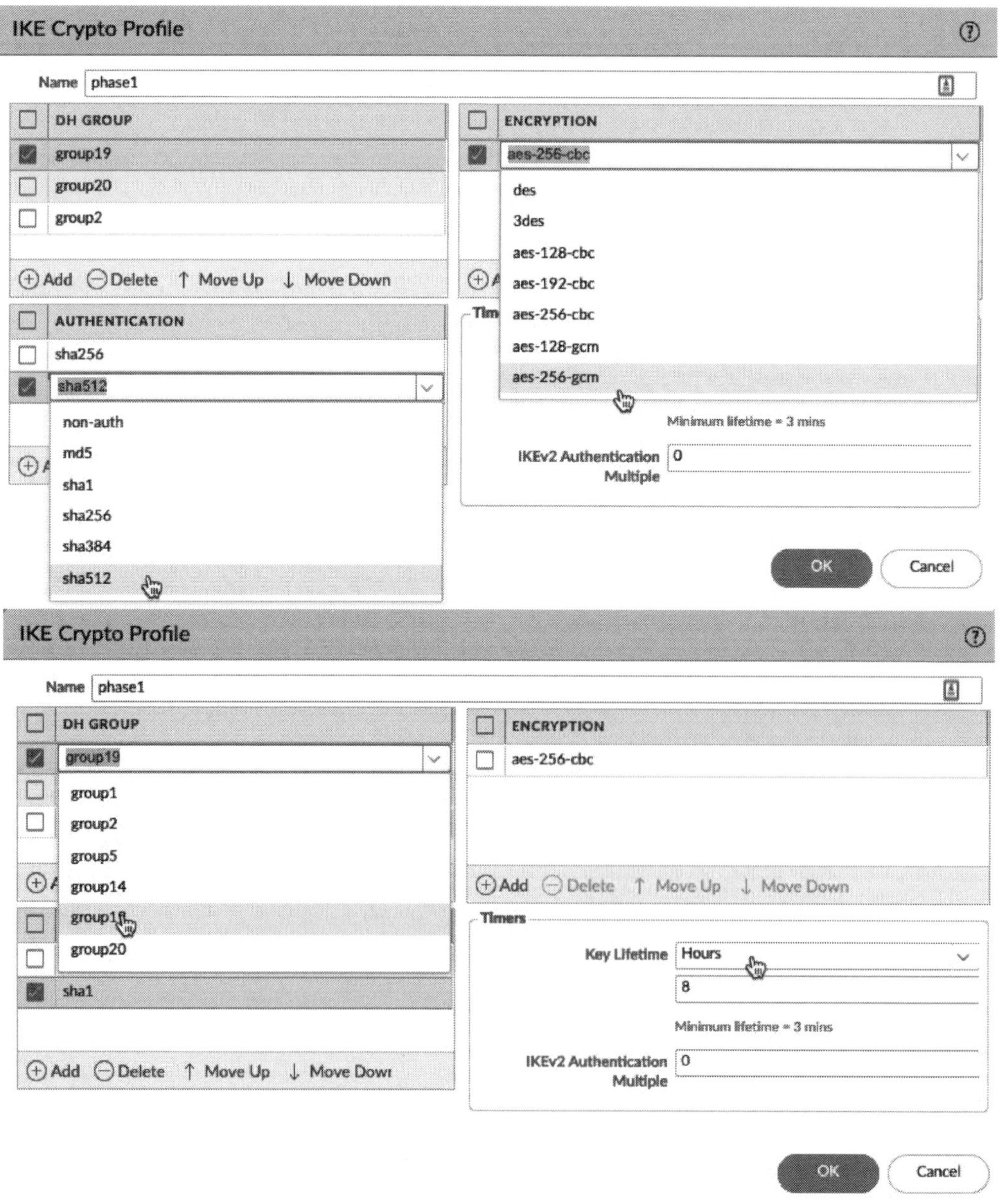

Figure 3.1 – IKE Crypto Profile

> **Important note**
>
> `Aes-128-gcm` and `aes-256-gcm` require PAN-OS 10.0.3, or later, and IKEv2 and DH groups `19` or `20` to be used. `non-auth` also requires PAN-OS 10.0.3 or later.

All of the settings that are needed to successfully negotiate `phase-1` with a remote peer are configured in **Network** > **Network Profiles** > **IKE Gateways**. As you can see, in *Figure 3.2*, both the local and remote settings are defined in the IKE Gateway object.

Version allows you to set the following options:

- **IKEv1 only mode**: In this mode, the `phase-1` negotiation will only use IKEv1.
- **IKEv2 only mode**: In this mode, `phase-1` will be completed in IKEv2. Both peers need to be able to use this mode for negotiation to succeed.
- **IKEv2 preferred mode**: This mode bridges the gap where your gateway will try to negotiate IKEv2 but can fall back to IKEv1 if the remote peer is unable to comply.

  The primary difference between IKEv1 and IKEv2 is that IKEv1 will use nine messages for main mode and six messages for aggressive mode. In comparison, IKEv2 will always use four messages. Additionally, IKEv2 has improved NAT-T functionality if one or both peers are located behind a NAT device (NAT-T must be enabled on both devices to take advantage of this functionality). IKEv2 also uses a child SA, while IKEv1 uses a `phase-1` SA and a `phase-2` SA.
- Both **Interface** and **Local IP Address** allow you to choose which interface the tunnel will be bound to and which IP to use when connecting to the peer. The interface can be any physical interface, a sub interface, a loopback, or a `vlan` interface.

> **Important note**
>
> To attach the IPSec tunnel to an IP address that is different from the external interface, create a loopback interface in the same zone, set it to the desired IP address, and attach the IKE Gateway to the loopback.

- **Peer IP Address Type** can either be an **IP** or **Fully Qualified Domain Name** (**FQDN**). Alternatively, it can be set to `Dynamic` if the remote peer has a dynamic IP address. In the latter case, the **Peer Address** field will disappear.
- **Authentication**: Some form of authentication is required so that both sides can determine whether they can communicate. A `Pre-Shared` **key** can be set, which needs to be identical on both peers; alternatively, a *certificate* can be loaded.

By default, a peer uses its local IP address as identification during the `phase-1` negotiation. **Local Identification** and **Peer Identification** can be can be set to manually change identification of each peer. This could be useful if a peer is located behind a NAT device and is using a private IP on its interface. The peer would include the private IP in the negotiation, but the packets would originate from the NAT device's external IP, which will cause a mismatch. Manually setting the internal IP as an accepted identifier will rectify that issue. For dynamic hosts that use a different source IP every time, it is also possible to set an FQDN or an agreed-upon email address instead of an IP. This setting needs to be applied to both members. Local identification is used to inject an ID into outbound packets while peer identification is used to override the peer's source IP as a match.

If the peer is **Cisco ASA** (**Adaptive Security Appliance**), or another vendor that uses `Key-ID` (`KEYID`), the identifier can also be set to `KEYID`. On Palo Alto, the Key-ID needs to be a `HEX` value, so if the remote is using an ASCII string, the ASCII will need to be converted into `HEX`. An ASCII to HEX converter can be found at `https://www.pangurus.com/tools`:

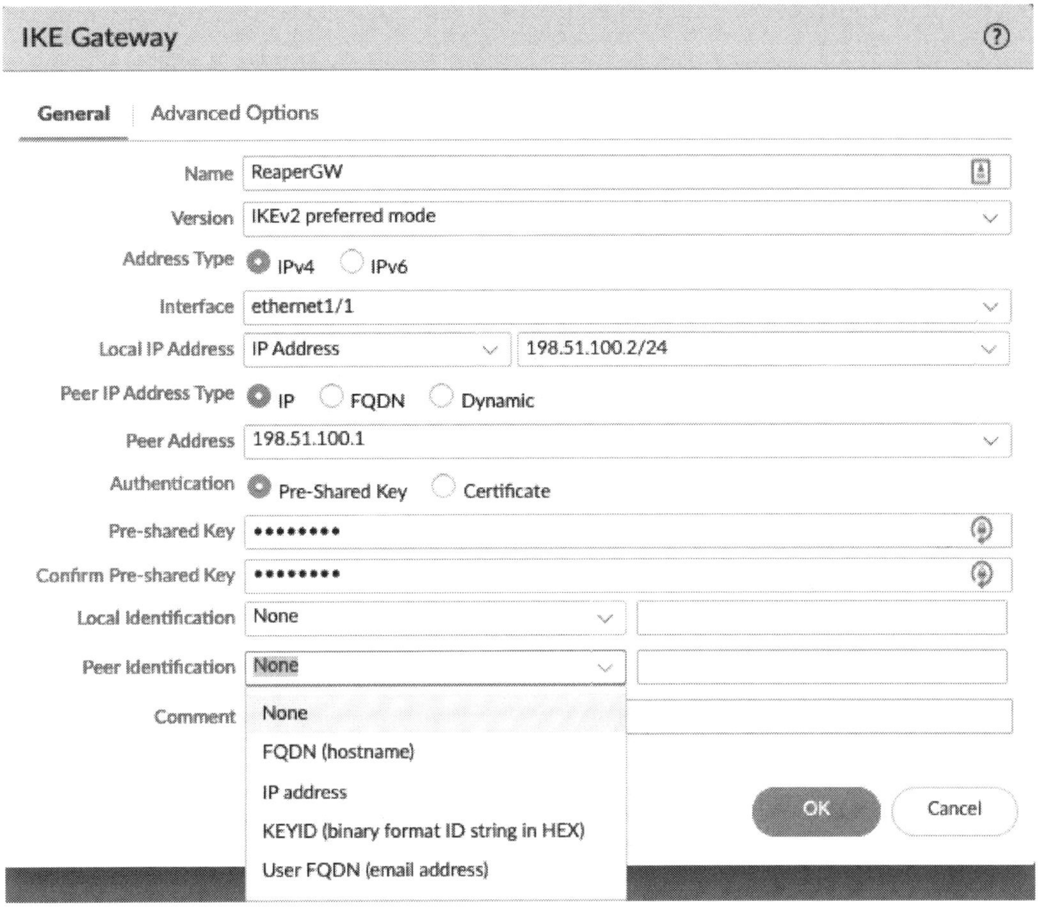

Figure 3.2 – IKE Gateway with static peer and a pre-shared key

In *Figure 3.3*, you can view the certificate authentication configuration. The **Local Certificate** must be a server certificate with a private key, which is signed by the same **Certification Authority** (**CA**) certificate as the remote peer's certificate. A `certificate profile` containing the aforementioned CA and CRL or URL information must be attached so that the identity of the remote peer certificate can be verified.

If a wildcard certificate is used, the **Peer ID Check** must be toggled to **Wildcard** instead of **Exact** (this requires an exact match to the peer certificate **Common Name** or **CN**).

Permit peer identification and certificate payload identification mismatch allows you to skip matching the peer certificate payload so that the SA can be created without verification. *This option should only be used for troubleshooting*:

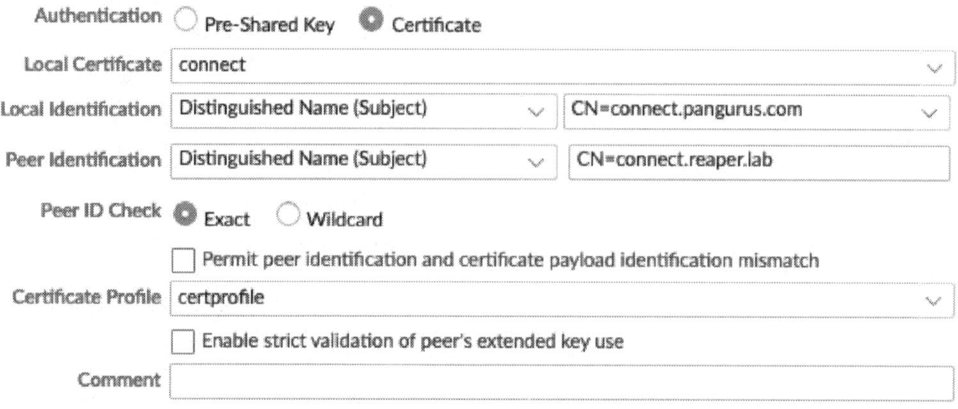

Figure 3.3 – Certificate authentication in IKE Gateway

In the **Advanced** tab, additional configuration for the selected IKE version should be set. If the version is set to a preferred mode of IKEv1 or IKEv2, only the selected IKE version will be displayed. If IKEv2 is set as the preferred mode, both IKE versions will be listed and can be configured individually. As you can see, in *Figure 3.4*, the available configuration is as follows:

1. **Enable Passive Mode** will set the firewall as a responder only; it will never try to initiate an outgoing connection to the peer. This can be useful if the peer is a dynamic host or is not online all the time to prevent the firewall from endlessly trying to connect.
2. **Enable NAT Traversal** (NAT-T) is required if one or both peers are located behind a NAT device. This setting needs to be enabled on both peers to be effective.
3. In IKEv1, **Exchange Mode** can be `auto`, `main`, or `aggressive`. In `auto` mode, both modes are accepted with a preference for `main` mode.
4. The **IKE Crypto Profile** must be set to the profile that contains the appropriate crypto suite for this peer. *Do not use the default.*
5. **Enable Fragmentation** can be enabled to accept fragmented IKE packets; the maximum fragmented packet size is 576 bytes.
6. **Dead Peer Detection** is enabled by default; leave this as is unless the peer doesn't support it or requires alternative settings.

7. In IKEv2, select the appropriate **IKE Crypto Profile** for this peer and *do not use the default.*
8. **Strict Cookie Validation** can be enabled as an added security measure, as it will require the initiator to always send an `IKE_SA_INIT` containing a cookie. If this option is disabled, the firewall will allow half-open SAs until a threshold is reached, and only then will it enforce initiators to send an `IKE_SA_INIT` containing a cookie.
9. **Liveness Check** is always enabled in IKEv2, as all packets serve as liveness checks. This option is used to send empty message packets if no regular packets have been transmitted for the configured amount of time. If no liveness packets are received after 10 attempts, both `IKE_SA` and `CHILD_SA` are torn down and a new `IKE_SA_INIT` must be sent:

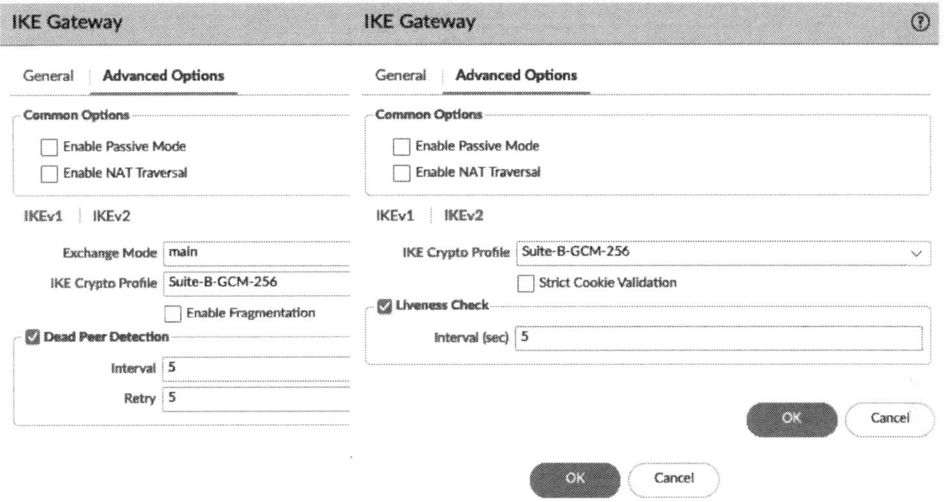

Figure 3.4 – IKE Gateway Advanced Options

After configuring the `phase-1` settings, the `phase-2` settings need to be prepared. Firstly, an **IPSec Crypto Profile** needs to be prepared, which contains settings that the peer is also able to accommodate. As you can see, in *Figure 3.5*, there are, again, many options that need to be carefully considered. Ideally, the Crypto Profile is tailored to contain only the desired algorithms.

IPSec Protocol can be set to **Encapsulated Security Payload** (**ESP**), which is full encryption, or **Authentication Header** (**AH**), which adds a signed header to a packet indicating it has not been tampered with in transit but does not encrypt the payload.

In **Authentication**, the available algorithms are `sha256`, `sha384`, `sha512`, and `none`. Note that `sha1` and `md5` should be avoided.

In **Encryption**, there's `aes-128-cbc`, `aes-192-cbc`, and `aes-256-cbc` as CBC, and `aes-128-gcm` and `aes-256-gcm` as GCM.

DH Groups of `1`, `2`, `5`, `14`, `19`, and `20` are available. Alternatively, if the IKE key created in `phase-1` does not need to be renewed, `no-pfs` (that is, no perfect forward secrecy) will reuse the key for every `phase-2` rekey.

The default **Lifetime** is 1 hour, but this can be changed to seconds, minutes, hours, or days.

Optionally, a **Lifetime** in KB, MB, GB, or TB can be enabled. This allows you to rekey whenever a certain amount of data has traversed the tunnel:

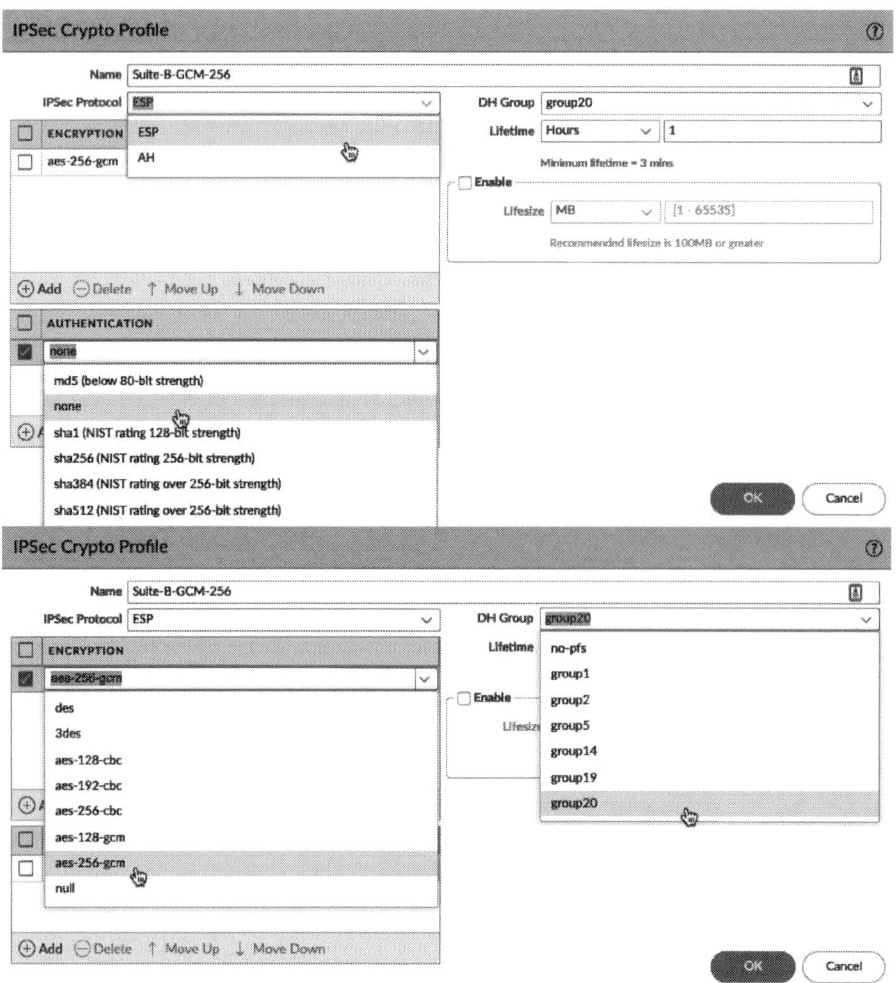

Figure 3.5 – IPSec Crypto Profile

After configuring the IPSec Crypto Profile, a tunnel interface should be created in **Network** > **Interfaces** > **Tunnel** to terminate the tunnel connection. The zone used on the interface should be unique enough for it to be identified easily, and security rules can be created without accidentally opening access to unexpected network segments. Therefore, it is not advisable for you to reuse the *untrust* zone that is configured to the external interface on the tunnel interface. As illustrated in *Figure 3.6*, the tunnel interface must be attached to a virtual router so that packets can be routed into it, but it does not need to have an IP address assigned to it per se. An IP configured on the interface could serve as a tunnel monitoring destination for the remote peer, or it could be used to facilitate **source NAT** (**SNAT**) if there is a subnet overlap:

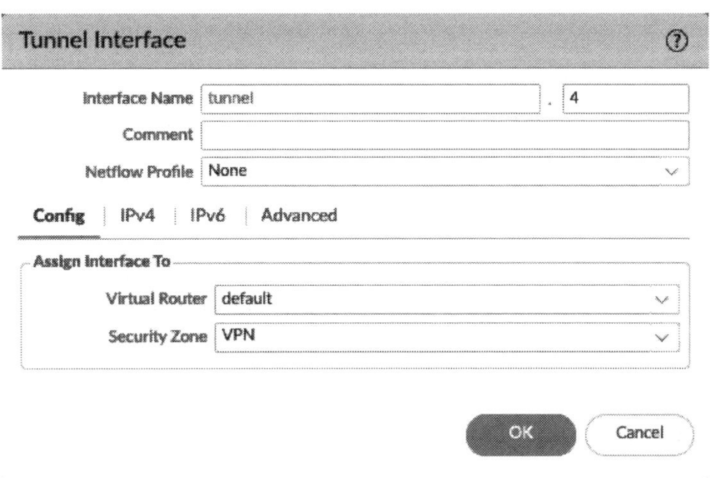

Figure 3.6 – Tunnel Interface

The final step involves creating an IPSec tunnel in **Network** > **IPSec Tunnels** and attaching the newly created tunnel interface, IPSec Crypto Profile, and IKE Gateway, as illustrated in *Figure 3.7*.

There are not a lot of things to configure in the IPSec tunnel as most parameters have already been created in the IKE Gateway. The type of tunnel can be set to one of the following:

- **Auto Key**: This will let the firewall negotiate cryptographic parameters based on the IKE and IPSec Crypto Profiles and the IKE Gateway object.
- **Manual Key**: This allows you to completely predefine all the parameters of the `phase-2` negotiation.
- **GlobalProtect Satellite**: This is a simplified site-to-site connection based on GlobalProtect. We will cover this, in more detail, later in this chapter.

Enable Replay Protection is enabled by default and adds a bit of unique data to the message. There are only rare occasions in which this setting would need to be disabled, but if the IPSec connection flows through a proxy server, replay attacks might be detected and packets discarded unjustly.

If **Type of Service** (**ToS**) headers are used internally, **Copy ToS Headers** can be enabled to attach any internal ToS IP headers to the external IP header.

If a tunnel is being built to a legacy device that requires a GRE tunnel, **Add GRE Encapsulation** can be enabled to add a GRE header after the IPSec header.

The **Tunnel Monitor** can be enabled to send pings to a remote IP to ensure the tunnel is still "up" and passing traffic. The *Tunnel Interface* needs to be configured with an IP in order for tunnel monitoring to function. This is because the outbound ping will originate from the tunnel interface. The two actions available in the monitoring profile are as follows:

- **Wait-recover**: The firewall will report in the log that tunnel monitoring has failed but will keep sending packets into the tunnel.
- **Fail Over**: The tunnel is brought down and the static route is removed from the routing table (forwarding information base); a backup route and a secondary tunnel should be configured to take advantage of the failover action.

> **Important note**
>
> The tunnel monitoring outbound packets can't be manipulated with policy-based forwarding or security policies.

In *Figure 3.7*, you can view an example of the IPSec Tunnel object:

Figure 3.7 – The IPSec Tunnel object

The **Proxy IDs** are used if a tunnel needs to be created with a peer device that uses policy-based VPN. This is because those devices create an SA for each remote and local subnet pair, whereas the Palo Alto, as a route-based VPN device, negotiates `0.0.0.0/0 to 0.0.0.0/0` by default and relies on static routes or policy-based forwarding to decide which packets to send into the tunnel.

As illustrated in *Figure 3.8*, the Proxy IDs should either be left empty for a full `0.0.0.0/0` tunnel or have individual subnet pairs. These subnet pairs need to be identically configured on each side, as a unique SA will be negotiated for each of them. If each side has multiple subnets that all need to communicate with each other, the list of Proxy IDs could grow pretty quickly:

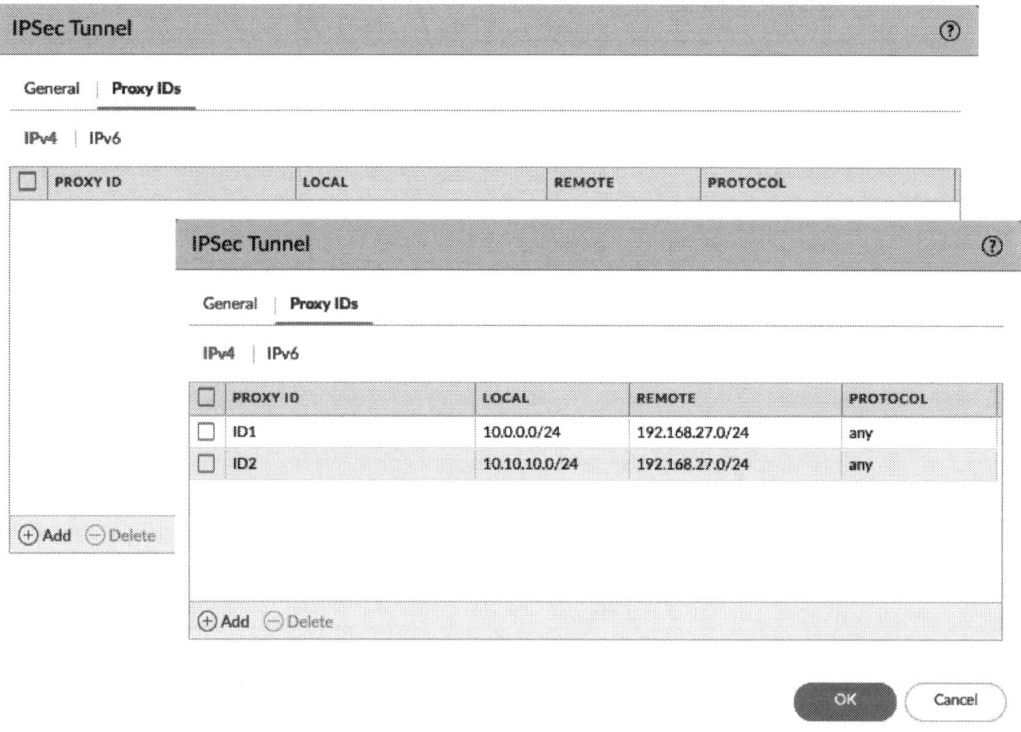

Figure 3.8 – Proxy IDs for a route-based and policy-based tunnel

The last step is to add a route to the virtual router in **Network** > **Virtual Routers**. This is so the remote subnet is properly routed into the tunnel. The route will look like the `vpn LA` route depicted in *Figure 3.9*: the remote network is set as the destination and the interface is indicated as the appropriate tunnel interface. There does not need to be an additional hop as packets will simply be put into the tunnel for the remote router to take care of:

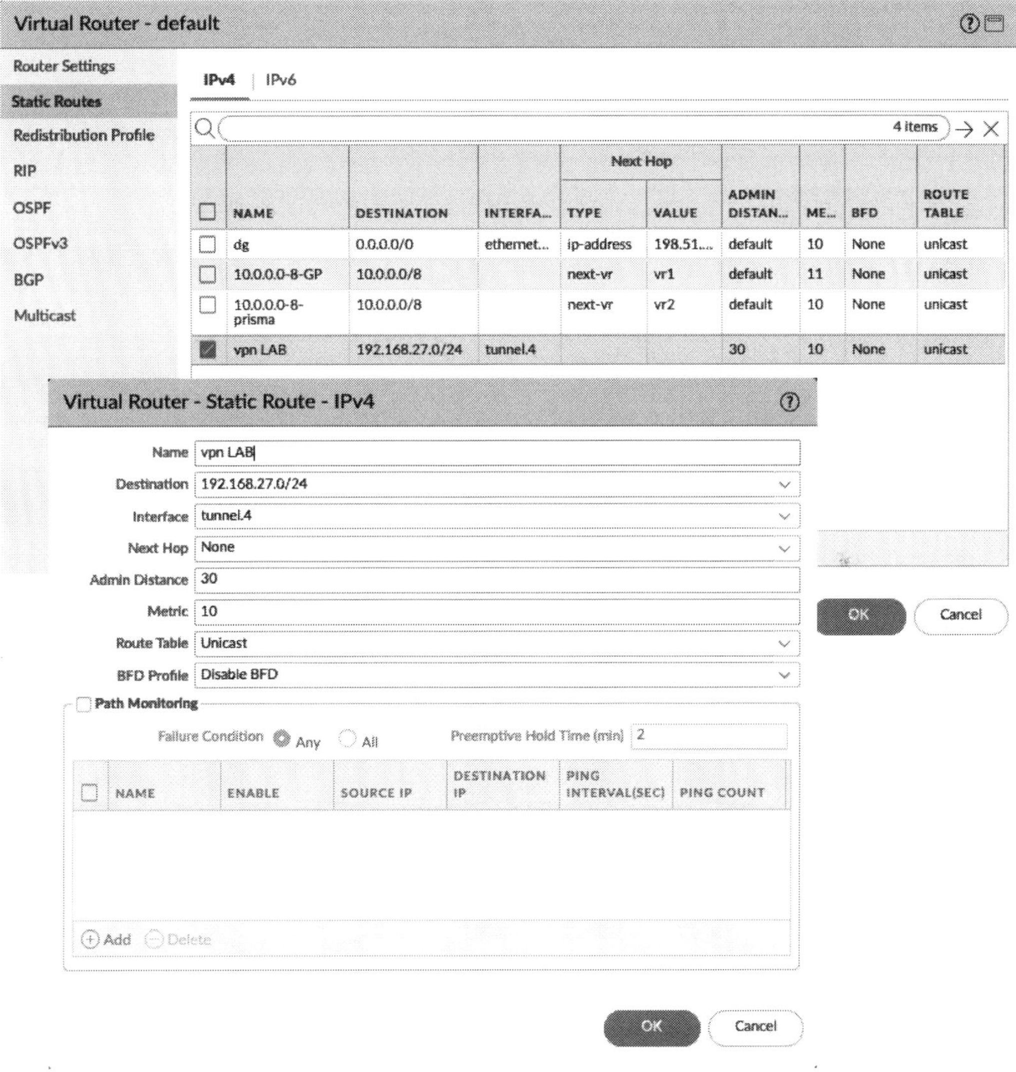

Figure 3.9 – The VPN remote network route into the tunnel

Now that we have covered the basics of how to set up tunnels, let's take a closer look at a few different implementations.

Static site-to-site tunnels

We will start with the most common tunnel configuration, that is, with both sides on a static IP address, which is the easiest to configure. The first thing that we need to do is to create a checklist of all the information we require to build a tunnel. The following is a simple lab setup with `192.168.27.0/24` as the remote subnet, `198.51.100.1` as the remote peer, `198.51.100.2` as the local untrust interface, and `10.0.0.0/24` as the local subnet, as illustrated in *Figure 3.10*:

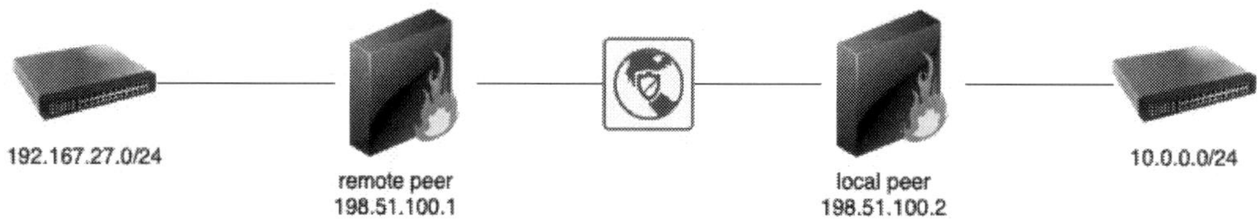

Figure 3.10 – A simple lab setup

The configuration for `phase-1` is as follows:

IKE version for both sides of support	IKEv2 preferred mode
Local IP	198.51.100.2
Remote IP	198.51.100.2
Preshared key or certificate	**********
DH group	19
Authentication algorithm	Sha256
Encryption algorithm	Aes-128-cbc
Key lifetime	8 hours

Figure 3.11 – Phase-1

The configuration for `phase-2` is as follows:

Tunnel interface	Tunnel.4
DH group	19
Encryption algorithm	Aes-128-gcm
Authentication algorithm	None
Lifetime	1 hour
Remote subnet	192.168.27.0/24
If needed, Proxy ID 1	10.0.0.0/24 – 192.168.27.0/24
Proxy ID 2	

3.12 – Phase-2

The configuration for this setup will be fairly straightforward. The IKE Gateway object will look similar to *Figure 3.13*. The remote site will look the same except that **Local IP Address** and **Peer Address** are switched:

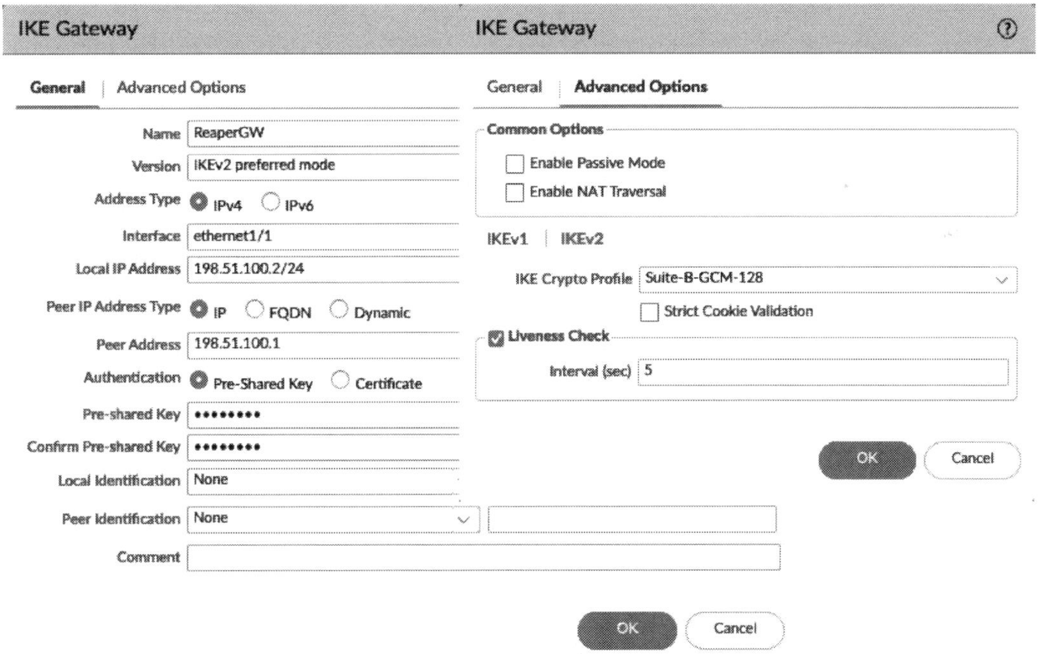

Figure 3.13 – The lab IKE Gateway

The tunnel configuration will look similar to *Figure 3.14*. The **LOCAL** and **REMOTE** Proxy IDs will be switched on the remote firewall:

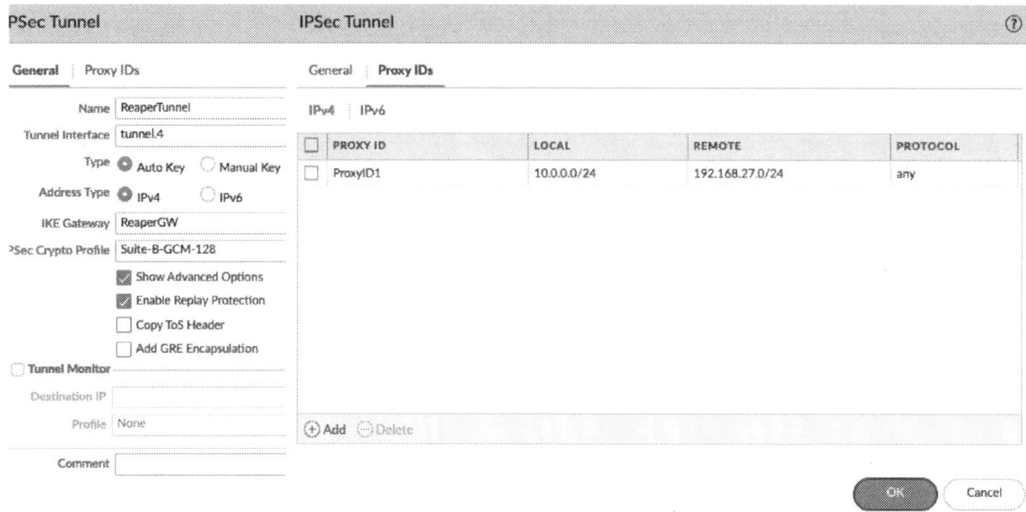

Figure 3.14 – The lab IPSec Tunnel

Let's take a look at how to troubleshoot a couple of issues that could go wrong when setting up a tunnel.

Proposal mismatching

Once the tunnel has been configured on both sides, `phase-1` and `phase-2` can be manually started to verify whether everything was set up properly. Use the following two commands to initiate each phase. If you execute the commands without including the gateway or tunnel, all of the gateways or tunnels will be negotiated:

```
test vpn ike-sa gateway <gatewayobject>
```

```
test vpn ipsec-sa tunnel <tunnelobject>:<proxyid>
```

If there are no Proxy IDs, just set the tunnel name, as follows:

```
reaper@PA-VM2> test vpn ike-sa gateway ReaperGW
Start time: Jan.26 23:13:59
Initiate 1 IKE SA.

reaper@PA-VM2> test vpn ipsec-sa tunnel ReaperTunnel:ProxyID1
Start time: Jan.26 23:14:16
Initiate 1 IPSec SA for tunnel ReaperTunnel:ProxyID1.
```

We can then check, in the **Web Interface** at **Network** > **IPSec Tunnels**, whether the tunnel is up by two green status indicators. As you can see, in *Figure 3.15*, the two indicators are red, and the interface icon is green. The green interface icon indicates that the tunnel interface has not been shut down and is ready to work:

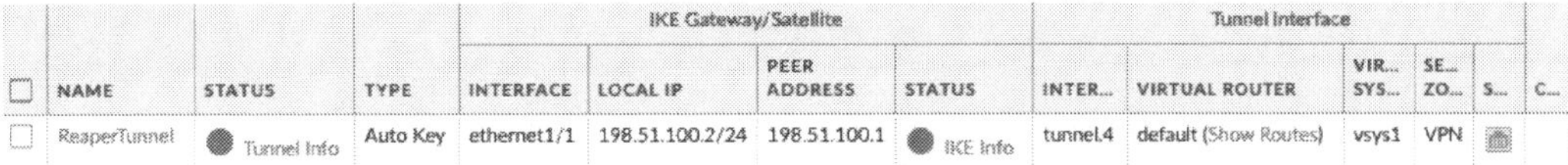

			IKE Gateway/Satellite				Tunnel Interface					
NAME	STATUS	TYPE	INTERFACE	LOCAL IP	PEER ADDRESS	STATUS	INTER...	VIRTUAL ROUTER	VIR... SYS...	SE... ZO...	S...	C...
ReaperTunnel	Tunnel Info	Auto Key	ethernet1/1	198.51.100.2/24	198.51.100.1	IKE Info	tunnel.4	default (Show Routes)	vsys1	VPN		

Figure 3.15 – The IPSec tunnel status

The next step is to find out why the tunnel is not coming up. The first place you can search for more information is the system log. We can look up the system log using the `show log system direction equal backward subtype equal vpn` command. Adding `direction equal backward` will ensure that the latest logs are presented first. Also, adding the `subtype eq vpn` filter will ensure that only VPN logs are displayed:

```
reaper@PA-VM2> show log system direction equal backward subtype
equal vpn
Time                    Severity Subtype Object EventID ID
Description
==============================================================
================
2021/01/26 23:41:11 info      vpn     Reaper ike-neg 0   IKE
phase-1 SA is deleted SA: 198.51.100.2[500]-198.51.100.1[500]
cookie:20af4534796f0f71:0000000000000000.
2021/01/26 23:41:11 info      vpn     Reaper ike-neg
0  IKE phase-1 negotiation is failed as initiator, main
mode. Failed SA: 198.51.100.2[500]-198.51.100.1[500]
cookie:20af4534796f0f71:0000000000000000. Due to timeout.
2021/01/26 23:40:38 info      vpn     Reaper ike-neg
0  IKE phase-1 negotiation is started as initiator, main
mode. Initiated SA: 198.51.100.2[500]-198.51.100.1[500]
cookie:20af4534796f0f71:0000000000000000.
2021/01/26 23:40:38 info      vpn     Reaper ikev2-n 0   IKEv1 is
used in IKEv2 preferred mode.
2021/01/26 23:40:38 info      vpn            ike-gen 0   IKE_SA_
INIT retransmission failed for gateway ReaperGW SN 2, trying
IKEv1.
2021/01/26 23:38:22 info      vpn     Reaper ikev2-n 0   IKEv2
IKE SA negotiation is started as initiator, non-rekey.
```

```
Initiated SA: 198.51.100.2[500]-198.51.100.1[500] SPI:75dc0c769
c7978cf:0000000000000000.
```

The web interface version of the logs will look similar to *Figure 3.16*, and, depending on your circumstances, it might be a little easier to read:

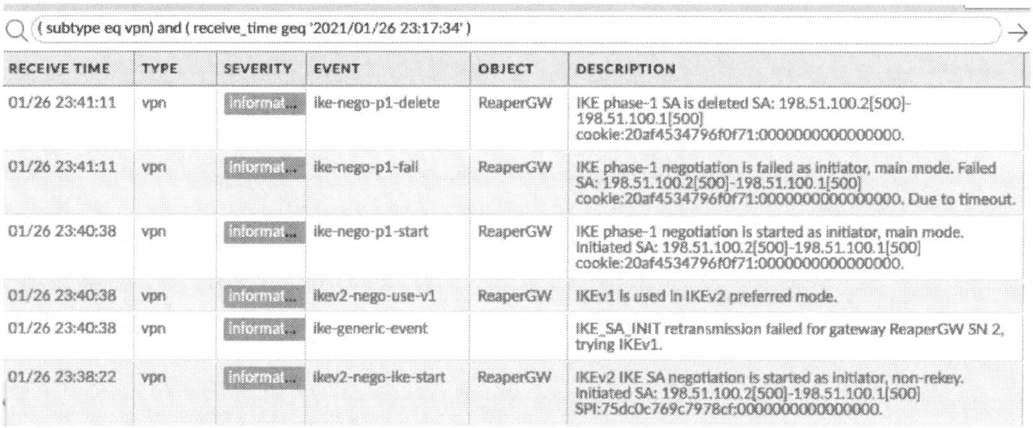

(subtype eq vpn) and (receive_time geq '2021/01/26 23:17:34')

RECEIVE TIME	TYPE	SEVERITY	EVENT	OBJECT	DESCRIPTION
01/26 23:41:11	vpn	informat...	ike-nego-p1-delete	ReaperGW	IKE phase-1 SA is deleted SA: 198.51.100.2[500]-198.51.100.1[500] cookie:20af4534796f0f71:0000000000000000.
01/26 23:41:11	vpn	informat...	ike-nego-p1-fail	ReaperGW	IKE phase-1 negotiation is failed as initiator, main mode. Failed SA: 198.51.100.2[500]-198.51.100.1[500] cookie:20af4534796f0f71:0000000000000000. Due to timeout.
01/26 23:40:38	vpn	informat...	ike-nego-p1-start	ReaperGW	IKE phase-1 negotiation is started as initiator, main mode. Initiated SA: 198.51.100.2[500]-198.51.100.1[500] cookie:20af4534796f0f71:0000000000000000.
01/26 23:40:38	vpn	informat...	ikev2-nego-use-v1	ReaperGW	IKEv1 is used in IKEv2 preferred mode.
01/26 23:40:38	vpn	informat...	ike-generic-event		IKE_SA_INIT retransmission failed for gateway ReaperGW SN 2, trying IKEv1.
01/26 23:38:22	vpn	informat...	ikev2-nego-ike-start	ReaperGW	IKEv2 IKE SA negotiation is started as initiator, non-rekey. Initiated SA: 198.51.100.2[500]-198.51.100.1[500] SPI:75dc0c769c7978cf:0000000000000000.

Figure 3.16 – Web interface system logs

From the preceding logs, we can determine that the firewall first attempted to negotiate IKEv2, which timed out. Then, it attempted to negotiate IKEv1, which also timed out. After this, the firewall gave up and deleted its SA. At this time, there's not much that can be done except to contact the peer device administrator and ask whether any clear error messages can be seen or check whether the outbound connection might be getting blocked by a firewall. If the administrator does not have logging permissions to such a degree that they can tell you what is going on, the next step is to have the remote end initiate a connection to see whether we can determine what is going on. When troubleshooting VPN, it is always ideal to be the responder, as the error messages will be far more detailed.

As you can see, in *Figure 3.17*, being the responder has some advantages, that is, we can immediately see that the proposal does not match the IKE Crypto Profile that we configured earlier:

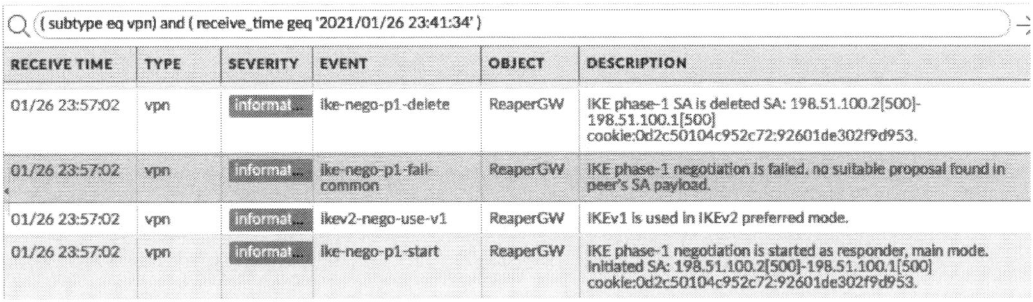

(subtype eq vpn) and (receive_time geq '2021/01/26 23:41:34')

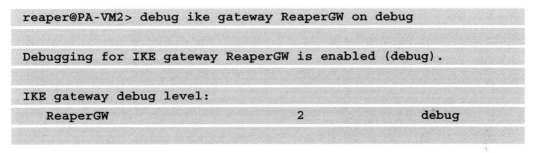

RECEIVE TIME	TYPE	SEVERITY	EVENT	OBJECT	DESCRIPTION
01/26 23:57:02	vpn	informat...	ike-nego-p1-delete	ReaperGW	IKE phase-1 SA is deleted SA: 198.51.100.2[500]-198.51.100.1[500] cookie:0d2c50104c952c72:92601de302f9d953.
01/26 23:57:02	vpn	informat...	ike-nego-p1-fail-common	ReaperGW	IKE phase-1 negotiation is failed. no suitable proposal found in peer's SA payload.
01/26 23:57:02	vpn	informat...	ikev2-nego-use-v1	ReaperGW	IKEv1 is used in IKEv2 preferred mode.
01/26 23:57:02	vpn	informat...	ike-nego-p1-start	ReaperGW	IKE phase-1 negotiation is started as responder, main mode. Initiated SA: 198.51.100.2[500]-198.51.100.1[500] cookie:0d2c50104c952c72:92601de302f9d953.

Figure 3.17 – No suitable proposal found in peer's SA payload

To find which proposal is being sent over, we can enable debugging in the `ikemgr` process via the following command line:

```
reaper@PA-VM2> debug ike gateway ReaperGW on debug

Debugging for IKE gateway ReaperGW is enabled (debug).

IKE gateway debug level:
  ReaperGW                          2              debug
```

We can then use the `tail` command to follow along with the debug log while the remote end sends over its negotiation: `tail follow yes mp-log ikemgr.log`.

The result will look somewhat similar to *Figure 3.18*. We will need to go through each line with due care. This is because the issue might be in smaller detail within a single line, and there is an abundance of information to check through, as you will see in a moment:

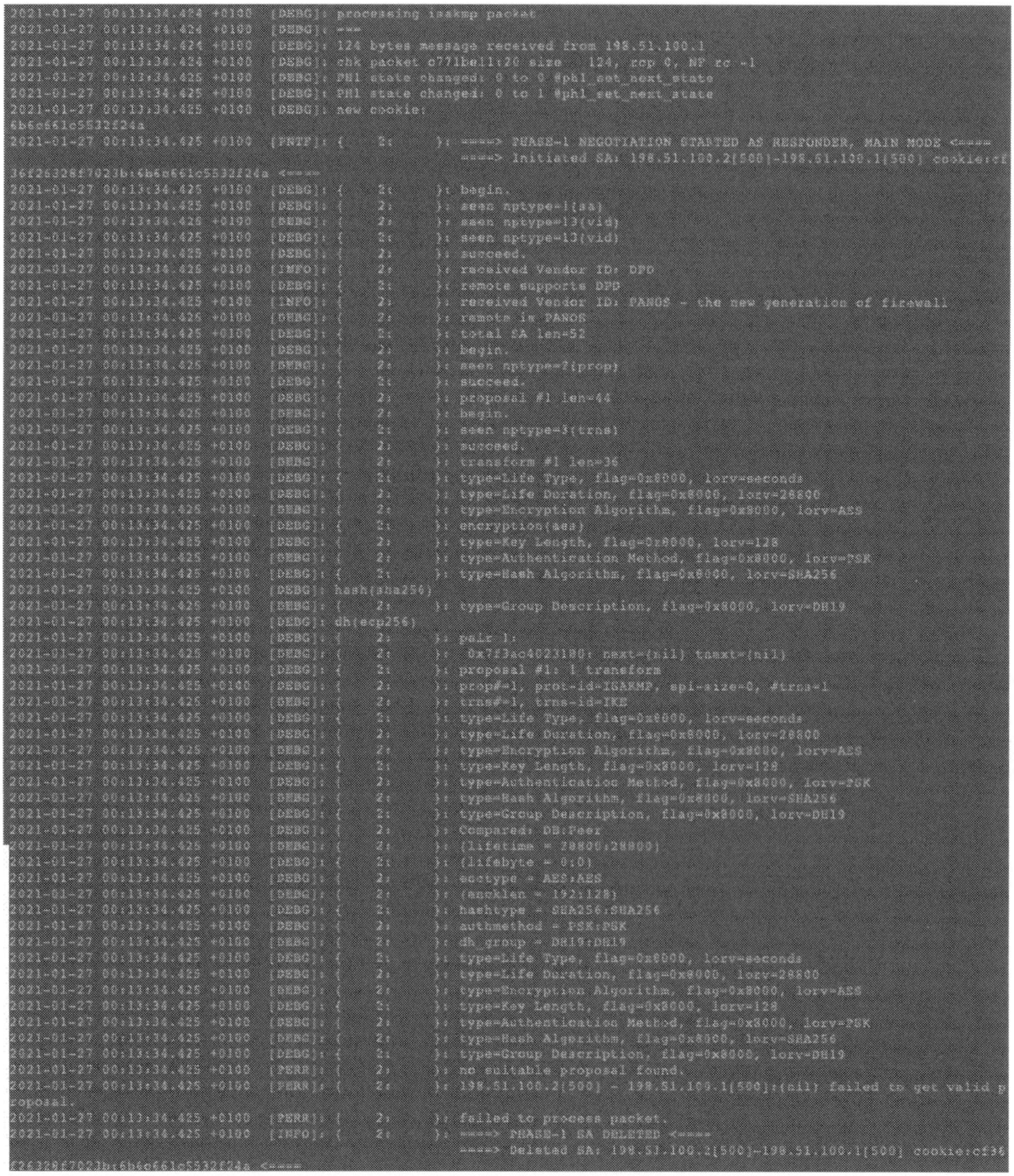

```
2021-01-27 00:13:34.424 +0100  [DEBG]: processing isakmp packet
2021-01-27 00:13:34.424 +0100  [DEBG]: ===
2021-01-27 00:13:34.424 +0100  [DEBG]: 124 bytes message received from 198.51.100.1
2021-01-27 00:13:34.424 +0100  [DEBG]: chk packet c771be11:20 size   124, rcp 0, NP rc -1
2021-01-27 00:13:34.425 +0100  [DEBG]: PH1 state changed: 0 to 0 #ph1_set_next_state
2021-01-27 00:13:34.425 +0100  [DEBG]: PH1 state changed: 0 to 1 #ph1_set_next_state
2021-01-27 00:13:34.425 +0100  [DEBG]: new cookie:
6b6c661c5532f24a
2021-01-27 00:13:34.425 +0100  [PNTF]: {     2:      }: ====> PHASE-1 NEGOTIATION STARTED AS RESPONDER, MAIN MODE <====
                                                          ====> Initiated SA: 198.51.100.2[500]-198.51.100.1[500] cookie:cf
36f26328f7023b:6b6c661c5532f24a <====
2021-01-27 00:13:34.425 +0100  [DEBG]: {     2:      }: begin.
2021-01-27 00:13:34.425 +0100  [DEBG]: {     2:      }: seen nptype=1(sa)
2021-01-27 00:13:34.425 +0100  [DEBG]: {     2:      }: seen nptype=13(vid)
2021-01-27 00:13:34.425 +0100  [DEBG]: {     2:      }: seen nptype=13(vid)
2021-01-27 00:13:34.425 +0100  [DEBG]: {     2:      }: succeed.
2021-01-27 00:13:34.425 +0100  [INFO]: {     2:      }: received Vendor ID: DPD
2021-01-27 00:13:34.425 +0100  [DEBG]: {     2:      }: remote supports DPD
2021-01-27 00:13:34.425 +0100  [INFO]: {     2:      }: received Vendor ID: PANOS - the new generation of firewall
2021-01-27 00:13:34.425 +0100  [DEBG]: {     2:      }: remote is PANOS
2021-01-27 00:13:34.425 +0100  [DEBG]: {     2:      }: total SA len=52
2021-01-27 00:13:34.425 +0100  [DEBG]: {     2:      }: begin.
2021-01-27 00:13:34.425 +0100  [DEBG]: {     2:      }: seen nptype=2(prop)
2021-01-27 00:13:34.425 +0100  [DEBG]: {     2:      }: succeed.
2021-01-27 00:13:34.425 +0100  [DEBG]: {     2:      }: proposal #1 len=44
2021-01-27 00:13:34.425 +0100  [DEBG]: {     2:      }: begin.
2021-01-27 00:13:34.425 +0100  [DEBG]: {     2:      }: seen nptype=3(trns)
2021-01-27 00:13:34.425 +0100  [DEBG]: {     2:      }: succeed.
2021-01-27 00:13:34.425 +0100  [DEBG]: {     2:      }: transform #1 len=36
2021-01-27 00:13:34.425 +0100  [DEBG]: {     2:      }: type=Life Type, flag=0x8000, lorv=seconds
2021-01-27 00:13:34.425 +0100  [DEBG]: {     2:      }: type=Life Duration, flag=0x8000, lorv=28800
2021-01-27 00:13:34.425 +0100  [DEBG]: {     2:      }: type=Encryption Algorithm, flag=0x8000, lorv=AES
2021-01-27 00:13:34.425 +0100  [DEBG]: {     2:      }: encryption(aes)
2021-01-27 00:13:34.425 +0100  [DEBG]: {     2:      }: type=Key Length, flag=0x8000, lorv=128
2021-01-27 00:13:34.425 +0100  [DEBG]: {     2:      }: type=Authentication Method, flag=0x8000, lorv=PSK
2021-01-27 00:13:34.425 +0100  [DEBG]: {     2:      }: type=Hash Algorithm, flag=0x8000, lorv=SHA256
2021-01-27 00:13:34.425 +0100  [DEBG]: hash(sha256)
2021-01-27 00:13:34.425 +0100  [DEBG]: {     2:      }: type=Group Description, flag=0x8000, lorv=DH19
2021-01-27 00:13:34.425 +0100  [DEBG]: dh(ecp256)
2021-01-27 00:13:34.425 +0100  [DEBG]: {     2:      }: pair 1:
2021-01-27 00:13:34.425 +0100  [DEBG]: {     2:      }:  0x7f3ac4023180: next=(nil) tnext=(nil)
2021-01-27 00:13:34.425 +0100  [DEBG]: {     2:      }: proposal #1: 1 transform
2021-01-27 00:13:34.425 +0100  [DEBG]: {     2:      }: prop#=1, prot-id=ISAKMP, spi-size=0, #trns=1
2021-01-27 00:13:34.425 +0100  [DEBG]: {     2:      }: trns#=1, trns-id=IKE
2021-01-27 00:13:34.425 +0100  [DEBG]: {     2:      }: type=Life Type, flag=0x8000, lorv=seconds
2021-01-27 00:13:34.425 +0100  [DEBG]: {     2:      }: type=Life Duration, flag=0x8000, lorv=28800
2021-01-27 00:13:34.425 +0100  [DEBG]: {     2:      }: type=Encryption Algorithm, flag=0x8000, lorv=AES
2021-01-27 00:13:34.425 +0100  [DEBG]: {     2:      }: type=Key Length, flag=0x8000, lorv=128
2021-01-27 00:13:34.425 +0100  [DEBG]: {     2:      }: type=Authentication Method, flag=0x8000, lorv=PSK
2021-01-27 00:13:34.425 +0100  [DEBG]: {     2:      }: type=Hash Algorithm, flag=0x8000, lorv=SHA256
2021-01-27 00:13:34.425 +0100  [DEBG]: {     2:      }: type=Group Description, flag=0x8000, lorv=DH19
2021-01-27 00:13:34.425 +0100  [DEBG]: {     2:      }: Compared: DB:Peer
2021-01-27 00:13:34.425 +0100  [DEBG]: {     2:      }: (lifetime = 28800:28800)
2021-01-27 00:13:34.425 +0100  [DEBG]: {     2:      }: (lifebyte = 0:0)
2021-01-27 00:13:34.425 +0100  [DEBG]: {     2:      }: enctype = AES:AES
2021-01-27 00:13:34.425 +0100  [DEBG]: {     2:      }: (encklen = 192:128)
2021-01-27 00:13:34.425 +0100  [DEBG]: {     2:      }: hashtype = SHA256:SHA256
2021-01-27 00:13:34.425 +0100  [DEBG]: {     2:      }: authmethod = PSK:PSK
2021-01-27 00:13:34.425 +0100  [DEBG]: {     2:      }: dh_group = DH19:DH19
2021-01-27 00:13:34.425 +0100  [DEBG]: {     2:      }: type=Life Type, flag=0x8000, lorv=seconds
2021-01-27 00:13:34.425 +0100  [DEBG]: {     2:      }: type=Life Duration, flag=0x8000, lorv=28800
2021-01-27 00:13:34.425 +0100  [DEBG]: {     2:      }: type=Encryption Algorithm, flag=0x8000, lorv=AES
2021-01-27 00:13:34.425 +0100  [DEBG]: {     2:      }: type=Key Length, flag=0x8000, lorv=128
2021-01-27 00:13:34.425 +0100  [DEBG]: {     2:      }: type=Authentication Method, flag=0x8000, lorv=PSK
2021-01-27 00:13:34.425 +0100  [DEBG]: {     2:      }: type=Hash Algorithm, flag=0x8000, lorv=SHA256
2021-01-27 00:13:34.425 +0100  [DEBG]: {     2:      }: type=Group Description, flag=0x8000, lorv=DH19
2021-01-27 00:13:34.425 +0100  [PERR]: {     2:      }: no suitable proposal found.
2021-01-27 00:13:34.425 +0100  [PERR]: {     2:      }: 198.51.100.2[500] - 198.51.100.1[500]:(nil) failed to get valid p
roposal.
2021-01-27 00:13:34.425 +0100  [PERR]: {     2:      }: failed to process packet.
2021-01-27 00:13:34.425 +0100  [INFO]: {     2:      }: ====> PHASE-1 SA DELETED <====
                                                          ====> Deleted SA: 198.51.100.2[500]-198.51.100.1[500] cookie:cf36
f26328f7023b:6b6c661c5532f24a <====
```

Figure 3.18 – IKE proposal

The preceding screenshot might be a little difficult to read. So, let's zoom in on what really matters, which, in this case, is the start of `Compared: DB:Peer`. This highlights the *local* versus *remote* crypto settings. In the following output, you might notice that, on *line 5*, after the snip, `local` has an `encklen` of `192`, while `remote` has `128`. This means that both ends are trying to negotiate a different key length (I have removed the timestamps to make this section a little more readable). The tail is started by executing `tail follow yes mp-log ikemgr.log`. Here, `tail` is a live read of the `log` file, which is keeping an open connection to the `log` file and immediately displaying new entries in the console. This can be useful when you are tracking issues on the fly. The tail can be ended by hitting *Ctrl-C*:

```
reaper@PA-VM2> tail follow yes mp-log ikemgr.log

...snip
 [DEBG]: {    2:      }: Compared: DB:Peer
 [DEBG]: {    2:      }: (lifetime = 28800:28800)
 [DEBG]: {    2:      }: (lifebyte = 0:0)
 [DEBG]: {    2:      }: enctype = AES:AES
 [DEBG]: {    2:      }: (encklen = 192:128)
 [DEBG]: {    2:      }: hashtype = SHA256:SHA256
 [DEBG]: {    2:      }: authmethod = PSK:PSK
 [DEBG]: {    2:      }: dh_group = DH19:DH19
 [DEBG]: {    2:      }: type=Life Type, flag=0x8000,
lorv=seconds
 [DEBG]: {    2:      }: type=Life Duration, flag=0x8000,
lorv=28800
 [DEBG]: {    2:      }: type=Encryption Algorithm, flag=0x8000,
lorv=AES
 [DEBG]: {    2:      }: type=Key Length, flag=0x8000, lorv=128
 [DEBG]: {    2:      }: type=Authentication Method,
flag=0x8000, lorv=PSK
 [DEBG]: {    2:      }: type=Hash Algorithm, flag=0x8000,
lorv=SHA256
 [DEBG]: {    2:      }: type=Group Description, flag=0x8000,
lorv=DH19
 [PERR]: {    2:      }: no suitable proposal found.
 [PERR]: {    2:      }: 198.51.100.2[500] -
198.51.100.1[500]:(nil) failed to get valid proposal.
 [PERR]: {    2:      }: failed to process packet.
```

```
  [INFO]: {     2:       }: ====> PHASE-1 SA DELETED <====
                                                        ====>
Deleted SA: 198.51.100.2[500]-198.51.100.1[500]
cookie:cf36f26328f7023b:6b6c661c5532f24a <====
```

If the remote side is unable to change its `phase-1` encryption to match `192` bits, we can lower ours to `128`.

If all goes well, the next attempt will look similar to the following output. Note that I've removed the timestamps to make it a little more readable:

```
  [DEBG]: {     2:       }: begin encryption.
  [DEBG]: {     2:       }: encryption(aes)
  [DEBG]: {     2:       }: pad length = 16
  [DEBG]: {     2:       }: encryption(aes)
  [DEBG]: {     2:       }: with key:
  [DEBG]: {     2:       }: encrypted payload by IV:
  [DEBG]: {     2:       }: save IV for next:
  [DEBG]: {     2:       }: encrypted.
  [DEBG]: {     2:       }: 92 bytes from 198.51.100.2[500] to
198.51.100.1[500]
  [DEBG]: 198.51.100.2[500] - 198.51.100.1[500]:(nil) 1 times of
92 bytes message will be sent over socket 1024
  [DEBG]: {     2:       }: add packet bc3e74e8:20 size    92, rcp
3
  [DEBG]: {     2:       }: PH1 state changed: 8 to 13 @ph1_set_
next_state
  [PNTF]: {     2:       }: ====> PHASE-1 NEGOTIATION SUCCEEDED AS
RESPONDER, MAIN MODE <====
                                                        ====>
Established SA: 198.51.100.2[500]-198.51.100.1[500]
cookie:9f9ed23b50e87b5b:d721c43e9a1b9566 lifetime 28800 Sec
<====
```

We can now use the remote side to try to initiate the `phase-2` negotiation, which we can easily track in the system log or by watching the little indicator lights in **Network** > **IPSec Tunnels**.

As indicated in *Figure 3.19*, there is another proposal issue in `phase-2` this time:

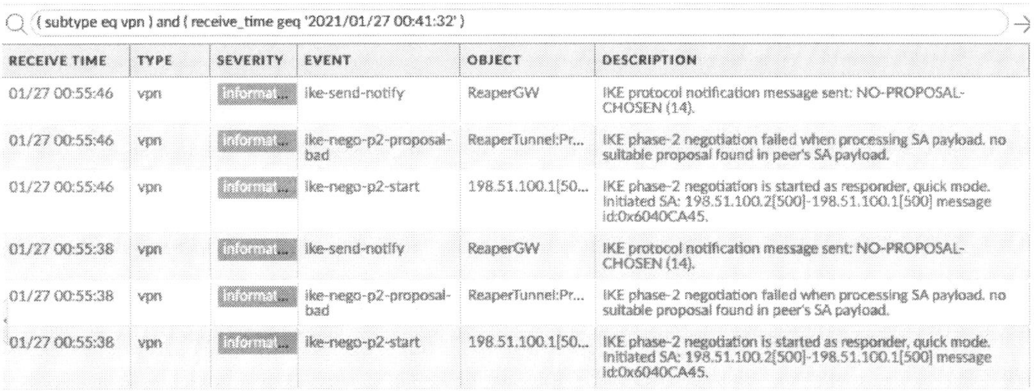

(subtype eq vpn) and (receive_time geq '2021/01/27 00:41:32')

RECEIVE TIME	TYPE	SEVERITY	EVENT	OBJECT	DESCRIPTION
01/27 00:55:46	vpn	informat...	ike-send-notify	ReaperGW	IKE protocol notification message sent: NO-PROPOSAL-CHOSEN (14).
01/27 00:55:46	vpn	informat...	ike-nego-p2-proposal-bad	ReaperTunnel:Pr...	IKE phase-2 negotiation failed when processing SA payload. no suitable proposal found in peer's SA payload.
01/27 00:55:46	vpn	informat...	ike-nego-p2-start	198.51.100.1[50...	IKE phase-2 negotiation is started as responder, quick mode. Initiated SA: 198.51.100.2[500]-198.51.100.1[500] message id:0x6040CA45.
01/27 00:55:38	vpn	informat...	ike-send-notify	ReaperGW	IKE protocol notification message sent: NO-PROPOSAL-CHOSEN (14).
01/27 00:55:38	vpn	informat...	ike-nego-p2-proposal-bad	ReaperTunnel:Pr...	IKE phase-2 negotiation failed when processing SA payload. no suitable proposal found in peer's SA payload.
01/27 00:55:38	vpn	informat...	ike-nego-p2-start	198.51.100.1[50...	IKE phase-2 negotiation is started as responder, quick mode. Initiated SA: 198.51.100.2[500]-198.51.100.1[500] message id:0x6040CA45.

Figure 3.19 – The proposal issue in phase-2

To see what's going on in `phase-2`, we can enable debugging on the tunnel. If no Proxy IDs are being used, you can simply add the tunnel name. If Proxy IDs are being used, each one needs to be added individually. If you are not sure which one is going to be used for this test, it may be prudent to enable debugging on all of them:

```
reaper@PA-VM2> debug ike tunnel ReaperTunnel:ProxyID1 on debug

Debugging for IPSec tunnel ReaperTunnel:ProxyID1 is enabled
(debug).

IKE gateway debug level:
  ReaperGW                         2              debug
IPSec tunnel debug level:
  ReaperTunnel:ProxyID1            2              debug

```

Now, let's zoom in on `begin compare proposals` to see where there could be a mismatch. We can see that `encklen` is, again, mismatched; this time it is `256 remote` and `128 local`. The `pfs` (perfect forward secrecy) DH group is also mismatched with `19 local` and `20 remote`:

```
 [DEBG]: {      :     2}: begin compare proposals.
 [DEBG]: {      :     2}: pair[1]: 0x7f3ac4043b30
 [DEBG]: {      :     2}:  0x7f3ac4043b30: next=(nil) tnext=(nil)
 [DEBG]: {      :     2}: prop#=1 prot-id=ESP spi-size=4 #trns=1
```

```
trns#=1 trns-id=GCM16
 [DEBG]: {        :      2}: type=SA Life Type, flag=0x8000,
lorv=seconds
 [DEBG]: {        :      2}: type=SA Life Duration, flag=0x8000,
lorv=3600
 [DEBG]: {        :      2}: lifetime 3600 seconds
 [DEBG]: {        :      2}: type=Encryption Mode, flag=0x8000,
lorv=Tunnel
 [DEBG]: {        :      2}: type=Key Length, flag=0x8000, lorv=256
 [DEBG]: {        :      2}: type=Group Description, flag=0x8000,
lorv=20
 [DEBG]: {        :      2}: peer's single bundle:
 [DEBG]: {        :      2}:   (proto_id=ESP spisize=4 spi=e8918aeb
spi_p=00000000 encmode=Tunnel reqid=0:0)
 [DEBG]: {        :      2}:    (trns_id=GCM16 encklen=256
authtype=254)
 [DEBG]: {        :      2}: my single bundle:
 [DEBG]: {        :      2}:   (proto_id=ESP spisize=4 spi=00000000
spi_p=00000000 encmode=Tunnel reqid=0:0)
 [DEBG]: {        :      2}:    (trns_id=GCM16 encklen=128
authtype=254)
 [PERR]: {      2:       }: pfs group mismatched: my:19 peer:20
 [PERR]: {        :      2}: not matched
 [PERR]: {        :      2}: no suitable policy found.
```

Once the proposals have been corrected, the tunnel interface should look similar to *Figure 3.20*. Here, both indicators will be green:

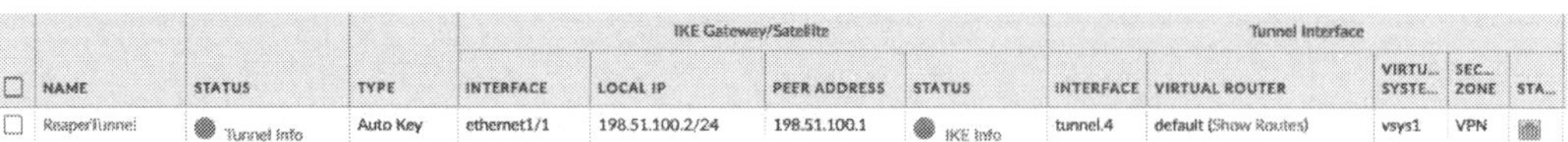

Figure 3.20 – The IPSec tunnel in fully connected status

The tunnel can also be checked in the CLI via the `show vpn flow` command:

```
reaper@PA-VM2> show vpn flow

total tunnels configured:                                    1
filter - type IPSec, state any

```

```
total IPSec tunnel configured:                                  1
total IPSec tunnel shown:                                       1

id name                   state monitor local-ip      peer-ip
tunnel-i/f
-- ----                   ----- ------- --------      -------
----------
2  ReaperTunnel:ProxyID1 active off 198.51.100.2 198.51.100.1
tunnel.4
```

This command will return the tunnels that are up, and, if any Proxy IDs were configured, the pairs that are currently connected. This takes us to the next section.

Proxy ID mismatching

Another common mismatch is the Proxy ID; this could happen if one side has the IDs configured and the other side does not, or if one side has smaller subnets than the other. In the case where the remote peer initiates the connection, these will be fairly easy to spot as they are reported in the system log, as shown in *Figure 3.21*. Here, the `remote` peer proposes a Proxy ID with a local subnet of `10.0.0.0/24` and a remote subnet of `192.168.27.0/24`. The local configuration does not contain a matching pair in the Proxy IDs, so the negotiation fails:

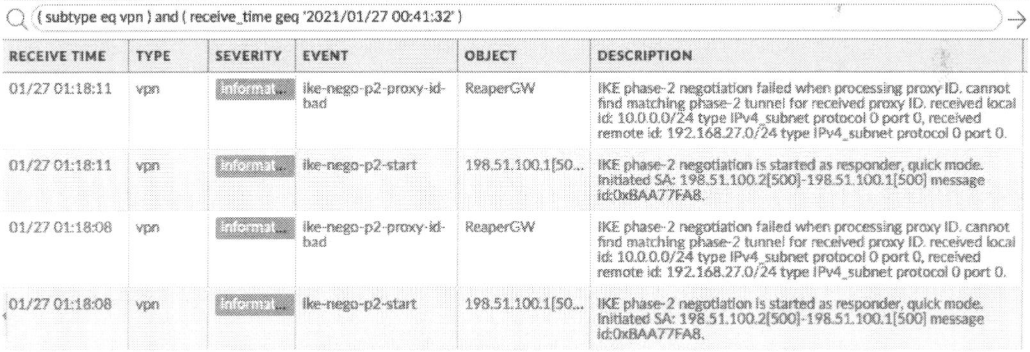

(subtype eq vpn) and (receive_time geq '2021/01/27 00:41:32')

RECEIVE TIME	TYPE	SEVERITY	EVENT	OBJECT	DESCRIPTION
01/27 01:18:11	vpn	informat...	ike-nego-p2-proxy-id-bad	ReaperGW	IKE phase-2 negotiation failed when processing proxy ID. cannot find matching phase-2 tunnel for received proxy ID. received local id: 10.0.0.0/24 type IPv4_subnet protocol 0 port 0, received remote id: 192.168.27.0/24 type IPv4_subnet protocol 0 port 0.
01/27 01:18:11	vpn	informat...	ike-nego-p2-start	198.51.100.1[50...	IKE phase-2 negotiation is started as responder, quick mode. Initiated SA: 198.51.100.2[500]-198.51.100.1[500] message id:0xBAA77FA8.
01/27 01:18:08	vpn	informat...	ike-nego-p2-proxy-id-bad	ReaperGW	IKE phase-2 negotiation failed when processing proxy ID. cannot find matching phase-2 tunnel for received proxy ID. received local id: 10.0.0.0/24 type IPv4_subnet protocol 0 port 0, received remote id: 192.168.27.0/24 type IPv4_subnet protocol 0 port 0.
01/27 01:18:08	vpn	informat...	ike-nego-p2-start	198.51.100.1[50...	IKE phase-2 negotiation is started as responder, quick mode. Initiated SA: 198.51.100.2[500]-198.51.100.1[500] message id:0xBAA77FA8.

Figure 3.21 – The remote peer proposing Proxy IDs while the local peer has none

Dynamic site-to-site tunnels

When a peer is connected to a dynamic-IP internet connection, such as a cable or xDSL, several changes need to be made to the regular configuration to accommodate for this missing factor. Let's use the following scenario, as depicted in *Figure 3.22*, to build a new configuration:

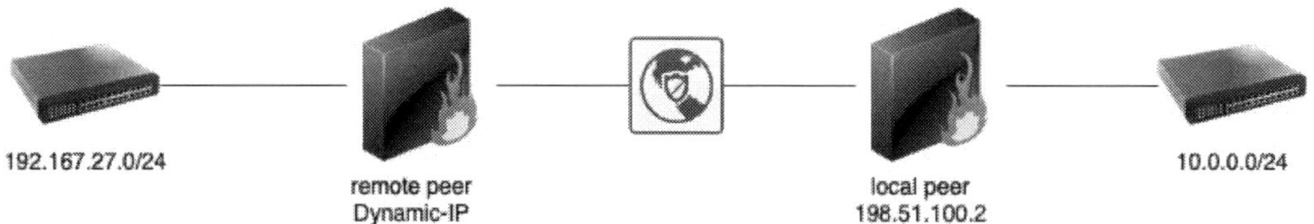

Figure 3.22 – A lab layout with one dynamic peer

In the IKE Gateway object, the `Peer IP Address object` will need to be adjusted so that it is no longer static. One hybrid solution to keep a static configuration is to use an FQDN instead of an IP address if the peer is capable of setting up a dynamic DNS service. One drawback of this workaround is that the tunnel will depend on the existence of a DNS record, and how fast the record is updated if the peer IP address changes. Some ISPs may force an IP address refresh every day to discourage running services, which could cause frequent disconnects and extended downtime if the DNS is not updated quickly. The **Dynamic** setting will provide the quickest reconnect if the peer IP changes. One drawback of this is that a factor of identification is lost. To make up for this, peer identification can be set to serve as an alternative proof of identity.

As illustrated in *Figure 3.23*, when the peer is dynamic, peer identification is *required* to make up for the missing IP the peer can offer during negotiation to prove its identity. An `FQDN`, `IP`, `KEYID`, or `email address` can be set on both sides to help in this respect. The peer will need to set the ID to `local`, whereas the local device will need to have it set to `remote`:

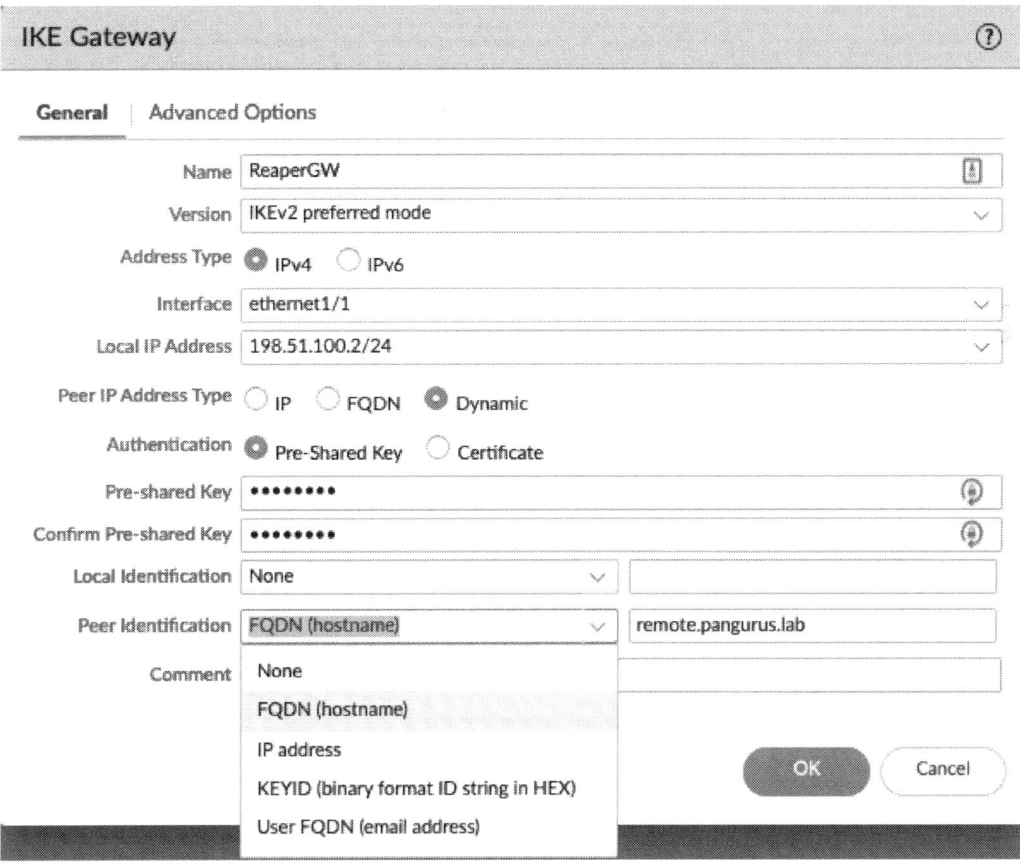

Figure 3.23 – IKE Gateway for the dynamic peer

In the **Advanced Options** tab, a few changes will need to be made as well: the local firewall needs to be set to `Passive Mode` to prevent the firewall from trying to make an outbound connection to the dynamic host as it may be offline. If **IKEv1** is used, the exchange mode needs to be set to `aggressive`. This is because, in main mode, the IP addresses are taken into account as part of the negotiation:

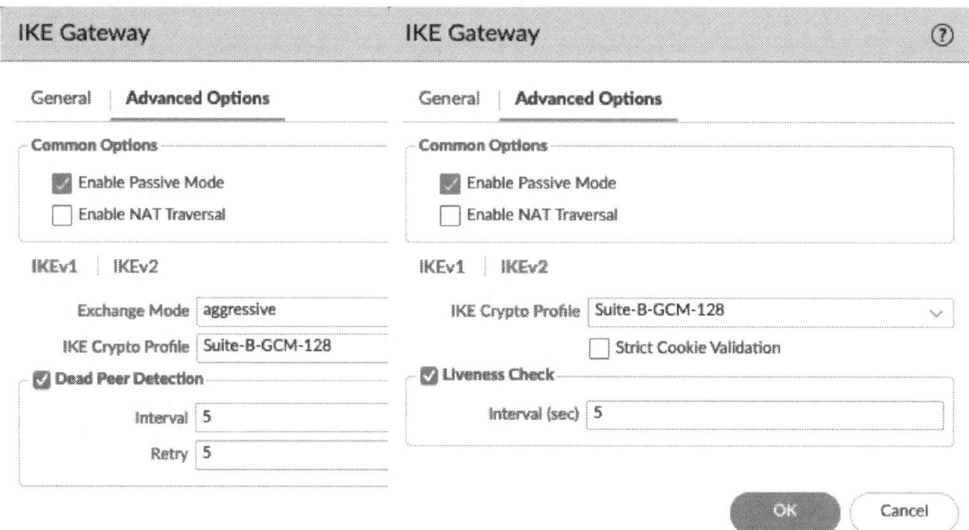

Figure 3.24 – IKE Gateway Advanced Options for the dynamic peer

When configuring a dynamic connection, identification becomes an important factor to consider. Here are a few troubleshooting steps.

Troubleshooting dynamic VPN

If a dynamic peer tries to connect to the firewall while not providing the configured identification string, that is, it is either missing or wrong, the error message will clearly indicate that the firewall received an `IKE phase-1` but is unable to match it to a gateway object. If the peer tries to use main mode instead of aggressive, the following error will appear also (main mode requires both sides to authenticate their identity using their IP, which one site will not be able to provide). Note that the timestamps have been removed for legibility:

```
reaper@PA-VM2> tail follow yes mp-log ikemgr.log
 [PERR]: Couldn't find configuration for IKE phase-1 request
for peer IP 198.51.100.1[500].
 [PERR]: Couldn't find configuration for IKE phase-1 request
for peer IP 198.51.100.1[500].
```

```
 [PERR]: Couldn't find configuration for IKE phase-1 request
for peer IP 198.51.100.1[500].
 [PERR]: Couldn't find configuration for IKE phase-1 request
for peer IP 198.51.100.1[500].
 [PERR]: Couldn't find configuration for IKE phase-1 request
for peer IP 198.51.100.1[500].
 [PERR]: Couldn't find configuration for IKE phase-1 request
for peer IP 198.51.100.1[500].
```

When using IKEv2, the error message will actually show more detail. The following is a mismatch in the FQDN host ID (timestamps have been removed for legibility):

```
[INFO]: {    2:      }: received IKE request 198.51.100.1[500]
to 198.51.100.2[500], found IKE gateway ReaperGW
[PNTF]: {    2:      }: ====> IKEv2 IKE SA NEGOTIATION STARTED
AS RESPONDER, non-rekey; gateway ReaperGW <====
                                                      ====>
Initiated SA: 198.51.100.2[500]-198.51.100.1[500]
SPI:ed6a32e92a028544:a4305ee9a6e5f494 SN:32 <====
[DEBG]: {    2:      }: see whether there's matching transform
[DEBG]: {    2:      }: found same ID. compare attributes
[DEBG]: {    2:      }: OK; advance to next of my transform type
[DEBG]: {    2:      }: see whether there's matching transform
[DEBG]: {    2:      }: found same ID. compare attributes
[DEBG]: {    2:      }: OK; advance to next of my transform type
[DEBG]: {    2:      }: see whether there's matching transform
[DEBG]: {    2:      }: found same ID. compare attributes
[DEBG]: {    2:      }: OK; advance to next of my transform type
[DEBG]: {    2:      }: see whether there's matching transform
[DEBG]: {    2:      }: found same ID. compare attributes
[DEBG]: {    2:      }: OK; advance to next of my transform type
[DEBG]: {    2:      }: success
[DEBG]: {    2:      }: update request message_id 0x0
[DEBG]: {    2:      }: received notify type ESP_TFC_PADDING_
NOT_SUPPORTED
[PERR]: {    2:      }: 198.51.100.1[500] -
198.51.100.2[500]:0x5594946b97f0 received ID_I (type fqdn
[domote.pangurus.lab]) does not match peers id
[DEBG]: {    2:      }: update request message_id 0x1
```

```
[INFO]: {     2:       }: 198.51.100.2[500] -
198.51.100.1[500]:(nil) closing IKEv2 SA ReaperGW:32, code 13
[PNTF]: {     2:       }: ====> IKEv2 IKE SA NEGOTIATION FAILED AS
RESPONDER, non-rekey; gateway ReaperGW <====
```

There is also a third option that can be used that connects to a dynamic remote Palo Alto; this leverages GlobalProtect instead of the traditional IPSec configuration.

Setting up the LSVPN

LSVPN is a feature that simplifies the connection of remote Palo Alto firewalls, called **satellites**. Typically, but not exclusively, smaller devices that have a very dynamic nature can be onboarded rapidly and deployed where they need to be. Connections are managed in very much the same way as GlobalProtect agents. Here, a portal is used to service clients and provide configuration updates, while one or several gateways provide connectivity based on preference and availability.

If a GlobalProtect setup already exists, satellite configuration can be added to it to simplify the deployment process. Alternatively, a new deployment can be set up specifically for the LSVPN. In **GlobalProtect Portal Configuration**, navigate to the **Satellite** tab, as depicted in *Figure 3.25*.

Besides the satellite configuration, there are also two certificate configuration options, as follows:

- **TRUSTED ROOT CA**: This is the root certificate that signs the GlobalProtect Gateway server certificate and is pushed out to connecting satellites, so they know they can trust the gateway server certificate.
- **Client Certificate**: This is used to issue a certificate to a connecting satellite as a client certificate after it successfully authenticates:

1. **OCSP Responder**: This will be used by the satellite to verify the validity of the issuing certificate. This can be set to **none**, so the satellite does not validate the issuing certificate.
2. **Validity Period**: This is the time the client certificate is valid and can be set to between 7 and 365 days.
3. **Certification Renewal Period**: This is the number of days before the client certificate expires and in which the certificate is automatically renewed:

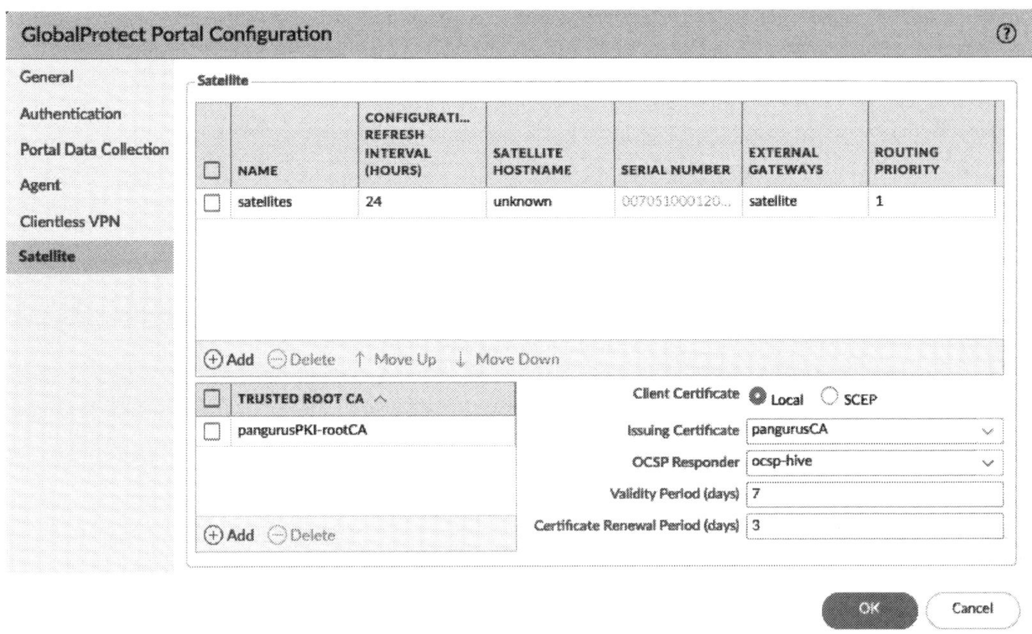

Figure 3.25 – The satellite portal configuration

As illustrated in *Figure 3.26*, the satellite portal configuration is very straightforward:

- **General** takes a friendly name for the profile and an interval between the configuration updates.
- In **Devices**, the serial numbers of known devices can be added to facilitate onboarding. The portal can accept authentication by either a serial number or user credentials. If a device connects with an unknown, or no, serial, it will be required to authenticate. If it connects with a serial number added here, no further authentication is required. The **SATELLITE HOSTNAME** is issued once the satellite has been authenticated.
- **Enrolment User/User Group** is used as the user credentials in lieu of a known serial number. If no authentication is set, only known and configured serials will be allowed to authenticate.
- In **Gateways**, all the GP gateways can be configured, and a routing preference can be provided to indicate which gateway is preferred. The routing preference serves two purposes:
    - It indicates which gateway has priority, with the lowest number having the highest priority. Routing priorities can be set to any number from 1 to 25.

- The routes published by the gateway to the satellite receive a metric that is 10 times the value of the gateway priority (that is, the "preferred" gateway with a routing priority of 1 will publish routes with a metric value of 10 to the satellites, and the backup gateway with a routing priority of 2 will publish routes with a metric value of 20 to the satellite):

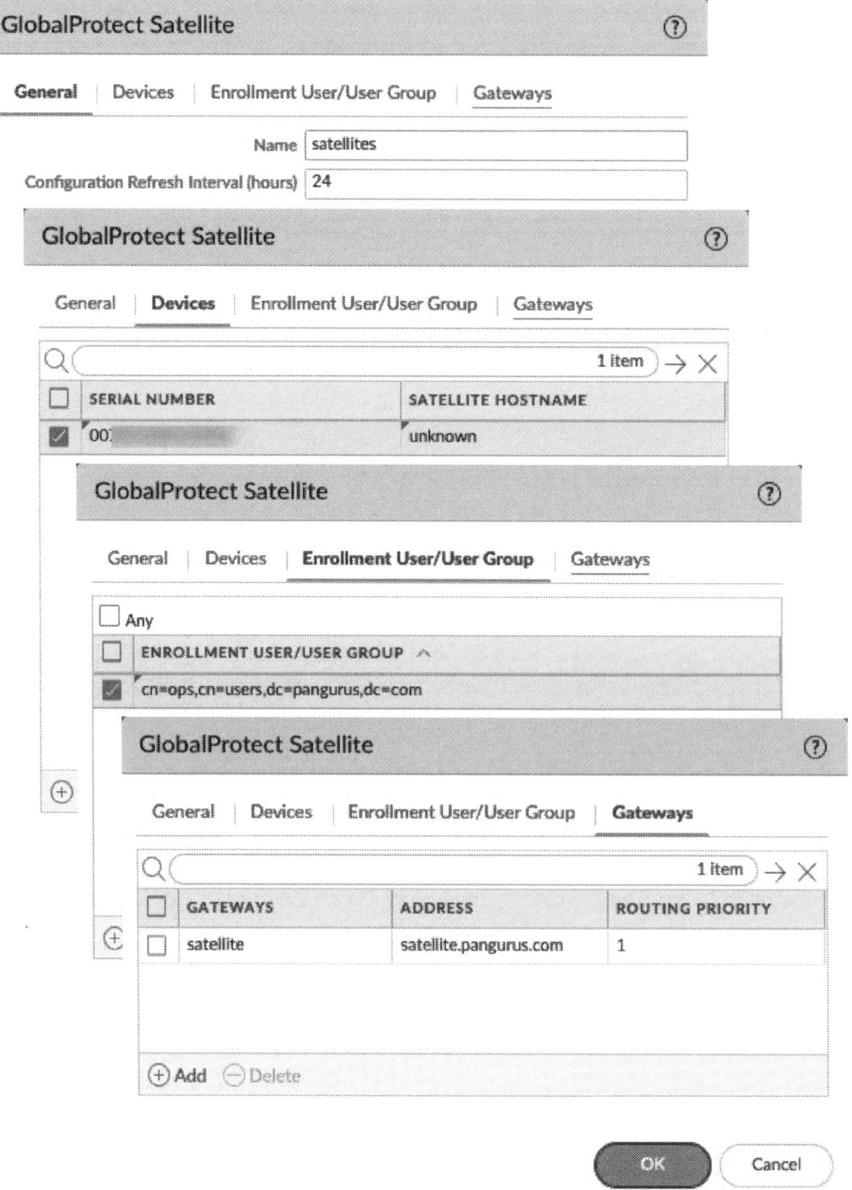

Figure 3.26 – The satellite portal configuration

The next step is to configure the gateway so that the satellite can connect. This configuration can also be added to an existing GlobalProtect gateway or a standalone gateway that is used exclusively for satellite connections.

As shown in *Figure 3.27*, in the **GlobalProtect Gateway Configuration Satellite** tab, **Tunnel Configuration** needs to be enabled to activate the gateway for the satellite. Next, a tunnel interface needs to be added to serve as an egress point of tunnelled sessions. Interestingly, another **Configuration Refresh Interval** can be configured here for the satellite to check for a new configuration on the portal.

In **Tunnel Monitoring**, an IP can be added so that the satellite monitors an IP address on the network beyond the gateway. If the monitor fails, the satellite will fail over to the next gateway in the routing priority list. If the tunnel interface has an IP assigned, the **Tunnel Monitoring** > **Destination Address** can be left blank, and the tunnel interface IP will automatically be used as the monitoring destination.

Crypto Profiles will determine which algorithms will be used once the tunnel is established in the same way that `phase-2` is established in a regular IPSec tunnel:

Figure 3.27 – The GlobalProtect Gateway Satellite configuration

In *Figure 3.28*, in the **Network Settings** tab, the configuration is very similar to the GlobalProtect agent's IDs provided for the satellites:

- **Inheritance Source** can be used to pass the local ISP DNS servers onto the satellite gateway.
- **Primary DNS** and **Secondary DNS** servers are used to provide the remote satellite with the preferred DNS configuration.
- **DNS Suffix** can be added to control the search domain for local domain names.
- **IP POOL** provides each satellite with a dynamic IP address inside the tunnel and should be large enough to accommodate all satellites with an IP address. This IP address is not passed on to the local network of the satellite but serves as a tunnel interface IP on the satellite.
- **ACCESS ROUTE** can be used to control which subnets are routed through the tunnel in a similar way that GlobalProtect uses split tunnels. That is, if left blank, all traffic is routed through the tunnel, and if subnets are added, then only traffic destined to these subnets are routed through the tunnel:

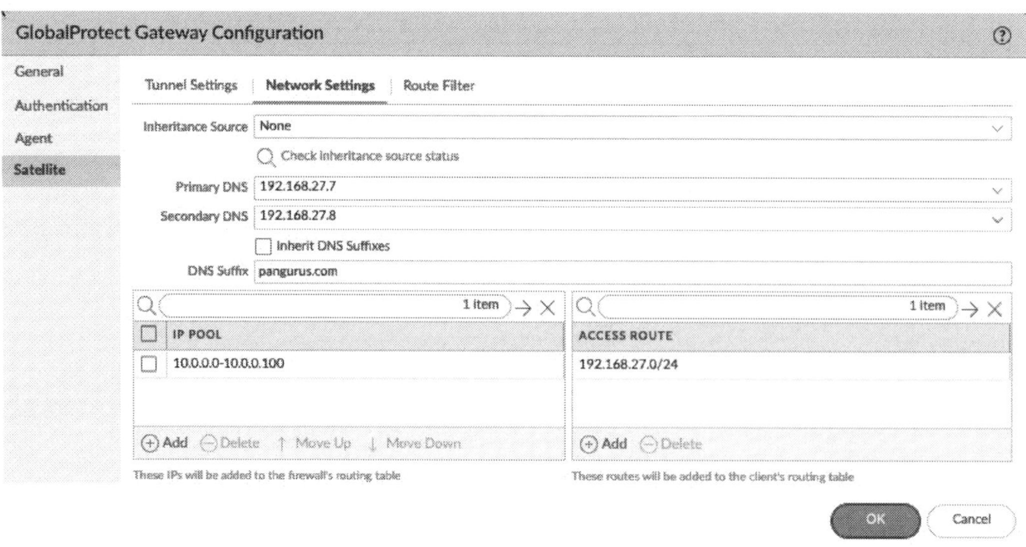

Figure 3.28 – The Gateway Satellite Network Settings

> **Important note**
>
> If multiple satellites have the same, or overlapping, local subnets, outbound connections from the satellite to the gateway need to be placed behind the tunnel IP that is assigned by the **IP Pool**.

In the **Route Filter** tab, **Accept published routes** can optionally be enabled. This option will import the local routes from the satellite onto the gateway; if disabled, no routes are reimported. With the option disabled, only inbound connections from clients behind the satellite can be set up. With the option enabled, outbound connections from the gateway's local subnets to the satellite's local subnets can also be set up. This can come in handy if, for example, the IT team needs to be able to reach out to remote machines. As illustrated in *Figure 3.29*, **Permitted Subnets** can also be set to limit the subnets that can be published; this is to prevent any overlap with local routes on the gateway:

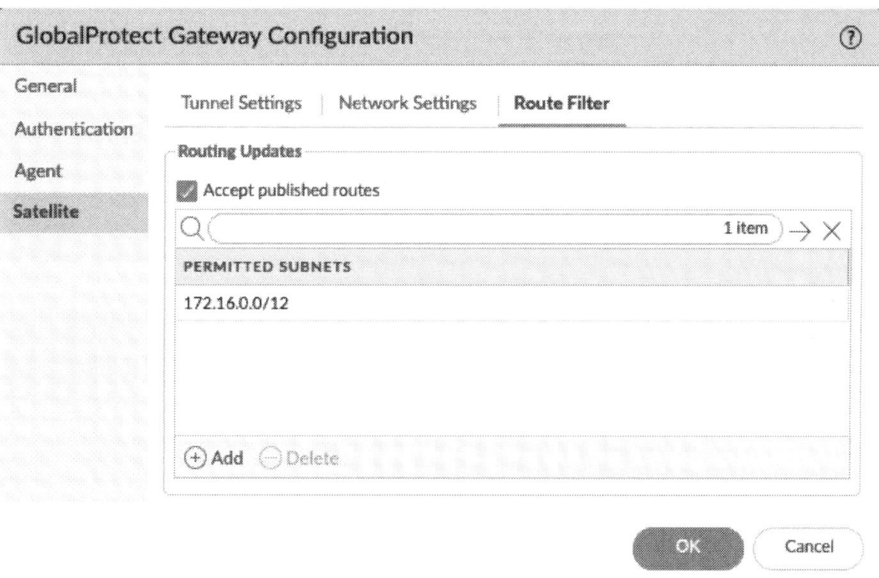

Figure 3.29 – The Gateway Satellite Route Filter

With this configuration in place, the satellite firewalls will now be able to set up a simplified connection. Rather than needing to configure an IKE Gateway object just as you would with a traditional site-to-site IPSec tunnel, only the IPSec tunnel configuration needs to be provided. As illustrated in *Figure 3.30*, setting the **tunnel type** to **GlobalProtect Satellite** will prepare the tunnel for the satellite connection. In the **General** tab, a new field for **Portal Address** will appear.

The external interface, or a loopback interface, needs to be assigned so that the tunnel can bind to a physical interface to initiate the connection. Additionally, a tunnel interface is required to provide the egress point for outbound connections to the remote network behind the gateway:

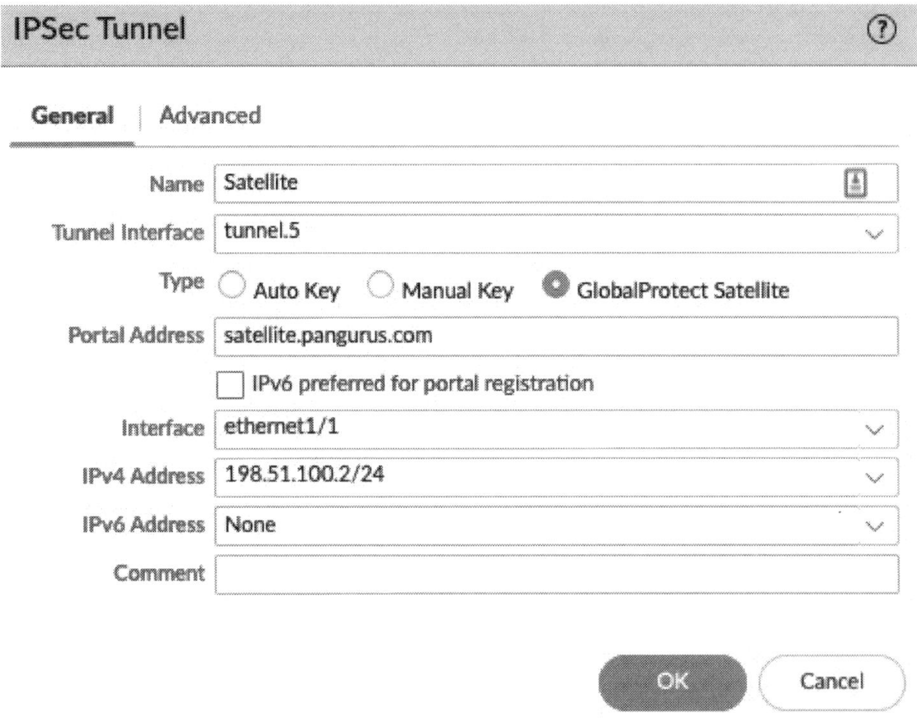

Figure 3.30 – The Satellite IPSec Tunnel configuration

In the **Advanced** tab, the **Publish all static and connected routes to Gateway** option can be enabled to publish local routes to the remote gateway. If that includes too many subnets, subnets can be specified in the following **Subnet** field so that only relevant subnets are published to the gateway.

Additionally, **External Certificate Authority** can optionally be loaded if the certificates are managed by an external CA. This is so the satellite can trust and verify the certificates it receives from the gateway:

Figure 3.31 – The Satellite IPSec Tunnel Advanced configuration

Once the configuration is set up, the satellite and gateway will report a connected state, as illustrated in *Figure 3.32*:

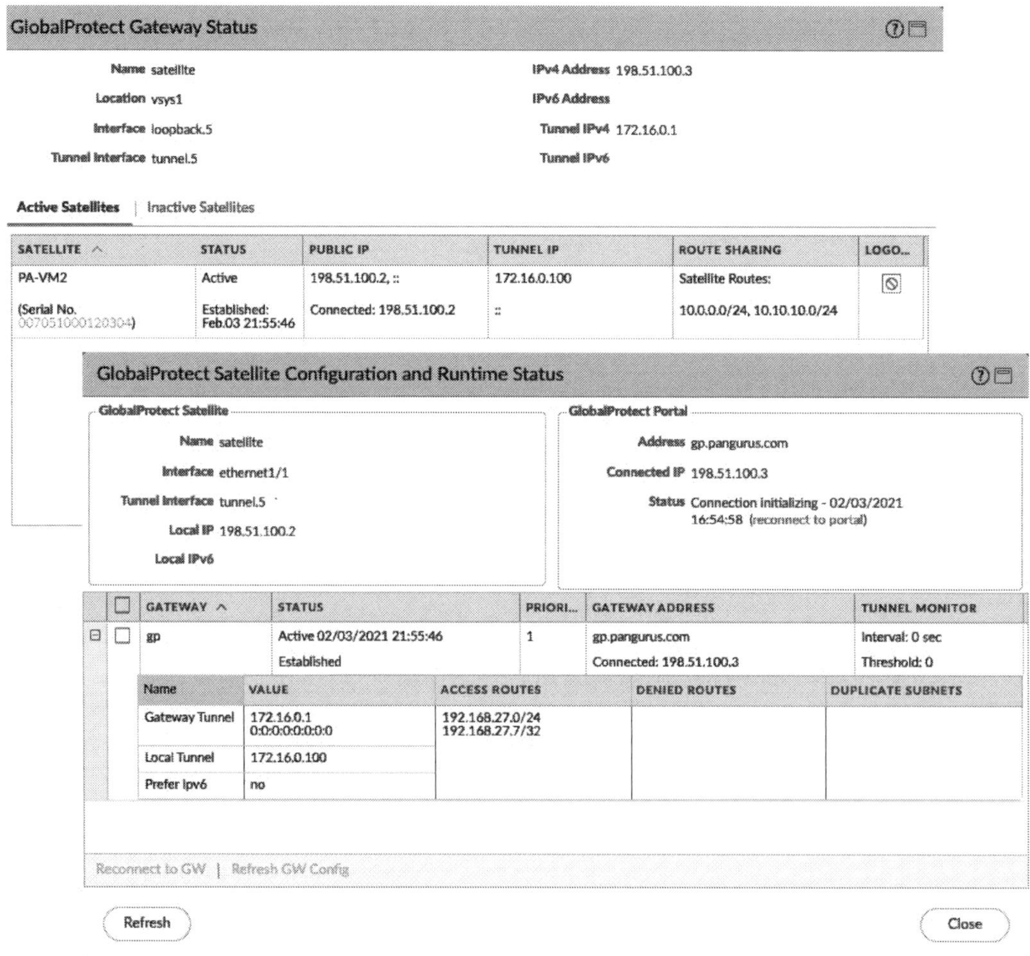

Figure 3.32 – The connected gateway and satellite

Once the configuration is implemented, you could still run into some issues that require troubleshooting.

Troubleshooting the LSVPN

In the previous sections, we learned about troubleshooting IPSec issues. Additionally, in *Chapter 3, Setting up site-to-site VPNs and Large Scale VPNs*, we saw how GlobalProtect uses its own logs. Although the LSVPN makes use of the GlobalProtect configuration in the portal and the gateway and is tied to the IPSec tunnel on the satellite, on the client side, troubleshooting happens in an entirely different process, called **satd** (**satellite daemon**). In contrast, server-side troubleshooting will happen mostly in the SSL-VPN process. In the system log, there is a dedicated subtype for satellite logs, as illustrated in *Figure 3.33*, which is also called satd. The satellite will initially behave like a GlobalProtect agent when connecting to the portal to collect the configuration. This offers the benefit of logging, so it can provide a verbose description of what is going wrong. In the following example, first, I set the IP address as the portal address; this is instead of the FQDN that is used by the server certificate installed on the GlobalProtect portal. The error message reads as follows:

```
GlobalProtect Satellite connection to portal failed.  Satellite
failed to connect to Portal 198.51.100.3 due to certificate
common name does not match the configured hostname on the
satellite. subject=/CN=gp.pangurus.com
```

Then, I corrected the portal address; however, the certificate issuer was not a trusted root certificate. The error reads as follows:

```
GlobalProtect Satellite connection to gateway failed.
Satellite failed to connect to Gateway gp.pangurus.com  due
to certificate was not trusted. subject=/CN=gp.pangurus.com;
issuer=/C=AT/O=ZeroSSL/CN=ZeroSSL RSA Domain Secure Site CA;
not before=Dec 28 00:00:00 2020 GMT; not after=Mar 28 23:59:59
2021 GMT
```

Here is the error message, as shown in the **System** log:

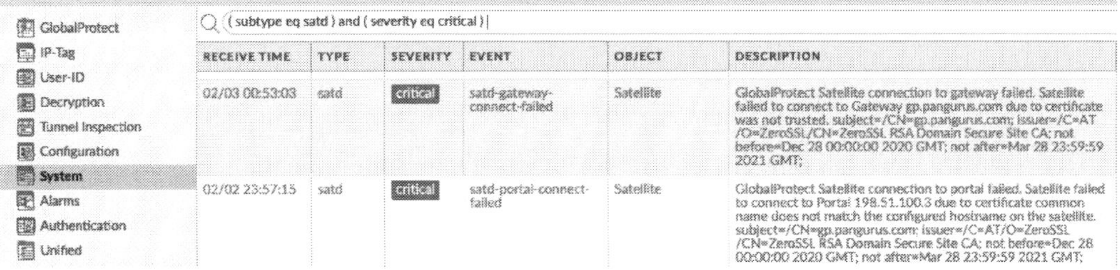

Figure 3.33 – System logs for the satd subtype

The last issue that could occur is using a server certificate that was self-signed, issued by an internal CA, or issued by a not very well-known public CA. This issue can be solved by manually importing the root CA certificate onto the satellite and setting it as a trusted root certificate. Alternatively, you can push the certificate out to all the satellites from the portal satellite configuration, as illustrated in *Figure 3.34*:

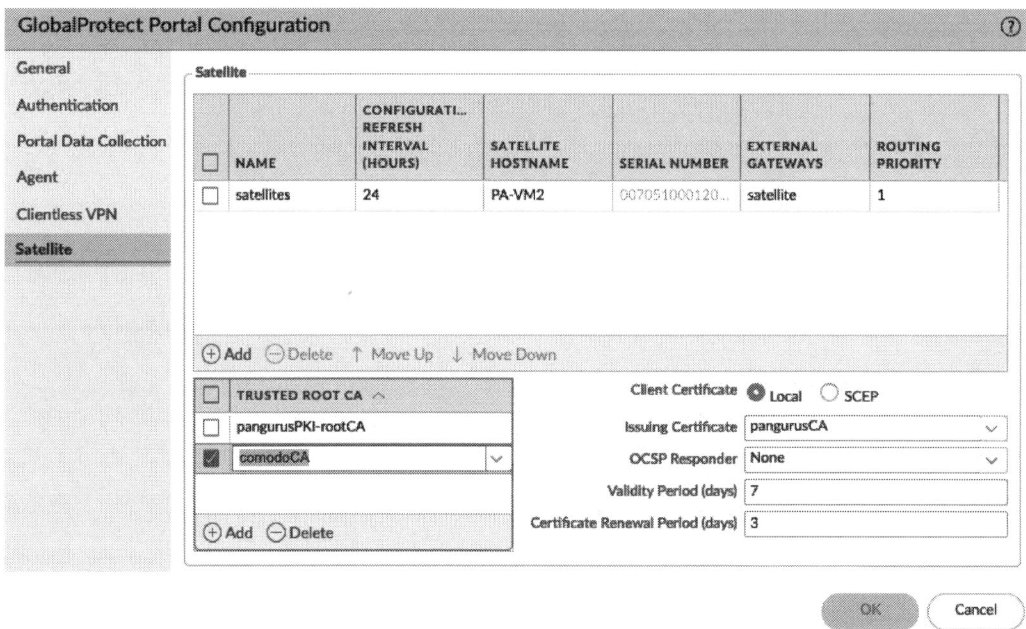

Figure 3.34 – Pushing trusted root CA certificates out to the satellites to establish trust

The daemon can also be set to debug mode from CLI using the `debug satd on debug` command, to troubleshoot any issues that might occur if the satellite is unable to connect. The following example illustrates a failure to connect because the DNS is not resolving to the correct address.

First, enable debugging on the process to ensure that all of the details are revealed. The debug command will also show what the previous level of debugging was, so you can revert to the default setting after you have finished troubleshooting:

```
reaper@PA-VM2> debug satd on debug

sw.satd.debug.global: normal
```

Next, you can use `tail follow yes mp-log satd.log` to view a live scroll by of the logs while you test the connection, or you can wait until you have completed the connection attempt and then read the logs using `less mp-log satd.log` (timestamps have removed for legibility):

```
reaper@PA-VM2> tail follow yes mp-log satd.log

debug: pan_tcp_sock_open_i(server_utils.c:510): pan_util_
connect_server(203.0.113.1(203.0.113.1):443) failed: -9999
Error:  pan_ssl_conn_open(pan_ssl_utils.c:755): pan_tcp_sock_
open() to 203.0.113.1 port 443 failed; errno=115
debug: satd_http_request(src/pan_satd_http.c:395): (conn) satd_
http_request: new connection sock_fd=0, port=0
Error:  satd_proc_portal_register(src/pan_satd_proc.c:1562):
request to 203.0.113.1
Error:  satd_proc_portal_register(src/pan_satd_proc.c:1563):
request POST /global-protect/satelliteregister.esp HTTP/1.1
User-Agent: GlobalProtect Satellite
Host: 203.0.113.1
Content-Type: application/x-www-form-urlencoded
Content-Length: 86
```

We can manually manipulate the client connecting, disconnecting, or reconnecting to the GlobalProtect gateway by using the following three commands:

```
reaper@PA-VM2> test global-protect-satellite gateway-disconnect
gateway-address gp.pangurus.com method activation satellite
satellite

Please use "show global-protect-satellite current-gateway
gateway gp.pangurus.com satellite satellite" to check gateway
info

reaper@PA-VM2> test global-protect-satellite gateway-connect
gateway-address gp.pangurus.com method activation satellite
satellite

```

```
Please use "show global-protect-satellite current-gateway
gateway gp.pangurus.com satellite satellite" to check gateway
info

reaper@PA-VM2> test global-protect-satellite gateway-reconnect
gateway-address gp.pangurus.com method activation satellite
satellite

Please use "show global-protect-satellite current-gateway
gateway gp.pangurus.com satellite satellite" to check gateway
info
```

As indicated by the preceding commands, you can verify the current status by executing `show global-protect-satellite current-gateway gateway <gatewayFQDN> satellite <satellite-name>`:

```
reaper@PA-VM2> show global-protect-satellite current-gateway
gateway gp.pangurus.com satellite satellite
GlobalProtect Satellite : satellite (1 gateways)
Gateway Info: gp.pangurus.com
    Get Config State:
        Refresh Time (seconds)             : 86400
        Failed Refresh Time (seconds)      : 300
        Current Get Config                 : success
        Max Get Config Retries             : 16777215
        Number Get Config Failed           : 0
        Config Timer Activated             : yes
        Next Get Config Time (seconds)     : 86240
        Cached Get Config Time (seconds)   : 0
        Failed Reason                      :

    Portal Config:
        GlobalProtect Gateway Name         : gp
        GlobalProtect Gateway Address      : gp.pangurus.com
        Priority                           : 1
        Gateway connected IP               : 198.51.100.3
        Ipv6 preferred                     : no

    Gateway Config:
```

```
Gateway Tunnel Name                  : satellite-S
Gateway Tunnel Interface             : tunnel.5
Gateway Tunnel id                    : 2
Gateway Tunnel IP                    : 172.16.0.1
Gateway Tunnel Ipv6                  : 0:0:0:0:0:0:0:0
Gateway Additional Tunnel IPs        :
Gateway Additional Tunnel Ipv6s      :

Status                               : Active
Status Time                          : Feb.03 15:48:44
Reason                               : Established

Config Refresh Time (hours)          : 24
IP Address                           : 172.16.0.100
Default Gateway                      : 172.16.0.1
Netmask                              : 255.255.255.255
Ipv6 Address                         :
Ipv6 Default Gateway                 :
Access Routes                        : 192.168.27.0/24
                                     : 192.168.27.7/32
Denied Routes                        :
Duplicate Routes                     :
DNS Servers                          : 192.168.27.7
DNS Suffixes                         :

Tunnel Monitor Enabled               : No
Tunnel Monitor Interval              : 0 seconds
Tunnel Monitor Action                : wait-recover
Tunnel Monitor Threshold             : 0 attempts
Tunnel Monitor Source                : 172.16.0.100
Tunnel Monitor Destination           : 172.16.0.1
Tunnel Monitor Source Ipv6           : 0:0:0:0:0:0:0:0
Tunnel Monitor Destination Ipv6      : 0:0:0:0:0:0:0:0
Tunnel Monitor in Ipv6               : no
Tunnel Monitor Status                : No data available
Encryption                           : aes-128-cbc
```

```
        Authentication                    : sha256

 -------------------------------------------------------------
---------------
```

On the GlobalProtect gateway, further troubleshooting can be performed by debugging the SSL-VPN process. First, enable debugging on the SSL-VPN process by executing `debug ssl-vpn on debug`; note that logs for this process are written to `appweb3-sslvpn.log`. The logs can be followed live during testing by running `tail follow yes mp-log appweb3-sslvpn.log`.

In the following output, you can see an operation to disconnect is executed by the client:

```
debug: sslvpnHandler_run(sslvpnHandler.c:563): sslvpnHandler_
run: Begin...
debug: sslvpnHandler_run(sslvpnHandler.c:572): sslvpnHandler_
run: method=2, port=20177, url=/clientcert-info.sslvpn
debug: sslvpnHandler_run(sslvpnHandler.c:606): sslvpnHandler_
run: SSLVPN_SSL_APPWEB_NAT
debug: sslvpnHandler_run(sslvpnHandler.c:618): sslvpnHandler_
run: do_panSslVpnClientCert
debug: conn_get_local_remote_addr_port_
internal(sslvpnHandler.c:723): conn_get_local_remote_addr_port_
internal: soc
k=23, port=20177, is_ipv4=1
debug: conn_get_local_remote_addr_port_
internal(sslvpnHandler.c:753): conn_get_local_remote_addr_port_
internal: X-R
eal-IP=198.51.100.2
debug: conn_get_local_remote_addr_port_
internal(sslvpnHandler.c:754): conn_get_local_remote_addr_port_
internal: X-R
eal-PORT=45560
debug: conn_get_local_remote_addr_port_
internal(sslvpnHandler.c:758): conn_get_local_remote_addr_port_
internal: pan
_getlocaladdr... is_proxy=1
debug: sslvpn_clcertmap_get_key(modsslvpn_portalmap.c:822):
sockfd:23, remote:198.51.100.2[45560], local:198.51.100
.3[20077]
debug: sslvpn_clcertmap_insert(modsslvpn_
```

```
portalmap.c:883): sslvpn_clcertmap_insert:
key=remote:198.51.100.2[45560],local:198.51.100.3[20077],
insert=1
debug: sslvpnHandler_run(sslvpnHandler.c:690): sslvpnHandler_
run: send_response code 552 to DP
debug: sslvpnHandler_run(sslvpnHandler.c:684): sslvpnHandler_
run: send_response
debug: panSslVpnSatelliteLogout(panPhpSslVpn.c:6811): client
software version 3.0.0
debug: sslvpn_request_send(modsslvpn_rasmgr.c:467): sending
command to sw.rasmgr.sslvpn.satellite_logout:
<?xml version="1.0" encoding="UTF-8"?><request><global-
protect-gateway><satellite-logout><gateway>satellite-S</
gateway><reason>satellite logout</
reason><serialno>007011000111111</serialno></satellite-
logout></global-protect-gateway></request>
debug: sslvpn_request_send(modsslvpn_rasmgr.c:477): response:

        <response status="success">
                <gateway>satellite-S</gateway>
                <serialno>007011000111111</serialno>
        </response>
```

Although the LSVPN is very easy to deploy, consider using a traditional site-to-site configuration for static locations. Static locations do not require regular configuration updates and IPSec provides a more robust VPN solution.

Summary

In this chapter, we learned the difference between static and dynamic site-to-site IPSec VPN tunnels, and we looked at several ways to troubleshoot mismatched algorithms. We also learned about the LSVPN and the benefits it could bring when lots of mobile devices need to be deployed quickly and easily.

You will now be able to effectively decide which of the preceding scenarios will be most beneficial to you depending on your needs. Additionally, you can also decide how to troubleshoot if a tunnel still does not connect after you have configured it.

In the next chapter, we will learn about *Prisma Access*, which is a VPN consolidation product that is intended to replace traditional site-to-site VPN connections with a more resilient cloud-based variant.

4
Configuring Prisma Access

In this chapter, we will learn about **Prisma Access**. Prisma Access is positioned as a **Secure Access Service Edge** (**SASE**) solution that aims to decentralize connectivity from the traditional data centre into the cloud, which it does by combining user VPNs and site-to-site VPNs and providing a service layer in the cloud that manages security. The cloud aspect enhances the user experience by providing users and remote offices with a geographically nearby point-of-presence, all while maintaining the same level of security wherever they are located.

In this chapter, we're going to cover the following main topics:

- Configuring Prisma Access
- Configuring the service infrastructure
- Configuring the service connections
- Configuring directory sync
- Configuring mobile users
- Configuring remote networks
- Configuring the remote firewalls
- Configuring Cortex Data Lake

Technical requirements

In this chapter, we will focus on deploying Prisma Access via Panorama as this will give you the most hands-on experience. Working experience with Panorama device groups and templates is recommended to easily follow along with the topics discussed in this chapter.

Check out the following link to see the Code in Action video:
`https://bit.ly/3fosfXf`

Configuring Prisma Access

SASE, or **Secure Access Service Edge**, is a term that was coined by *Gartner* to describe a cloud-centric approach to network architecture, where secure services and connectivity are delivered directly to the source of a connection rather than a data centre. With Prisma Access, connectivity and security can be taken out of the data centre where, historically, a bulky firewall would provide a focal point of partner VPN tunnels and remote users dialling in to reach resources in the DMZ, while doubling up as the perimeter firewall protecting the office users and server farm. As shown in the following diagram, all connectivity is shifted toward the cloud. The data centre is still represented but could also be a cloud-based service, such as an Azure-based Active Directory and Office 365 environment, while remote users and remote offices connect to a cloud instance that's geographically closest to them rather than the central site. This cuts down on direct connection latency and improves the user experience:

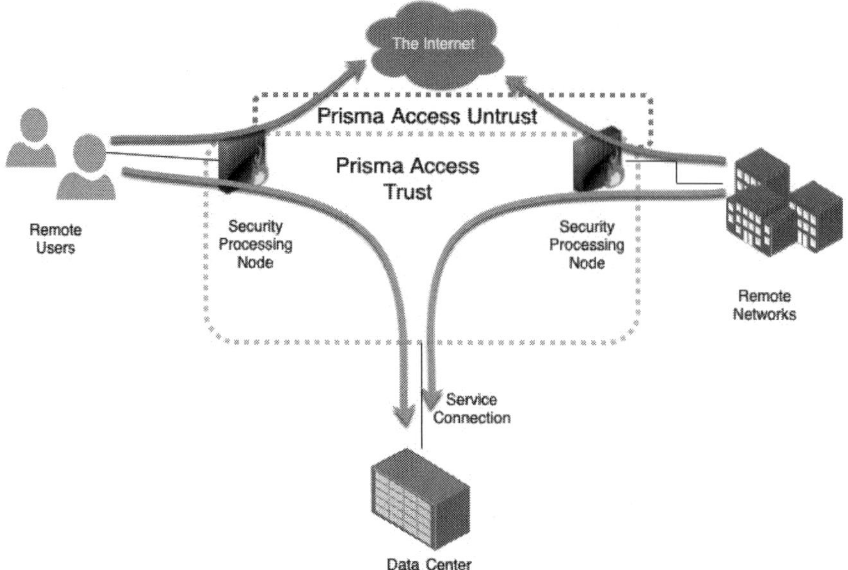

Figure 4.1 – Prisma Access basic design

There is a cost associated with shifting to the cloud, however. While traditional site-to-site VPNs and GlobalProtect are free with the platform, Prisma Access requires at least two licenses, with a third one depending on your deployment, with optional add-ons and features if required. Sizing and prices will vary, depending on the *size* of certain licenses, but these are the ones that are required just to get started:

- **Cortex Data Lake** (**CDL**), as all logs related to Prisma Access can only be stored in CDL.
- A Business/Business Premium, Enterprise, or **Zero Trust Network Access Secure Internet Gateway** (**ZTNA SIG**) Prisma Access license.
- Panorama is optional as the configuration can either be controlled through Panorama or the Prisma Access app via the app portal (`https://apps.paloaltonetworks.com`).

The following are its add-ons and additional feature licenses:

- Additional service connections can be added as additional licenses.
- The **interconnect license** is *required* if remote networks need to communicate with each other and not just the internet or the service connections.
- **Data Loss Prevention** (**DLP**) can be added to scan for sensitive data that should not leave the network.
- **Internet of Things** (**IoT**) can be added to scan for IoT devices so that security rules can be applied.
- **Autonomous Digital Experience Management** (**ADEM**) is a feature that provides visibility into the connectivity pathway and can help troubleshoot issues such as latency and jitter.

Panorama licenses are scaled against the number of devices that will be managed. Depending on the number of on-premises devices, it could be beneficial to get a Panorama license and consolidate all configuration into it or use the app if no physical firewalls are currently deployed. CDL licenses are scaled against the total volume of logs in terabytes that need to be stored.

The Prisma Access license types come in four flavours: Business, Business Premium, ZTNA, and Enterprise.

The following table provides an overview of each license and its features and capabilities:

		Business	Business Premium	ZTNA	Enterprise
Core Capabilities	URL Filtering	X	X	X	X
	DNS Security	X	X		X
	Threat Prevention		X	X	X
	WildFire		X		X
	Service Connection			Two with Local Five with Global	Two with Local Five with Global
Add-on	Additional service Connections			X	X
	Interconnect				X

For each of these flavours, the license is based on the number of active users over a period of 90 days, and/or the sum of all the throughput capacity for all the remote networks you intend to onboard to Prisma Access.

There's also a number of user licenses, and the total data transfer per year is capped based on a calculation of 250 GB per year per endpoint times the number of endpoints.

For reference, a license guide can be found here; more changes may be made to licenses soon: `https://www.paloaltonetworks.com/resources/datasheets/prisma-access-licensing-guide`.

Once your order has been placed, you should receive an email from your sales contact with an easy activation link to activate your licenses.

Before following the activation link, make sure that you complete the following two steps:

1. On the Palo Alto Networks Support Portal (`support.paloaltonetworks.com`), make sure the account that will be used to perform the activation and registration is set as a **Super User** and that, on the Hub portal (`apps.paloaltonetworks.com`), all roles have been assigned to the account.
2. If you do not have an active Panorama server set up, download an appropriate base image from `https://support.paloaltonetworks.com`, and then configure and update the server so that it's in a good working condition. A complete procedure can be found in *Mastering Palo Alto Networks*.

For Prisma Access, it is imperative that Panorama is set to the appropriate time zone, is connected to an NTP server, and that **Telemetry** has also been set to the correct region, as shown in the following screenshot:

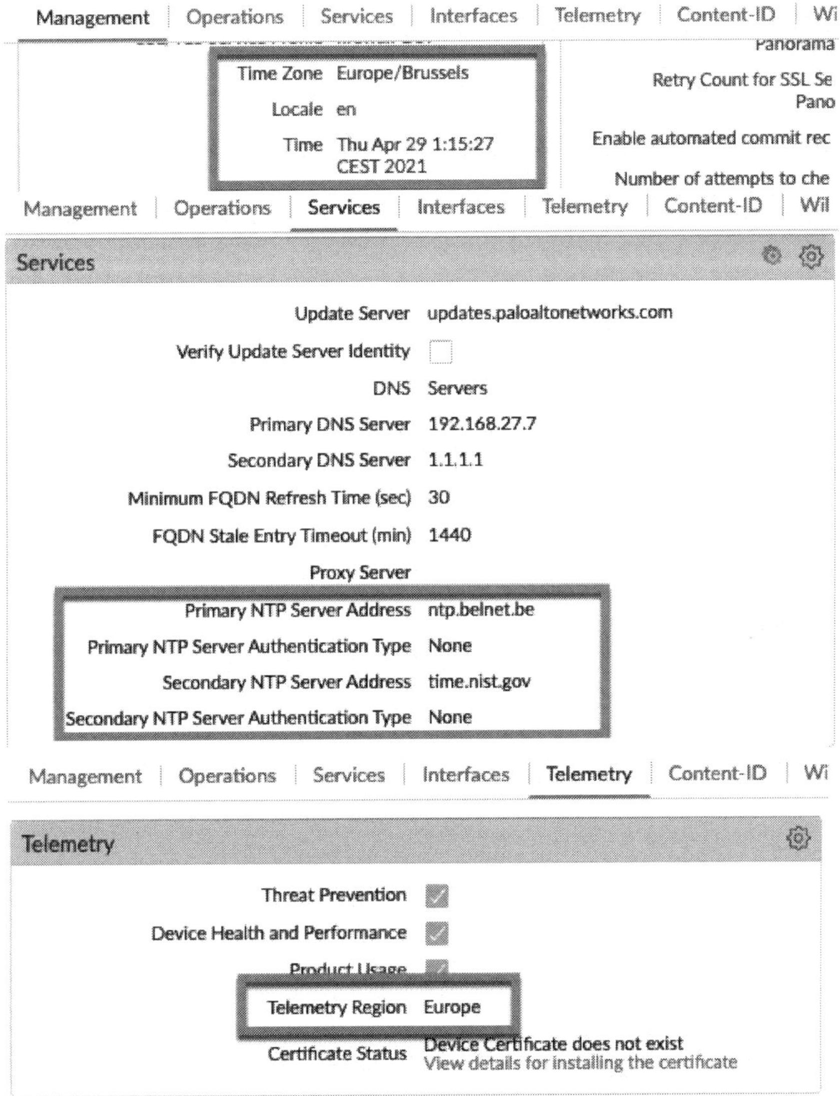

Figure 4.2 – Region, time zone, and NTP configuration in Panorama

Next, the Cloud Services plugin needs to be installed. Prisma Access can only be configured through this plugin in Panorama. Ensure that the latest plugin is installed. The plugin page should look as follows. Once the plugin has been downloaded and installed, a new **Cloud Services** menu item will also appear under the **Plugins** menu. Make sure to click **Check Now** to retrieve the latest available plugins:

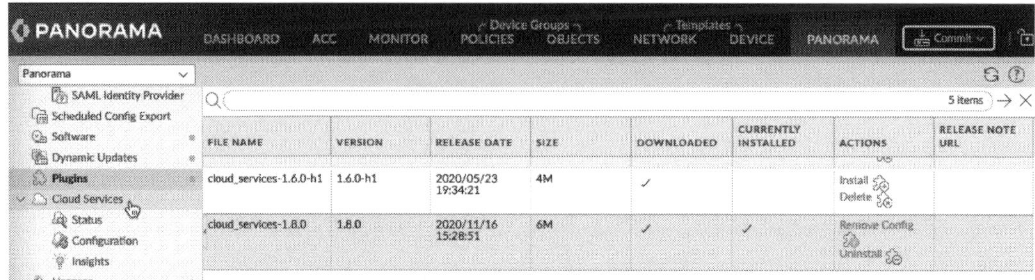

Figure 4.3 – Required cloud services plugin

Once the plugin has been installed correctly and the licenses have been activated, Panorama still needs to be "connected" to Prisma Access, which can be accomplished with a **One-Time Password** (**OTP**).

If you complete the registration process via the self-enrolment email, the last page will present you with the OTP ready to use, as shown in the following screenshot:

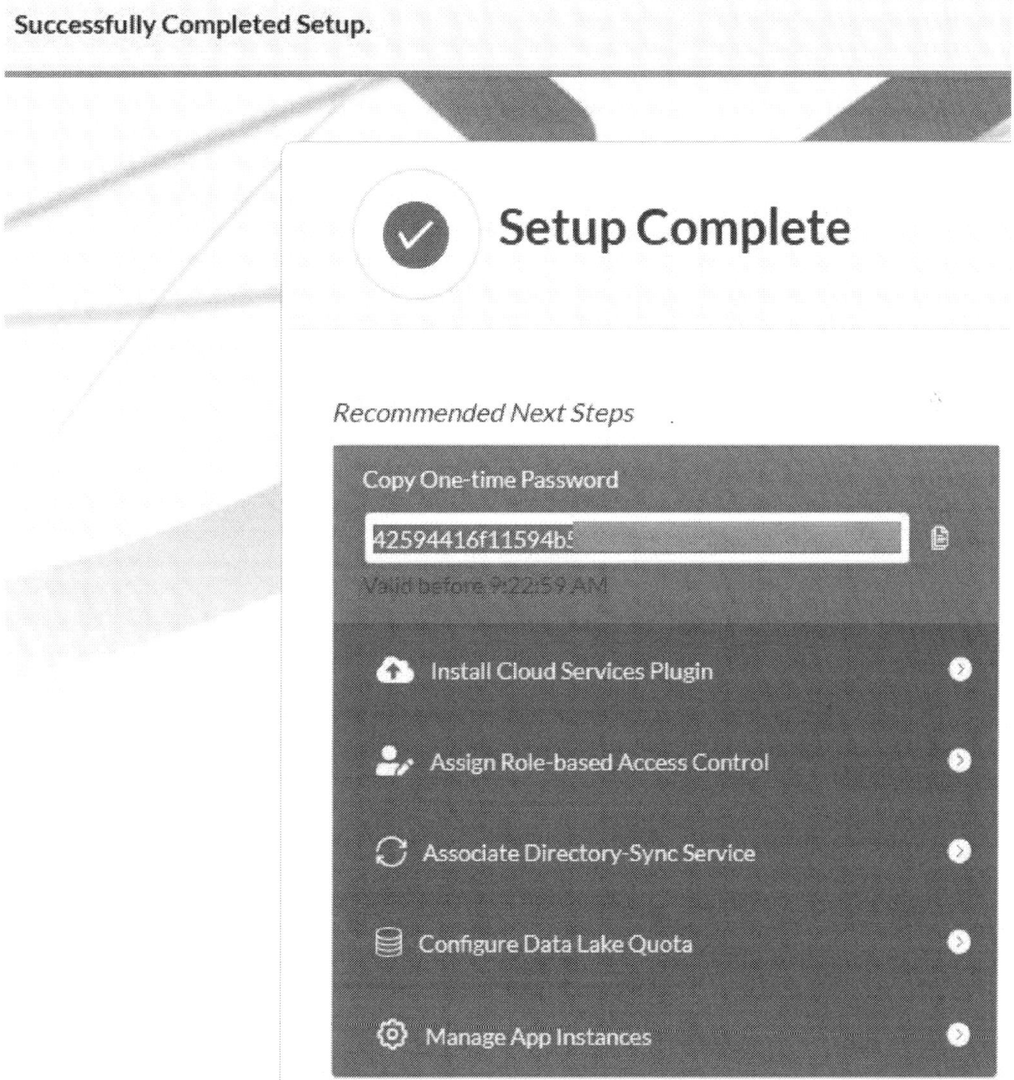

Figure 4.4 – Panorama activation OTP at the end of auto-setup

Alternatively, if the licenses were activated earlier or via the regular process via the support portal, you can generate an OTP in the support portal (`https://support.paloaltonetworks.com`) via **Assets** > **Cloud Services** > **Generate OTP**, as shown here:

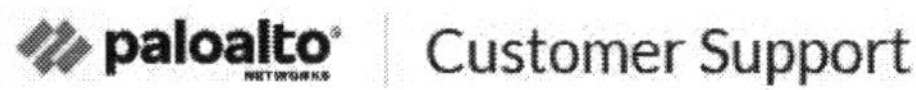

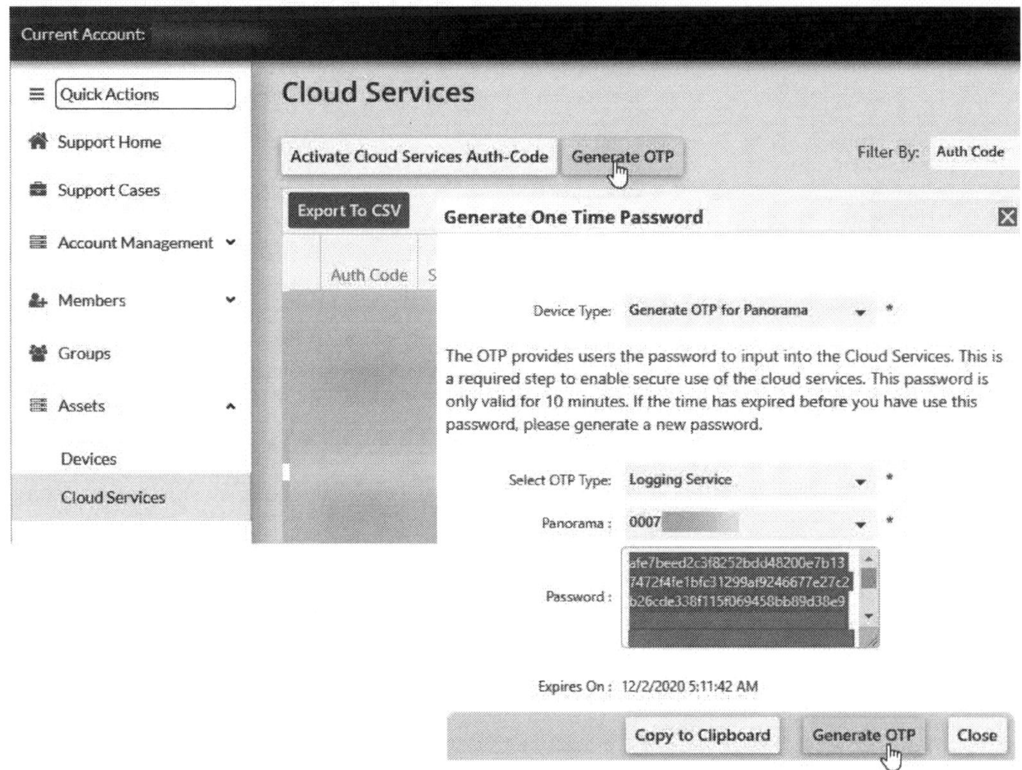

Figure 4.5 – Generating the Panorama OTP for the Prisma Access Cloud Services plugin

Once the OTP has been copied, it can be entered into Panorama by accessing the new **Cloud Services** > **Status** menu and clicking **Verify**. As shown in the following screenshot, a popup will appear that the OTP can be pasted into. Once you click **OK**, Panorama will connect to the cloud services to sync up with Prisma Access:

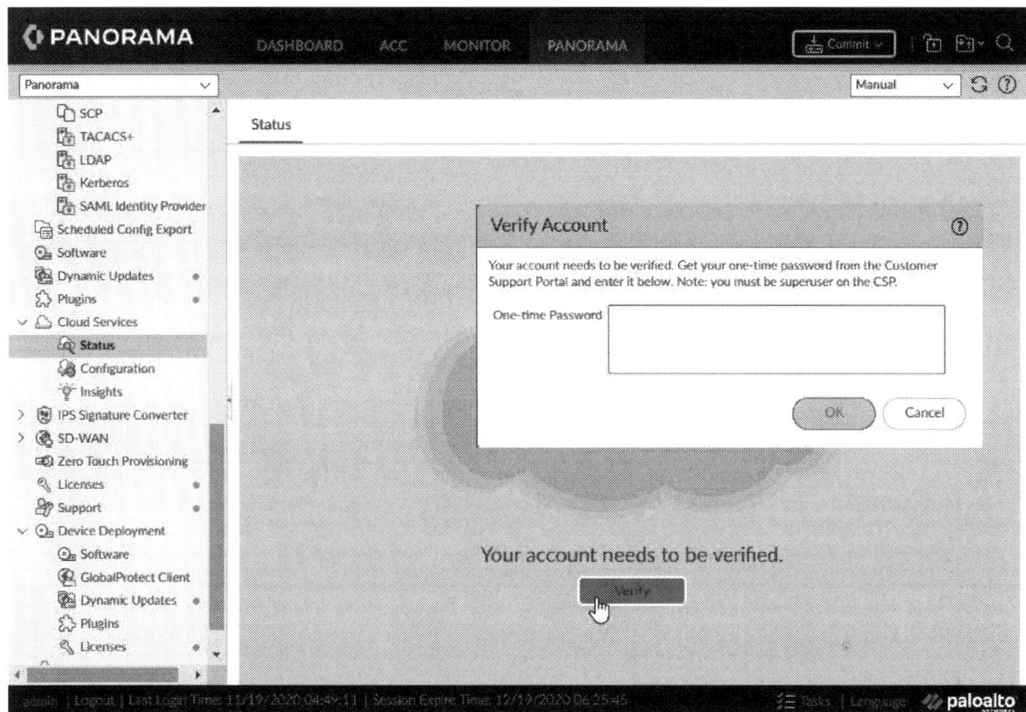

Figure 4.6 – Attaching Panorama to Prisma Access

Once the OTP has been accepted, some unconfigured objects will appear in the **Cloud Services** > **Status** window, and new configuration options will become available in **Cloud Services** > **Configuration**.

Configuring the service infrastructure

The first thing that needs to be configured is the **service infrastructure**, as illustrated in the following screenshot. This is essentially the virtual network "inside" Prisma Access that serves as the backbone between remote networks, service connections, GlobalProtect users, and the internet. This needs to exist before any other component can be configured and needs a subnet that does not overlap anywhere else in the company.

On the **Service Setup** menu item, click the *cog wheel* to configure the service infrastructure.

In the **General** tab, do the following:

- Provide an infrastructure subnet that does not overlap with any internal networks. Choose wisely because once this network has been configured, *it can't be changed.*
- A **Border Gateway Protocol Autonomous System** (**BGP AS**) is present and can be changed if an internal BGP is used for enterprise-wide routing. If no dynamic routing is used, the BGP AS can remain unchanged and will not impact regular routing decisions.
- Take note of `Service_Conn_Template_Stack` and `Service_Conn_Template` as these are automatically generated and will be used to push configuration, such as zones and VPN information for the **service connections**, onto the service network. `Service_Conn_Template` is read-only and managed by Palo Alto Networks. Additional templates can be added to `Service_Conn_Template_Stack`.
- An automatically generated device group is also added so that policies can be pushed. If a device group hierarchy already exists, **Service_Conn_Device_group** can be added as a child. Otherwise, it can be placed directly into **shared**.

On the **Internal Domain List** tab, add any domain names that have an internal DNS server, and then add the primary and secondary DNS servers. This information can be used as a **Proxy DNS** configuration for all the connected remote networks and users.

In the **Cortex Data Lake** tab, make sure the correct **Theatre** is selected as restrictions may apply where logs can be stored.

In the **Advanced** tab, routing can be changed from **Default**, which lets Prisma Access perform all the routing, to **Hot Potato Routing**, which sets Prisma Access to hand off routing to the company's WAN as quickly as possible. **HIP Redistribution** can also be enabled so that Prisma Access can share HIP information from its GlobalProtect and remote network users with the service connections:

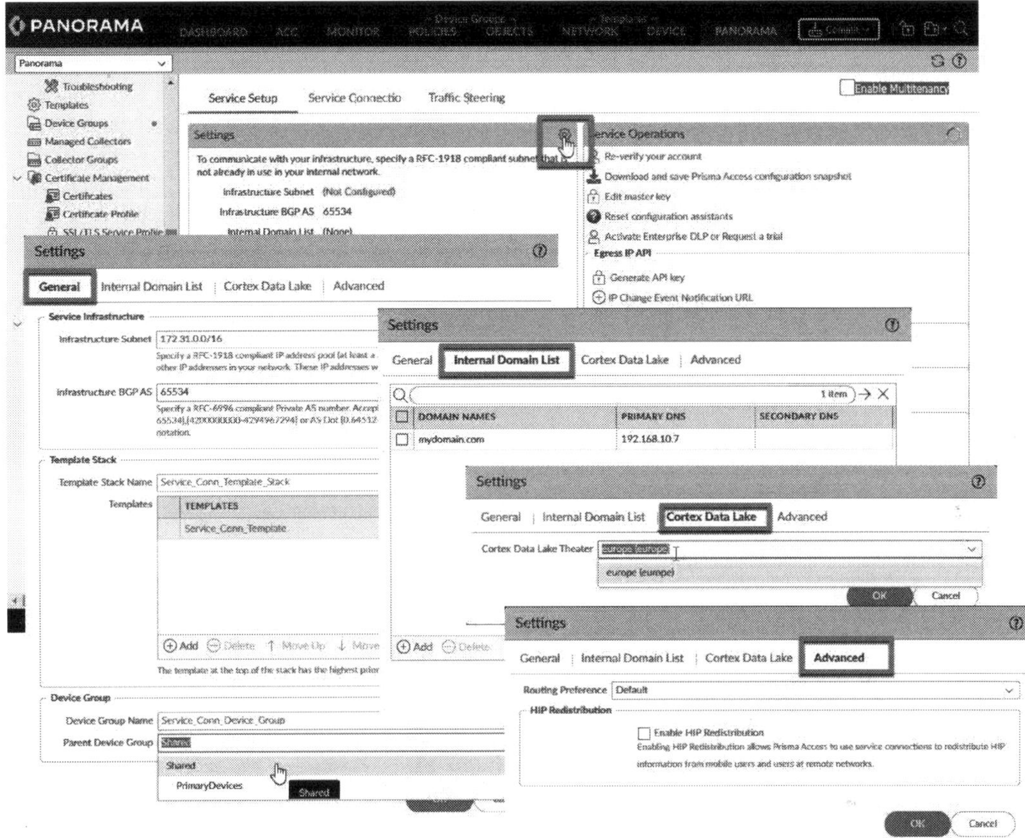

Figure 4.7 – Service infrastructure configuration

Activating the service infrastructure requires a two-phase commit – **First Commit to Panorama** (do not use **Commit and Push** when dealing with Prisma Access) and then **Push to Devices**:

1. Click **Edit Selection** at the bottom left.
2. Navigate to the **Prisma Access** tab in the **Push Scope Selection** window.
3. Check the **Service Setup** checkbox, as shown in the following screenshot.

4. The commit scope will now contain the new **Device Groups** and **Templates** for the Prisma Access service.
5. Proceed with **Commit And Push**:

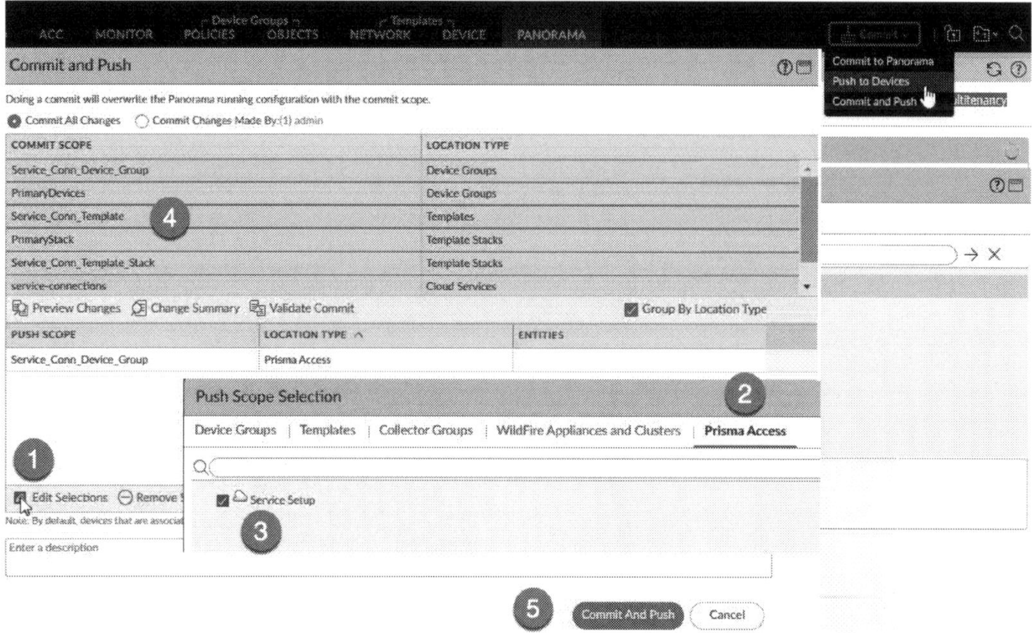

Figure 4.8 – Push scope selection

The service infrastructure will now be provisioned on Prisma Cloud. This process can take quite a while, so rather than waiting for this process to complete, start creating the service connection IPSec configuration.

Configuring the service connection

In **Templates** > **Network** > **Network Profiles** > **IKE Gateways**, first, switch the template to `Service_Conn_Template`, which will ensure the IPSec tunnel is created in the service connection part of the Prisma infrastructure. As we learned in *Chapter 2, Configuring Advanced GlobalProtect Features*, the IKE gateway is configured based on local and remote parameters.

> **Important note**
>
> The IPSec tunnel configuration is created as a service on the Prisma Access service infrastructure, so the physical firewall connecting to Prisma Access will need its own configuration.

The Prisma Access side interface will receive a static IP address, while the remote service connection can either be a static or dynamic host. In the following screenshot, my service connection is hosted on a dynamic ISP, so **Peer IP Address Type** is set to **Dynamic** and is behind a NAT device, and **Local Identification** and **Remote Identification** have been set to accommodate this. Follow these steps:

1. Add a new IKE gateway.
2. Set your preferred IKE **Version**, taking into account what the HQ or DataCentre firewall will be able to support.
3. Add the DC/HQ IP address or set **Peer IP Address Type** to **Dynamic**.
4. Set a **Pre-shared Key** or import and set a **certificate**.
5. Set up **Local Identification** and **Remote Identification**.

In the **Advanced Options** section, do the following:

1. Tick **Enable Passive Mode** so that the service connection waits for the peer to initiate the connection.
2. Ticking **Enable NAT Traversal** is only needed if the remote peer is behind a NAT device.
3. Select or create an appropriately secure **IKE Crypto Profile**.
4. Enable **Liveness Check** or **Dead peer Detection** if you must use IKEv1:

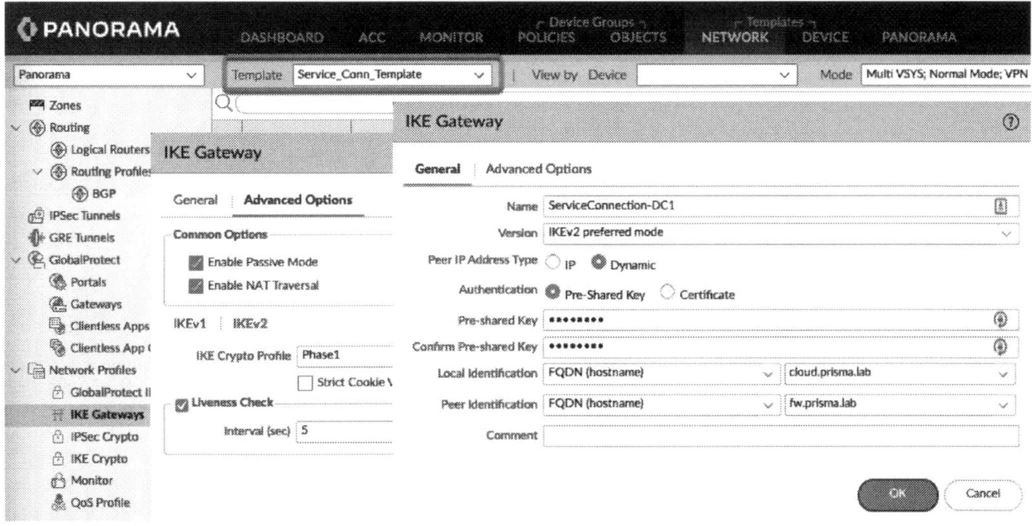

Figure 4.9 – Service connection IKE gateway

Next, we need to set up the IPSec tunnel configuration. Navigate to **Profiles** > **Network** > **IPSec Tunnels** and create a new tunnel. Notice in the following screenshot that unlike a regular IPSec tunnel configuration, there is no tunnel interface to be configured, since these are automatically attached to the backend when the configuration is committed to Prisma Access:

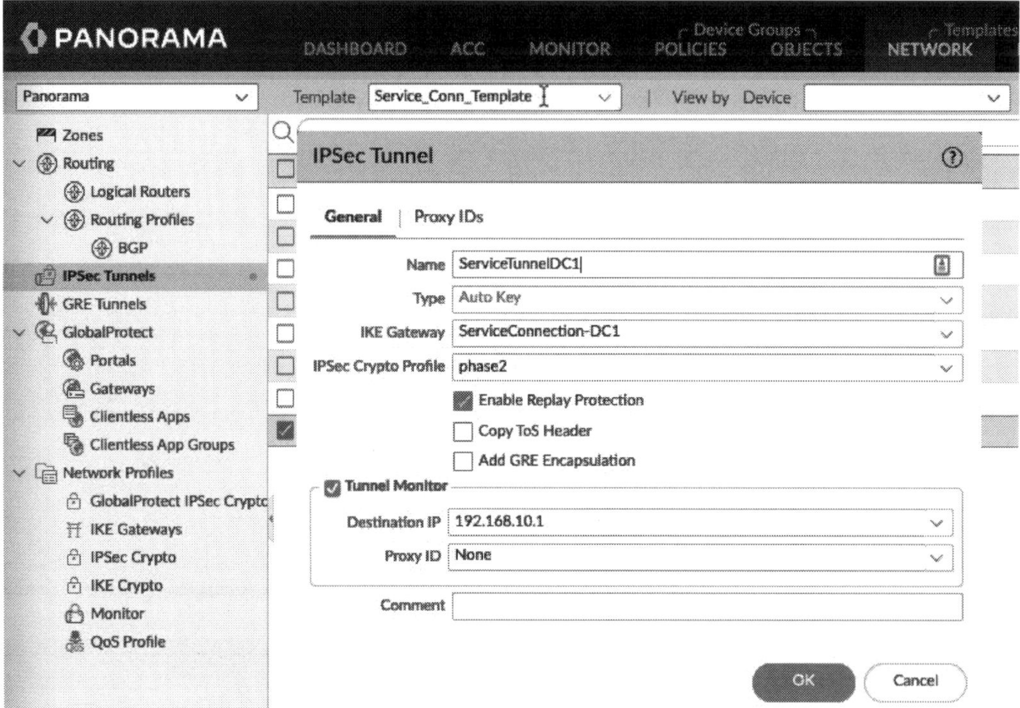

Figure 4.10 – Service connection IPSec tunnel

Repeat the preceding process (creating an IKE gateway and IPSec tunnel) for all the service connection sites and any backup IPSec tunnel each site has.

The newly created service connection (IPSec tunnel) must be added to **Service Connection Onboarding** via **Panorama** > **Cloud Services** > **Configuration** > **Service Connection** > **Onboarding**. As shown in the following screenshot, add a new onboarding and set the appropriate **Region**. This will ensure the tunnel interface is deployed in the same regional cloud instance that the service connection site is located in.

If another service connection exists, this can be added as a **Backup SC**. Prisma will automatically fail over to that service connection in case of a link failure on the current one.

If the current service connection site can support a backup IPSec tunnel through a secondary ISP, the tunnel for that link can be added to the **Enable Secondary WAN** section.

In the **Static Routes** and **BGP** tabs, you can configure routing parameters for the subnets located at the remote site. In the **QoS** tab, a simple QoS profile can be added:

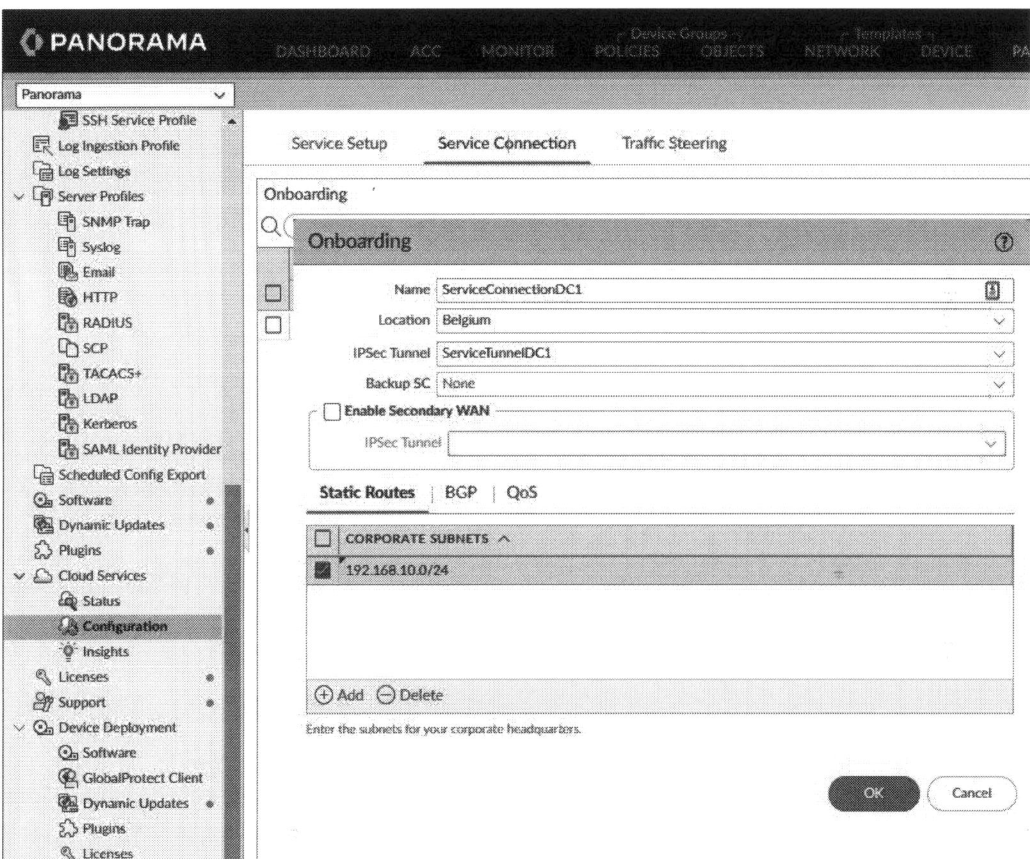

Figure 4.11 – Service connection onboarding

Now that the service connection has been set up, we can move on to **mobile users**.

Configuring directory sync

Before we configure mobile users, we need to consider how user information such as group membership can be learned. An on-premises Panorama server can connect directly to the Active Directory servers to gather the required information, but a cloud-based management server does not have this access. For a cloud-based Panorama instance, we need to set up an additional service called **Directory Sync** so that it can collect user information. The remote networks and mobile users can also use Directory Sync or connect directly to Active Directory through the service connection.

Directory Sync can be activated via **the Hub** at `https://apps.paloaltonetworks.com`. On the landing, page scroll down until you see the corresponding tile, as shown in the following figure:

1. Click **Activate** on the Directory Sync tile.

   On the next page, you can change the company account if you have multiple accounts, and set a user-friendly name for the connection. Make sure you select the appropriate region as Directory Sync needs to interface with your Active Directory environment.

2. Click **Agree & Activate**.
3. On the main landing page, click the *bento* menu and select the newly created Directory Sync app:

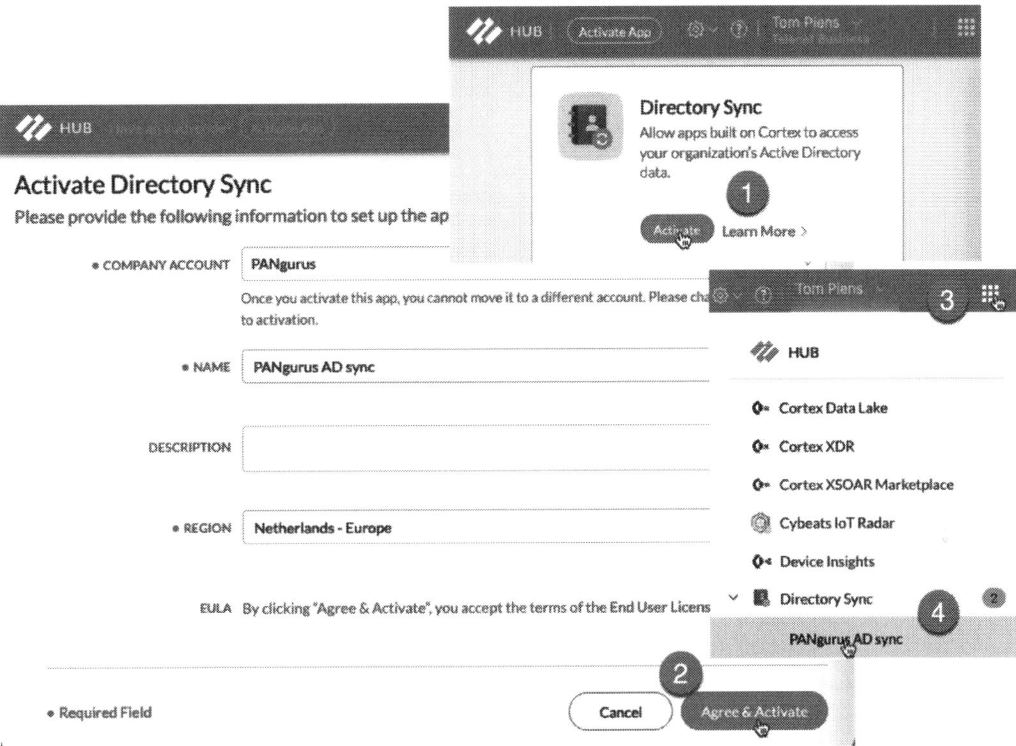

Figure 4.12 – Activating Directory Sync

Once the app has been activated, you will be taken to the configuration wizard, as shown in the following screenshot, to select which type of Active Directory to configure. Currently, the options are **Azure Active Directory** or **On-Premises**:

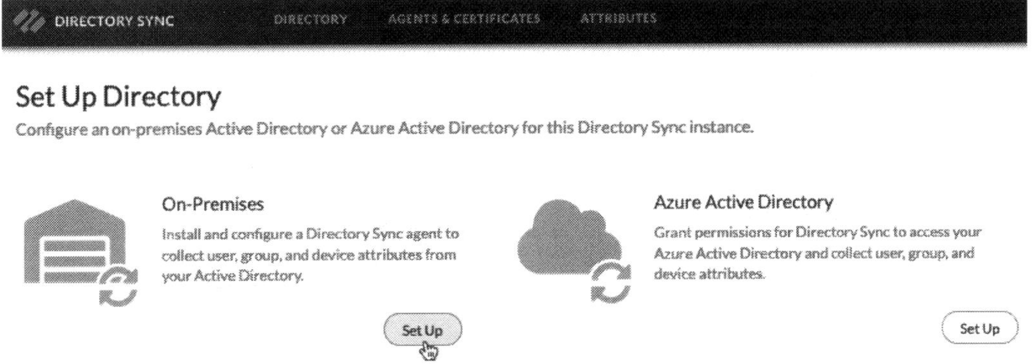

Figure 4.13 – Cloud or on-premises Active Directory configuration

Setting up a connection with Azure is fairly simple: a user needs to exist on Azure that is allowed to connect and collect information. Use this user to log in from the Directory Sync app.

The on-premises connection requires that you accomplish a few more steps on the first page. Here, you are prompted to download an agent and a certificate, as shown in the following screenshot. This agent needs to be installed on your Active Directory server:

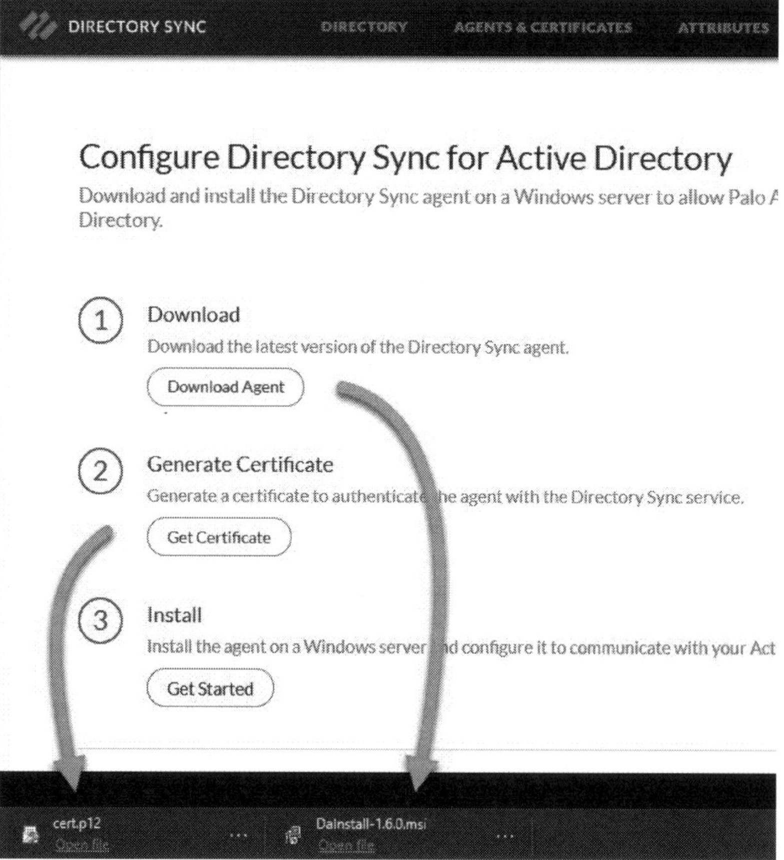

Figure 4.14 – Downloading the required components for on-premises Directory Sync

The certificate must be installed in the server's trusted root CA certificate store. After completing this, double-click the executable file and follow the installation wizard. Once the wizard completes, the Directory Sync agent will be installed in `C:\Program Files (x86)\Palo Alto Networks\Directory-Sync Agent\`.

Open the executable and configure the Directory Sync service, as shown in the following screenshot.

For **Directory Sync Configuration**, set the appropriate regional FQDN so that it matches the region in the app:

`United States (US)`	`agent-directory-sync.us.paloaltonetworks.com`
`European Union (EU)`	`agent-directory-sync.eu.paloaltonetworks.com`
`United Kingdom (UK)`	`agent-directory-sync.uk.paloaltonetworks.com`
`Singapore (SG)`	`agent-directory-sync.sg.paloaltonetworks.com`
`Canada (CA)`	`agent-directory-sync.ca.apps.paloaltonetworks.com`
`Japan (JP)`	`agent-directory-sync.jp.apps.paloaltonetworks.com`
`Australia (AU)`	`agent-directory-sync.au.apps.paloaltonetworks.com`

In **LDAP configuration**, set the bind DN to a username that has sufficient rights to read group memberships. A regular user should suffice but there may need to be specific privileges for your environment. Check with your domain admin that the account is allowed to collect group membership information. The bind DN can be **User Principal Name (UPN)**, **sAMAccountName**, or a proper LDAP formatted (**distinguishedName**) user, as long as the server supports said format.

Set the appropriate protocol to **LDAP**, **LDAPS**, or **LDAP with STARTTLS** and add the server IP.

Once these parameters have been added, make sure the agent is running; you should start seeing messages in the **Monitor** tab. At the top, **Directory Sync Service** should state **Connected**. If not, review your logs and make sure the agent can connect to the configured Directory Sync FQDN:

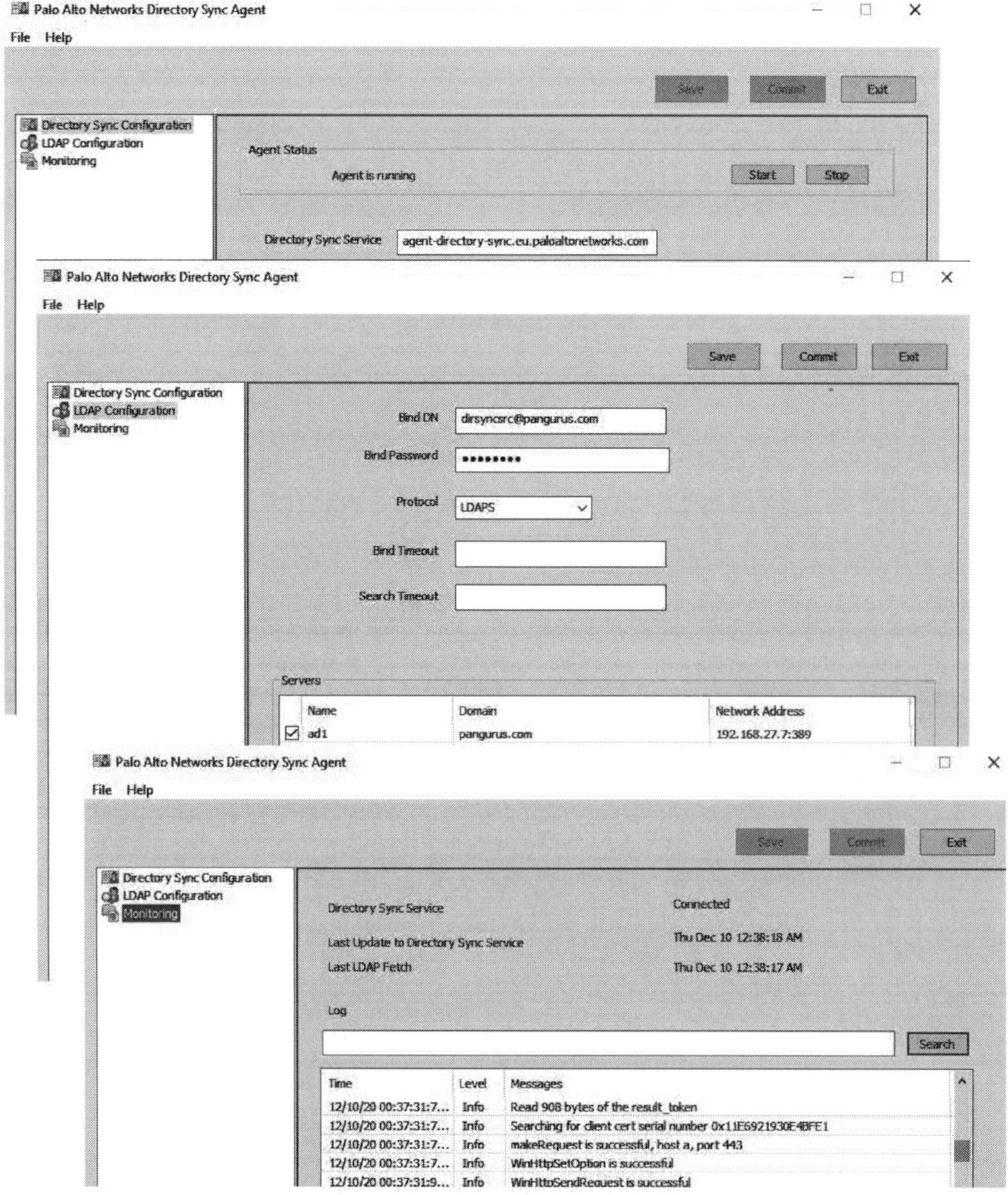

Figure 4.15 – Configuring the Directory Sync agent

Once the agent is connected to the cloud, it needs to be attached to cloud-based management. Open the Hub via `app.paloaltonetworks.com` and find the **Panorama** pictogram on the landing page, as shown on the right in the following screenshot. Click it and attach the **Directory Sync** service:

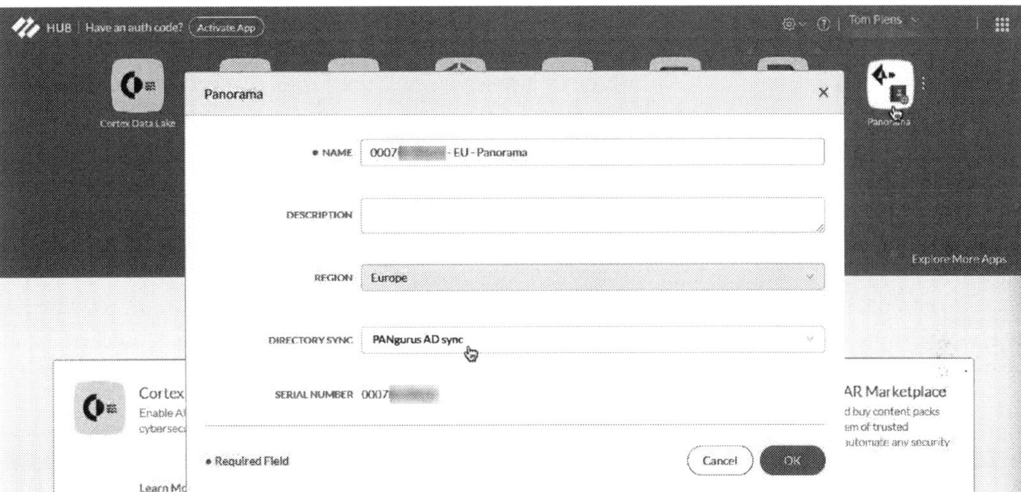

Figure 4.16 – Attaching the Directory Sync service to the cloud Panorama instance

An on-premises Panorama instance can connect directly to Active Directory, of course, and the service connection, remote networks, and mobile users can use the **Service connection tunnel** to connect to the Active Directory environment directly. For each service, the configuration needs to be added under the appropriate **Template**, as shown here:

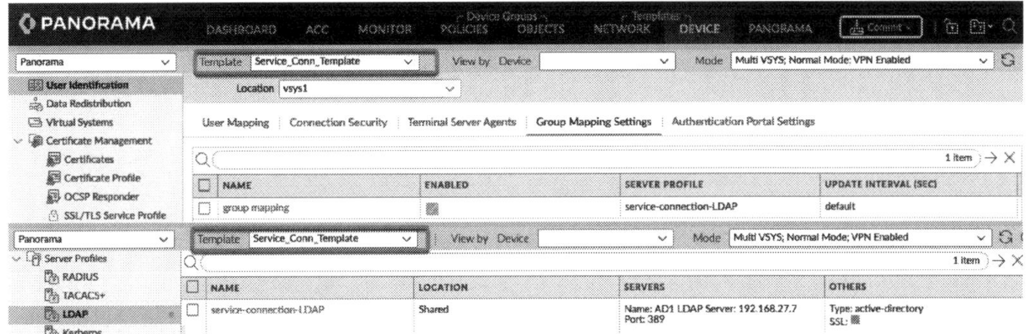

Figure 4.17 – Regular user-ID configuration for Prisma Access service connections, mobile users, and remote networks

With Directory Sync and LDAP configuration in place, we can move on to configuring mobile users.

Configuring mobile users

Once the service infrastructure has been provisioned (you can check its status from the **Panorama** > **Cloud Services** > **Status** menu; a percentage will indicate its progress and a green light will indicate its completion), the **Mobile Users** tab will also become available.

To activate mobile users, we need to activate the **Template** and **Template Stack** options for mobile users, create a zone inside `Mobile_User_Template`, and then assign those zones inside **Mobile User Zone Mapping**. Follow these steps to get that set up:

1. In **Panorama** > **Cloud Services** > **Configuration** > **Mobile Users**, click **Settings**.
2. Review the **Template Stack** and **Template** information and, if needed, change the **Device Group** parent. Click **OK**.
3. Navigate to **Templates** > **Network** > **Zones** and switch to `Mobile_User_Template`.
4. Create a `prisma-trust` zone and a `prisma-untrust` zone: in the context of Prisma Access, the **prisma-trust** zone will not only encompass remote users connected to GlobalProtect, but also the **service infrastructure**, **service connections**, and **remote networks**. **prisma-untrust** is used for internet access exclusively.
5. Navigate back to **Panorama** > **Cloud Services** > **Configuration** > **Mobile Users** and click **Zone Mapping**. Move **prisma-trust** to **Trusted Zones** by selecting it and clicking **Add**.

Your view should now be similar to the following:

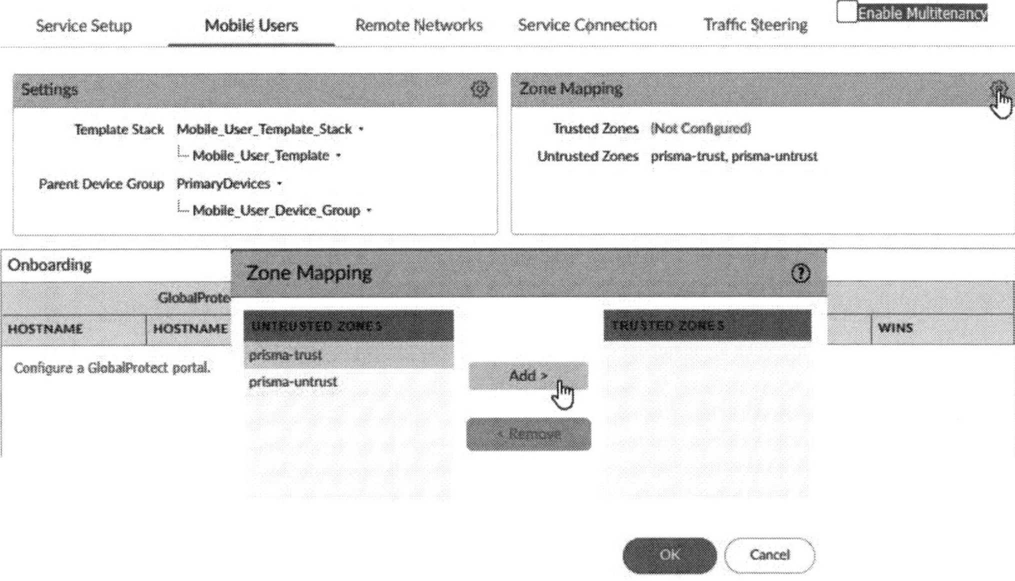

Figure 4.18 – Preparing mobile users

Once the settings and zone mapping have been taken care of, we can move on to the onboarding configuration. Click **Configure** from the **Onboarding** section. As shown in the following screenshot, on the **General** tab of the onboarding configuration, you can select whether the portal name will use a **company domain FQDN** or a subdomain of `gpcloudservice.com`. Since `gpcloudservice.com` is shared with all customers, a generic name may no longer be available: if you do opt for the default domain, pick a descriptive subdomain such as `acmecompany-portal`.

Add an LDAP profile for **Client Authentication**. Alternatively, you can create a SAML profile, which we covered in *Chapter 2, Configuring Advanced GlobalProtect Features.*

Internal Host Detection is used to disable the GlobalProtect agent if the host can **reverse lookup** an internal IP to the configured FQDN. This can only be accomplished by having direct access to the company DHCP server before setting up a tunnel:

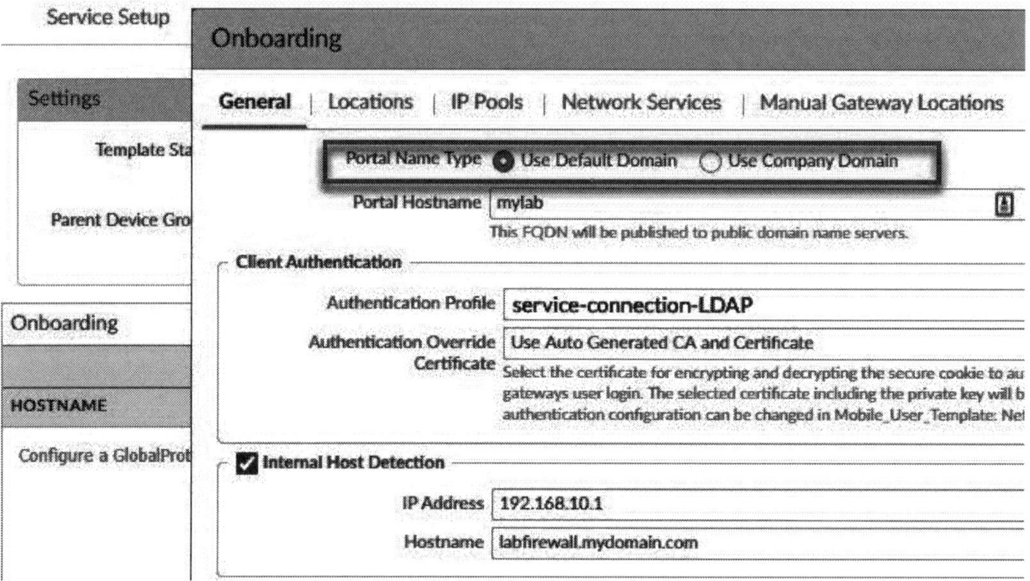

Figure 4.19 – General onboarding configuration

In the **Locations** tab, we can select where GlobalProtect gateways will be spun up to accommodate users. Depending on the subscription, this can range from five locations to "all" locations. If you have a smaller subscription, you can zoom into every region and select which locations to activate. In the following screenshot, locations in and around Belgium were activated to accommodate for me traveling. At the top, you can enable all the locations in an entire region, so you don't need to click every individual dot on the map:

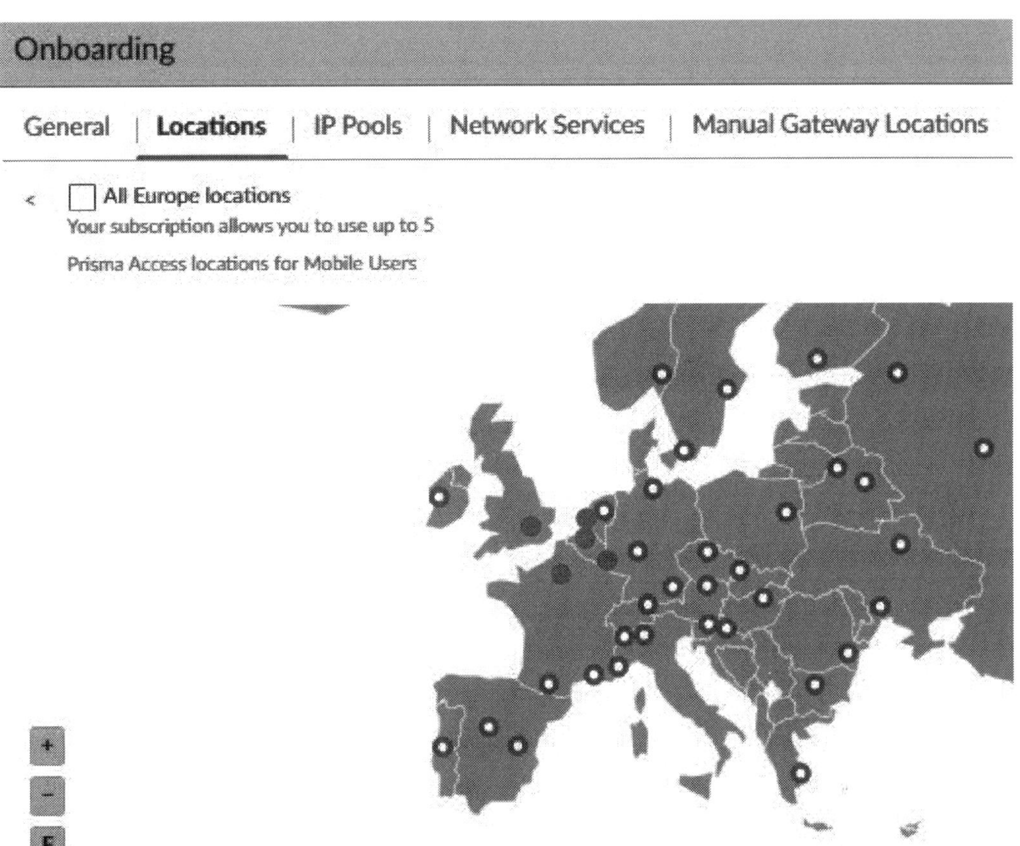

Figure 4.20 – Mobile user locations

On the **IP Pool** tab, the IP subnets that will be used by mobile users need to be configured per region. Take into account that each location will require a `/24` subnet, so a regional IP pool should be large enough to accommodate the minimum number of `/24` subnets. In the following screenshot, the IP pool that's available in the EMEA region is a `/19` subnet, so there are more than enough IP addresses for the five locations that were configured. The minimum subnet that must be used in this example is `/21`, which provides eight locations, since there are five locations, and `/20` will only split up into four class C subnets (`/24`). If there are fewer locations in a region, you can, of course, use even smaller subnets.

IP pools can be configured per region or worldwide. If a region depletes its IP pool, new users will be assigned an IP from the worldwide pool. If no worldwide pool has been configured, a warning message will pop up:

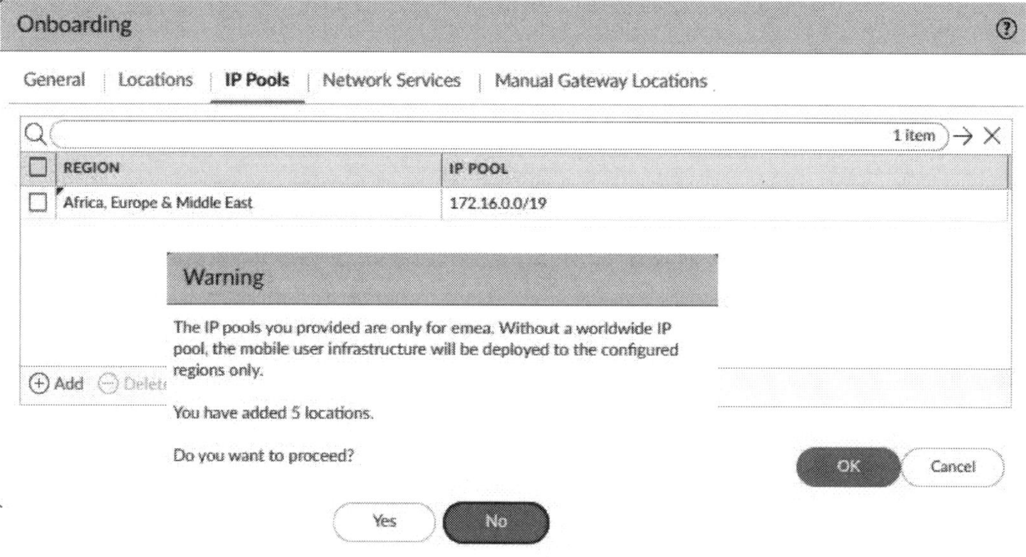

Figure 4.21 – Mobile user IP pool

In the **Network Services** tab, as shown in the following screenshot, some regional client configuration can be provided. If there is a service connection per region, the *local* DNS servers can be added, and the default public DNS can also be replaced if needed:

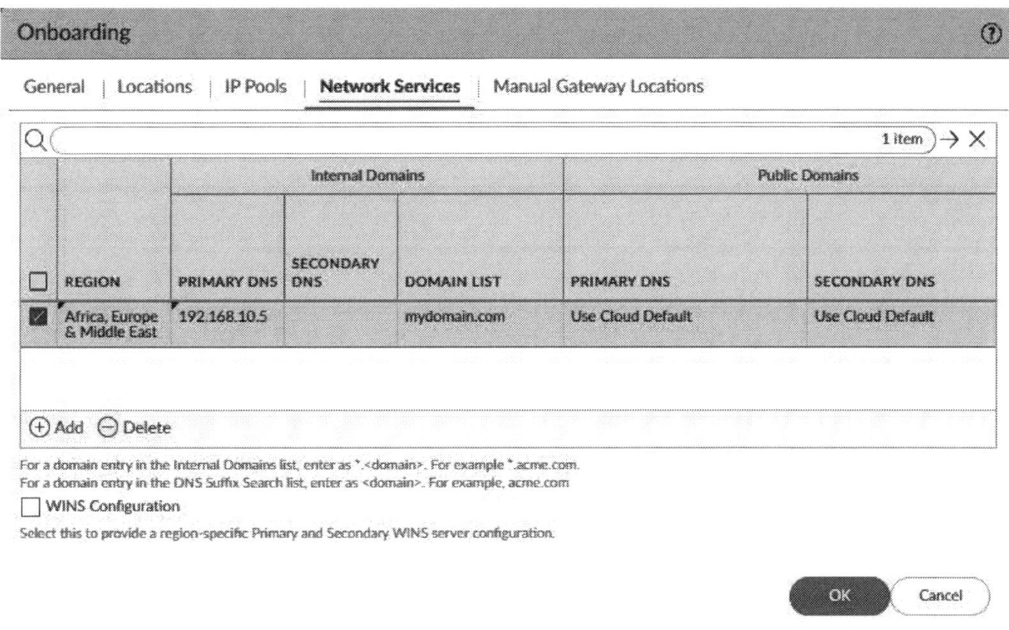

Figure 4.22 – Mobile user network services

In the **Manual Gateway Locations** tab, you can select whether users are allowed to connect to any gateways by choice. Leaving this tab as-is will ensure gateway selection is fully automatic.

Commit this configuration by selecting **Commit to Panorama** and then **Push to Devices**. As with the service infrastructure and as shown in the following screenshot, you must edit **Push Scope Selection**, navigate to **Prisma Access**, and select **Mobile Users** and **Service Setup**. Then, click **OK** and continue with the **Commit** process:

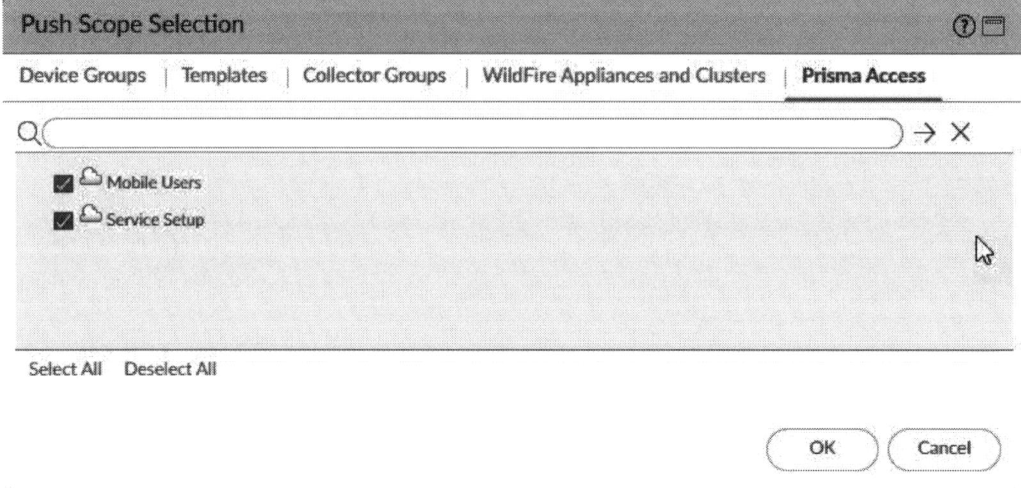

Figure 4.23 – Committing the Service Setup and Mobile Users configuration

> **Important Note**
>
> If any of your physical sites have a gateway configured, this gateway can also be added to the portal configuration. All Prisma Access mobile users will then be able to connect to this physical location as well.

Additional tuning can be accomplished by accessing the template configuration for the portal and gateway, since the preceding configuration steps create a GlobalProtect portal and gateway configuration. As shown in the following screenshot, you can access **Template** > **Network** > **GlobalProtect** and edit **Portal** or **Gateway** as needed:

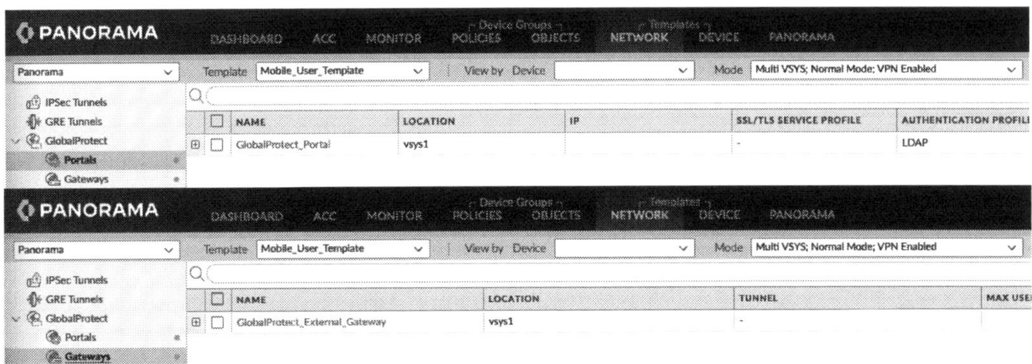

Figure 4.24 – Modifying the GlobalProtect properties

In the next section, we will look into remote network configuration.

Configuring remote networks

The **remote networks** are different from a service connection as they have firewall rules, security profiles, and can connect to the internet. Just like mobile users, the remote network configuration needs the device group, template, and template stack to be activated. Navigate to **Remote Network** via **Panorama** > **Cloud Services** > **Configuration** > **Remote Network** and open the **Settings** menu to see the menu items, as shown in the following screenshot. In the **Settings** tab, make sure the templates have been populated properly and assign `Remote_Network_Device_Group` to the appropriate **Parent Device Group**. In **DNS Proxy**, a DNS proxy object can be configured to serve as an upstream DNS server to remote network clients. This DNS proxy will need to be assigned somehow to the clients, most likely by a DHCP server configuration on the local firewall in the office. In the **Group Mapping Settings** section, the username attribute needs to be set so that it matches the user in Active Directory (or other directory service). The default setting is `sAMAccountName` but any other attribute, such as UPN, `distinguishedName`, or an email address, can be used. If you are not sure about the proper attribute name, use an LDAP browser tool to verify which attribute matches the desired username.

Directory Sync is enabled by default but can be disabled in favour of a regular LDAP connection via the service connection. LDAP needs to be configured in **Remote_Network_Template**:

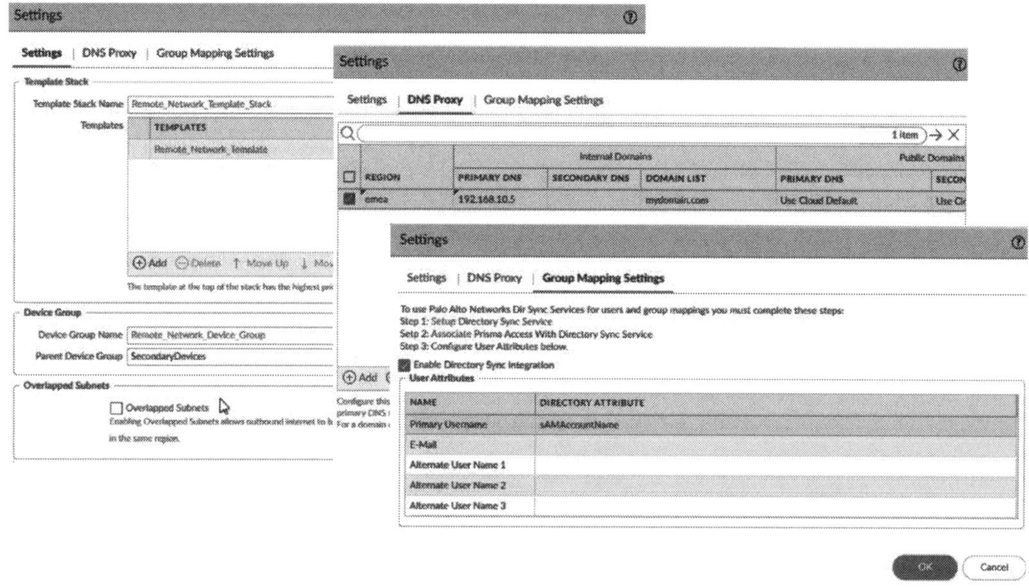

Figure 4.25 – Remote network activation

Once these settings have been enabled, the zones must be created for remote networks for internal and external areas. Internal is considered for all services and is connected directly to the service infrastructure, while external is the internet. As shown in the following screenshot, access **Templates** > **Network** > **Zones** > **Remote_Network_Template** and add at least two zones:

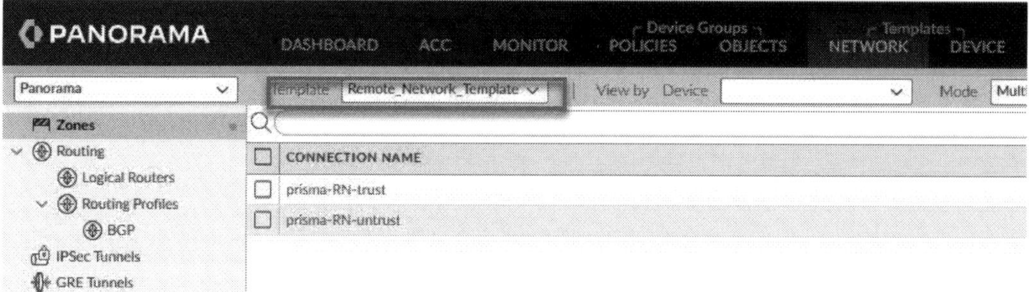

Figure 4.26 – Remote network zones

Next, the IKE gateway(s) need to be created so that our remote networks can set up a connection to Prisma Access. Navigate to **Templates** > **Network** > **Network Profiles** > **IKE Gateways** and set the **Template** aspect to Remote_Network_Template. Create a new IKE gateway. As shown in the following screenshot, the configuration is similar to the service connection. Follow these steps to configure the object:

1. Provide a friendly and identifiable name.
2. Set the appropriate **version**. IKEv2-only is the preferred setting but some remote peers may not be able to use this version yet. If you aren't sure which protocol version the remote end will be able to entertain, use IKEv2-preferred.
3. **Peer IP Address Type** can accommodate both a peer with a static IP and a dynamically assigned one, so choose the most appropriate option for each remote network site.
4. For **Authentication**, either set an imported certificate or a pre-shared key.
5. If the peer has a static IP, then **Local** and **Peer Identification** are not required. Only set these if the peer has a dynamic IP or is located behind a NAT device.
6. In the **Advanced** tab, set up **Enable Passive Mode** in case the peer has a dynamic IP or if the connection should always be initiated by the remote network.
7. Set up **Enable NAT Traversal** if the remote peer is located behind a NAT device, such as an ISP router or modem.

8. If **IKEv1** is being used, set **Exchange Mode** to **Aggressive** for peers with a dynamic IP or **Main** for peers with a static IP (auto is the default setting, but pick a specific setting to ensure no negotiation mismatches cause issues). Also, set a proper crypto profile.
9. For **IKEv2**, make sure the appropriate crypto profile is selected.
10. Click **OK**:

Figure 4.27 – Remote network IKE gateway

Once the IKE gateway has been created, navigate to **Templates** > **Network** > **IPSec Tunnels**. Make sure **Remote_Network_Template** is selected and create a new IPSec tunnel object. Follow these steps:

1. Set an identifiable name in the **Name field**.
2. Add the newly created **IKE Gateway**.
3. Select the **IPSec Crypto Profile**.

4. If the remote tunnel interface can be assigned an IP address, enable **Tunnel Monitor** and add our IP address. Don't use tunnel monitoring if you intend to bundle multiple tunnels to increase bandwidth to a single remote network:

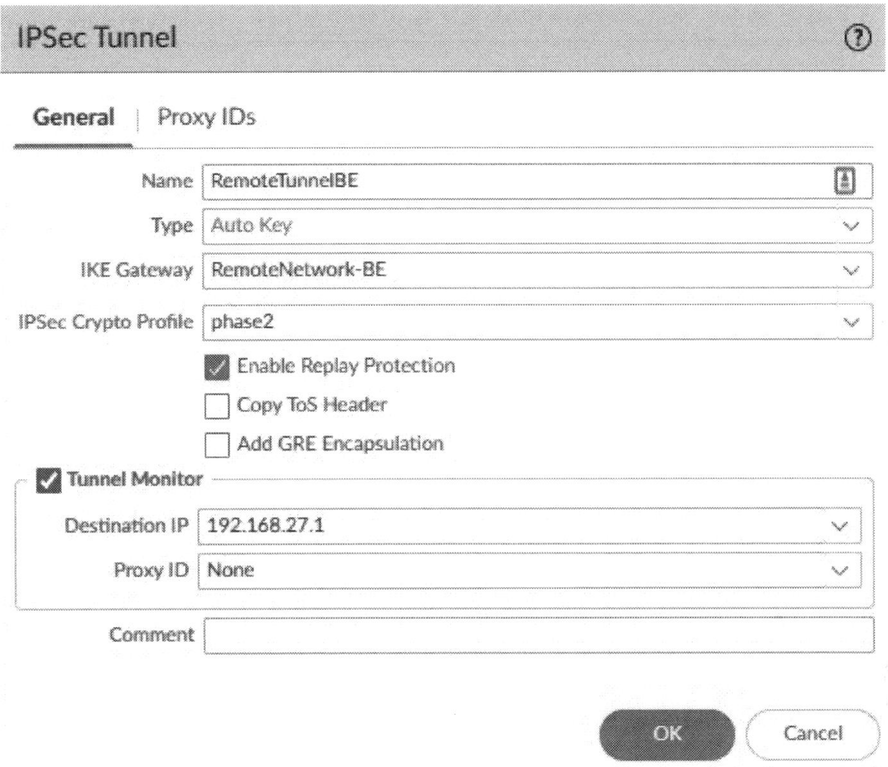

Figure 4.28 – Remote network IPSec tunnel

To complete the remote network configuration, go back to **Panorama** > **Cloud Services** > **Configuration** > **Remote Network** and assign the newly created zones to **Zone Mapping**. Then, open **Bandwidth Allocation.**

As shown in the following screenshot, the available bandwidth associated with your subscription will be available as one big pool that can be assigned to individual remote networks or **compute locations** (for example, **US East**, **Europe North**, and so on) with a starting minimum of 50 Mbps. When the bandwidth is assigned to a compute location, all the remote networks connected to that location will share the bandwidth, with a limit of 500 Mbps for a single remote network connection:

Bandwidth Allocation

Allocated Total : 0 / 200 Mbps

Click each bandwidth allocation to edit bandwidth allocated to com

Bandwidth Allocation (Mbps)	Compute Location
0	Canada Central
0	US Northwest
0	US Southeast
0	US Southwest
0	US Central
0	US East
0	South America East
0	Europe Central
0	Europe North
200	Belgium
0	Europe West

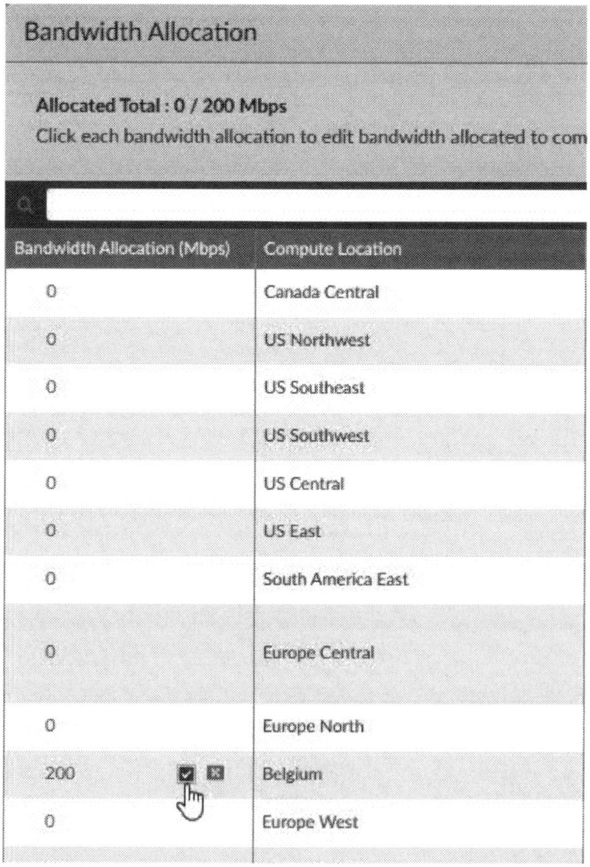

Figure 4.29 – Remote network bandwidth allocation

Finally, the onboarding connection needs to be configured, as illustrated in the following screenshot.

ECMP Load Balancing can be configured so that you can bundle multiple IPSec tunnels into a remote network connection. For ECMP to optimally utilize all these tunnels, BGP needs to be enabled (static routing must be left empty). Do not enable tunnel monitoring on the IPSec tunnels as BGP will determine which tunnels can pass traffic and move routes, if a tunnel is determined to be down.

A **Compute Location** must be selected so that this profile provides onboarding configuration. An onboarding profile should be created for each compute location that will be used.

You must fill the **IPSec Termination Node** field. Multiple nodes may be available per location.

The corresponding **IPSec Tunnel** field needs to be filled, so pick the one that will be applied to the profile.

A secondary WAN can be enabled, thus binding a second tunnel to this same profile for redundancy. This tunnel will be used as a passive standby connection.

The **Static Routes tab** can be used for a remote location to indicate which subnets are located at this site. Prisma will use these routes to direct packets destined for this subnet to the appropriate compute node and into the tunnel to the office.

BGP can also be set up if a larger network of offices exist that require dynamic routing to shift subnets and routes around. BGP is also required for *link aggregation* using ECMP across multiple tunnels:

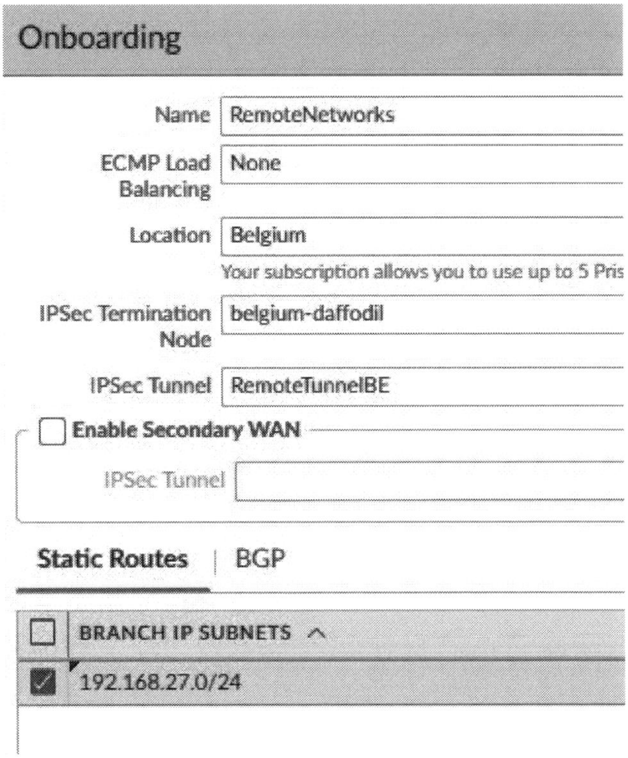

Figure 4.30 – Remote network onboarding

Now that all the components have been configured, the **Remote Networks** page will look similar to the following:

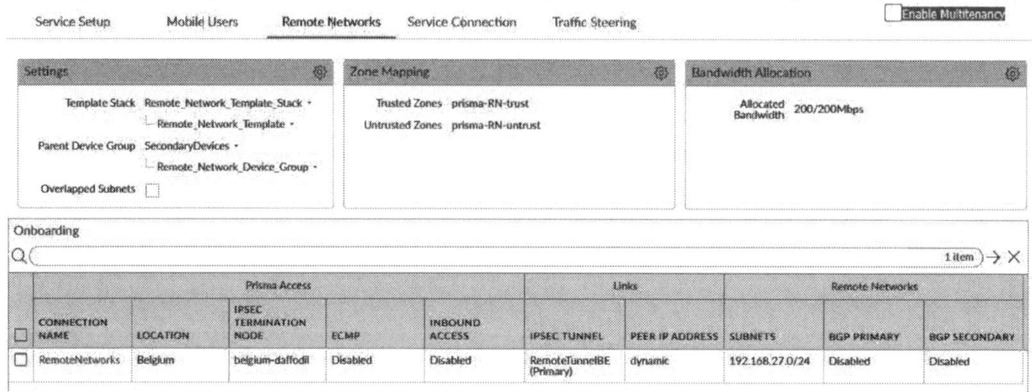

Figure 4.31 – Remote network configuration

Now, it's time to configure the service connections and remote networks on the remote devices. The first information that needs to be collected before this step can be started is the remote IP that's used by the Prisma Access service infrastructure for each connection.

As shown in the following screenshot, the service connection information can be gathered from **Panorama** > **Cloud Services** > **Status** > **Network Details** > **Service Connection**. The SC IP is listed, so it can be entered as a remote peer in the remote firewall IKE gateway (or another vendor equivalent) configuration. The service infrastructure User-ID Agent IP is also listed, so remote firewalls can connect to this agent to collect User-to-IP mapping information for connected mobile users:

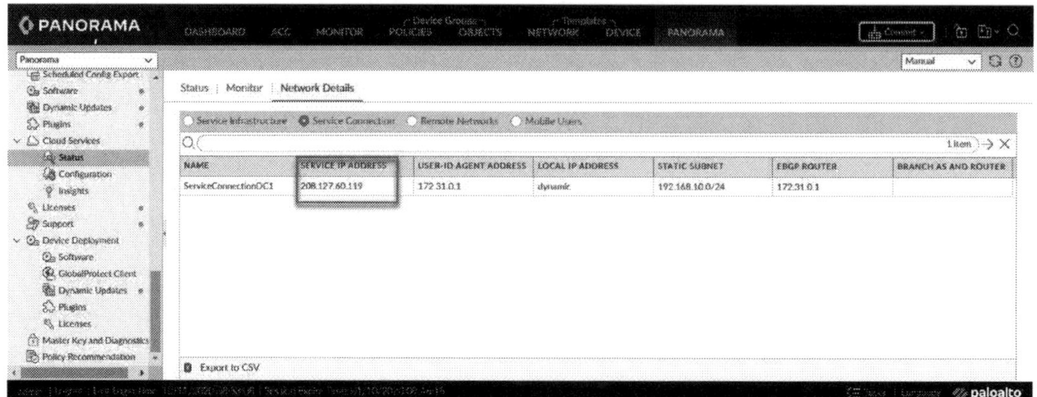

Figure 4.32 – Service connection IP information

The same information can be collected for remote networks by navigating to **Panorama** > **Cloud Services** > **Status** > **Network Details** > **Remote Network**, as shown here:

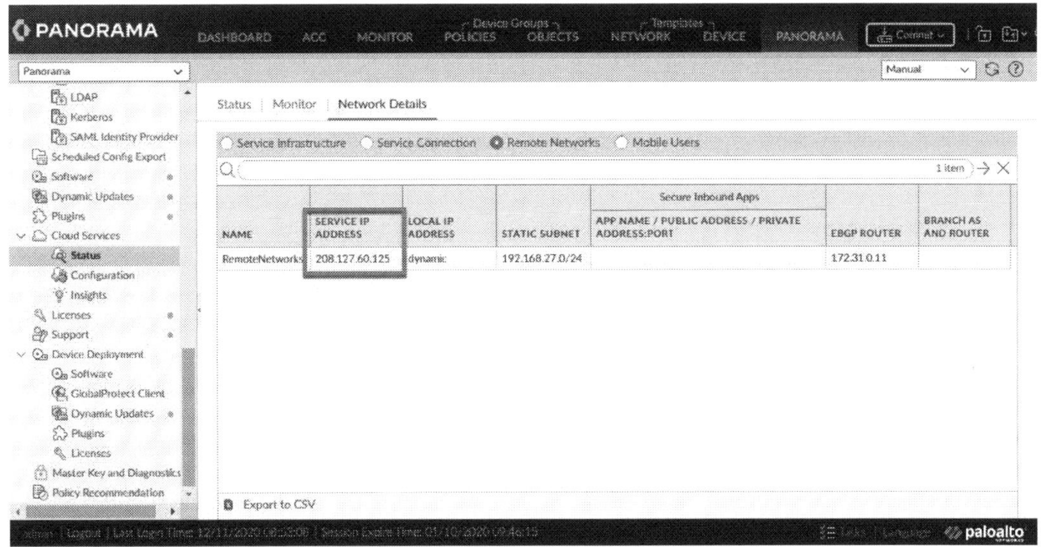

Figure 4.33 – Remote network IP information

Commit to Panorama and then push to devices. Make sure that you edit `Push Scope Selection` so that it includes the **Remote Network** cloud service.

We can now configure the remote peers.

Configuring the remote firewalls

Once Prisma Access has been fully configured, the remote firewalls still need to be configured so that they can connect to Prisma to establish the virtual network.

In the *Configuring the service connections* section earlier in this chapter, I set the remote peer to dynamic and behind a NAT device. The corresponding configuration on the remote firewall should look similar to what's shown in the following screenshot. While setting up your environment, set the configuration so that it reflects the actual situation in your deployment (that is, it will be likely that an actual data centre or HQ location will have a static IP and will not be behind a NAT device; these settings were set purely for demonstration purposes):

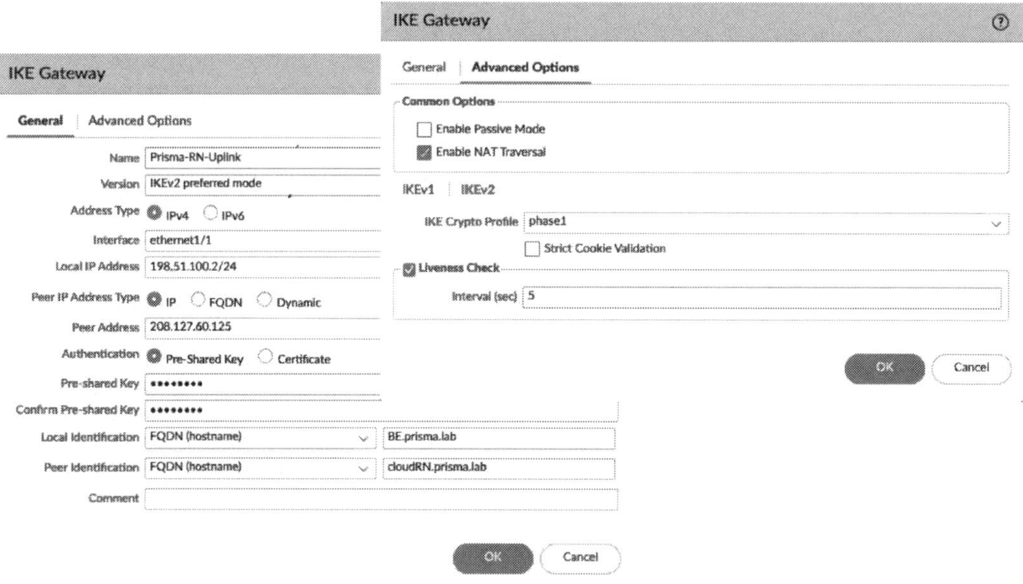

Figure 4.34 – Configuring the HQ firewall IKE gateway

The next step is to create an IPSec tunnel so that the firewall can establish the service connection. Make sure that you add all the relevant subnets to the routing table:

- The service infrastructure
- All the remote network subnets that need to be able to connect to the service connection
- The mobile user IP pool:

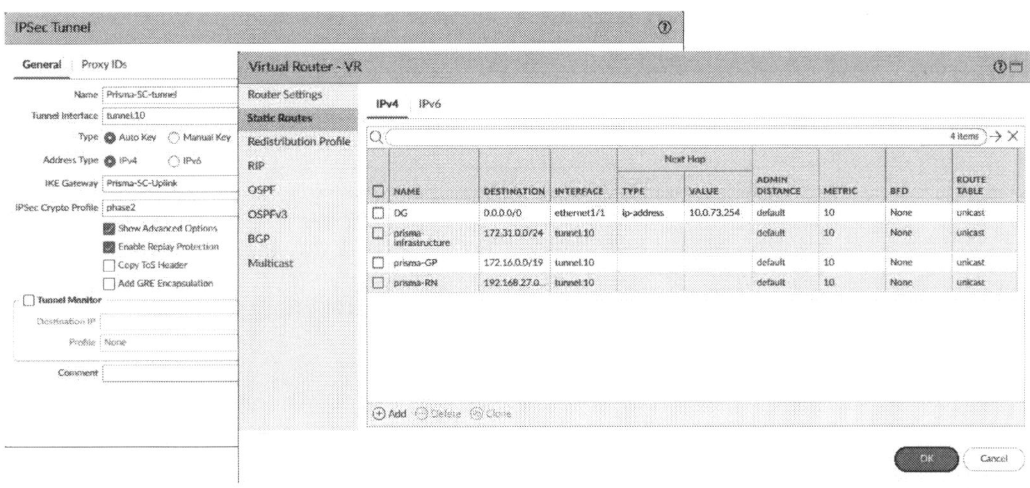

Figure 4.35 – Service connection remote firewall IPSec tunnel and virtual router

As shown in the following screenshot, more or less the same configuration will apply to all the remote network firewalls: the local IKE gateway needs to be set up so that it matches the parameters you configured on the service infrastructure, with **Peer Address** set to the IP corresponding to the node IP found in **Panorama** > **Cloud Services** > **Status** > **Network Details** > **Remote Network**:

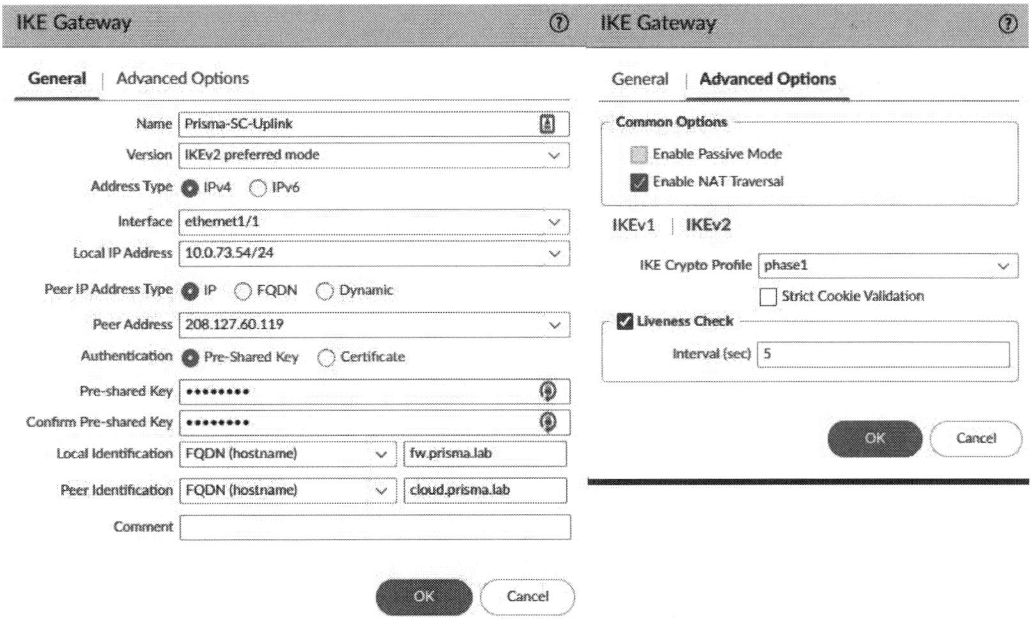

Figure 4.36 – IKE gateway on the remote network local firewall

Also, for the IPSec tunnel and virtual router, the service connection gateway needs to be added and routes toward the service infrastructure, service connection, and mobile users, as shown in the following screenshot:

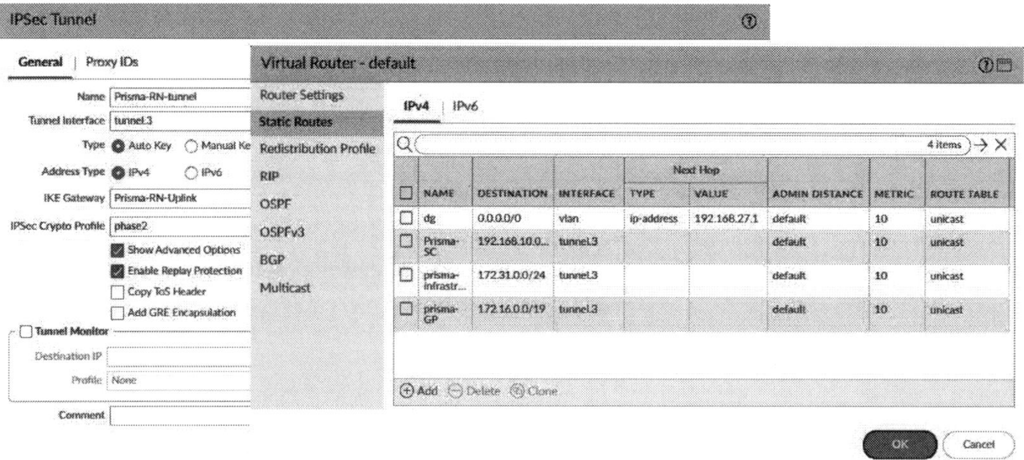

Figure 4.37 – Remote network local firewall IPSec tunnel and virtual router

The virtual router should contain your local routes, such as the default route, and the routes that comprise the Prisma Access connected networks:

- Prisma infrastructure .
- Service connection(s): These are the HQ or data centre location subnets, routed through Prisma Access to a physical location or hybrid cloud such as Azure, AWS, or GCS.
- Mobile user routes are optional: If the remote network should be reachable by mobile users, a route to the IP pool needs to lead back to Prisma Access.

Make sure these subnets are also included in any security rules that control incoming and outgoing connections.

Configuring Cortex Data Lake

The last step is to make sure **CDL** storage is distributed across the different log types. By default, the total log space is unassigned, so no logs will be collected until a certain number of logs have been assigned to each type of log you are interested in. Access CDL directly via https://logging-service.apps.paloaltonetworks.com/storage/status?instance=<instancename> if you know the instance name, or go to apps.paloaltonetworks.com and click the **Cortex Data Lake** tile.

As shown in the following screenshot, access the **Configuration** menu and set storage quotas (in %) for the log types that are of interest. Any log types that are left empty will not receive quotas:

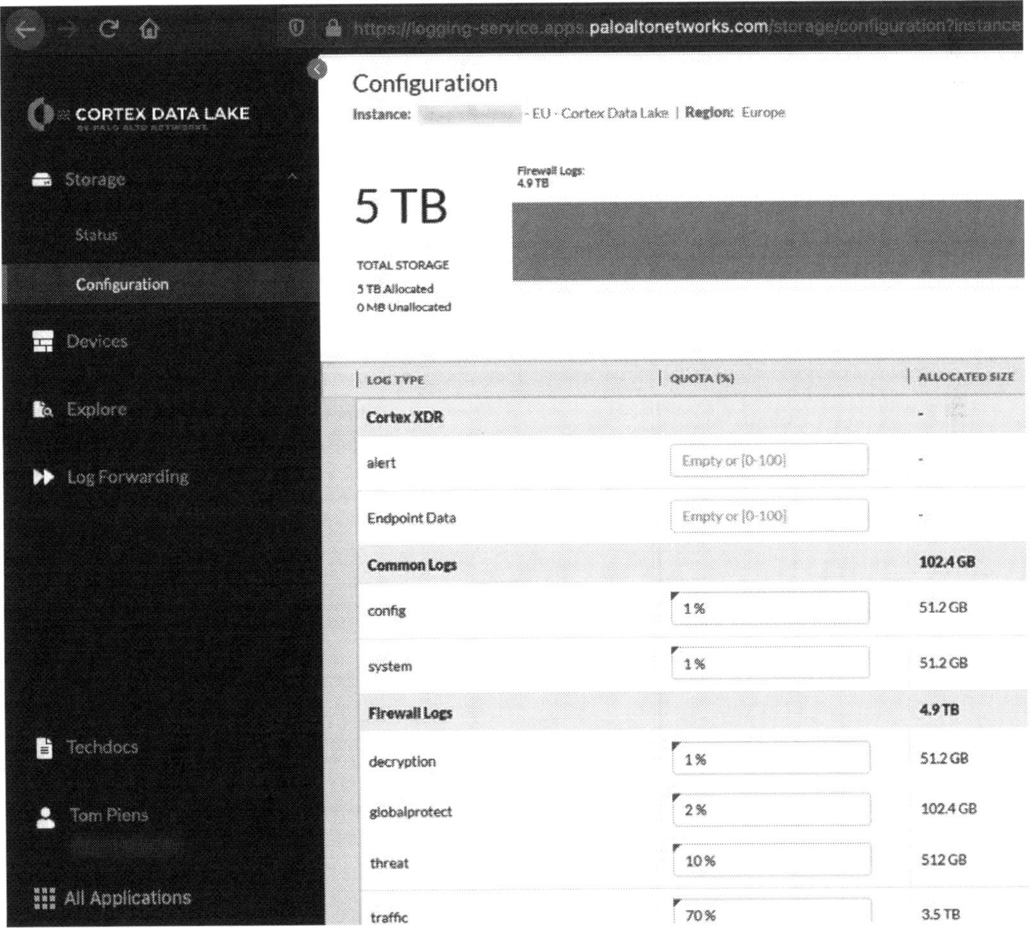

Figure 4.38 – Assigning log storage to log types

Once storage has been assigned, logs can be viewed in the **Explore** section. If some troubleshooting needs to be done, the Prisma system logs can be accessed through the **Explore** menu as well.

Summary

In this chapter, we learned about Prisma Access and how to configure Panorama to control how all the remote networks and users interact, as well as which security policies are applied. With this knowledge, you can determine if and when Prisma Access can provide added value to you or your customers and how to quickly set up all its components.

In the next chapter, we will review the best practices surrounding hardening the management interface and how to leverage dynamic user groups.

Section 2: Tools, Troubleshooting, and Best Practices

In this section, you will learn about best practices and features that can help strengthen your security posture, as well as exploring tools that facilitate the deployment of new and existing sites.

The following chapters will be covered in this section:

- *Chapter 5, Enabling features to improve your security posture*
- *Chapter 6, Anti Phishing with User Credential Detection*
- *Chapter 7, Practical troubleshooting and Best Practice Tools*

5
Enabling Features to Improve Your Security Posture

In this chapter, you will learn methods to improve your devices' **security posture** by applying some security *best practices*. The **management interface** and **administrator access** are of particular interest, as there's possibly nothing worse than a firewall being compromised by weak security measures.

In this chapter, we're going to cover the following main topics:

- Hardening the management interface
- **External dynamic lists** (EDLs)

Technical requirements

This chapter will cover general topics regarding the management interface, the **graphical user interface** (GUI), the **command-line interface** (CLI), and configuration tweaks. A lab device to test things out before applying your new knowledge in a production environment is recommended.

Check out the following link to see the Code in Action video:
`https://bit.ly/3vnbFwn`

Hardening the management interface

From a security perspective, it is best practice to ensure all your vulnerable and critical systems are always hardened. Thus, any unneeded services must be turned off, access should be restricted to only specific hosts, **role-based access control** (**RBAC**) principles should be upheld, and protocols should be restricted to the most secure version. The default configuration of the Palo Alto Networks appliances is actually relatively weak. This is intentional, to allow administrators to quickly deploy a firewall or panorama out of the box without too much hassle to get it running. Securing the appliance is left for after the initial deployment, but this stage is often overlooked. The following sections will provide you with knowledge you will need in order to harden your appliances.

FIPS-CC mode

FIPS-CC mode sets the system to comply with standards described in the **Federal Information Processing Standard** (**FIPS**) *140-2* and **Common Criteria** (**CC**). Enabling this mode does not cause any direct impact on resource consumption, but it will make these changes to the system:

- The management web service is set to **Transport Layer Security** (**TLS**) 1.1 minimum (even though TLS 1.1 is technically compliant to the standard, it is strongly recommended to set it to at least TLS 1.2).
- Password minimum length is set to 6 characters (while 6 characters meets compliance, a longer password is recommended).
- Management idle timeout can no longer be `0`.
- **Failed Attempts** and **Lockout Time** in **authentication settings** can no longer be `0`.

- Weak encryption algorithms and cipher suites are removed as options, thus **Message Digest 5** (**MD5**), **Data Encryption Standard** (**DES**), and 3DES encryption algorithms are removed and only **Diffie-Hellman** (**DH**) groups 14, 19, and 20 remain available.
- Certificates must contain a public key that is RSA-2048 or higher (where **RSA** stands for **Rivest-Shamir-Adleman**), or ECDSA-256 or higher (where **ECDSA** stands for **Elliptical Curve Digital Signature Algorithm**). The digest must be SHA-256 or greater (where **SHA** stands for **Secure Hash Algorithm**).
- Weak management connection protocols **Trivial File Transfer Protocol** (**TFTP**), Telnet, and **HyperText Transfer Protocol** (**HTTP**) are permanently disabled.
- HA1 (**High Availability control link**) encryption is required if the firewall is part of a cluster.
- The console port can no longer be used for CLI access and only outputs limited system status messages.
- The default login is changed to `admin/paloalto` if the admin password has not yet been changed.

You can manually invoke maintenance mode by executing `debug system maintenance-mode`, as follows:

```
reaper@PA-VM2> debug system maintenance-mode
Executing this command will disconnect the current session
and reboot the system into maintenance mode. Do you want to
continue? (y or n)

Broadcast message from root (Sat Feb 27 00:28:42 2021):

The system is going down for reboot NOW!
```

Once the device is rebooted, you can log in via `ssh`, setting the username to `maint`, as follows:

```
$ ssh -l maint 192.168.27.11
The system is in maintenance mode. Connect via serial console
or with user 'maint' through ssh to access the recovery tool.

maint@192.168.27.11's password:
```

The password is the device's serial number. Once logged in and past the **Welcome** screen, you will be presented with the **Maintenance Mode options** menu, as illustrated in the following code snippet:

```
              Welcome to the Maintenance Recovery Tool

 < Maintenance Entry Reason
 < Get System Info
 < Factory Reset
 < Set FIPS-CC Mode
 < FSCK (Disk Check)
 < Log Files
 < Disk Image
 < Select Running Config
 < Content Rollback
 < Set IP Address
 < Diagnostics
 < Debug Reboot
 < Reboot
```

FIPS-CC mode can be enabled by using the arrow keys to *scroll* to the **Set FIPS-CC Mode** option, and on the next screen, select the **Enable FIPS-CC Mode** option at the bottom, as illustrated in the following code snippet:

```
                          FIPS-CC Mode Enable/Disable

***WARNING: Changing FIPS-CC mode will remove all logs and
configuration.***

Using Image: panos-10.0.4

WARNING: Scrubbing will iteratively write patterns on pancfg,
panlogs, and any extra disks to make retrieving the data more
difficult.
NOTE: This could take up to 48 hours if selected.  Scrubbing is
not recommended unless explicitly required.

     [ ] Scrub
```

```
If scrubbing, select scrub type:
    (X) nnsa                              ( ) dod

FIPS-CC Mode is currently: Disabled

NOTE: Login via the console will be disabled in FIPS-CC Mode

< Enable FIPS-CC Mode
```

A progress bar will indicate how far along the process of converting the system is. Once the operation is completed, the screen will display a `Success` message, after which you need to reboot to boot into the **Palo Alto Networks operating system** (**PAN-OS**), as illustrated in the following code snippet:

```
Set FIPS-CC Mode Status: Success

< Back
< Reboot

```

Besides switching to FIPS mode, there are several other steps you can take to strengthen your device.

Replacing the default certificates

On the firewall are a handful of services that rely on certificates to run securely. Out of the box, the factory certificates perform these functions as a placeholder. Very often, these certificates are overlooked and the system is left vulnerable, as an attacker could exploit default certificates. Admins may also grow used to dismissing certificate errors, which could lead to credentials getting stolen.

With the default certificate still enabled, an error message such as the one shown in the following screenshot will appear while accessing the management web interface:

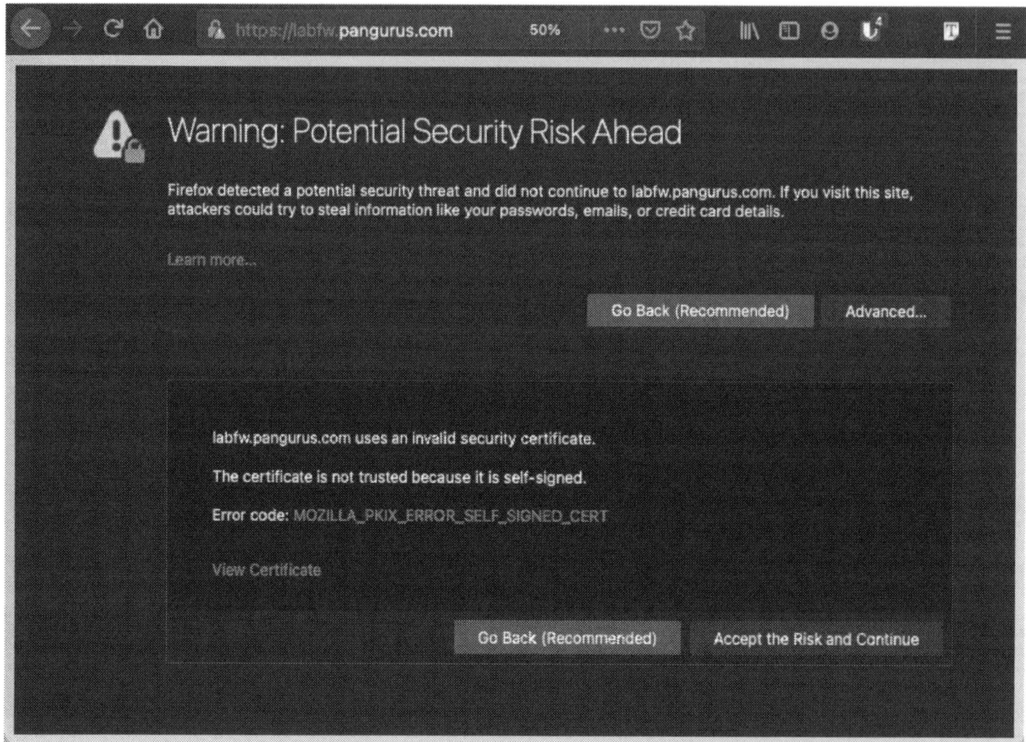

Figure 5.1 – Certificate error message

To get rid of this error message, a new certificate first needs to be loaded into the certificate store. One option is to get a commercial server certificate, but if an internal **certificate authority** (**CA**) is available a certificate can be retrieved from there, which will be much cheaper. Once you're logged in to the firewall, navigate to **Device** > **Certificate Management** > **Certificates** and click **Generate** to create a new certificate. In the **Generate Certificate** popup, fill out all the values, as illustrated in the following screenshot. Select **External Authority** (**CSR**) as the **Signed By** value. This generates an exportable **certificate signing request** (**CSR**) that can be used both for a commercial CA and an internal CA:

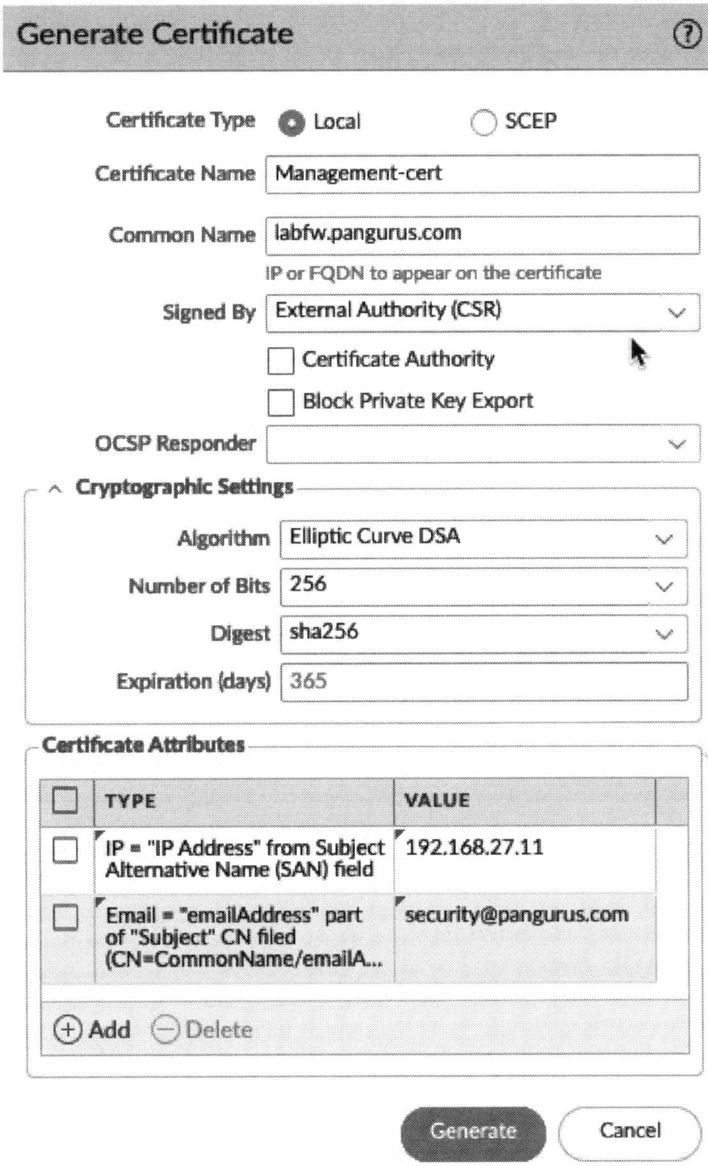

Figure 5.2 – Generating a new certificate

The exported CSR file needs to be provided to the CA. Your experience may vary, as each CA will have its own procedure to process a CSR, but the overall procedure will be similar to the **Active Directory Certificate Services** (**AD CS**) procedure you see in *Figure 5.3*.

Access the AD CS portal and follow these steps:

1. Click **Request a certificate**.
2. Select the **advanced certificate request** link under **Or, submit an advanced certificate request**.
3. Paste the content of the CSR file and select **Web Server** as the certificate template.
4. Click **Submit**.
5. Select **Base64 encoded** and click **Download certificate**.

The preceding steps are illustrated in the following screenshot:

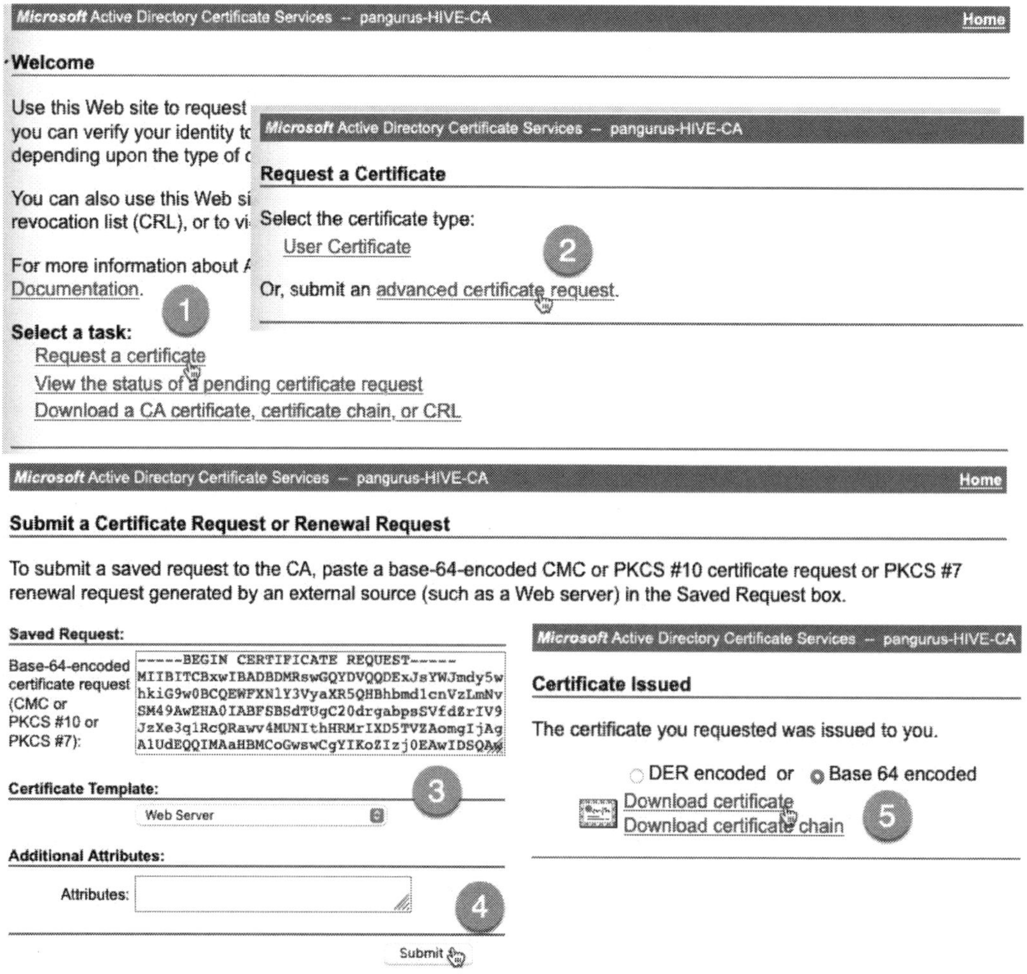

Figure 5.3 – AD CS requesting a certificate via CSR

The downloaded file can now be imported onto the firewall as a response to the CSR. As illustrated in *Figure 5.4*, click **Import** at the bottom of **Device** > **Certificate Management** > **Certificates**, set the certificate name, and select the file downloaded from the CA. Once the certificate response has been imported properly, the orange CSR shown in the following screenshot will turn into a blue certificate, with the **Private Key** checkbox checked:

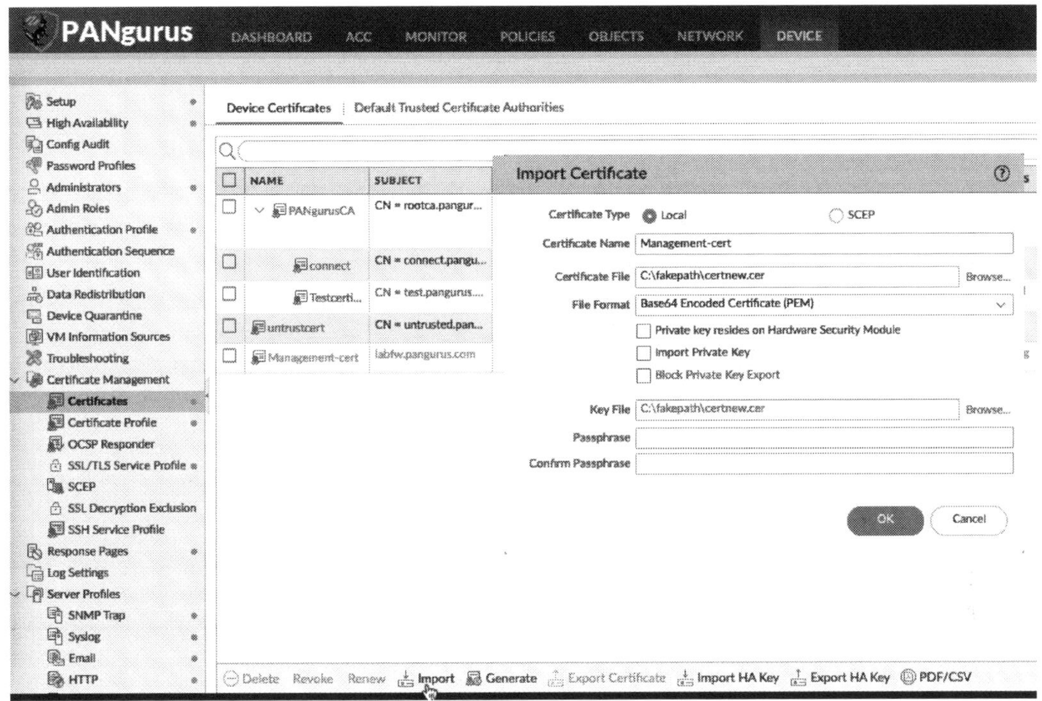

Figure 5.4 – Importing the certificate response

> **Important note**
>
> The certificate name that is set during the import must match the CSR name exactly. If a different name is chosen, the certificate is imported without a private key and the orange CSR will remain.

Next, we need to create a **Secure Sockets Layer** (**SSL**)/TLS profile, so navigate to **Device** > **Certificate Management** > **SSL/TLS Service Profile** and create a new profile.

Give the profile a friendly name and select the newly created server certificate. Set the minimum TLS version (**Min Version**) to `TLSv1.2`, as illustrated in the following screenshot:

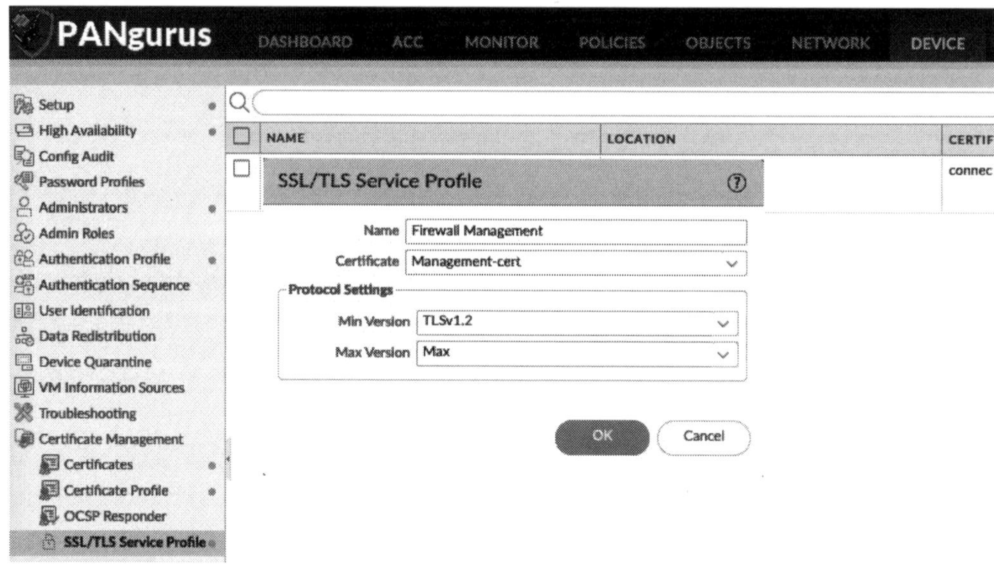

Figure 5.5 – Creating an SSL/TLS service profile

Lastly, in **Device** > **Setup** > **Management** > **General settings**, add the **SSL/TLS Service Profile**, as illustrated in the following screenshot, and commit the change:

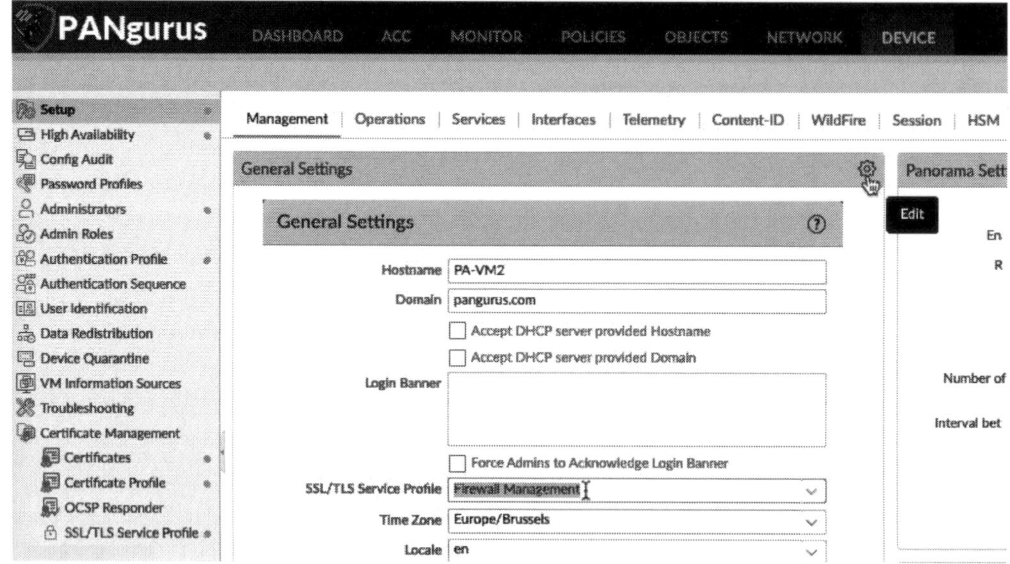

Figure 5.6 – Adding the SSL/TLS profile to the management interface

Notice that the **commit** window includes the following notification:

```
Web server will be restarted upon a successful commit of this
configuration.
Please refresh your browser window.
```

When the commit job reaches 99%, it will appear as if the operation is hanging. This is due to the web server restart, so go ahead and refresh your browser at this time.

Some browsers may not pick up on the new certificate right away, so it may be necessary to close your browser and reconnect to the **firewall management**. Once the certificate is seen by your browser, the address bar should look similar to this:

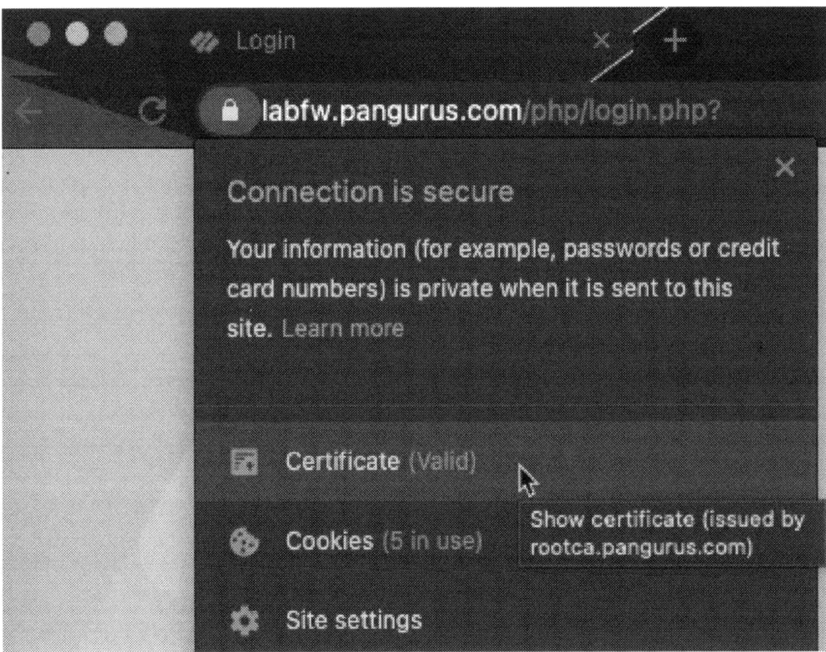

Figure 5.7 – Secure connection indicator in browser

Some browsers such as Firefox may require an additional step to import the root certificate if the SSL/TLS certificate was signed by the internal CA as opposed to a commercial CA. Firefox uses its own certificate store, so any root certificates loaded into the system store will be ignored. Type `about:preferences#privacy` into the address bar and scroll down to the **Certificates** section, click **View Certificates**, and then click **Import...** to import the root certificate, as illustrated in the following screenshot:

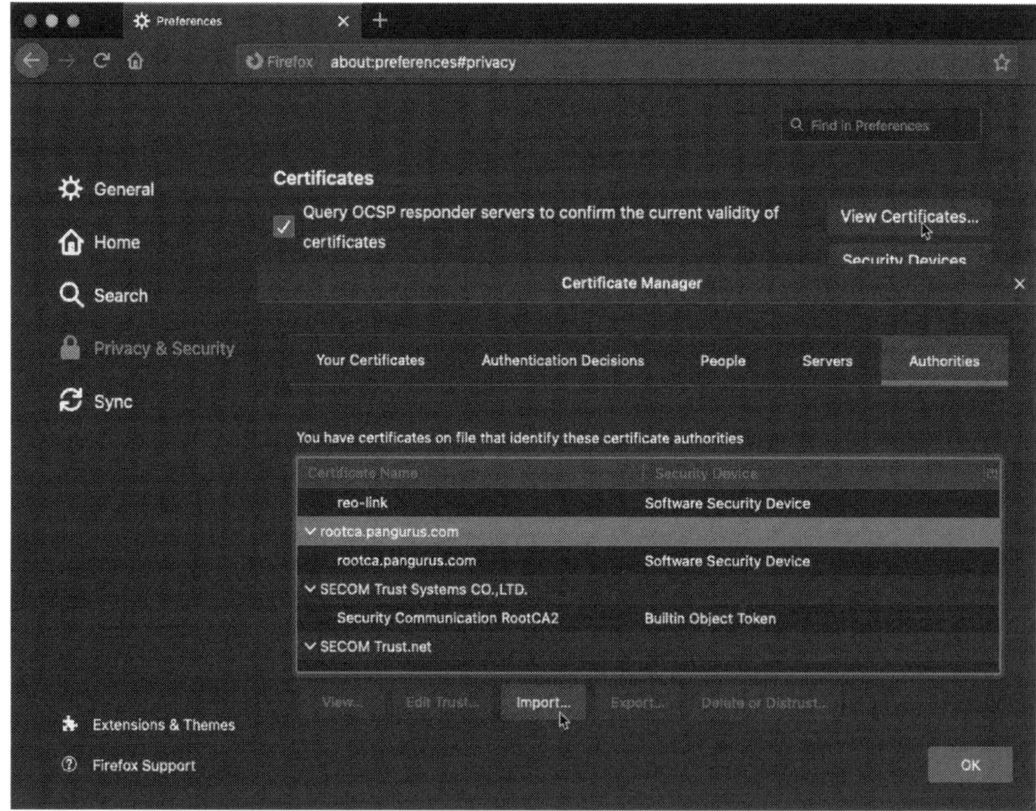

Figure 5.8 – Importing a root CA into Firefox

Another important hardening configuration setting is the **Minimum Password Complexity** setting.

Setting minimum password complexity

For administrator accounts that have been set up to use an external authentication, such as **Remote Authentication Dial-In User Service** (**RADIUS**), **Terminal Access Controller Access-Control System+** (**TACACS+**), or the **Lightweight Directory Access Protocol** (**LDAP**), a minimum password complexity policy should exist on the external device that ensures passwords are not overly simple, are changed regularly, and are not reused. For local administrator accounts, this configuration setting is often overlooked, which could lead to administrator passwords that remain unchanged for many years and could be guessed. **Minimum Password Complexity** can be enabled in **Device** > **Setup** > **Management** > **Minimum Password Complexity** by checking the **Enabled** box at the top left. Once the setting is enabled and the change committed, the counter will start for any time limitations. You can set the following password format parameters:

- **Minimum Length**: A minimum of `8` characters is recommended and up to 15 characters are supported.
- **Minimum Uppercase Letters**: Lets you set a minimum number of uppercase letters. A minimum of `1` is recommended.
- **Minimum Lowercase Letters**: Lets you set a minimum number of lowercase letters. A minimum of `1` is recommended.
- **Minimum Numeric Characters**: Lets you set a minimum number of numeric letters. A minimum of `1` is recommended.
- **Minimum Special Characters**: Lets you set a minimum number of non-alphanumerical letters. A minimum of `1` is recommended.
- **Block Repeated Characters**: Lets you prevent users from repeating the same character *n* times in a row. The range is `2` to `15`, with `0` disabling this check. If `2` is set, two identical characters are allowed to be used in a password, but not three.
- **Block Username Inclusion (Including Reversed)**: Lets you block users from adding their username in the password. This box should be checked.

The **Functional Requirements** are outlined as follows:

- **New Password Differs By Characters**: Forces how *different* a new password must be compared to the last. This helps prevent users from changing `password1` to `password2`.

- **Require Password Change on First Logon**: A great way to have new administrators customize their password if they are being assigned a new user by a different administrator.
- **Prevent Password Reuse Limit**: Prevents an admin from reusing a previous password. The count sets the number of passwords that need to be set before an admin is allowed to reuse an old password—for example, if the value is set to `3`, the fourth password can't be any of the previous three, but the fifth can be the same as the first. The range is `0` (disabled) to `50`.
- **Block Password Change Period (days)**: Prevents an admin from changing their password more than once in a given period, which helps prevent admins from recycling through passwords to be able to reuse an old password.
- **Required Password Change Period (days)**: Sets the length of time a password can be used for until it needs to be changed.
- **Expiration Warning Period (days)**: Sets the number of days before a password expires that an admin will receive a notification when they log on to notify them their password will expire and that they need to change it.
- **Post Expiration Admin Login Count**: The number of times that an admin is allowed to log on after their password has expired, to grant them a last chance to change their password before locking them out of the account.
- **Post Expiration Grace Period (days)**: The number of days after a password has expired that an admin is still allowed to log on. If admins don't log on regularly, it may be useful to allow a sufficient grace period to allow for the opportunity to change a password even after it has already expired. To be used in conjunction with the **Post Expiration Admin Login Count** setting.

> **Important note**
>
> In case you still need to build a password policy, the **National Institute of Standards and Technology** (**NIST**) publishes *Digital Identity Guidelines* as part of *Special Publication 800-63* (current revision, 3), which provides some great guidelines about password policy. It can be found here: `https://pages.nist.gov/800-63-3/sp800-63b.html`.

Once updated, your **Minimum Password Complexity** configuration should look similar to this:

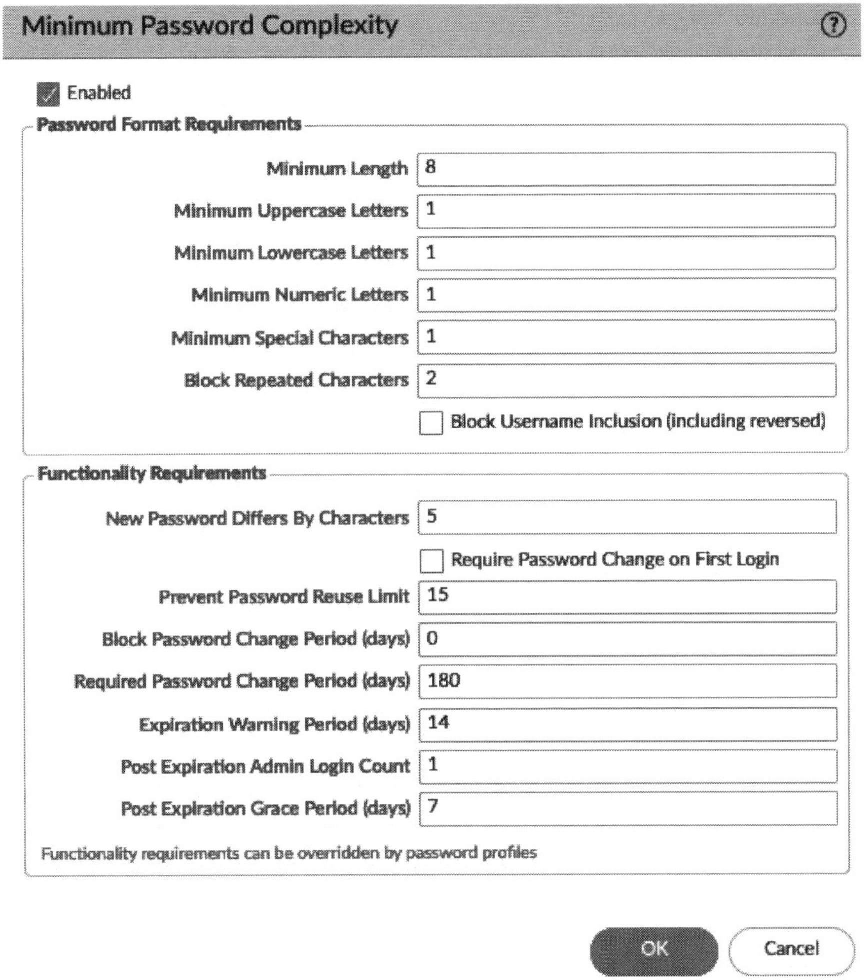

Minimum Password Complexity

☑ Enabled

Password Format Requirements

Minimum Length	8
Minimum Uppercase Letters	1
Minimum Lowercase Letters	1
Minimum Numeric Letters	1
Minimum Special Characters	1
Block Repeated Characters	2

☐ Block Username Inclusion (including reversed)

Functionality Requirements

New Password Differs By Characters	5

☐ Require Password Change on First Login

Prevent Password Reuse Limit	15
Block Password Change Period (days)	0
Required Password Change Period (days)	180
Expiration Warning Period (days)	14
Post Expiration Admin Login Count	1
Post Expiration Grace Period (days)	7

Functionality requirements can be overridden by password profiles

OK Cancel

Figure 5.9 – Minimum Password Complexity configuration

The password policy enforced by **Minimum Password Complexity** is global for all administrators. Some administrators may need to be set up with slightly different password reset controls, for which a **Password** profile can be created in **Device** > **Password Profiles**. **Password** profiles override **Minimum Password Complexity** profiles. As illustrated in *Figure 5.10*, a **Password** profile can be configured with the following parameters, and is attached directly to an administrator account:

- **Name**: Sets the administrator's username.
- **Required Password Change Period (days)**: Here, a different expiration time from the global setting can be added. Some admins may need to change their password more frequently, while others may have longer times attributed to them as required.

- **Expiration Warning Period (days)**: The number of days before the password expires that an administrator receives a reminder to change their password.
- **Post Expiration Admin Login Count**: The number of times an administrator is allowed to log on after their password expired.
- **Post Expiration Grace Period (days)**: The number of days after the password expired that an administrator is still allowed to log on with their old password.

The **Administrator** profile and **Password** profile should look similar to this:

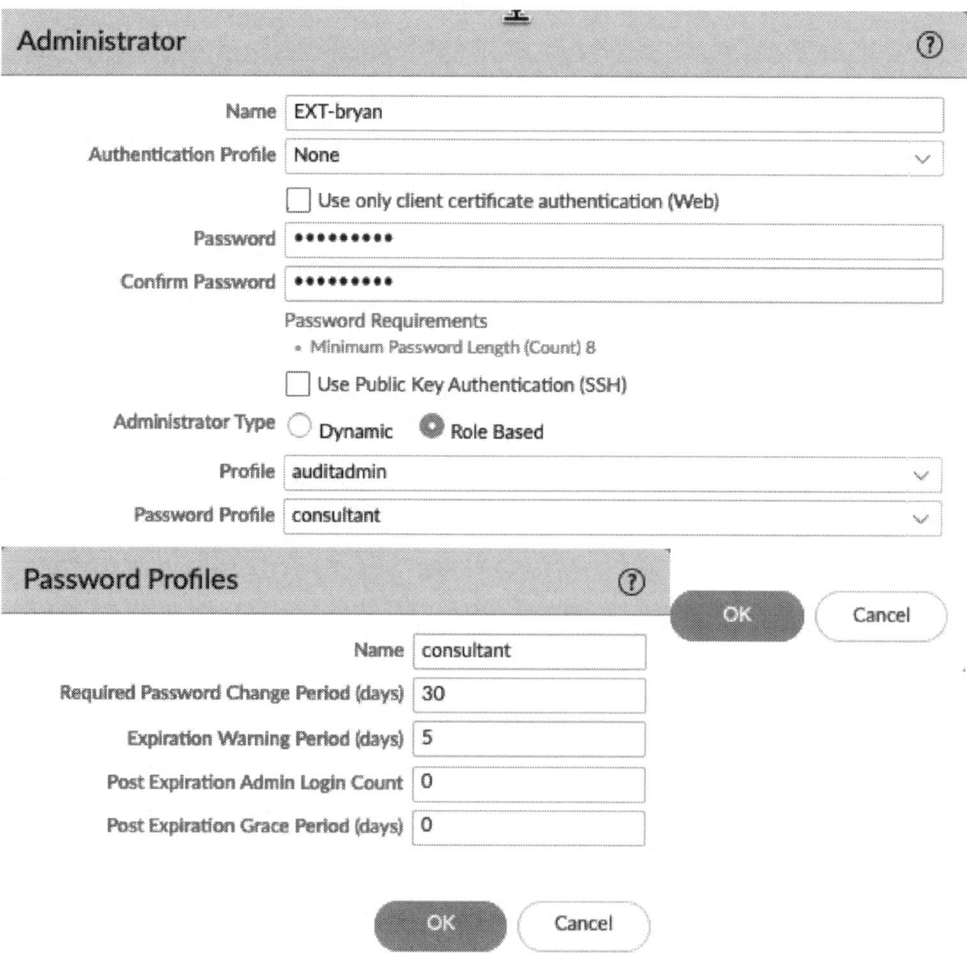

Figure 5.10 – Password profile attached to an administrator account

When additional administrators need to be added, RBAC may also be an important consideration to keep in mind.

Configuring administrator roles

Not all admins are created equally, and some may need more access while others require less. Via **Device** > **Admin Roles**, we can create different roles and assign them to each individual admin account so that the person behind the keyboard gets access to the things they need and not the things they don't need.

A few preconfigured roles are available that can provide some inspiration while building your own admin role. As you can see in the following screenshot, there is a `cryptoadmin` role that allows the admin account access to all crypto-related settings such as **IPsec tunnels** and **GlobalProtect config and certificates** settings, and allows the admin to perform a partial commit (only their changes). The `auditadmin` role has access to all logs, but nothing else:

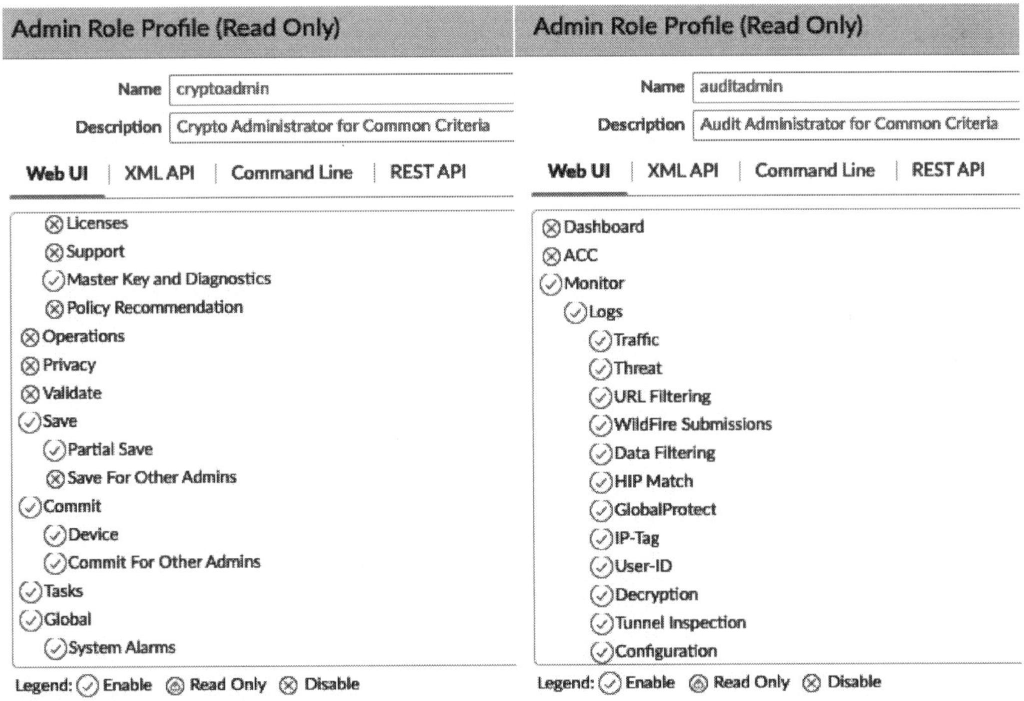

Figure 5.11 – Preconfigured admin roles

You can create as many of these Admin Role Profiles as needed and select **Enable**, **Read Only**, or **Disable** on any section or subsection. Subsections can be set individually but they can't be set as less restrictive than their parent section—for example, as you can see in the following screenshot, if the **Network** section is set to **Enable**, you can set **Interfaces** and **Zones** and others to **Read Only**, but if you change access for a parent such as **GlobalProtect**, the subsections will also disappear:

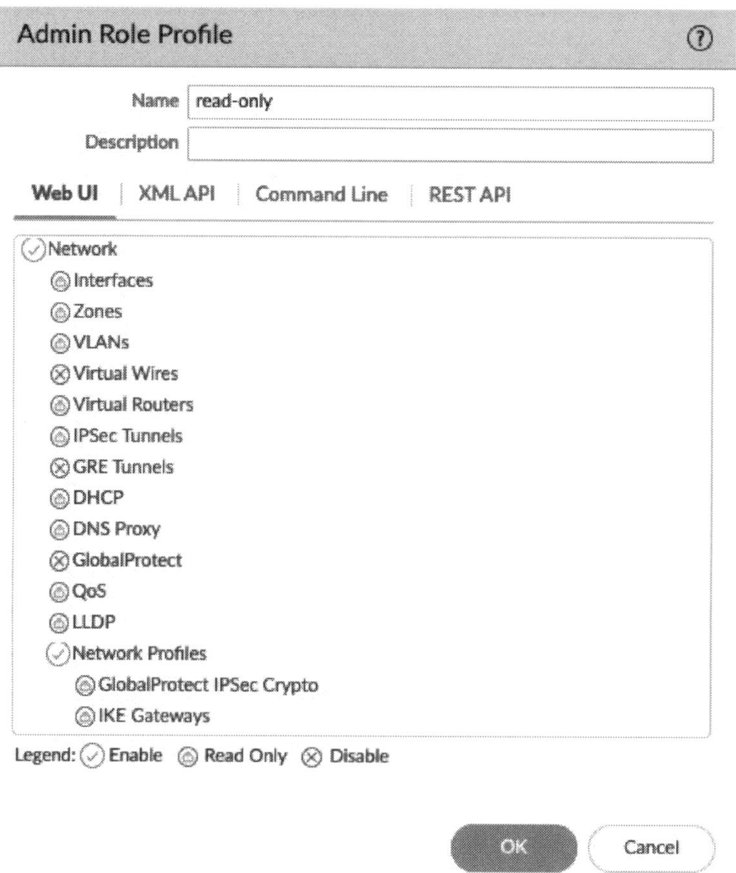

Figure 5.12 – Controlling access granularly

Another powerful feature is the ability to grant partial access to actions that can impact how the firewall performs. First, access to configuration parts can be controlled so that admins are only able to make changes that are relevant to their role: admins may be allowed to make changes to security rules, but not be allowed to change decryption policies.

Secondly, they can be restricted to only be able to commit changes they have made. In an environment where multiple admins are making changes, one administrator could push another administrator's half-finished changes to the firewall. Preventing this from happening by only allowing administrators to commit their own updates can prevent mishaps.

Administrators can also be restricted from viewing sensitive **personal identifiable information** (**PII**) in logs by disabling **Internet Protocol** (**IP**) addresses and usernames from their view while still allowing access to logs, as illustrated in the following screenshot:

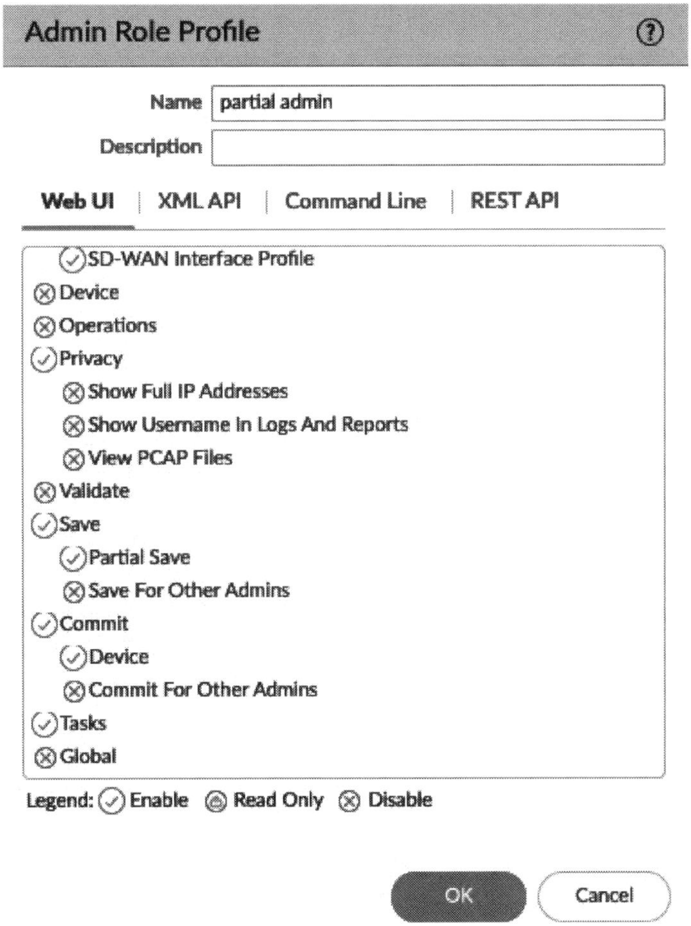

Figure 5.13 – Limiting administrators' actions and access to PII

As you can see in the following screenshot, for each admin role, access to the **XML API**, **REST API**, and **Command Line** access can also be controlled so that admins receive tailored access to the resources they need:

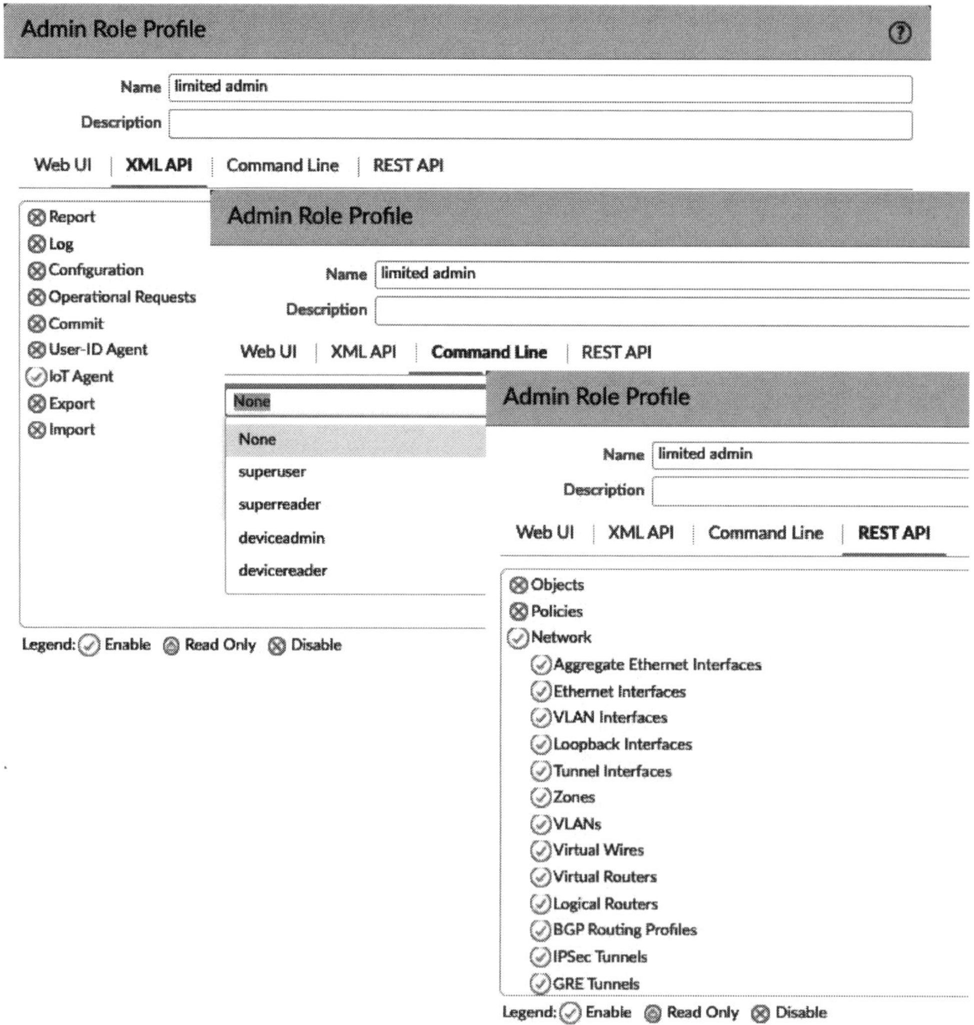

Figure 5.14 – Restricting access to the API and CLI

On top of limiting administrators' access, there are some other settings that can tighten down administrative access to prevent accidents or abuse.

In **Device** > **Setup** > **General Settings**, **Automatically Acquire Commit Lock** can be checked so that any admin making changes immediately acquires a lock on the system, preventing other admins from simultaneously making changes. This can be useful if administrators are not limited in their ability to commit other admins' changes.

As illustrated in the following screenshot, a login banner should also be added to notify any users accessing the management interface that they are connecting to a secure system and that their actions will be logged. This may deter regular users from trying to log on and may be required if any legal actions follow an unauthorized login:

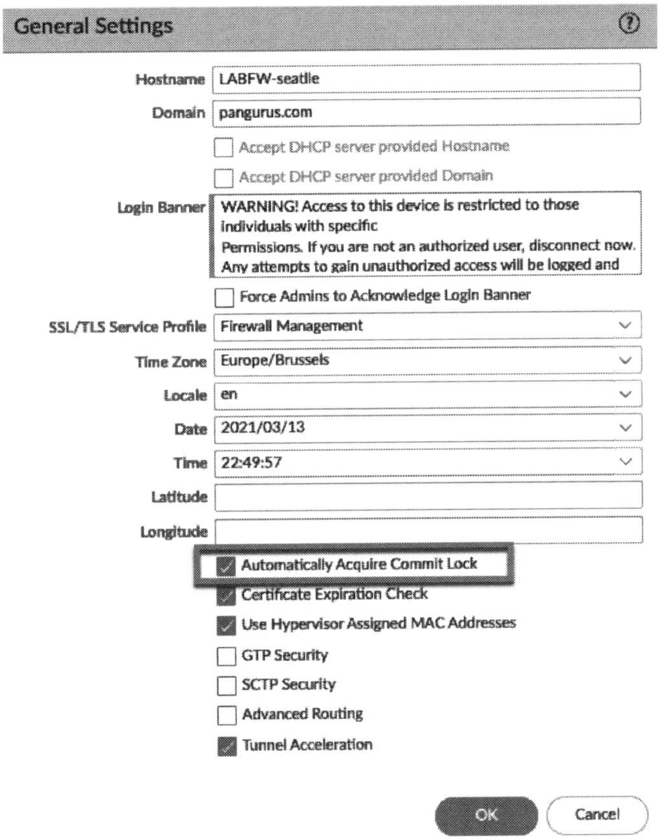

Figure 5.15 – Logon banner and automatically acquiring configuration lock

In **Device** > **Setup** > **Authentication Settings**, more security can be added to administrator logins by setting the following parameters, as shown in *Figure 5.16*:

- **Authentication Profile** can be set to a **TACACS+**, **RADIUS**, or **SAML** authentication profile (where **SAML** stands for **Security Assertion Markup Language**) to authenticate administrators for which a local account has not been created.
- **Certificate Profile**: Setting a certificate profile *enables client certificate authentication* for administrators. Client certificates need to be signed by the CA certificate configured in the certificate profile.

- **Idle timeout** determines how long an administrator can be idle before their session is logged off automatically. The default is 60 minutes, but a shorter period may be required by corporate policy.
- **API Key Lifetime** is an often-overlooked security risk as the default value is `0` (does not expire). An API key could have been generated years ago and is still functioning today. Set this to an acceptable timeframe.
- **Failed Attempts** should be set to prevent brute-force attacks on admin accounts. Once an admin account receives more than the number indicated, the account will be locked for a period of time.
- **Lockout Time** is the time an admin account is locked if more than the number of **Failed Attempts** were tried.
- **Max Session Count** is a limitation on the number of admins allowed to be logged on simultaneously. This can be useful to keep resource consumption of the management plane in check or to prevent too many administrators making changes at the same time.
- **Max Session Time** is a limitation on how long an admin is allowed to remain logged on before being logged out and needing to log back on again.

You can see the aforementioned settings here:

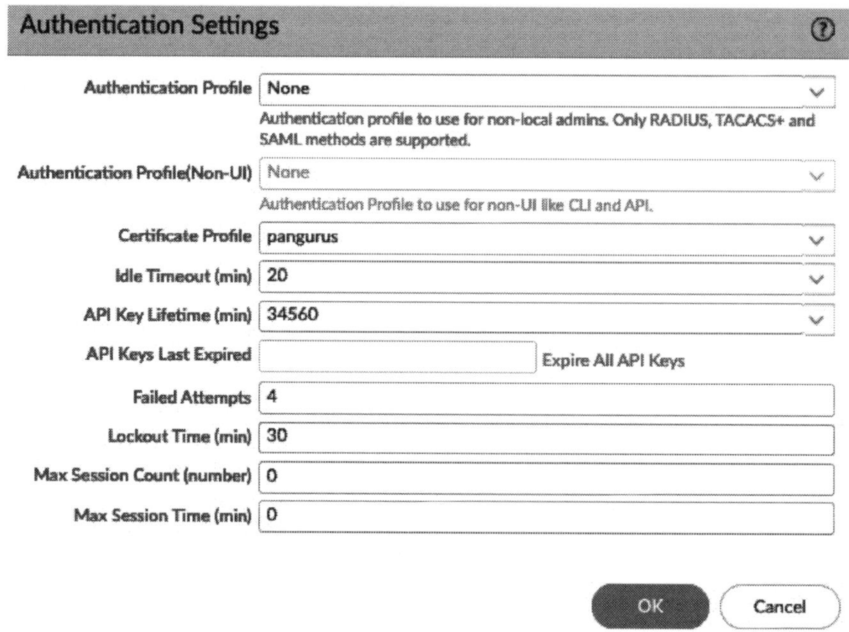

Figure 5.16 – Additional authentication settings

Preventing access altogether is a sound approach to protecting the management interface.

Restricting access to the management interface

Adding restrictions to the IP addresses allowed to connect to the management interface or management-enabled data plane interfaces is a solid approach and best practice. As illustrated in the following screenshot, multiple subnets or IP addresses can be set: take into account when defining these access lists that monitoring servers and peer firewalls that collect **User-ID** information from this firewall also need to be added for them to be allowed to access the management interface:

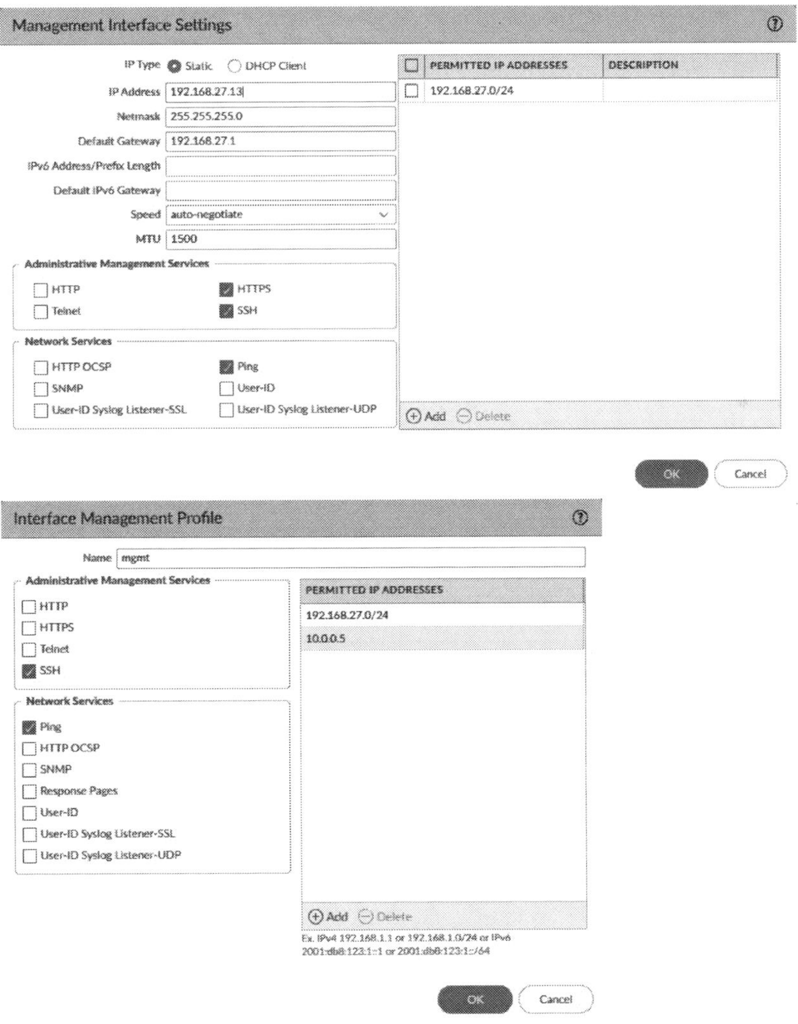

Figure 5.17 – Setting permitted IP addresses on the management interface profile

In addition to limiting access by source IP, it's best to disable all the weak protocols such as HTTP and Telnet and limit the others as much as possible. If only **Secure Shell** (**SSH**) is needed, consider whether enabling HTTPS adds more risk than convenience.

Setting the master key

All passwords and private keys are encrypted before they are written to the configuration file using the **Master Key**. By default, all firewalls and **Panorama** have the same Master Key, which allows for a *fresh* device to be quickly set up with a saved configuration file. This also introduces the risk that if a backup configuration file is released to the outside world somehow, certificates can have their private key stolen. It is recommended to change the Master Key as soon as possible, to ensure all private keys and passwords are secure.

As shown in the following screenshot, go to **Device** > **Master Key** and **Diagnostics** to change the key. On a regular device, only the Master Key can be changed. If FIPS-CC mode is enabled, an additional option becomes available to run scheduled cryptographic and software integrity self-tests:

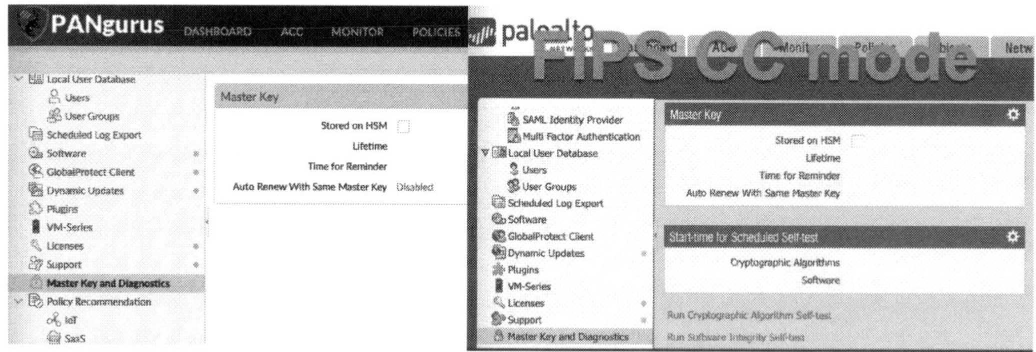

Figure 5.18 – Master key on a regular firewall and a Common Internet Firewall System (CIFS)- enabled firewall

The Master Key can be set with these considerations:

- A New Master Key must consist of exactly 16 characters.
- The **Lifetime** determines how long the Master Key will be valid for. The range is between 1 day and 50 years.

> **Important note**
>
> If the Master Key expires, the system will reboot into **maintenance** mode and will need to be factory reset.

- **Time for Reminder** can be set to display an alarm when the Master Key is about to expire. To enable these alarm popups, also set `Enable Alarms` in **Device** > **Log Settings** > **Alarm Settings**.
- **Auto Renew Master Key** can be set to automatically renew the master key. This can optionally be set to serve as a grace period after the Master Key expires to allow an admin to change the Master Key even past its intended expiration time.
- **HSM** can be set if a **hardware security module** (**HSM**) is configured in **Device** > **Setup** > **HSM**. The Master Key can then be owned and set by the module.

Each firewall should have a unique Master Key so that if one configuration file is compromised, all other firewalls are safe except under these two conditions:

1. A **HA** cluster needs to use the same Master Key on both devices.
2. In a deployment where **Panorama** pushes the configuration to the firewall, all the firewalls and Panorama need to share the same Master Key.

To reset the Master Key to the default value, clear the **Key** fields and uncheck the **Master Key** checkbox, as illustrated in the following screenshot:

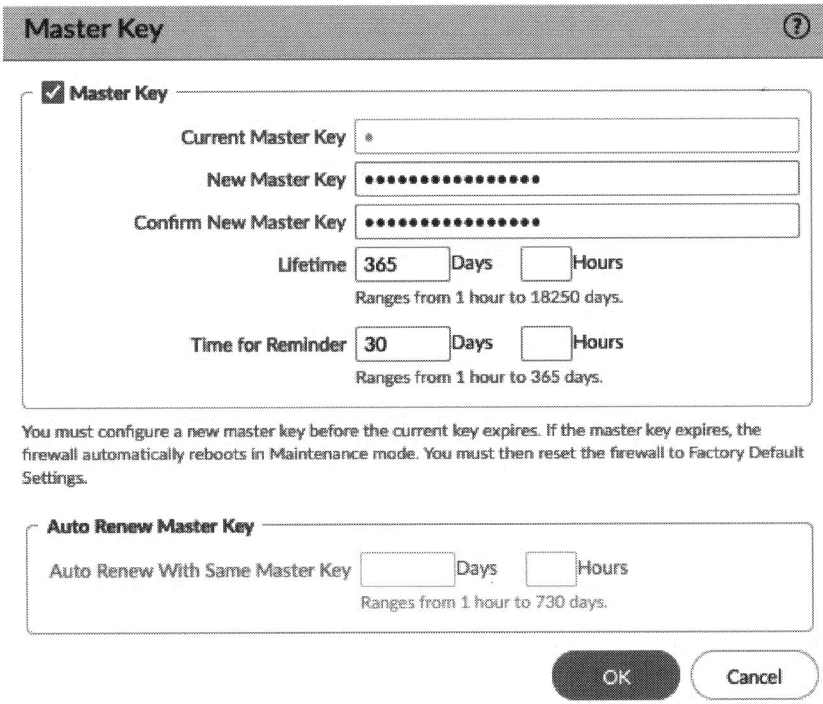

Figure 5.19 – Master key configuration

In this section, you learned the most important settings to ensure the attack surface on your management interface is as small as it can be. For even better security, consider enabling **Multi-factor Authentication** for admin users, but make sure there is a backup local admin account in case connectivity to external systems is lost.

EDLs

EDLs are dynamic objects that are periodically updated by fetching information from an external source. This source can be an external subscription-based or free threat-intelligence feed such as *Spamhaus*, Proofpoint's *Emerging Threats*, or *blocklist.de*, to name just a few.

Or, it can be an internally hosted tool such as **MineMeld** that can consolidate different feeds for ease of use.

When creating an EDL in **Objects** > **External Dynamic Lists**, there are five different types to choose from (which you can see in *Figure 5.21*), as follows:

- **Predefined IP List** lets you select one of the IP lists provided through dynamic updates (**Bulletproof**, known malicious IP, and **high-risk IP** as part of the **Threat Prevention** license).
- **Predefined URL List** lets you select one of the URL lists provided through content updates (a list of sites Palo Alto Networks trusts so that they can be excluded from authentication).
- **IP List** is a group of **IP version 4 (IPv4)** and/or **IP version 6 (IPv6)** addresses or subnets. These EDL objects can be used in security rules to block or allow a set of subnets (for example, allow all the Office 365 address space; block all known malware **command-and-control (C2)** servers).
- **Domain List** is a group of domains that can be used as part of the **Domain Name System (DNS)** sinkhole decision process in the **Anti Spyware** profile (for example, allow or sinkhole domains).

> Tip
>
> Blocking or sinkholing known malicious domains via DNS is a great way to conserve resources otherwise spent on scanning sessions, and obscures the presence of compromised hosts on a network to the outside world.

- **URL List** is a group of URLs that can be used in any of the **URL Filtering** profiles as a custom category.

Depending on the choice of type, a list will become available in different sections of the **Security Policy** or **Security Profiles**, as illustrated in the following screenshot:

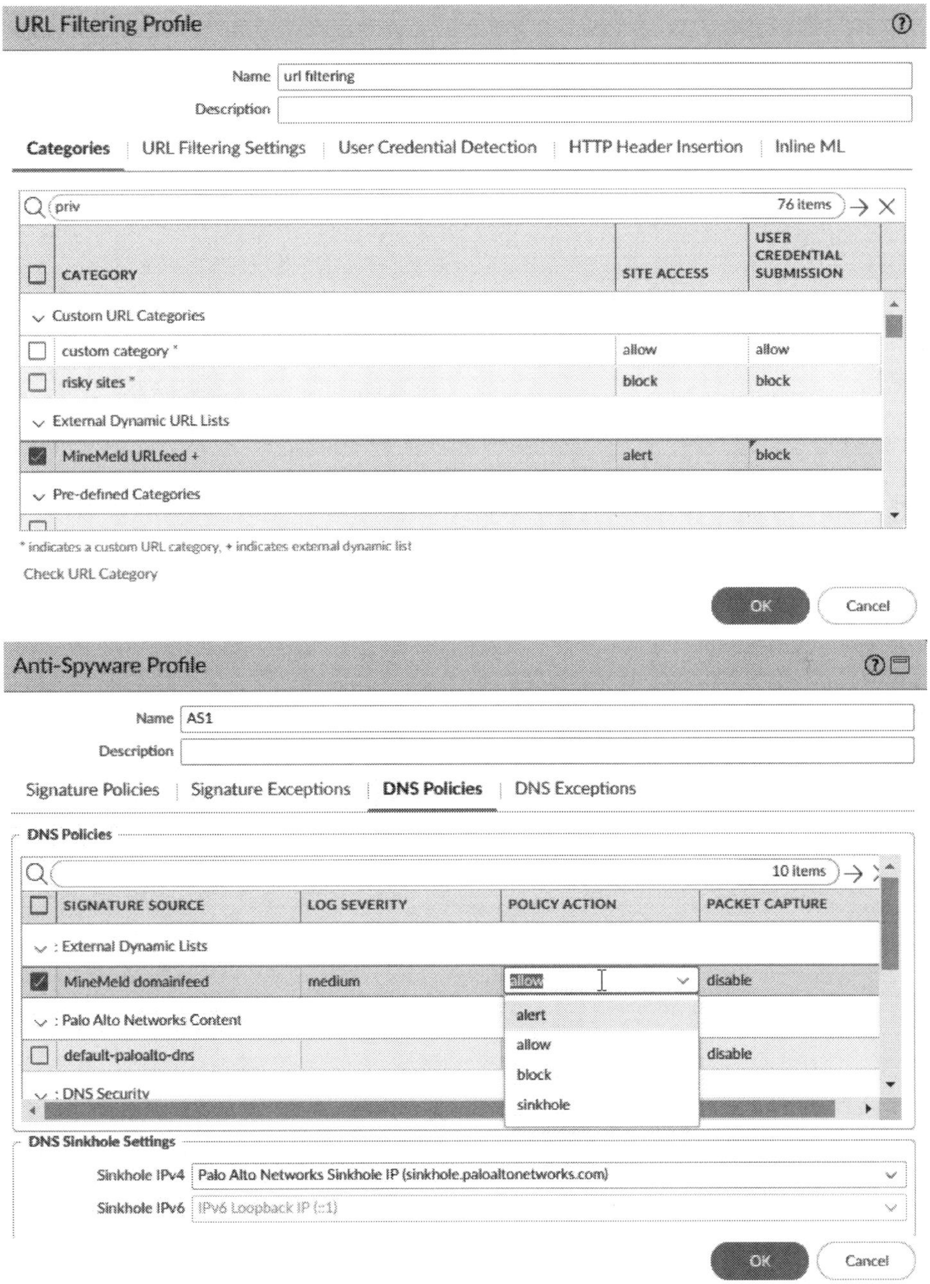

Figure 5.20 – Applying EDLs in security profiles

Besides the type, a source URL needs to be added to let the firewall know where to get the feed from. If the page is hosted on a TLS-enabled web server, it is recommended but not mandatory to add a certificate profile. An update schedule can be set for **Every five minutes**, **Hourly**, **Daily**, **Weekly**, or **Monthly**. If the website is unavailable at the time of the update, the previous entries will be kept.

On the **List Entries And Exceptions** tab, the currently loaded list of IPs, domains, or URLs is listed and, if needed, entries can be moved to the **Manual Exceptions** column, as illustrated in the following screenshot:

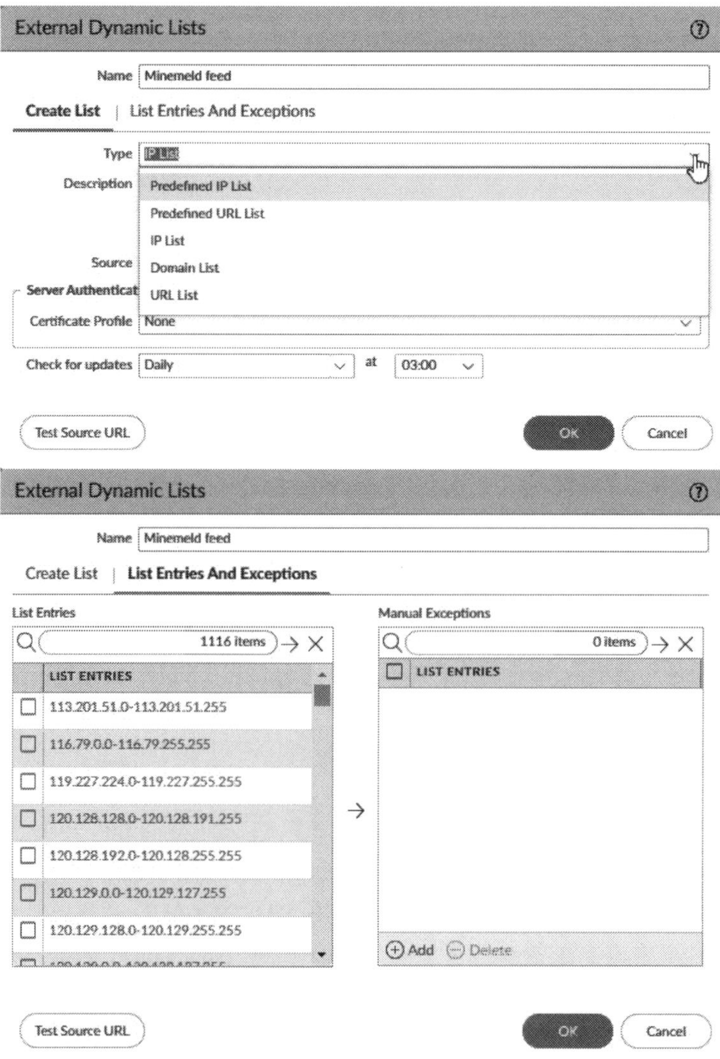

Figure 5.21 – EDL options

While an EDL input file can be hosted on any web server, it is highly recommended to set up a MineMeld instance to consolidate feeds from trusted external parties.

MineMeld

MineMeld can be installed in several different ways, but by far the easiest way to get an instance up and running is to use Docker as it can be run from nearly any system and operating system. Installing a *dockerized* version of MineMeld is also quite easy. You may first need to install Docker, so check if it is running by using the following command:

```
reaper@ubu20:~$ sudo docker run hello-world

Hello from Docker!
This message shows that your installation appears to be working
correctly.

To generate this message, Docker took the following steps:
 1. The Docker client contacted the Docker daemon.
 2. The Docker daemon pulled the "hello-world" image from the
Docker Hub.
    (amd64)
 3. The Docker daemon created a new container from that image
which runs the
    executable that produces the output you are currently
reading.
 4. The Docker daemon streamed that output to the Docker
client, which sent it
    to your terminal.

To try something more ambitious, you can run an Ubuntu
container with:
 $ docker run -it ubuntu bash

Share images, automate workflows, and more with a free Docker
ID:
 https://hub.docker.com/

For more examples and ideas, visit:
 https://docs.docker.com/get-started/
```

If Docker has not been installed yet, a desktop installer for Windows or Mac can be downloaded. Installation instructions for Windows, Mac, and several popular Linux distributions can be found here: `https://docs.docker.com/engine/install/`.

Once Docker is installed, we need to "pull" the latest MineMeld image, as follows:

```
reaper@ubu20:~$ sudo docker pull paloaltonetworks/minemeld
Using default tag: latest
latest: Pulling from paloaltonetworks/minemeld
8e097b52bfb8: Pull complete
a613a9b4553c: Pull complete
acc000f01536: Pull complete
73eef93b7466: Pull complete
3bcee6ae9997: Pull complete
4ffcdde85a27: Pull complete
Digest: sha256:64b12a73e70551e1a46b0c757daf2a2e8d15464aef
099d5b557774ed57f04d86
Status: Downloaded newer image for paloaltonetworks/
minemeld:latest
docker.io/paloaltonetworks/minemeld:latest
```

Some volumes (storage used by Docker) need to be created permanently, else all data will be lost if Docker ever restarts or the host is rebooted. This can be done with the following code:

```
reaper@ubu20:~$ sudo docker volume create minemeld-logs
minemeld-logs
reaper@ubu20:~$ sudo docker volume create minemeld-local
minemeld-local
```

Next, the image can be spun up. Decide which port MineMeld will be made available using the `-p` command followed by the `external:internal` port. If you want to access MineMeld on port `5000`, for example, set `-p 5000:443`, which redirects port `5000` on the host to port `443` in the container image, as illustrated in the following code snippet:

```
reaper@ubu20:~$ sudo docker run -dit --name minemeld
--restart unless-stopped --tmpfs /run -v minemeld-local:/opt/
minemeld/local -v minemeld-logs:/opt/minemeld/log  -p 443:443
paloaltonetworks/minemeld
```

We can verify whether the container is running with the following command:

```
reaper@ubu20:~$ sudo docker ps
CONTAINER ID   IMAGE                              COMMAND
CREATED              STATUS              PORTS                          NAMES
797f42520eb6   paloaltonetworks/minemeld   "/sbin/my_init"   25
minutes ago   Up 25 minutes   0.0.0.0:443->443/tcp   minemeld
```

We can now access MineMeld by accessing the IP and port of the host from a browser according to the following examples, assuming that the Docker host has an IP address of `192.168.27.10`:

- `0.0.0.0:443->443` will have the following URL: `https://192.168.27.10`.
- `0.0.0.0:5000->443` will have the following URL: `https://192.168.27.10:5000`.
- `0.0.0.0:5000->80` will have the following URL: `http://192.168.27.10:5000`.

The default username and password will be `admin/minemeld`.

The starting dashboard will not show much data as yet, so navigate to the **NODES** area.

In the **NODES** area, four miners are set up by default, one processor is present, and three outputs are available. These are detailed as follows:

- A **miner** is basically an external data source that MineMeld will ingest periodically.
- A **processor** is an aggregation process that combines the information collected by the miners associated with it into a single source.
- An **output** is the physical file and URL the firewall can then ingest.

Only one output contains indicators, as indicated by the number in the **Indicators** column. The output can be clicked for more details, including the **Feed Base URL**, which is the URL used by the EDL to fetch a list of objects, as illustrated in the following screenshot:

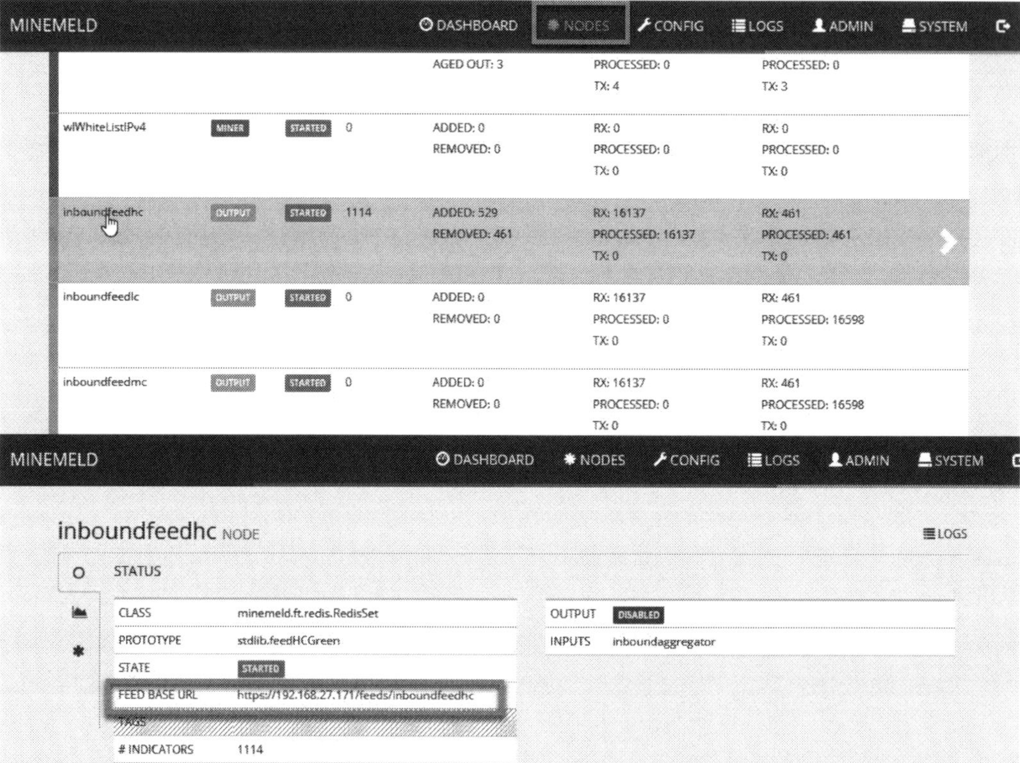

Figure 5.22 – Inspecting an output node

To add more miners, processors, or outputs, navigate to **Configuration**. To review the full list of available nodes, click the **hamburger** menu at the bottom right. You can search by **Name** or **Type**.

To add new nodes using **enable expert mode**, click on the little eye symbol at the bottom left. Click the **add node** plus (+) sign at the bottom right, as shown in the following screenshot:

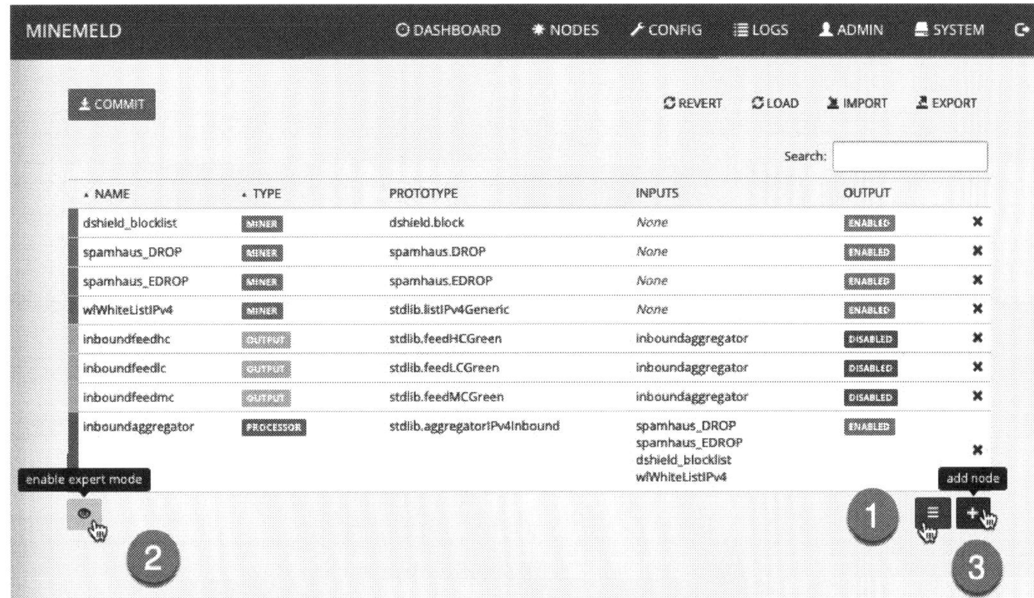

Figure 5.23 – Adding nodes to the configuration

We first add one or more miner nodes by selecting one of the preconfigured miners. You can type part of the name or search the entire list, as demonstrated here:

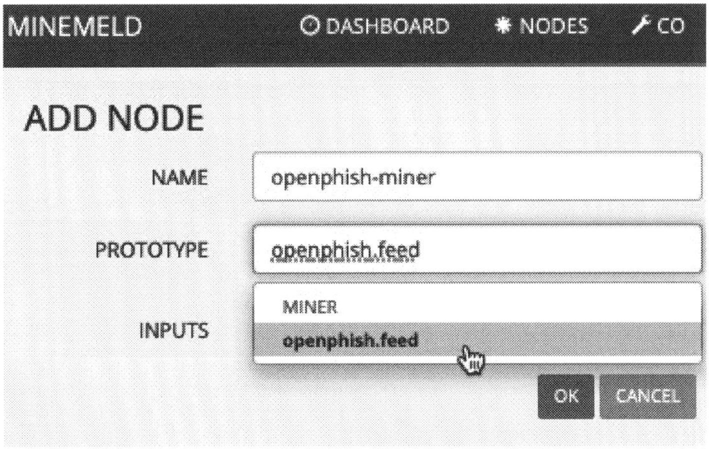

Figure 5.24 – Adding a miner node

Next, we create a **processor node**. First, select which type of input should be processed by selecting the appropriate prototype. The miner I selected is a **URL** type list containing URLs used in phishing attempts, so we enter an `aggregatorURL` processor.

Next, we select the miner we just created as the input node. Multiple miners can immediately be added if more miners are available for the type of processor, as illustrated in the following screenshot (`URL` miners will show up, but `IPv4`/`IPv6` miners will not as they are not compatible with the processor):

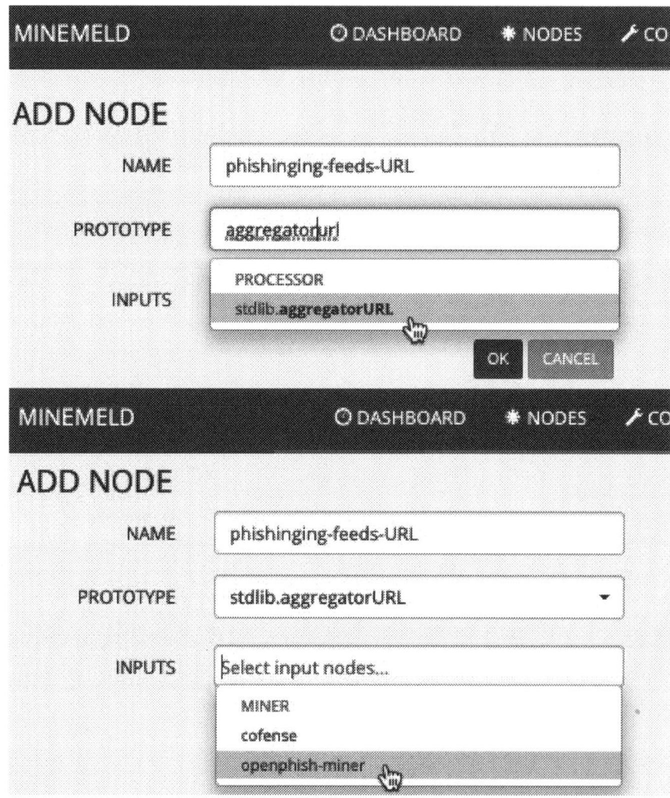

Figure 5.25 – Adding a processor node with input nodes

And lastly, we need to create an **output node**. As output prototype there are a few options available that include a confidence level (**HC**, **MC**, and **LC** for high, medium, and low confidence) and a colour. These are tags that can be used to determine how "safe" it is to block the content in the output node.

The colour is used for sharing purposes—for example, red feeds are private sources that should not be shared with partners, making them visually easy to classify. These tags also serve as filter for which information the output will accept from the processor. The miner I selected earlier has a **Medium Confidence** level and is `ShareLevelGreen`, so we pick the `stdlib.FeedMCGreen` prototype for the output. If multiple miners are combined into one processor, separate output feeds can be created for each confidence level. The process is illustrated in the following screenshot:

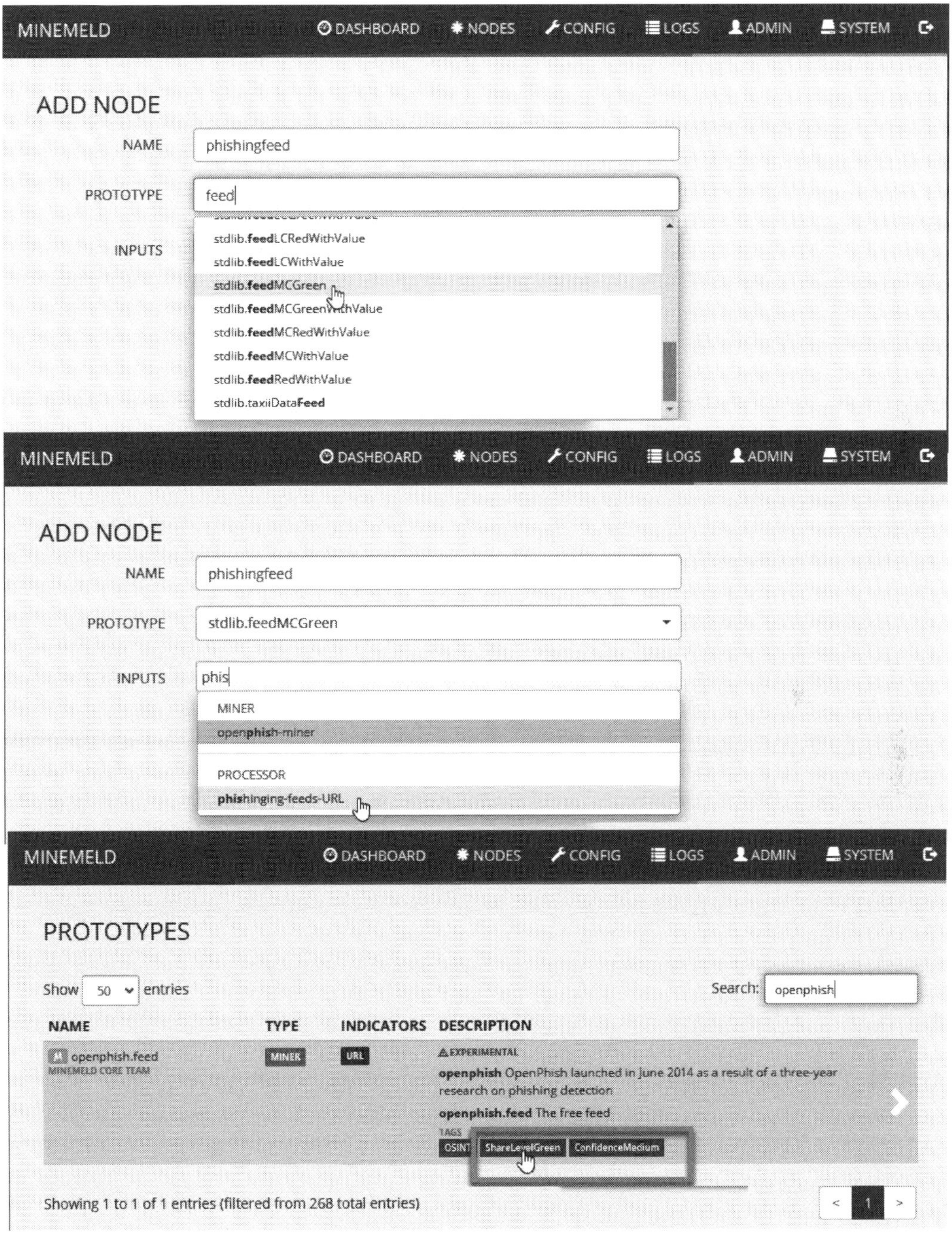

Figure 5.26 – Creating an output node

Once all the nodes have been added, the new configuration first needs to be committed, which will trigger the MineMeld engine to be restarted, as demonstrated in the following screenshot:

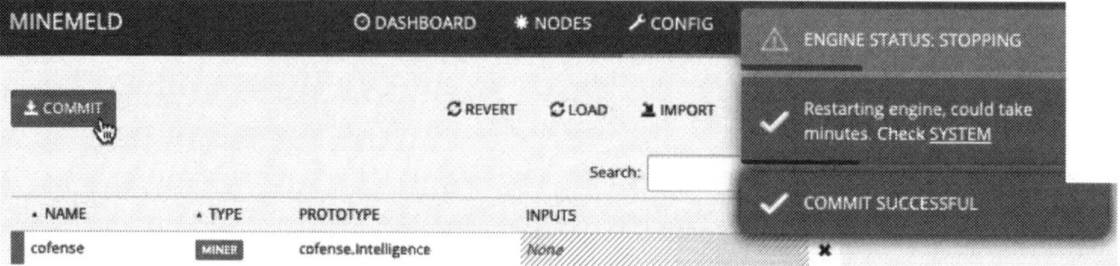

Figure 5.27 – Committing the new nodes to MineMeld

After the engine is restarted, the miners will start collecting data and feeding it to the processor, which will in turn aggregate all the data from all its miners into the output nodes. The output nodes will filter the information for the tags they support (**HC**, **MC**, **LC**, and colour) and add them to their corresponding output file. If you navigate to the **NODES** area, you can click the appropriate output node and find its **FEED BASE URL** setting, as indicated on the bottom of the following screenshot. This feed base URL needs to be added to the firewall EDL:

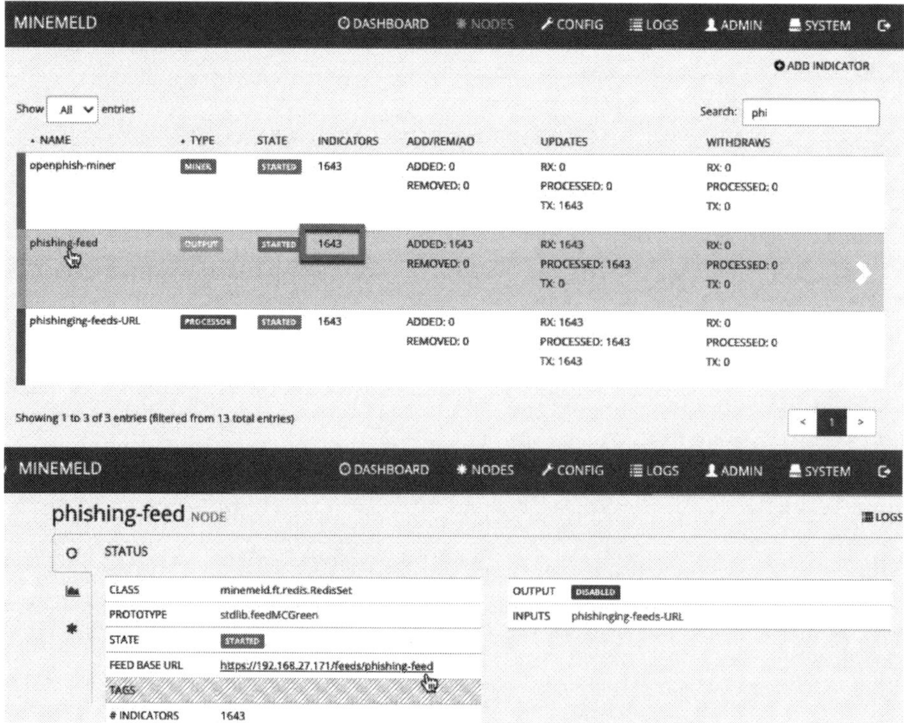

Figure 5.28 – Output node feed base URL

To add the feed to the firewall, navigate to **Objects** > **External Dynamic Lists** and create a new EDL, as follows:

1. Set the appropriate **Type** to match the output. For our output, this is a **URL List** type.
2. Set the **Source** as the feed base URL.
3. In **Check for updates**, set an update schedule that matches the update frequency of the feed. Some feeds may be very static so don't need frequent updates, while others may need very frequent updates.
4. Don't check the **List Entries And Exceptions** just yet. Just click **OK** and **Commit**, as shown in the following screenshot:

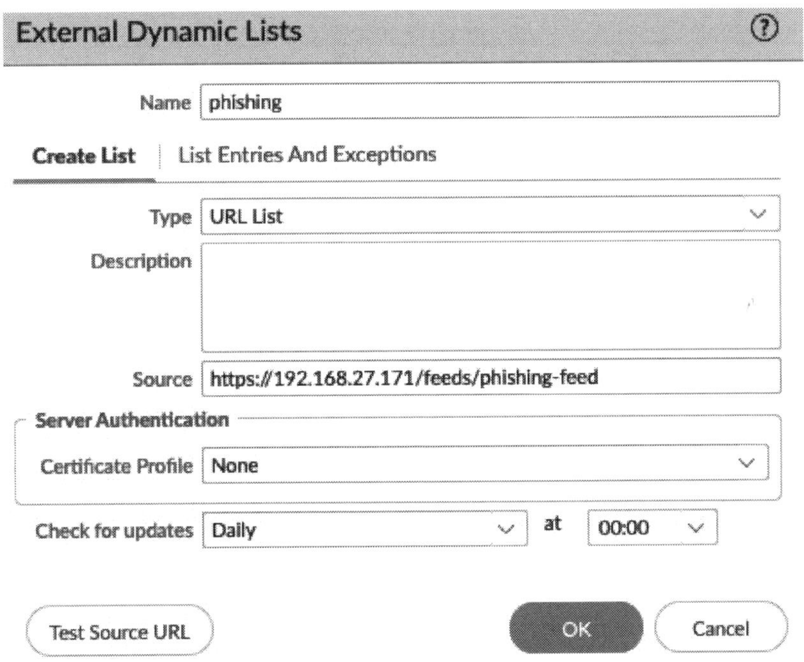

Figure 5.29 – Creating an EDL with the newly created output

The feed will be updated for the first time the first update schedule event takes place, so it could be many hours before the list is updated if you opted to update at midnight, as set in the preceding EDL. You can verify if the EDL was set up properly and is ready to be refreshed at the next interval. To do this, use the following command:

```
reaper@PANgurus> request system external-list stats type url
name phishing
```

```

vsys1/phishing:
        Next update at          : Tue Apr 13 00:00:00 2021
        Source                  : https://192.168.27.171/feeds/
phishing-feed
        Referenced              : Yes
        Valid                   : Yes
        Auth-Valid              : Yes
```

To manually update the list, use the following command:

```
reaper@PANgurus> request system external-list refresh type url
name phishing

EDL refresh job enqueued
reaper@PANgurus> show jobs all
Enqueued              Dequeued   ID    Type        Status
Result Completed
-----------------------------------------------------------------
-------------
2021/04/12 01:19:00   01:19:00   5625  EDLRefresh FIN    OK
01:20:50
2021/04/12 01:15:00   01:15:15   5623  Commit      FIN    OK
01:15:13

reaper@PANgurus> show jobs id 5625

Enqueued              Dequeued   ID   Type        Status Result
Completed
-----------------------------------------------------------------
-------------
2021/04/12 01:19:00   01:19:00   5625 EDLRefresh  FIN    OK
01:20:50
Warnings:
Details:EDL(vsys1/phishing url) Manual Refresh job success
```

We can now verify whether the EDL is populated with the following command:

```
reaper@PANgurus> request system external-list show type url
name phishing


phishing
        Total valid entries      : 0
        Total ignored entries    : 0
        Total invalid entries    : 806
        Total displayed entries : 100
        Invalid urls:
                http://3rdanniversarypubg.my.id/
                http://accountupdate.amazon86ez.xyz/
                http://adidasweb.buzz/amazon-bx
                http://aggiornamento-sicurezza-server.com/
                http://aldfhalsdj.ga/stop2
                http://allurdu.org/beechnut/shap/index/xb
                http://amaz0nbillingupdate.com/
                http://amazon.co.jp.twq56.com/signin
```

You will notice in the previous output there are invalid entries. This is due to the `http://` prefix still being attached to the URLs as they are collected from the upstream feed. PAN-OS URL filtering does not use these prefixes, so they need to be removed from the feed by adding a modifier to the source URL in the EDL configuration.

If we add `?v=panosurl` to the source, as illustrated in the following code snippet, the URLs are normalized:

```
reaper@PANgurus> request system external-list stats type url
name phishing



vsys1/phishing:
        Next update at          : Tue Apr 13 00:00:00 2021
        Source                  : https://192.168.27.171/feeds/
phishing-feed?v=panosurl
        Referenced              : Yes
        Valid                   : Yes
        Auth-Valid              : Yes
```

If we refresh the list and then query the URL list again, all URLs are now valid and the prefix is removed, as we can see in the following code snippet:

```
reaper@PANgurus> request system external-list refresh type url
name phishing

EDL refresh job enqueued
reaper@PANgurus> request system external-list show type url
name phishing

phishing
        Total valid entries     : 797
        Total ignored entries   : 0
        Total invalid entries   : 8
        Total displayed entries : 100
        Valid urls:
                h3rdanniversarypubg.my.id/
                haccountupdate.amazon86ez.xyz/
                adidasweb.buzz/amazon-bx
                aggiornamento-sicurezza-server.com/
                aldfhalsdj.ga/stop2
                allurdu.org/beechnut/shap/index/xb
                amaz0nbillingupdate.com/
                amazon.co.jp.twq56.com/signin
```

Other modifiers are available that can help integration of the MineMeld feed into other products. These are outlined as follows:

- `tr=1` translates IP ranges (for example, `10.0.0.0-10.0.0.255`) into **classless inter-domain routing** (**CIDR**) blocks (for example, `10.0.0.0/24`). This could cause ranges to increase the number of IP addresses included in the entry.
- `v=json` outputs the list in a **JavaScript Object Notation** (**JSON**)-friendly format.
- `v=csv` outputs the list in comma-separated values instead of a list.

With these feeds set up, you can now start building security rules that block known malicious hosts and networks, block phishing sites, prevent credentials being submitted to suspicious sites, or leverage DNS security to sinkhole malicious domains.

Summary

In this chapter, you learned how to make the management interface more resilient and secure. You are now able to enforce a security baseline on password complexity so that administrators are no longer able to set a weak password. You are also able to apply a more robust TLS profile to the management interface and you can limit access to the various interfaces. You are now able to set up MineMeld and activate threat feeds to tighten security against known malicious actors or dynamically load custom URL categories.

In the next chapter, we will learn to prevent phishing attacks by setting up **User-Credential Detection** by leveraging **URL Filtering** and **User Identification**.

6
Anti-Phishing with User Credential Detection

In this chapter, you will learn how we can mitigate phishing attacks and prevent users from using their corporate credentials outside company-approved web resources (for example, using their corporate username and password on Facebook).

In this chapter, we're going to cover the following main topics:

- Preparing the firewall for credential detection
- Using IP user mapping for credential detection
- Using group mapping for credential detection
- Using domain credential filter

Technical requirements

This chapter will cover topics concerning usernames and passwords. User ID integration is required so a lab containing **Write Active Directory (AD)**, and preferably a **Read-Only Domain Controller** (RODC) is desirable to reproduce the topics covered in this chapter.

Check out the following link to see the Code in Action video:
`https://bit.ly/3oRDZV1`

Preparing the firewall for credential detection

To control which websites users are allowed to submit corporate credentials to, we first need to be able to detect which credentials should be checked. URL filtering can be leveraged to perform user credential checking to ensure company usernames (and passwords, if enabled) are only shared with trusted websites.

As you can see in *Figure 6.1*, you can access the configuration options via **Objects** > **Security Profiles** > **URL Filtering** > **URL Filtering Profile** > **User Credential Detection**.

There are three options available to perform credential detection:

- **Use IP User Mapping**: Matches the submitted username to the user that is mapped to the source IP via IP user mapping.
- **Use Group Mapping**: Matches the submitted username to any corporate username in its user-to-group mapping table, which is learned by enabling LDAP group mapping.
- **Use Domain Credential Filter**: Verifies the submitted username and password match to a corporate credential and matches the user logged on to the source IP to the submitted username. This method is the most thorough but requires a **read-only domain controller** (**RODC**) to function:

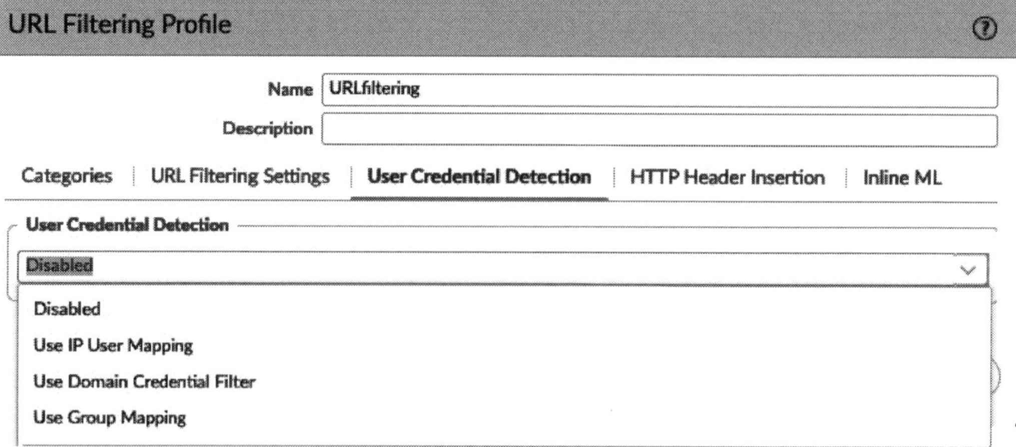

Figure 6.1 – User credential detection

Before we take a look at the previously mentioned detections, we first need to address prerequisites: SSL/TLS decryption is required to be able to detect any usernames submitted via HTTPS.

Configuring SSL/TLS decryption

Because most sites use TLS to create an encrypted session before ever transferring sensitive data such as a username and password, and malicious sites are no different, we first need to ensure that the firewall is able to look inside the encrypted packets before we can try to discern user credentials. To achieve seamless decryption, we first need to establish a trusted certificate chain the client browsers will trust. Outbound decryption works by proxying the session and creating two sessions out of one connection. One session will take place between the firewall and the server, using the target's own certificate to encrypt packets. The second session is established between the firewall and the client where the firewall impersonates the remote server by using a local certificate to encrypt the session. This is a typical example of a **Man in the Middle** (**MitM**) attack. The client needs to trust the certificate used by the firewall, however, or else the user will see a certificate warning page in their browser.

To get around this issue, as it will cause calls to the helpdesk if users keep seeing certificate warnings and could also create the bad user habit of *clicking away* the warning message, we must use a **Certificate Authority** (**CA**) certificate the client trusts to issue the server certificate used in the decryption session. The CA can be either of the following:

- A domain joined CA, which has the advantage of already being used on most of the clients or will be easily integrated in most cases
- A self-signed CA, which is easy to generate but may be more difficult to install on all endpoints

It cannot be a commercial certificate as you will most likely not be able to get a CA certificate with the private key from a public CA.

Whether self-signed or from an internal CA, the following attributes are necessary for a certificate to be used for SSL/TLS decryption:

- The private key must be included in the certificate as it is installed on the firewall.
- The certificate must be from a Certificate Authority as it will be used to sign the forged server certificate.

An appropriate certificate can be generated by a certificate-signing request as illustrated in the following screenshot, or by generating a new one signed by a self-signed root certificate:

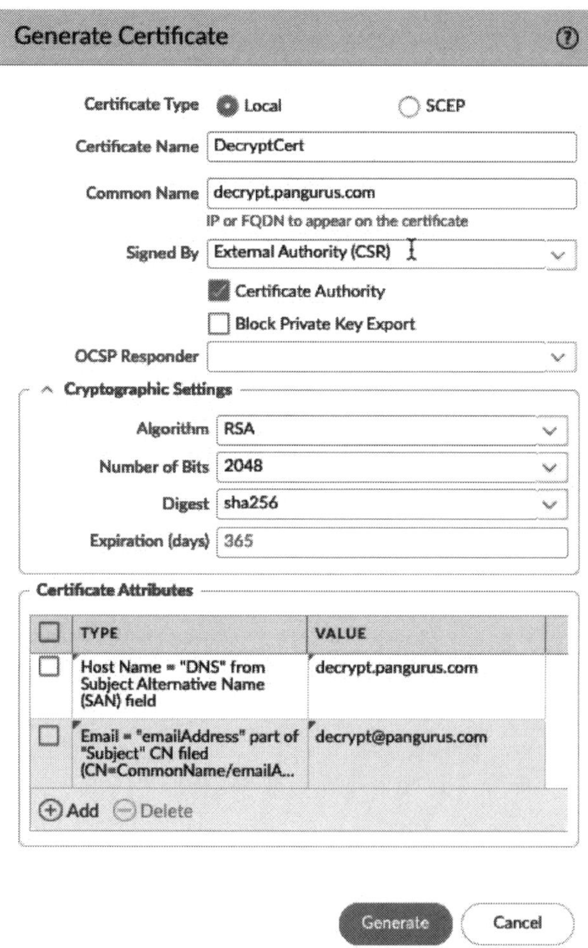

Figure 6.2 – Generating a certificate-signing request

Create a second certificate similar to *Figure 6.3*, which will be used for untrusted connections. Whenever there is something wrong with the real server's certificate that is not blocked by the **Secure Socket Layer** (**SLL**) decryption profile, that is, it is expired or signed by an untrusted authority, you can opt to still allow these connections. If such a session is decrypted with the trusted decrypt certificate, the user will not notice anything at all, which might be dangerous. If the session is decrypted by a certificate that the user does not trust either, there will still be a certificate warning page giving the user the opportunity to browse away if they were not expecting an error message:

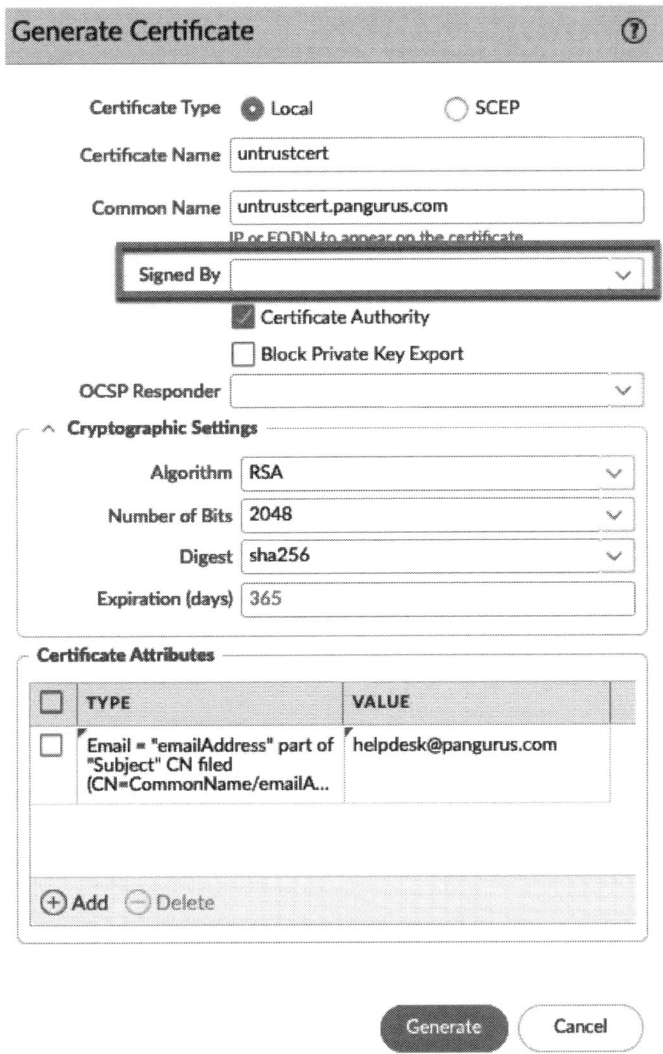

Figure 6.3 – Untrusted certificate generation

The newly generated certificates should look similar to *Figure 6.4* with both the **Private Key** and **Certificate Authority** checkboxes checked.

Click the trusted certificate's name and check **Forward Trust Certificate** to indicate this certificate will be used as the SSL decryption certificate.

Click the untrusted certificate's name and check **Forward Untrust Certificate** to indicate this certificate will be used as the SSL decryption certificate for untrusted remote certificates:

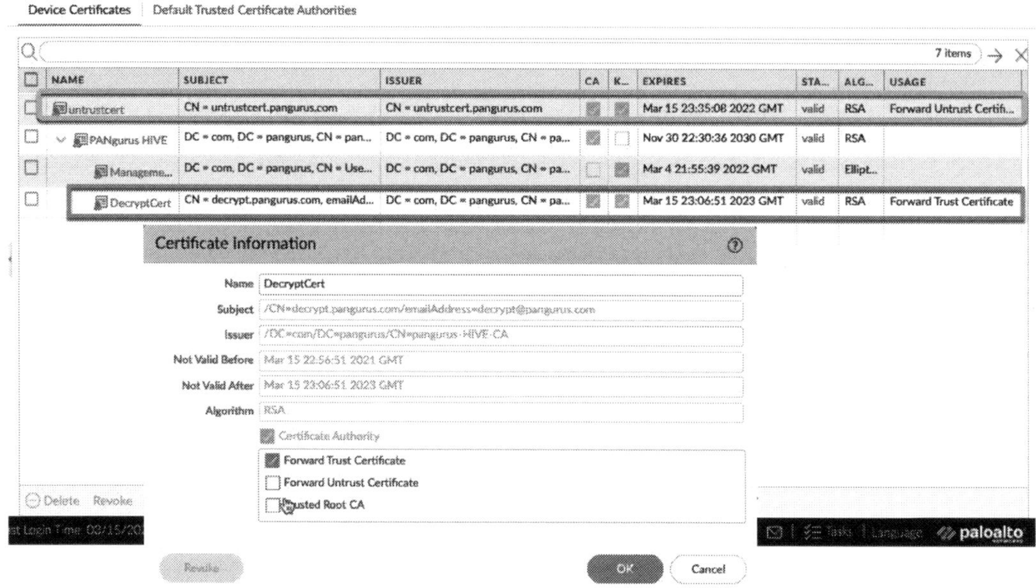

Figure 6.4 – Forward trust and untrust certificates

Now create a decryption profile as shown in *Figure 6.5* in **Objects** > **Decryption** > **Decryption Profile** to establish which types of certificate problems should be blocked. Only uncheck boxes if there is a necessity to do so (for example, if a partner is having certificate issues that are impacting your users, create a separate profile if possible, and create a separate decryption rule for these websites).

> **Important note**
>
> Sessions marked for `no decryption` will still be processed by the SSL forward proxy, as the session needs to be inserted into the proxy before it can be decided that the URL category should not be decrypted.

In the **SSL Protocol Settings** tab, make sure any weak algorithms are disabled and the minimum TLS version is set to **TLSv1.2** to ensure stronger encryption is enforced:

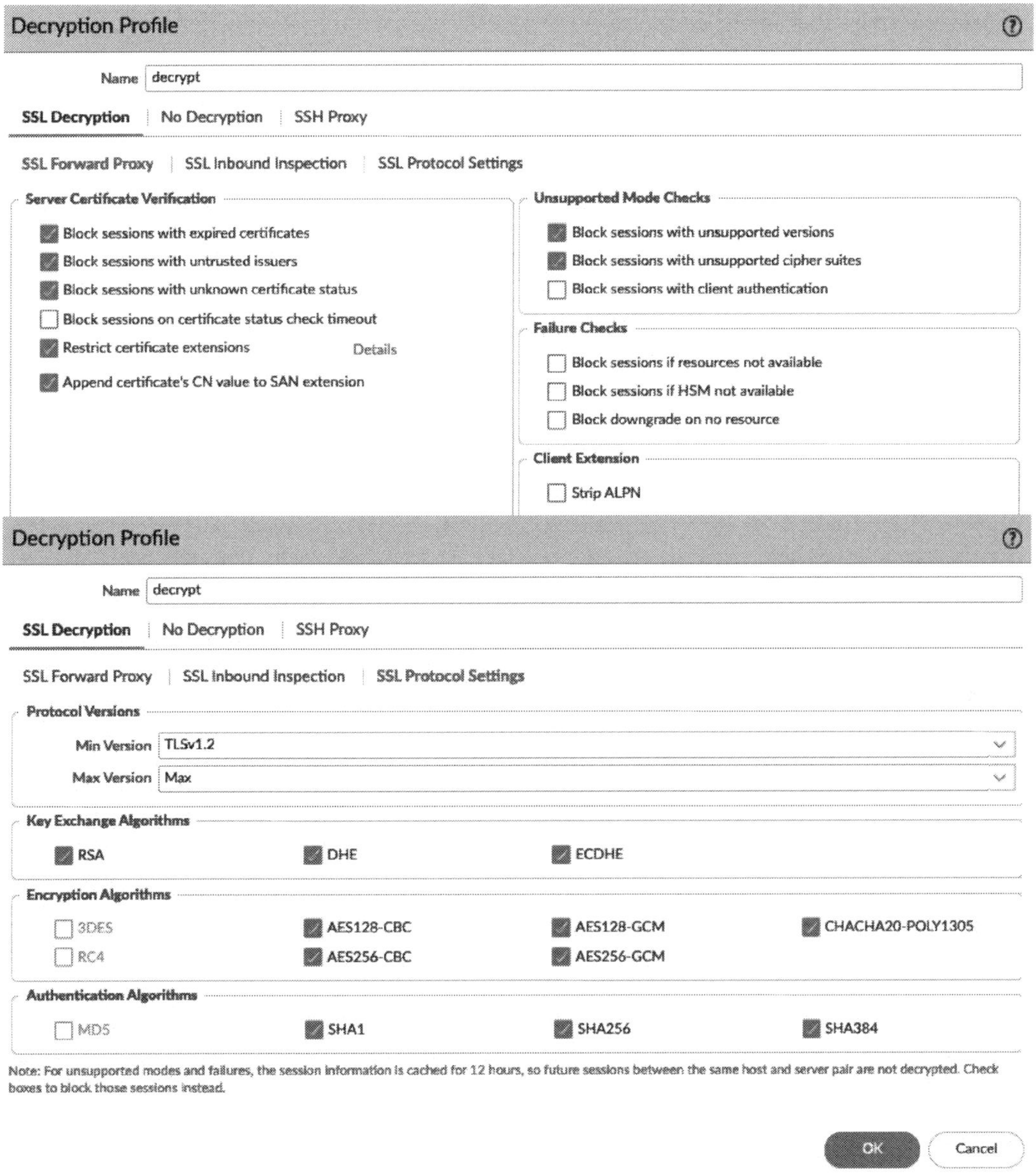

Figure 6.5 – Decryption profile

Also check **Block sessions with expired certificates** and **Block sessions with untrusted issuers** in the **No Decryption** tab as illustrated in the following screenshot:

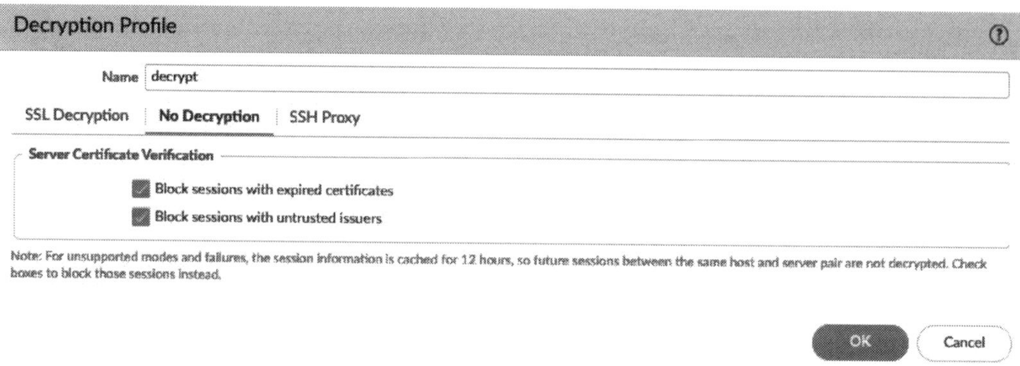

Figure 6.6 – No Decryption settings

Next, create a decryption rule in **Policies** > **Decryption** similar to *Figure 6.7*.

To keep things simple to reproduce, we will designate a **source zone** and **destination zone**. Subnets or hosts can be added in a source or destination to limit which traffic will be decrypted.

In the **Service/URL Category** tab, there are some things to consider:

- Setting the service port to `any` will ensure all SSL/TLS sessions regardless of their destination port are intercepted and decrypted. This will help catch any sessions that try to set up an SSL tunnel over a non-default port, which should be treated as suspicious behavior. Adding a service port will limit the ports that are inspected for SSL traffic.
- URL categories can be added to determine which types of websites should be decrypted or excluded from decryption.

> **Important note**
>
> Local laws such as the **General Data Protection Regulation** (**GDPR**) may prohibit the decryption of sites that process personal data. You will need to set up a No Decrypt rule at the top of the rule base for these categories. Typical categories include health - and - medicine, government, financial services, and religion.

In the **Options** tab, do the following::

- Set **Action** to **Decrypt**.
- Set the decryption **Type** to **SSL Forward Proxy**.
- Select the **Decryption Profile** we created in the previous step.
- Click **OK**.
- Commit the change.

This step will ensure all outbound traffic is decrypted and can be inspected for user credentials:

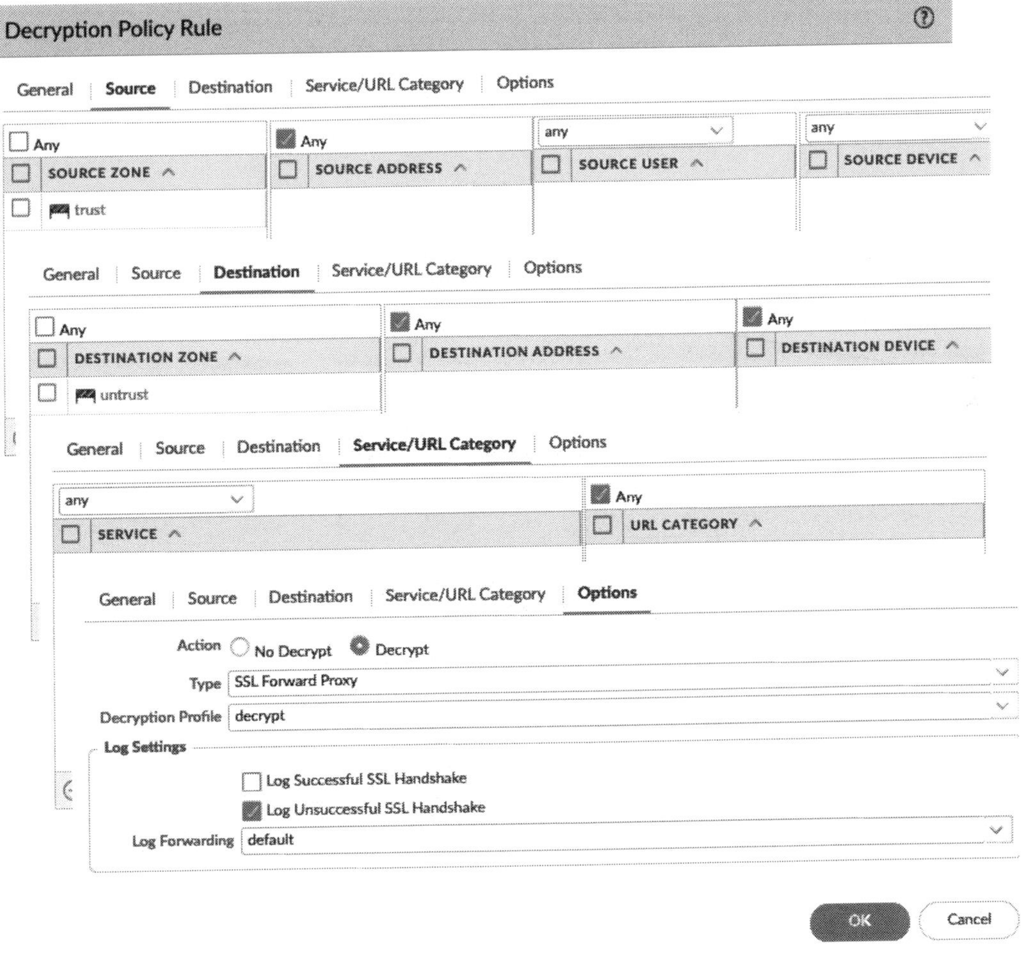

Figure 6.7 – Create an SSL decryption rule

We can now start configuring credential detection.

Enabling IP user mapping

The first option to intercept user credentials is based on **IP user mapping**. While any method of **User-ID** (for example, user-ID Agent, Captive Portal, GlobalProtect, and so on) will work, we will focus on **User-ID agentless deployment**.

The firewall will be set to read the AD event log and needs to be able to capture at least one of four possible event IDs from AD: 4768 (Authentication Ticket Granted), 4769 (Service Ticket Granted), 4770 (Ticket Granted Renewed), and 4624 (Logon Success). You will need to navigate to **Start** > **Windows Administrative Tools** > **Local Security Policy**. Then, in **Security Settings** > **Local Policy** > **Audit Policy**, set **Audit Logon Events** to `Success`, which will start logging all successful logon events that the user-ID agent(less) can use to map the user to their workstation's IP.

Next, in **Device** > **User Identification** > **User Mapping**, open the **Palo Alto Networks user-ID Agent Setup** configuration.

Add the **Username** and **Password** to a service account that will be used to read the event logs. Set the username as `domain\user` as illustrated in the following screenshot.

You can add the **Domain's DNS Name** and a **Kerberos Server Profile** to enable **WinRM over HTTP or HTTPS** as a transport mechanism:

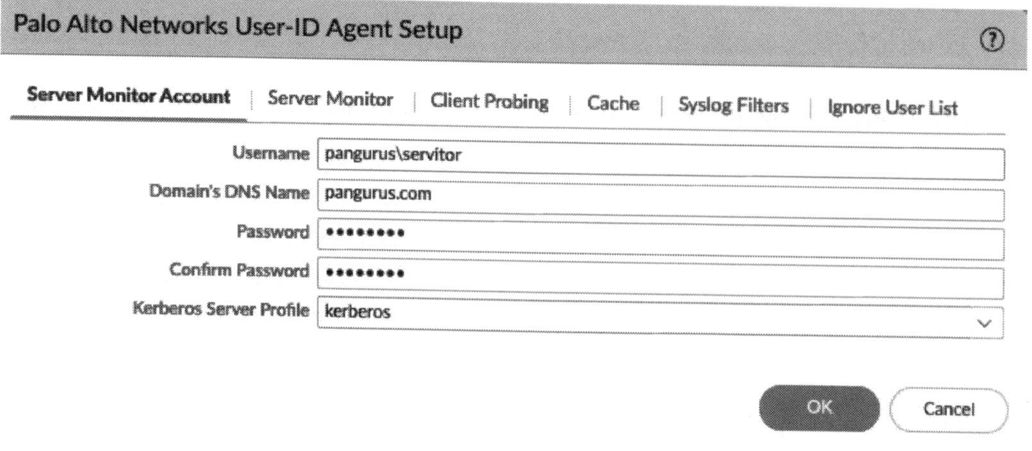

Figure 6.8 – Server Monitor Account with and without Kerberos

If a Kerberos profile is *not* attached, the firewall will use **WMI** to connect to Active Directory.

> **Important note**
>
> The user needs to be assigned **Distributed COM Users**, **Event Log Readers**, and **Remote Management Users** privileges in Active Directory and is allowed to connect.

On the **Server Monitor** tab, as seen in *Figure 6.9*, the frequency at which the firewall will read the AD event log can be set. By default, the frequency is set to 2 seconds. Relax this setting if there is latency between the firewall and AD. The **Enable Session** checkbox can be enabled if AD hosts mapped file shares, which the agent can monitor to collect user information. If shares are mapped using a different username, this could cause username conflicts.

The firewall can also receive syslog messages, from authentication servers or access points, for example, with username and IP information. In **Syslog Listener Settings**, an SSL/TLS certificate profile can be added in **Syslog Service Profile** if the syslog messages are encrypted:

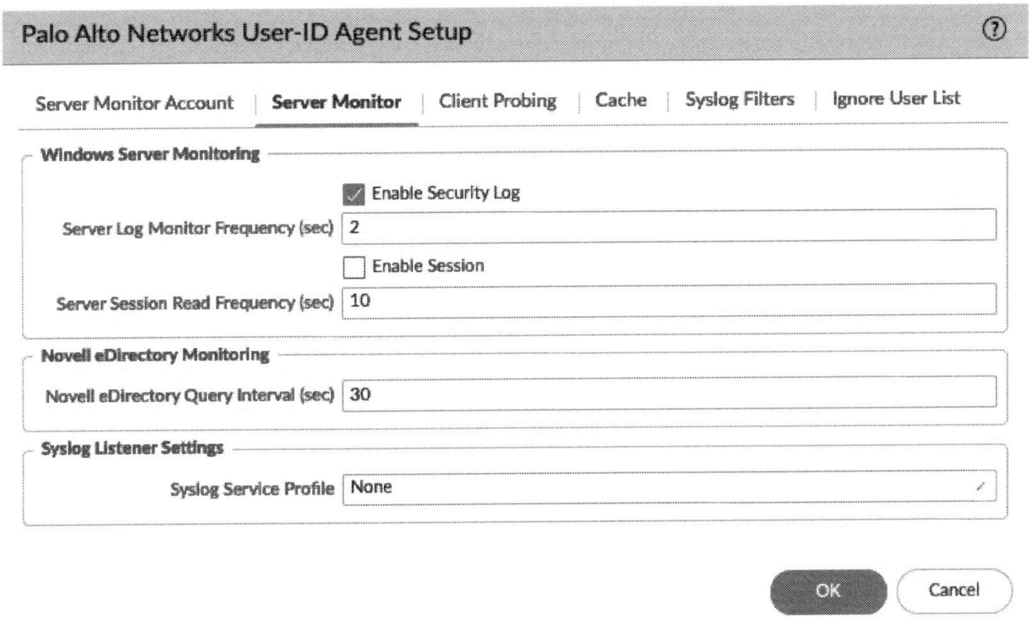

Figure 6.9 – Server Monitor

As illustrated in *Figure 6.10*, **Client Probing** should not be enabled: the probe will send WMI messages to endpoints to determine the logged-in user reactively to an unknown IP connecting to the firewall, or as a check that a known mapping is still active. Most secure networks will not allow WMI probes causing mappings to be deprecated by failed probes. Only enable probing if WMI probes can be allowed on all endpoints.

In **Cache**, **User Identification Timeout** should be increased to `900` minutes (the maximum length of a workday) for most office environments with static users.

The **Syslog Filters** tab contains predefined filters for syslog messages from several different vendors. Service accounts and admin accounts can be excluded from detection in **Ignore User List**:

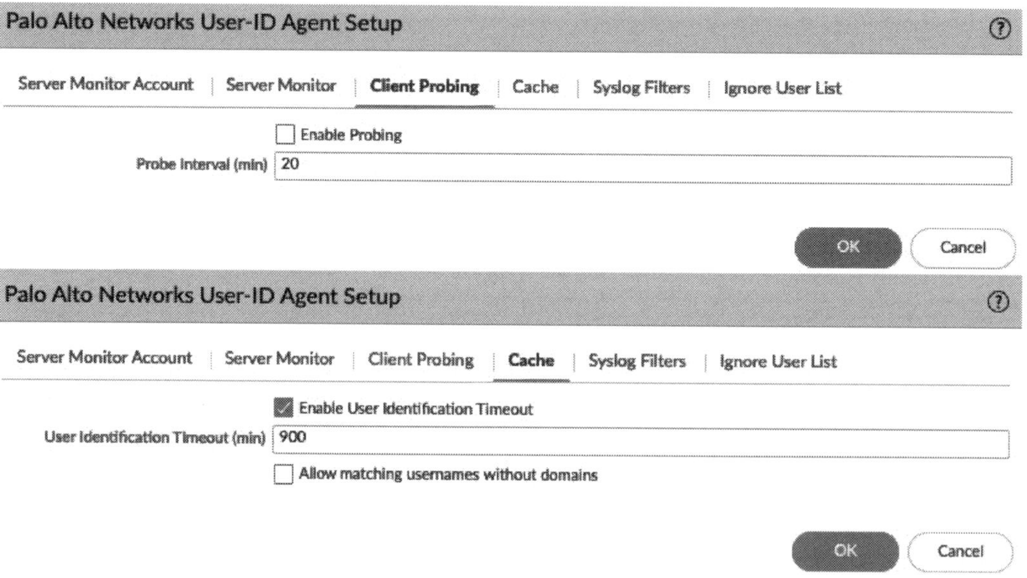

Figure 6.10 – Client Probing and Cache

Click **OK** and then click **Add** in **Server Monitoring** to add a server to be monitored. In **User Identification Monitored Server**, provide a name and set the server **Type**:

- **Microsoft Active Directory**
- **Microsoft Exchange**
- **Novell eDirectory**
- **Syslog Sender**

Then select the **Transport Protocol**:

- **WMI**: The default transport protocol
- **WinRM-HTTP**: Windows remote management over HTTP
- **WinRM-HTTPS**: Windows remote management over TLS, which is much more secure than HTTP:

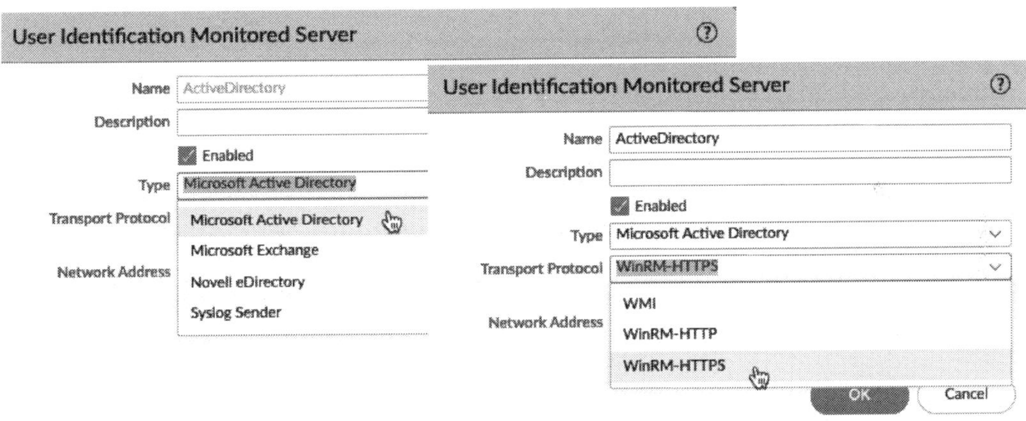

Figure 6.11 – User identification monitored server

Click **OK** and **Commit**.

The user mapping should now look like *Figure 6.12*. If the server monitor is unable to connect, it should show an error message telling you what went wrong:

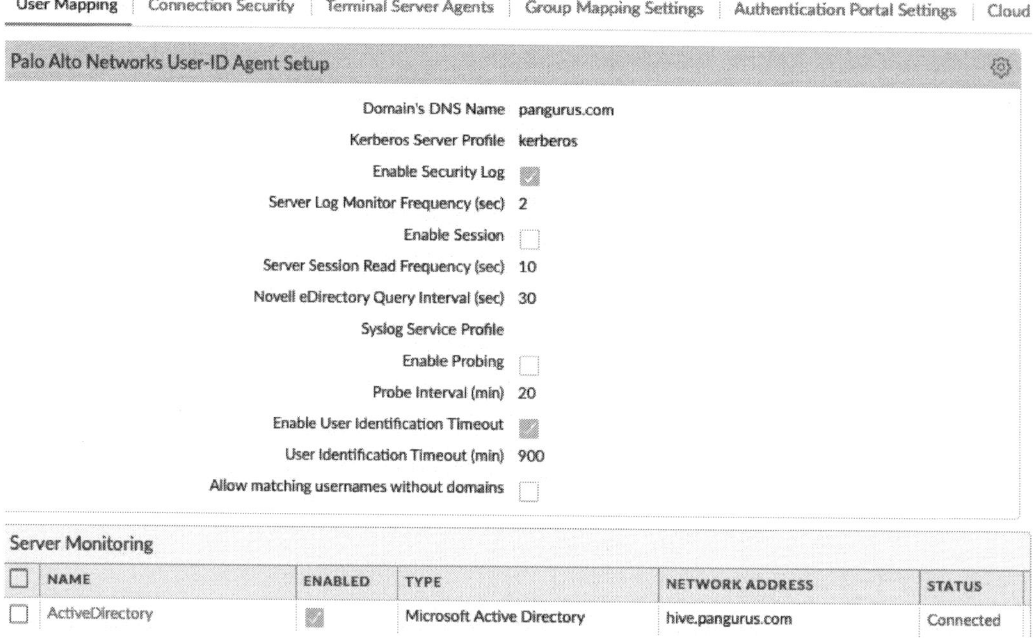

Figure 6.12 – Configure user mapping

The last step is to ensure user-ID is enabled on the internal zones where users are connecting. Check the zones via **Network** > **Zones** and **Enable User Identification** where needed, as you can see in *Figure 6.13*:

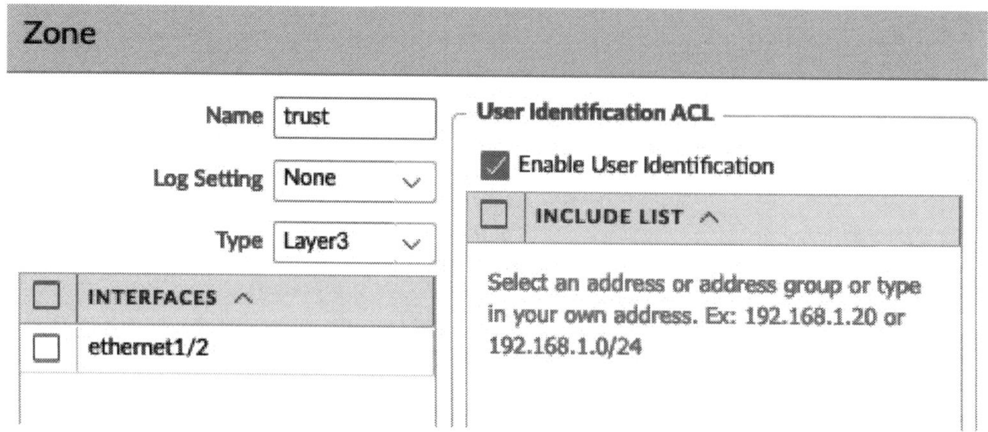

Figure 6.13 – Zone with user identification enabled

We can now set up user credential detection.

Using IP user mapping for credential detection

When IP user mapping is set up correctly, we can enable **Use IP User Mapping** in the **User Credential Detection** section of URL filtering. Open **URL Filtering Profile** in **Objects** > **Security Profiles** > **URL Filtering** and access the **User Credential Detection** tab. Set **User Credential Detection** to **Use IP User Mapping** and select the **severity** logs should have for detected credentials in the **Valid Username Detected Log Severity** field as illustrated next:

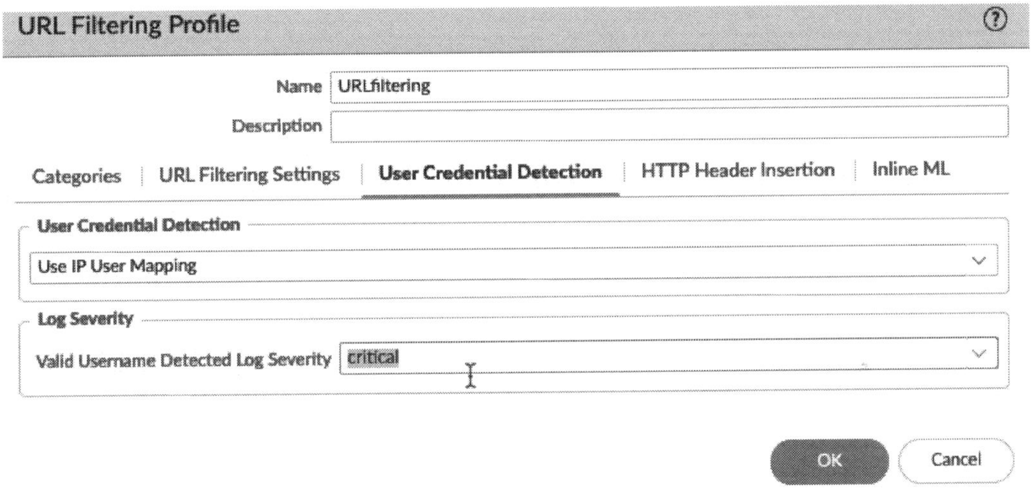

Figure 6.14 – Use IP user mapping in user credential detection

In the **Categories** tab, the action URL filtering will apply when user credentials are detected and can be set for each category individually. This way, corporate credentials can be blocked for undesirable categories, as shown in *Figure 6.15*. A **continue** action can be used for categories where users are technically allowed to use corporate credentials but encouraged to *think twice* before doing so. Alternatively, create a custom category for sites that are allowed and then block the pre-defined category. **Allow** the categories where corporate credentials are permitted.

> **Important note**
>
> A URL filtering license is not required to make this feature work, as you can see in the following screenshot, **custom URL categories** can also be used to enforce user credential submission.

If only a small number of sites are allowed, create a custom category and block all pre-defined categories:

URL Filtering Profile

Name: URLfiltering

Description:

Categories | URL Filtering Settings | User Credential Detection | HTTP Header Insertion | Inline ML

74 items

	CATEGORY	SITE ACCESS	USER CREDENTIAL SUBMISSION
	Custom URL Categories		
☐	updates *	allow	block
☐	corp sites *	allow	allow
	Pre-defined Categories		
☐	auctions	allow	continue
☐	abortion	allow	block
☐	abused-drugs	block	block

* indicates a custom URL category, + indicates external dynamic list

Check URL Category

OK | Cancel

Figure 6.15 – URL filtering with user credential submission actions

The security profile needs to be added to a security rule in **Policies** > **Security** before these settings will be applied. A simple rule, as illustrated next, will suffice to test this feature:

		Source		Destination					
	NAME	ZONE	USER	ZONE	APPLICATION	SERVICE	ACTION	PROFILE	OPTIONS
1	ssl	trust	any	untrust	any	application-...	Allow		
2	intrazone-default	any	any	(intrazone)	any	any	Allow	none	none
3	interzone-default	any	any	any	any	any	Deny	none	none

URL Filtering Profile: URLfiltering

Figure 6.16 – Security rule with URL filtering profile applied

The test user will now be able to access any URL for which **Site Access action** is set to **allow** (no log) or **alert** (log), but any logon attempt using a corporate username on a site that is not set to **allow** or **alert** on **User Credential Submission** will be blocked with an error message as shown in the next screenshot. For this exercise, I have not added my domain to the list of allowed user credential submission categories yet, which leads to my access getting denied:

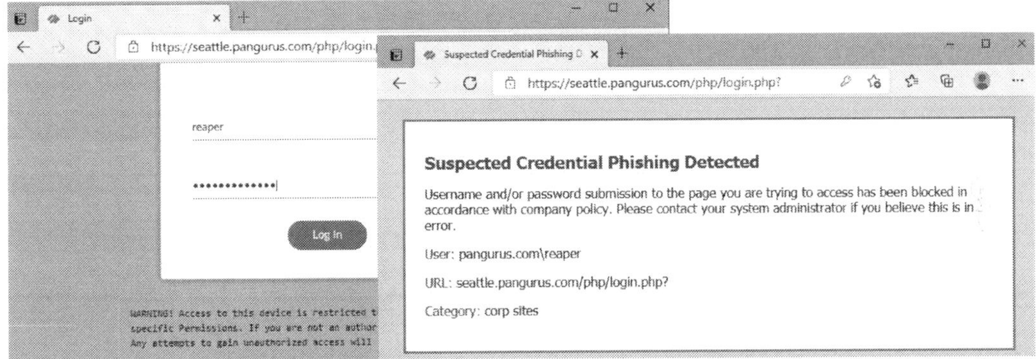

Figure 6.17 – Access blocked due to suspected credential phishing

The drawback of this method is that it is only able to check by username so there could be cases where the user's private username matches the corporate one. This method also only checks for the currently mapped user, so a user that has multiple corporate credentials can use all of the "other" usernames except the one they are logged on to the local machine with.

The Domain Credential Filter first requires group mapping to be enabled.

Enabling group mapping

Group mapping collects member information from **LDAP** groups and can be used for multiple purposes, such as building security rules that only apply to a certain group of users. To collect these groups, we first need to create an LDAP profile that creates a connection to an LDAP server. Go to **Device** > **Server Profiles** > **LDAP** and create a new profile:

1. Add a **Server** by its IP or FQDN. Set the port to `636` for SSL/TLS secured connections or `389` for cleartext connections if your server doesn't support TLS. **Global Catalog** can be set for multi-domain forests and uses ports `3268` and `3269`.
2. Select the **Type** from the dropdown. You can pick between **active-directory**, **e-directory**, **sun**, or other.

3. If the **Type** was set to **active-directory**, clicking the arrow in **Base DN** will show the available domains, else add the **domain component** (**DC**) string manually as `dc=domain,dc=tld` (**Top Level Domain**).
4. **Bind DN** is a username that is allowed to connect to the server and read all the group memberships. Unless the server has been locked down, a regular user is already able to collect this information.
5. **Bind Timeout** determines how long the firewall will try to connect to the first server in the list before connecting to the next server.
6. **Search Timeout** is the time limit on directory searches.
7. **Retry Interval** is the time the firewall waits before trying to connect again to a previously failed server.

> **Important note**
>
> Some cloud-based directory services may use the same base domain for all customers but add a `tennant dc` to distinguish between customers. In such cases, the **Base DN** could look like `dc=tennantID, dc=cloudprovider; dc=com`.

8. The **LDAP Server Profile** should look similar to *Figure 6.18*:

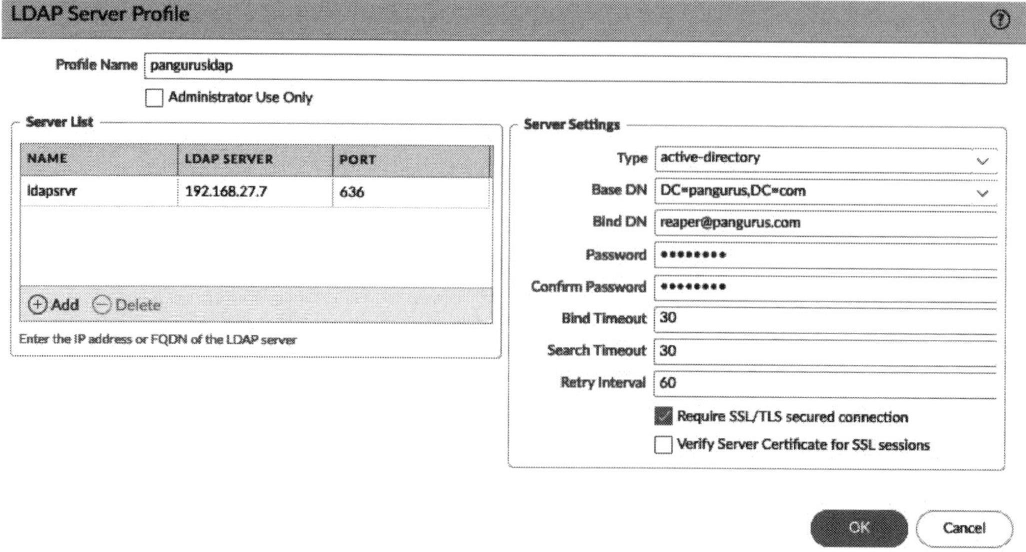

Figure 6.18 – LDAP Server Profile

Next, we need to enable group mapping by going to **Device** > **User Identification** > **Group Mapping Settings** and creating a new **Group Mapping**.

For this specific purpose, most of the default configuration will suffice to collect usable usernames for detection, but we'll cover some of the important fields so the user groups collected here can also be used for other purposes such as security rule enforcement:

1. In the **Server Profile** tab, add a new **Group Mapping**.
2. Add the **Server Profile** we created in the previous step.
3. **User Domain** can be filled with the `netbios` domain in case the user-ID agent picks up `netbios` domains and group mapping gets FQDNs from the LDAP queries (see *Troubleshooting user-ID*). Do not set **User Domain** if the LDAP server is set to the global catalog port as it will overwrite all user domains.
4. **Update Interval** is set to 60 minutes (3600 seconds) by default. This means that any user moved in or out of a group will take a maximum of 60 minutes to be updated on the firewall.
5. **Group Objects** will search for `group` as the **Object Class** associated with user groups. This can be changed if the desired user groups have a unique **Object Class** and additional filters can be added (for example, only a specific type of group needs to be included in group mapping and they have the **Object Class** `special` so the **Object Class** can be changed to only look for `special`).
6. **User Objects** are searched by the **Object Class** `person` by default, but this can also be changed if the user objects that need to be retrieved have a unique **Object Class** (for example, only a sub-section of users need to be included in group mapping and they have the **Object Class** `vip` so the **Object Class** can be changed to only look for `vip`).

7. The **Server Profile** tab should look similar to *Figure 6.19*:

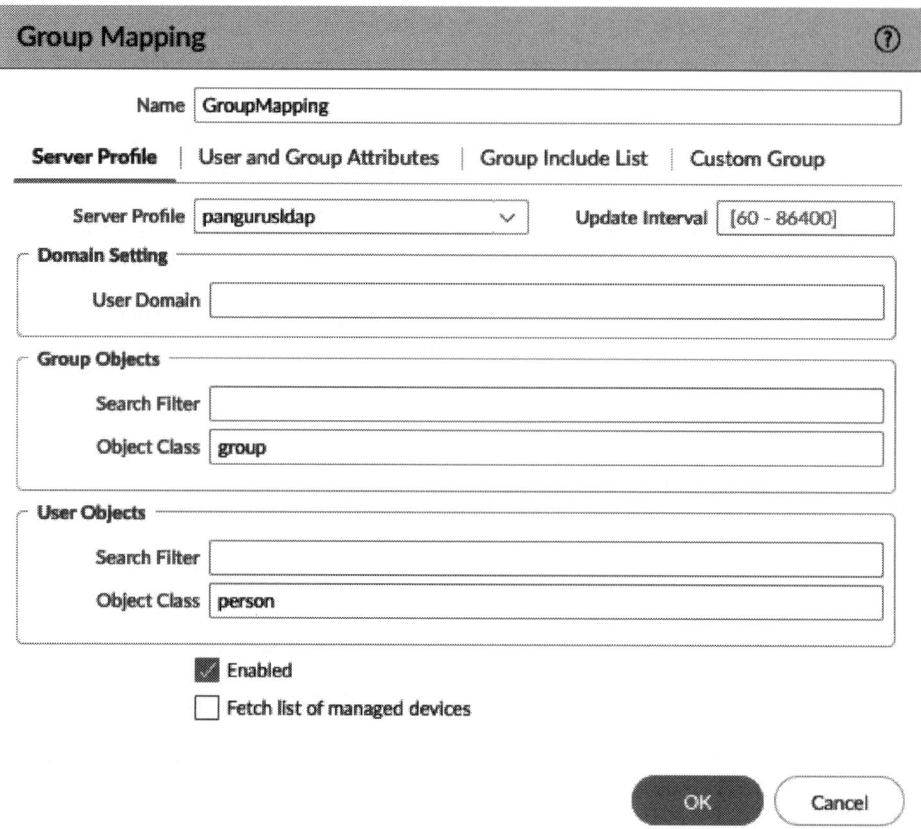

Figure 6.19 – Server Profile

8. In the **User and Group Attributes** tab, additional attributes can be set to control which objects are retrieved from the LDAP server. `sAMAccountName` is set as default but can be replaced by `UserPrincipalName` or any other attribute if needed. Some LDAP servers may use entirely different attributes as the username. This can be verified by connecting to the LDAP server using an LDAP browser and checking which attributes best match the required information.
9. As shown in *Figure 6.20*, in **Group Include List**, select all the appropriate groups for which user membership information should be collected, then click **OK**:

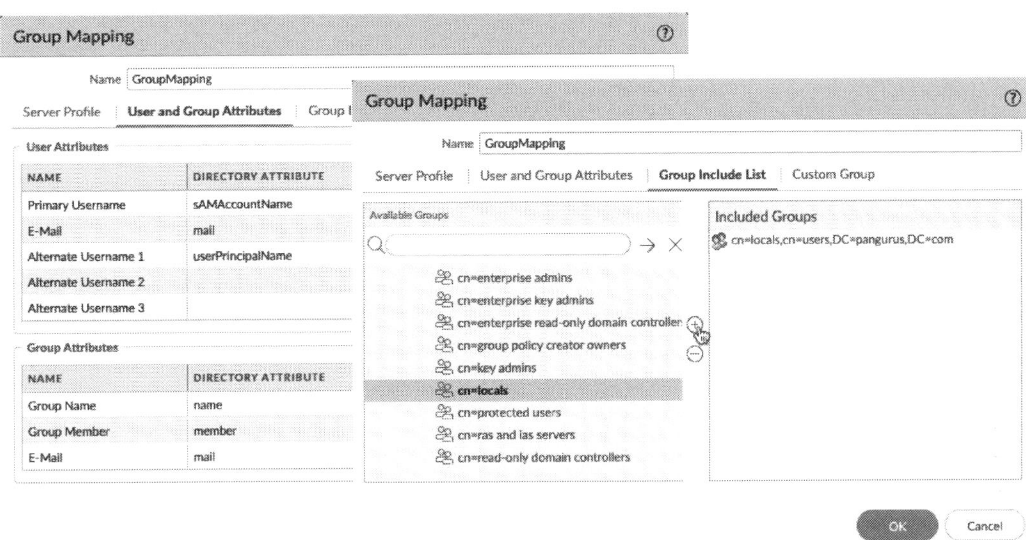

Figure 6.20 – Filtering logon attribute and adding user groups

To make sure user mapping works, double-check mapping in the CLI.

Troubleshooting user-ID

To check which user is mapped to a specific IP, we can use the following command:

```
reaper@LABFW> show user ip-user-mapping ip 10.0.0.10

IP address:     10.0.0.10 (vsys1)
User:           pangurus\reaper
From:           AD
Idle Timeout:   53661s
Max. TTL:       53661s
HIP Query:      Disabled
Group(s):       pangurus\reaper(5)
```

This command shows us the source where the user is learned from in the **From** field. In the preceding example, it is **AD**, which means the built-in User-ID agent. **GP** means GlobalProtect users, **UIA** is from an installed user-ID agent, and **CP** is captive portal.

To find out which groups are mapped on a system, we use the following command:

```
reaper@LABFW> show user group list

dynamic users
cn=locals,cn=users,dc=pangurus,dc=com

Total: 2
* : Custom Group
```

In the output, we can currently see only the `locals` group has been mapped. To see which users are members of this group, we can use the following command:

```
reaper@LABFW>show user group name
cn=locals,cn=users,dc=pangurus,dc=com

User group 'cn=locals,cn=users,dc=pangurus,dc=com' does not
exist or does not have members
```

The preceding command means no users have been added yet to the group. In this case, I only just added new users, but group mapping has not refreshed yet. We can force this by executing the following command:

```
reaper@LABFW> debug user-id refresh group-mapping all

group mapping 'GroupMapping' in vsys1 is marked for refresh.
```

And now users will show up when I query the group:

```
reaper@LABFW> show user group name
cn=locals,cn=users,dc=pangurus,dc=com

short name:  pangurus\locals
source type: ldap
source:      GroupMapping

[1     ] pangurus\reaper
[2     ] pangurus\tom
```

In the preceding output, we can see the `Group Mapping` usernames are identical to the user-ID usernames. This ensures there can be a positive match when parsing security rules for a source user against an allowed user group, for example. If the usernames do not match (one uses a slash, the other an @) you should tend to that first. In most cases, setting the **netbios User Domain** in the group mapping profile will help in correcting that issue as the UPN username gets overwritten with `netbios\domain`.

The firewall maintains a domain map for internal purposes and in a multi-domain forest, or a firewall that's been around for a while, it's possible that the firewall at one point learned the `FQDN` domain instead of `netbios`. This would manifest itself in users inexplicably being *stuck* in user-ID as UPN usernames (*user@domain*).

To verify this, use the following command:

```
reaper@LABFW> debug user-id dump domain-map

pangurus.com                                             : pangurus
 vsys1 dc=pangurus,dc=com
```

In the preceding example, the domain is registered under its `netbios` name. If you notice deviations, you can clear the domain map to relearn all domains:

```
reaper@LABFW> debug user-id clear domain-map
```

After clearing the domain map, make sure to refresh group mapping:

```
reaper@LABFW> debug user-id dump domain-map

reaper@LABFW> debug user-id refresh group-mapping all

group mapping 'GroupMapping' in vsys1 is marked for refresh.

reaper@LABFW> debug user-id dump domain-map

pangurus.com                                             : pangurus
 vsys1 dc=pangurus,dc=com
```

Now that we've made sure group mapping is working properly, we can move on to using group mapping for credential detection.

Using group mapping for credential detection

Before you proceed with this step, make sure you enabled SSL/TLS decryption, created a **Group Mapping** profile, and have a security rule with a URL filtering security profile set. Open **URL Filtering Profile** in **Objects** > **Security Profiles** > **URL Filtering** and access the **User Credential Detection** tab. Set the detection method to `Use Group Mapping`. An additional field will appear called **Group Mapping Settings**. The drop-down menu will show all the configured Group Mapping profiles, of which you can select one as illustrated in *Figure 6.21*:

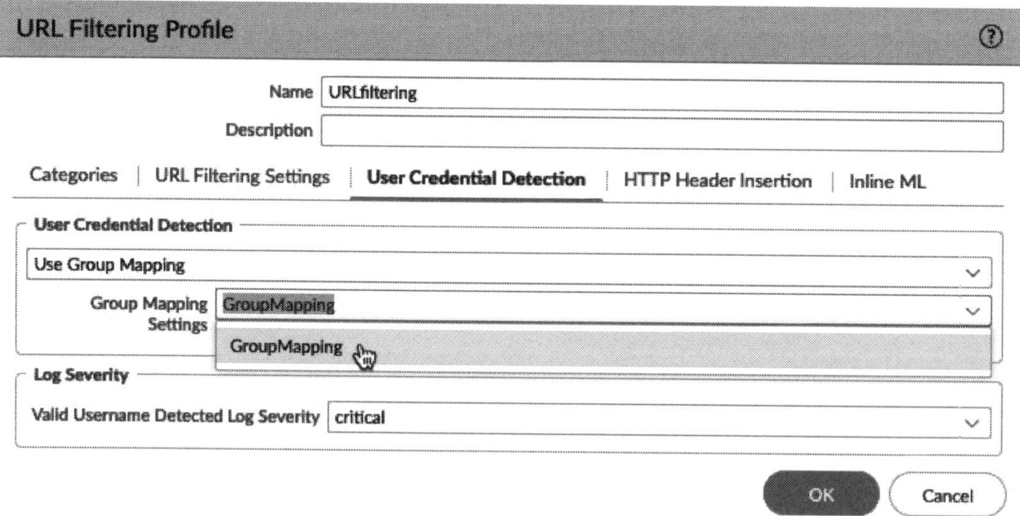

Figure 6.21 – Use Group Mapping User Credential Detection

All usernames collected via this Group Mapping profile will be used to match **User Credential Detection**. This means that where **Use IP User Mapping** could only be used to match the current user-to-IP-mapped username to a website submission, now multiple credentials can be intercepted from a single user, closing the gap for users logging on with one credential and submitting a secondary credential to a website. The drawback is that this method only matches the username and does not inspect the domain used to log in. This can lead to false positives when the username matches a private username, as illustrated in *Figure 6.22*:

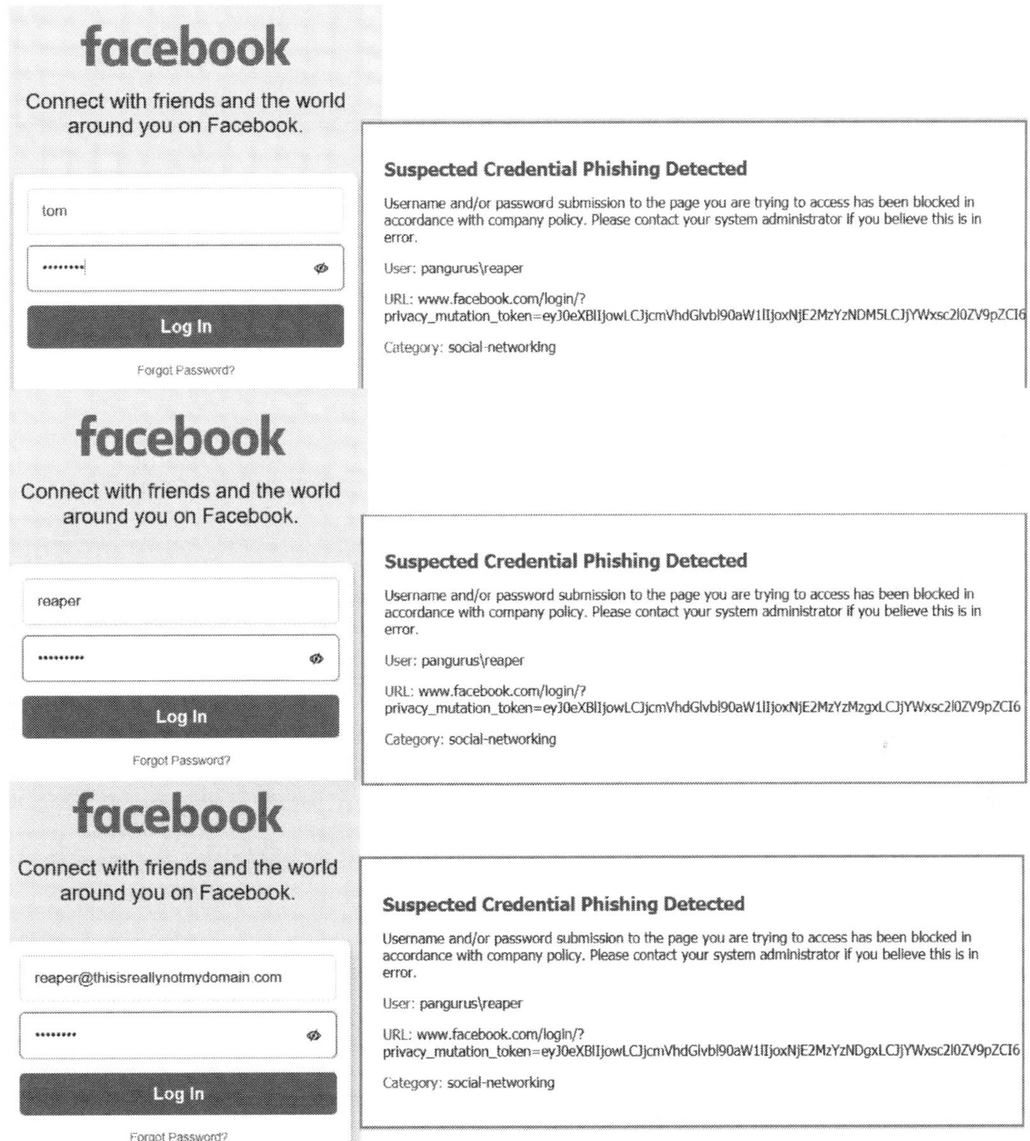

Figure 6.22 – User credential detection including a false positive

The last method checks both the username and password.

Using domain credential filter

Domain credential filter will check for a corporate username and the associated password: the firewall can check if the password entered on a website matches the actual password in a user's company account.

There are a few requirements to make this work: the Windows-based user-ID agent needs to be installed on an **RODC** and the user-ID credential service add-on needs to be added.

> **Important note**
>
> At this time, Windows Server 2012 or 2016 is recommended. 2019 is not yet supported.

The firewall also needs to be set up with traditional user-to-IP mapping, but this can be achieved by any of the user mapping methods. We already set up agentless User-IP mapping in a previous step, but an additional user-ID agent, Captive Portal or GlobalProtect, can be used instead or as well (a minimum of two agents is recommended for redundancy).

First, go into the support portal at `https://support.paloaltonetworks.com` and access **Software Updates**. Use the dropdown to find the **User Identification Agent** downloads and download both the `UaInstall` and `UaCredInstall` packages:

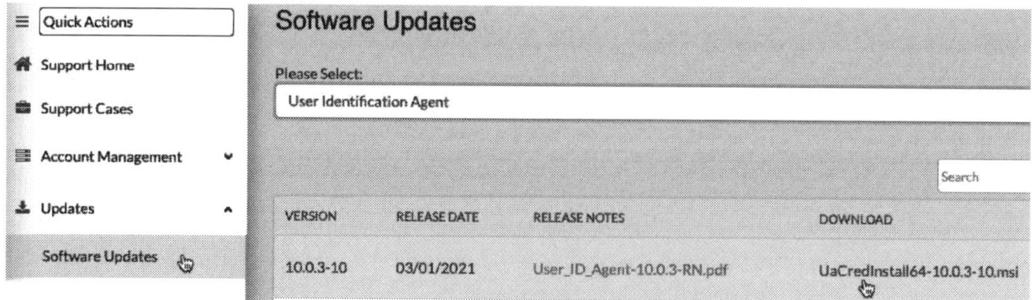

Figure 6.23 – Downloading the UID agent packages

Next, install the `UaInstall` package first, then install `UaCredInstall`.

Once both have been installed, configure the UserID agent. In the **Start** menu, find **Palo Alto Networks** and open **User-ID Agent**. In **Setup**, click **Edit** and fill out the required tabs:

- In **Authentication**, set an account that has appropriate privileges to run as a service and interact with Active Directory (server operator, Event Log Reader, Distributed COM User, and so on).

- In **Server Monitor**, disable **Security Log Monitor**, as we will not be using this User-ID agent for mapping users to IPs.
- In **Client Probing**, disable probing.
- In **Cache**, leave everything as the default.
- In **Agent Service**, verify the port the User-ID agent is listening to as this port will need to be added to the firewall later.
- The configuration should look similar to *Figure 6.24*:

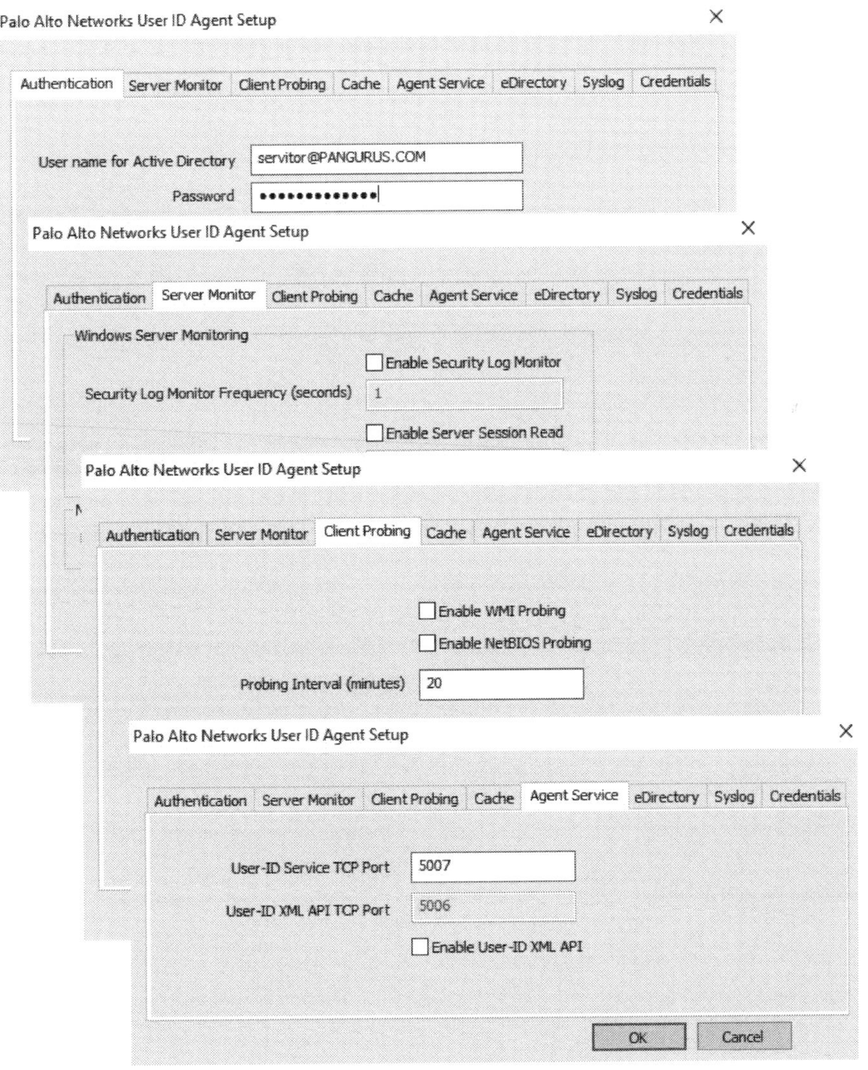

Figure 6.24 – Configuring the User-ID Agent

If the credential add-on was installed properly, the **Credentials** tab will appear. Make sure `Import from UserID Credential Agent` is enabled as this will enable the agent to import the bloom filter (bloom filters are a compact data structure that allow the firewall to quickly check whether an element is a member of a set of elements, that is, if a username and password hash belong together). A group DN can be added to filter which security group is included in the credential detection:

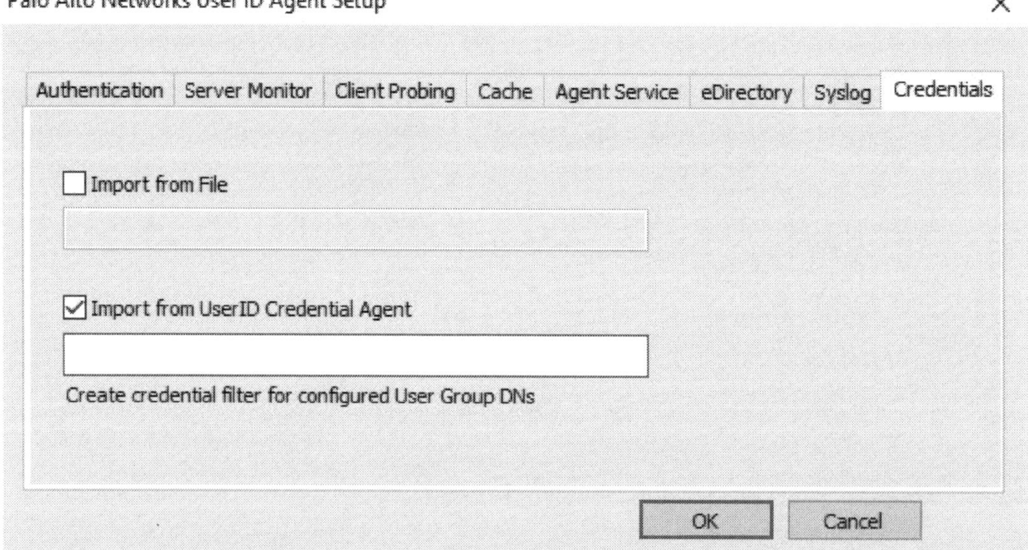

Figure 6.25 – Import from UserID credential agent

Next, in the **Discovery** tab, click **Discover** to find the **domain controllers**. If this action does not find any domain controllers, ensure the server is properly set up with internal DNS servers and has been joined to the domain. Add excluded and included networks as needed:

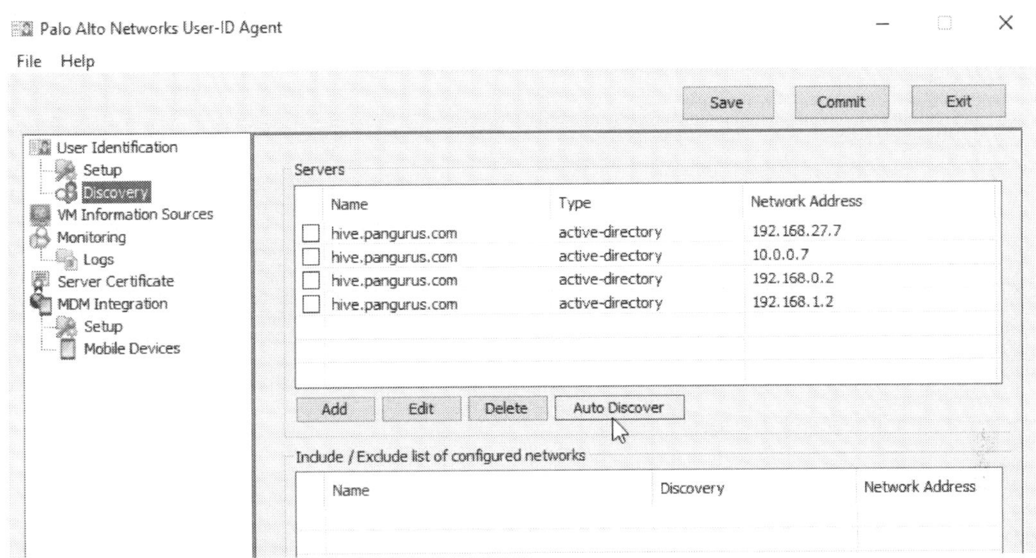

Figure 6.26 – Domain auto discovery

Make sure both services are running and the **Log On As** attribute is set as the appropriate service account: access the Windows `services.msc` and look for **User-ID Agent** and **User-ID Credential Agent**:

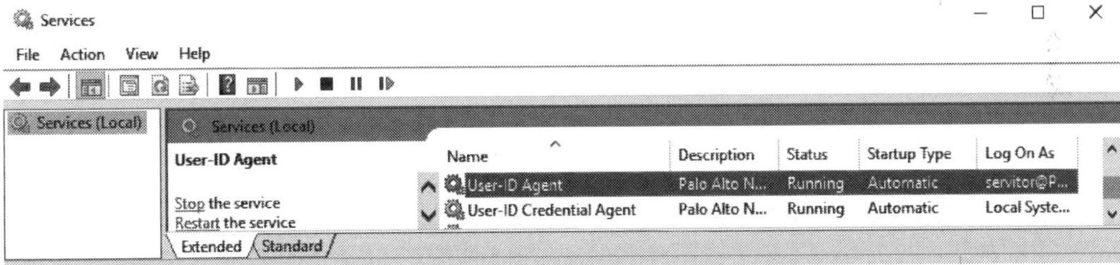

Figure 6.27 – Verify if services are running

The service account used for the UID agent *must be a local administrator account.* Administrator access can be set individually on an RODC (without promoting an account to administrator across the whole domain) by merit of **Administrator Role Separation** (**ARS**) on the RODC. The credential agent should be set as a local system account.

You can promote the service account by running Command Prompt as administrator and executing the following command:

```
dsmgmt "local roles" "add <serviceaccount> administrators"
```

```
C:\Users\Administrator.PANGURUS>dsmgmt "local roles" "add
servitor administrators"
```

```
dsmgmt: local roles
local roles: add servitor administrators
Successfully updated local role.
local roles:
local roles: quit
dsmgmt: quit
```

The next part is very important: All users that should have their credentials reinforced must be in the **Allowed RODC Password Replication Group** you can see in *Figure 6.27* to ensure the credentials are forwarded to the RODC, where the credential detection agent can pick them up and put them in the bloom filter. This group can be found in **Active Directory Users and Computers** > **Domain** > **Users**. Individual users or user groups can be added to the **Members** tab:

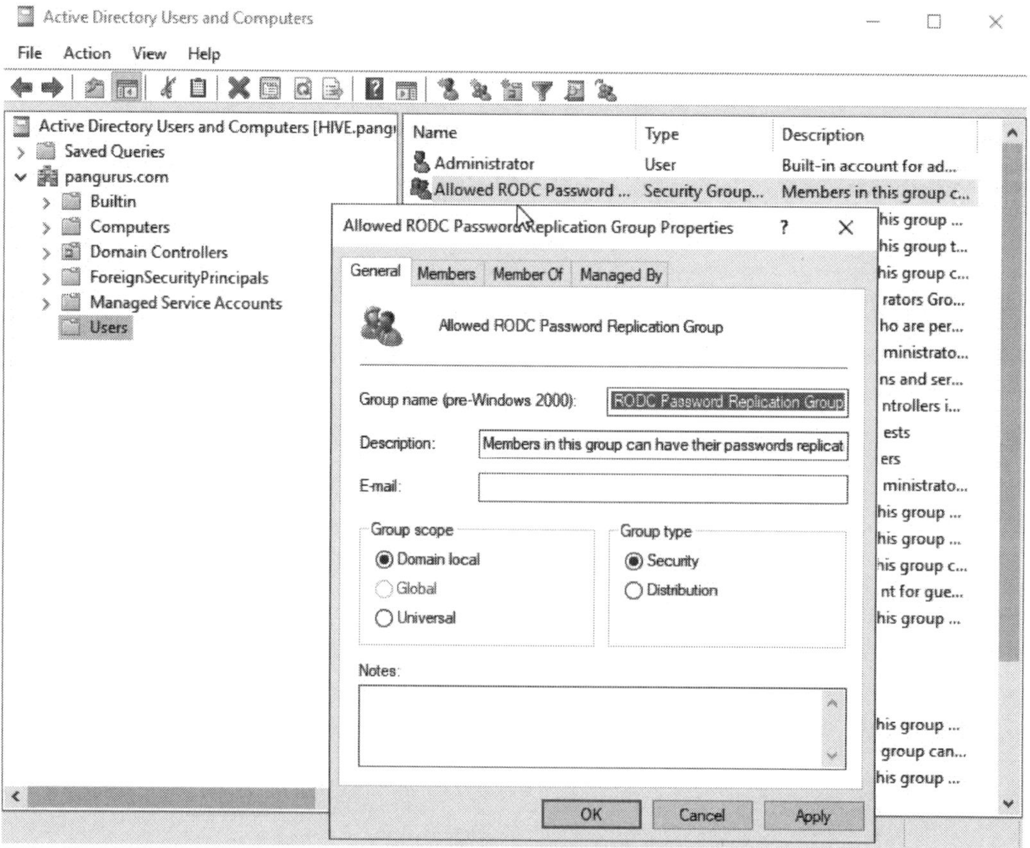

Figure 6.28 – Allowed RODC password replication group

There is also a **Denied RODC Password Replication Group**. Ensure none of the expected users are members of this group.

To add the agent to the firewall for enforcement, go to **Device** > **Data Redistribution** > **Agents** and add a new Agent:

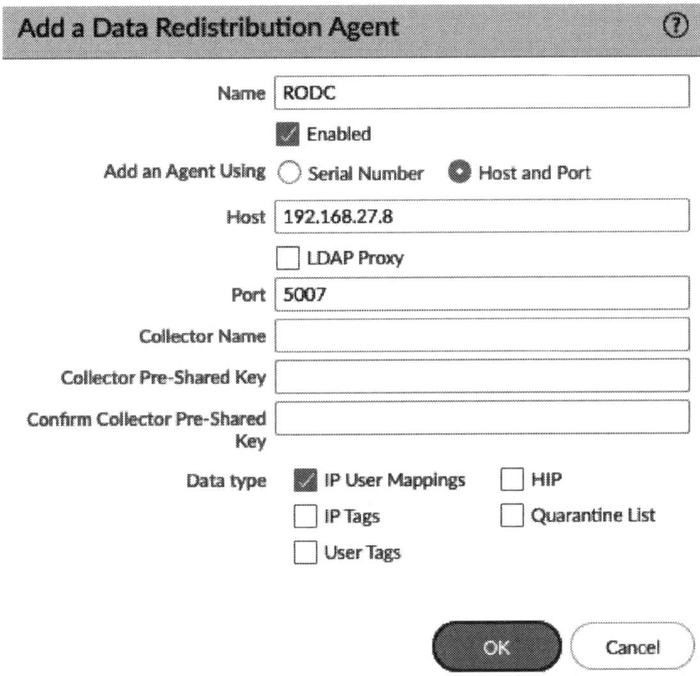

Figure 6.29 – Adding the user-ID agent

Lastly, set the **URL Filtering Profile User Credential Detection** to **Use Domain Credential Filter** as illustrated in *Figure 6.30* and commit to start using domain credential filter:

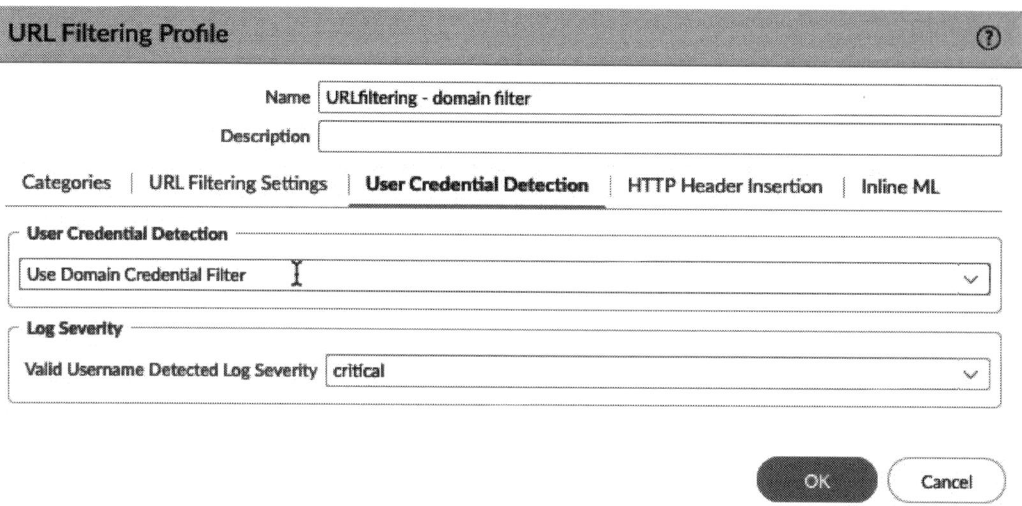

Figure 6.30 – URL filtering profile for domain credential filter

The firewall is now able to differentiate between a corporate username with a matching password and a username that matches a corporate credential but uses a different password, as you can see illustrated in *Figure 6.31*. The top login was attempted with the same username and password as my Active Directory user. The bottom login was done with the same username, but a different password:

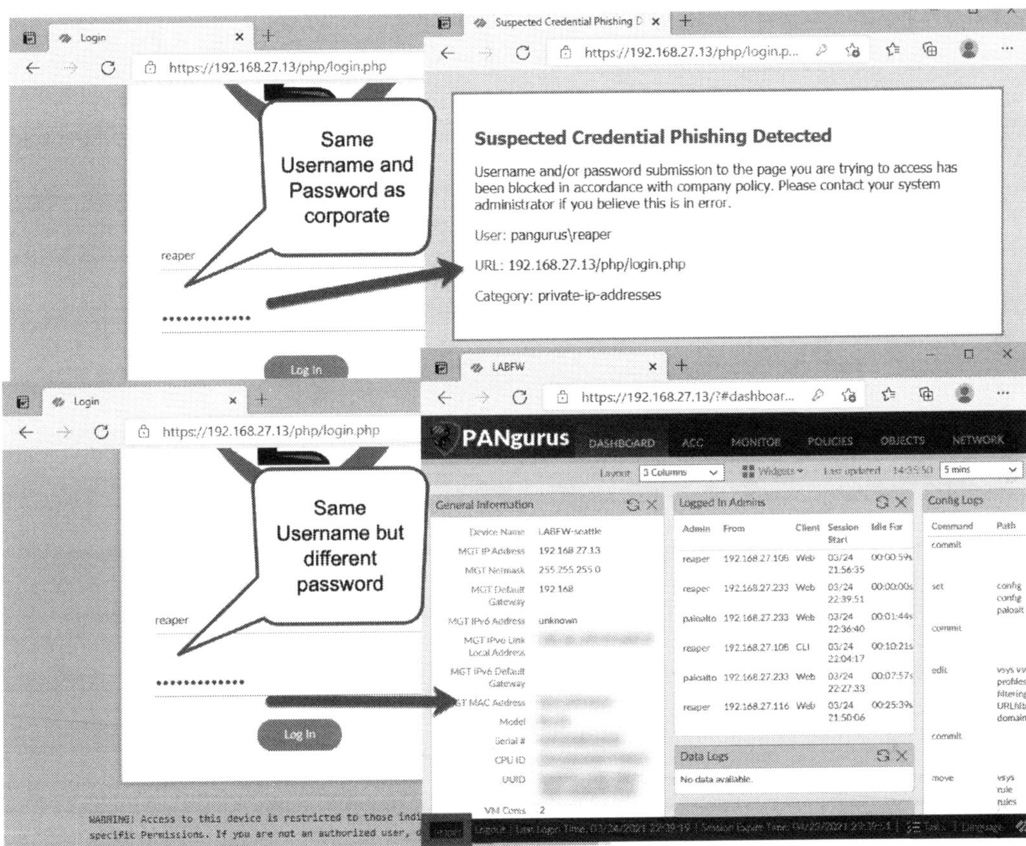

Figure 6.31 – User credential detection matching the corporate username and password

To verify that everything is working, and to troubleshoot any issues while setting up domain credential filter, we'll look at some useful commands.

Troubleshoot domain credential filter

There are quite a few gotchas while setting up Domain Credential Filter as the functionality depends on the RODC working as expected. The credential filtering statistics can be checked with the following command: `show user credential-filter statistics`.

As shown in *Figure 6.32*, there are indicators to show the following:

- If **GM (Group Mapping)** or **BF (Bloom Filter)** is configured
- How long ago the **DP (data plane)** was last updated
- How long it is since the last time the credential agent was consulted

- The number of credentials loaded
- The digest of the currently installed bloom filter:

```
reaper@LABFW> show user credential-filter statistics

Configuration       Delete Pending       Last DP Pushed (sec)       Last change check (sec)
GM        BF        GM        BF         GM          BF
------------------------------------------------------------------------------------------
No        Yes       No        No         88792       4551          37

VSYS ID  Group Mapping    Domain Credential
         Usernames        Credentials  Size (KB)  Digest
------------------------------------------------------------------------------------------
1        2                7            2          f4f28fe3485ba0aac3e6d57bda5540b4
```

Figure 6.32 – Show user credential-filter statistics

The command you can see in *Figure 6.33* can be used to check the user-ID agent state. At the bottom of the output, there is information regarding the credential enforcement and bloom filter: `show user user-id-agent state <agent name>`:

```
reaper@LABFW> show user user-id-agent state RODC

Agent: RODC(vsys: vsys1) Host: 192.168.27.9(192.168.27.9):5007
        Status                                            : conn:idle
        Version                                           : 0x5
        SSL config                                        : Default certificate
        num of connection tried                           : 1
        num of connection succeeded                       : 1
        num of connection failed                          : 0
        num of status msgs rcvd                           : 1161
        num of request of status msgs sent                : 1161
        num of request of ip mapping msgs sent            : 0
        num of request of new ip mapping msgs sent        : 0
        num of request of all ip mapping msgs sent        : 1
        num of user ip mapping msgs rcvd                  : 16
        num of ip msgs rcvd but failed to proc            : 0
        num of user ip mapping add entries rcvd           : 22
        num of user ip mapping del entries rcvd           : 4
        num of bloomfilter requests sent                  : 4
        num of bloomfilter response received              : 4
        num of bloomfilter response failed to proc        : 0
        num of bloomfilter resize requests sent           : 0
        Last heard(seconds ago)                           : 4
          Job ID                                          : 0
          Sent messages                                   : 1167
          Rcvd messages                                   : 1182
          Rcvd rate(msgs/s)                               : 0
          Rcvd peak rate(msgs/s)                          : 1
          Lost messages                                   : 0
          Failed to send messages                         : 0
          Failed to enqueue messages                      : 0
          Queued sending msgs with priority 0             : 0
          Queued sending msgs with priority 1             : 0
          Queued rcvring msgs with priority 0             : 0
        Credential Enforcement Status : In Sync
          Last BF digest received(seconds ago)            : 4
          Last BF request sent(seconds ago)               : 5129
          Last BF updated(seconds ago)                    : 5129
          Current BF digest : f4f28fe3485ba0aac3e6d57bda5540b4

reaper@LABFW>
```

Figure 6.33 – Output of show user user-id-agent state

All logs regarding the credential connection with the user-id agent will be written to `useridd.log`.

They can be read using the following command: `less mp-log useridd.log`.

On the RODC, there are a few things you can check as well to make sure everything is set up properly. To verify if the service account (that is used by the user-id agent service) is set up as local admin, run the following command:

```
C:\Users\Administrator.PANGURUS>dsmgmt
dsmgmt: local roles
local roles: show role administrators
        PANGURUS\servitor
local roles:
```

You can also see which usernames' credentials have been cached on the RODC. This is important as the cached credentials are used to create the bloom filter. Missing users will not be picked up in **User Credential Enforcement** on the firewall:

```
C:\Users\>repadmin /prp view RODC16 reveal
Reveal List (msDS-RevealedList):
RODC "CN=RODC16,OU=Domain Controllers,DC=pangurus,DC=com":
CN=paloalto,CN=Users,DC=pangurus,DC=com
CN=reaper,CN=Users,DC=pangurus,DC=com
CN=servitor,CN=Users,DC=pangurus,DC=com
CN=Tom,CN=Users,DC=pangurus,DC=com
CN=RODC16,OU=Domain Controllers,DC=pangurus,DC=com
CN=krbtgt_21772,CN=Users,DC=pangurus,DC=com
CN=cthulhu,CN=Users,DC=pangurus,DC=com
```

The `UaCredDebug.log` log file in `C:\Program Files\Palo Alto Networks\User-ID Credential Agent` contains all the logs relating to the credential agent. Error messages here can be used to track down issues:

```
C:\Program Files\Palo Alto Networks\User-ID Credential
Agent>more UaCredDebug.log
03/24/21 15:10:32:971 [ Info  667]: Sent BF to UaService.
ac9e9ed1166ad01280b8be8d1bacf4d1
03/24/21 15:15:33:665 [ Info  667]: Sent BF to UaService.
f4f28fe3485ba0aac3e6d57bda5540b4
```

On the domain controller, you may need to set some attributes through **Active Directory Users and Computers** (**ADUC**):

1. Access **Domain Controllers** and right-click on **RODC**.
2. In **Managed By**, set the account that is the administrator on the RODC. I set this to the same as the user-ID Agent as this RODC is used solely for this purpose.
3. In **Password Replication Policy**, carefully review all the groups that have been set to **Allow** or **Deny**, ensuring the right users are being picked up. Add or delete groups manually if needed:

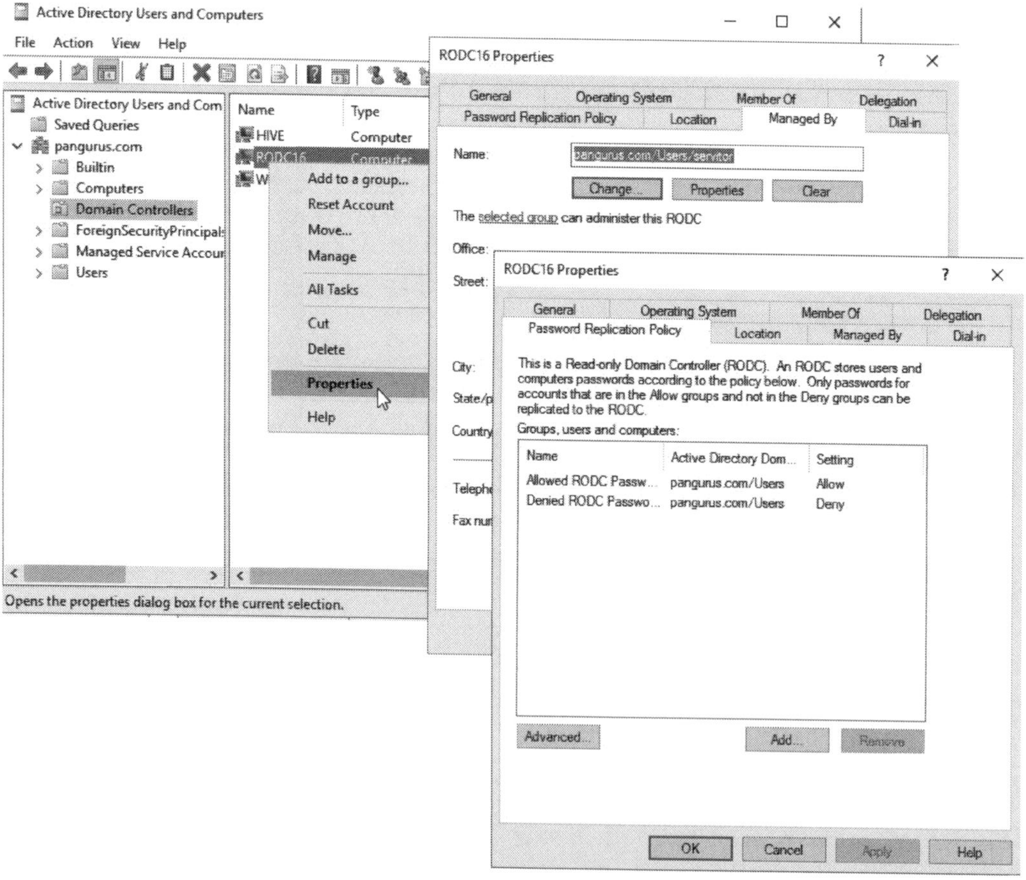

Figure 6.34 – Tweaking the RODC password replication policy

With this knowledge, you are now able to protect your organization from both phishing attacks and users reusing their corporate passwords on external sites.

All logs regarding the credential connection with the user-ID agent will be written to `useridd.log`.

They can be read using the following command: `less mp-log useridd.log`.

On the RODC, there are a few things you can check as well to make sure everything is set up properly. To verify if the service account (that is used by the user-ID agent service) is set up as local admin, run the following command:

```
C:\Users\Administrator.PANGURUS>dsmgmt
dsmgmt: local roles
local roles: show role administrators
        PANGURUS\servitor
local roles:
```

You can also see which usernames' credentials have been cached on the RODC. This is important as the cached credentials are used to create the bloom filter. Missing users will not be picked up in user credential enforcement on the firewall:

```
C:\Users\>repadmin /prp view RODC16 reveal
Reveal List (msDS-RevealedList):
RODC "CN=RODC16,OU=Domain Controllers,DC=pangurus,DC=com":
CN=paloalto,CN=Users,DC=pangurus,DC=com
CN=reaper,CN=Users,DC=pangurus,DC=Yom
CN=servitor,CN=Users,DC=pangurus,DC=com
CN=Tom,CN=Users,DC=pangurus,DC=com
CN=RODC16,OU=Domain Controllers,DC=pangurus,DC=com
CN=krbtgt_21772,CN=Users,DC=pangurus,DC=com
CN=cthulhu,CN=Users,DC=pangurus,DC=com
```

The `UaCredDebug.log` log file in `C:\Program Files\Palo Alto Networks\User-ID Credential Agent` contains all the logs relating to the credential agent. Error messages here can be used to track down issues:

```
C:\Program Files\Palo Alto Networks\User-ID Credential
Agent>more UaCredDebug.log
03/24/21 15:10:32:971 [ Info  667]: Sent BF to UaService.
ac9e9ed1166ad01280b8be8d1bacf4d1
03/24/21 15:15:33:665 [ Info  667]: Sent BF to UaService.
f4f28fe3485ba0aac3e6d57bda5540b4
```

On the domain controller you may need to set some attributes through **Active Directory Users and Computers** (**ADUC**):

- Access **Domain Controllers** and right-click the **RODC computer name** and open the **Properties**.
- In **Managed By**, set the account that is the administrator on the RODC, I set this to the same as the user-ID Agent as this RODC is used solely for this purpose.
- In **Password Replication Policy**, carefully review all the groups that have been set to **Allow** or **Deny** to ensure the right users are being picked up. Add or delete groups manually if needed:

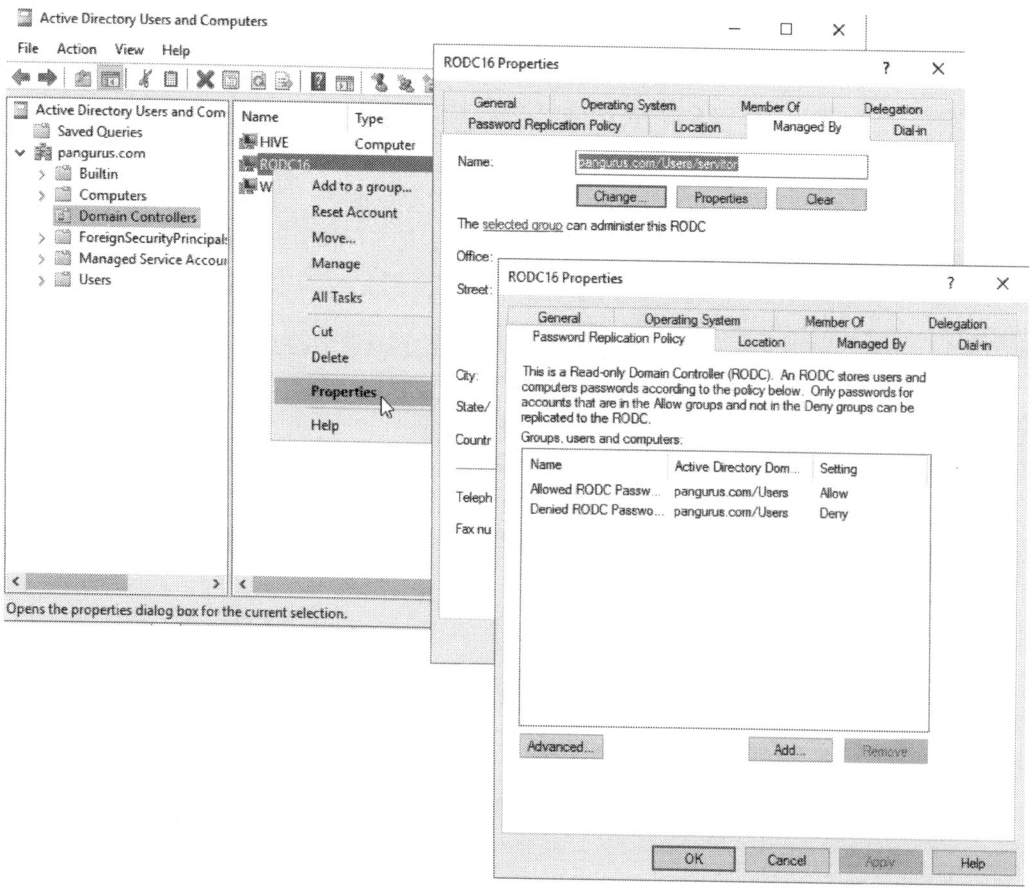

Figure 6.35 – Tweaking the RODC password replication policy

With this knowledge, you are now able to protect your organization from both phishing attacks and users reusing their corporate passwords on external sites.

Summary

In this chapter, you learned to prevent users from sharing corporate credentials with external parties either by reusing their corporate username and password on a web resource that was not approved for that use (for example, social media) or by phishing attacks that try to get users to submit their credentials on a malicious site.

In the next chapter, we will take a practical approach to troubleshooting and we will review which steps are needed to find the root cause of some common issues.

7
Practical Troubleshooting and Best Practices Tools

In this chapter, we will look into troubleshooting various issues that can arise during daily operation or while configuring the firewall. We will learn how to diagnose issues and which logical order of troubleshooting steps will lead to a solution or a better understanding of the cause of the problem.

In this chapter, we're going to cover the following main topics:

- Troubleshooting **User-ID**
- Troubleshooting **Network Address Translation** (NAT)
- The **Best Practice Assessment** (BPA) tool

Technical requirements

In this chapter, we will be covering practical examples of troubleshooting, so a functioning lab where issues can be reproduced to better acquaint yourself with the commands or concepts shown in each section will greatly help the learning process.

Check out the following link to see the Code in Action video: `https://bit.ly/3oQKyY0`

Troubleshooting User-ID

User-ID is the mechanism used to match a user by their username to an **Internet Protocol (IP)** address they are using on their mobile device, laptop, kiosk, or any other device or appliance they may be able to log on to. Additionally, by mapping a person by their username, membership to certain groups can be used to allow or block the user's access to resources.

There are many ways to map users to an IP address and there are many ways mapping may fail or behave unexpectedly. Luckily, troubleshooting is usually a case of deduction.

Users are not being mapped

The first thing we should verify when troubleshooting User-ID issues is that user-to-IP mappings actually exist. We can check for existing mappings with the following command:

```
reaper@PANgurus> show user ip-user-mapping all

IP  Vsys From User IdleTimeout(s) MaxTimeout(s)
-- ----- ---- ---- -------------- -------------
Total: 0 users
```

There are several reasons why mapping may not get populated. First, check if a **User-ID agent** has been configured and is in a connected state in **Device** > **Data Redistribution** > **Agents**, or an agentless **Server Monitoring** profile has been configured and shows as **Connected** in **DEVICE** > **User Identification** > **User Mapping**, as shown in the following screenshot:

User Mapping
Connection Security
Terminal Server Agents
Group Mapping Settings
Authentication Portal Settings
Server Monitoring
NAME
ENABLED
TYPE
NETWORK ADDRESS
STATUS
hive.pangurus.com
Microsoft Active Directory
hive.pangurus.com
Connected
Agents
Clients
Collector Settings
Include/Exclude Networks
2 items
NAME
ENABLED
HOST
PORT
LDAP PROXY
IP USER MAPPINGS
QUARANTI... LIST
USER TAGS
CONNECTED
AD
192.168.27.7
5007
yes
RODC
192.168.27.9
5007
no

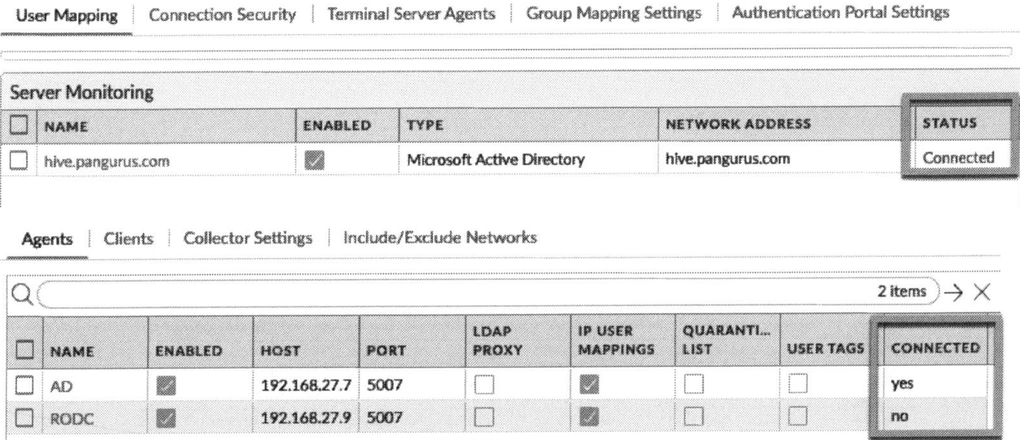

Figure 7.1 – User-ID agent and server monitoring connection state

Common issues that cause connectivity problems are an incorrect username or password, or insufficient privileges in the account configured in **Server Monitoring**. If the connection mode is set to `WMI`, an error message will indicate **Access denied**; if `WinRM` is used, a **Kerberos error** message will be shown, as illustrated in the following screenshot:

Server Monitoring
NAME
ENABLED
TYPE
NETWORK ADDRESS
STATUS
ActiveDirectory
Microsoft Active Directory
hive.pangurus.com
Kerberos error
Server Monitoring
NAME
ENABLED
TYPE
NETWORK ADDRESS
STATUS
ActiveDirectory
Microsoft Active Directory
hive.pangurus.com
Access denied

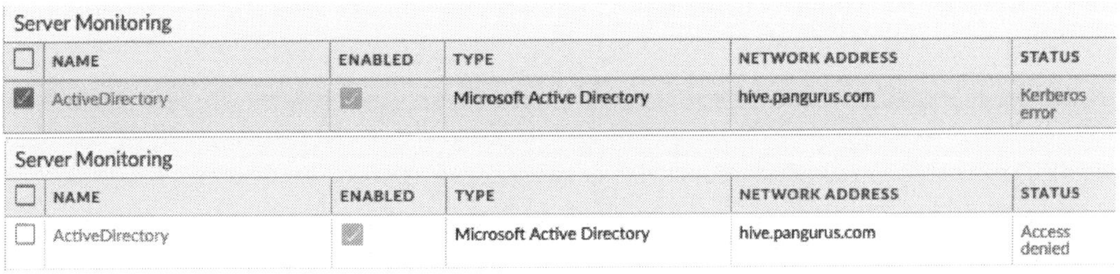

Figure 7.2 – Credential issue in server monitoring

If the connection is blocked by a firewall rule, for example, the **WMI** error message will be **Not connected**, while **WinRM** will still return **Kerberos error**. User-ID agents will simply show **yes** or **no**, as shown in the following screenshot:

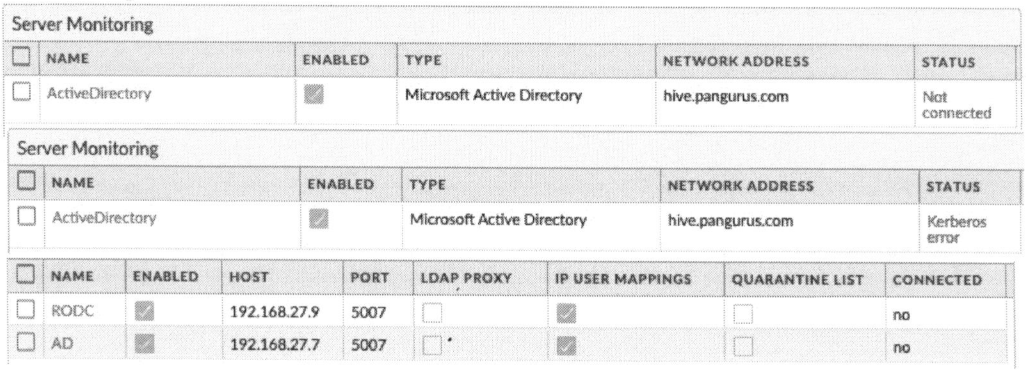

Server Monitoring

NAME	ENABLED	TYPE	NETWORK ADDRESS	STATUS
ActiveDirectory	☑	Microsoft Active Directory	hive.pangurus.com	Not connected

Server Monitoring

NAME	ENABLED	TYPE	NETWORK ADDRESS	STATUS
ActiveDirectory	☑	Microsoft Active Directory	hive.pangurus.com	Kerberos error

NAME	ENABLED	HOST	PORT	LDAP PROXY	IP USER MAPPINGS	QUARANTINE LIST	CONNECTED
RODC	☑	192.168.27.9	5007	☐	☑	☐	no
AD	☑	192.168.27.7	5007	☐	☑	☐	no

Figure 7.3 – Connection blocked

To troubleshoot connectivity issues, we can check logs in `useridd.log` to see if any indication is given why a connection is failing.

The following is a failed **Kerberos** connection:

```
reaper@LABFW> less mp-log useridd.logq
```

```
2021-04-02 23:29:20.103 +0200 Error:  pan_user_id_krb5_init_
ticket(pan_user_id_win.c:2094): krb5 error -1765328228: Cannot
contact any KDC for realm 'PANGURUS.COM'.
```

```
2021-04-02 23:29:20.103 +0200 Warning:  pan_user_id_krb5_
set(pan_user_id_win.c:2182): failed to acquire krb5 tgt ticket
on vsys 1 for server ActiveDirectory.
```

```
2021-04-02 23:29:20.103 +0200 Error: pan_user_id_winrm_
query(pan_user_id_win.c:2710): failed to prepare winrm
connection in vsys 1, server=ActiveDirectory.
```

And the following is a denied username:

```
2021-04-02 23:29:20.103 +0200 Error:  pan_user_id_win_wmic_log_
query(pan_user_id_win.c:1669): log query for ActiveDirectory
failed: NTSTATUS: NT_STATUS_ACCESS_DENIED - Access denied
```

```
2021-04-02 23:29:20.103 +0200 Error:  pan_user_id_win_get_
error_status(pan_user_id_win.c:1340): WMIC message from server
ActiveDirectory: NTSTATUS: NT_STATUS_ACCESS_DENIED - Access
denied
```

Agents unable to connect will also leave a log entry, as follows:

```
2021-04-03 00:11:38.844 +0200 Error:  pan_user_id_agent_send_
and_recv_msgs(pan_user_id_agent.c:4050): pan_user_msgs_recv()
failed
2021-04-03 00:11:38.844 +0200 Error:  pan_user_id_agent_uia_
proc_v5(pan_user_id_uia_v5.c:1254): pan_user_id_agent_send_and_
recv_msgs() failed for AD(1)
2021-04-03 00:11:38.845 +0200 [agent AD] useridd notify dist to
reconnect
```

Another tool to help verify if connections are being created or if there are any issues with packets flowing between the **firewall** and the **Active Directory** (**AD**) **server** is `tcpdump`, which captures packets on the *management interface*. This tool is illustrated in the following code snippet:

```
reaper@LABFW> tcpdump filter "host 192.168.27.7 and port 5007"
Press Ctrl-C to stop capturing

tcpdump: listening on eth0, link-type EN10MB (Ethernet),
capture size 65535 bytes
^C12 packets captured
12 packets received by filter
0 packets dropped by kernel
```

We can then review the packet capture using the following command:

```
View-pcap mgmt.pcap
```

We can add some parameters to disable `dns` lookup and port lookup so that actual values are returned instead of friendly names, as follows:

```
reaper@LABFW> view-pcap no-dns-lookup yes no-port-lookup yes
no-timestamp yes mgmt-pcap mgmt.pcap
IP 192.168.27.13.46604 > 192.168.27.7.5007: Flags [S],
seq 2598587376, win 29200, options [mss 1460,sackOK,TS val
2802743465 ecr 0,nop,wscale 7], length 0
IP 192.168.27.7.5007 > 192.168.27.13.46604: Flags [R.], seq 0,
ack 2598587377, win 0, length 0
IP 192.168.27.13.46620 > 192.168.27.7.5007: Flags [S],
seq 2878908722, win 29200, options [mss 1460,sackOK,TS val
2802748428 ecr 0,nop,wscale 7], length 0
```

```
IP 192.168.27.7.5007 > 192.168.27.13.46620: Flags [R.], seq 0,
ack 2878908723, win 0, length 0
IP 192.168.27.13.46628 > 192.168.27.7.5007: Flags [S], seq
27760118, win 29200, options [mss 1460,sackOK,TS val 2802753389
ecr 0,nop,wscale 7], length 0
IP 192.168.27.7.5007 > 192.168.27.13.46628: Flags [R.], seq 0,
ack 27760119, win 0, length 0
IP 192.168.27.13.46654 > 192.168.27.7.5007: Flags [S],
seq 2417573158, win 29200, options [mss 1460,sackOK,TS val
2802758399 ecr 0,nop,wscale 7], length 0
IP 192.168.27.7.5007 > 192.168.27.13.46654: Flags [R.], seq 0,
ack 2417573159, win 0, length 0
IP 192.168.27.13.46698 > 192.168.27.7.5007: Flags [S],
seq 3339357551, win 29200, options [mss 1460,sackOK,TS val
2802763441 ecr 0,nop,wscale 7], length 0
IP 192.168.27.7.5007 > 192.168.27.13.46698: Flags [R.], seq 0,
ack 3339357552, win 0, length 0
IP 192.168.27.13.46722 > 192.168.27.7.5007: Flags [S],
seq 553541829, win 29200, options [mss 1460,sackOK,TS val
2802768391 ecr 0,nop,wscale 7], length 0
IP 192.168.27.7.5007 > 192.168.27.13.46722: Flags [R.], seq 0,
ack 553541830, win 0, length 0
```

You may have noticed in the preceding packet capture output that there are reply packets coming back from the **Active Directory**: this can be an indication that **Windows Firewall** is blocking the connection or that the **User-ID service** is not running.

Once we've been able to establish a connection but still are not seeing mapped users, make sure **Security Settings** > **Local Policies** > **Audit logon events** has been set to **Success** (this is set to **No auditing** by default) in the AD **Local Security Policy**, as shown in the following screenshot:

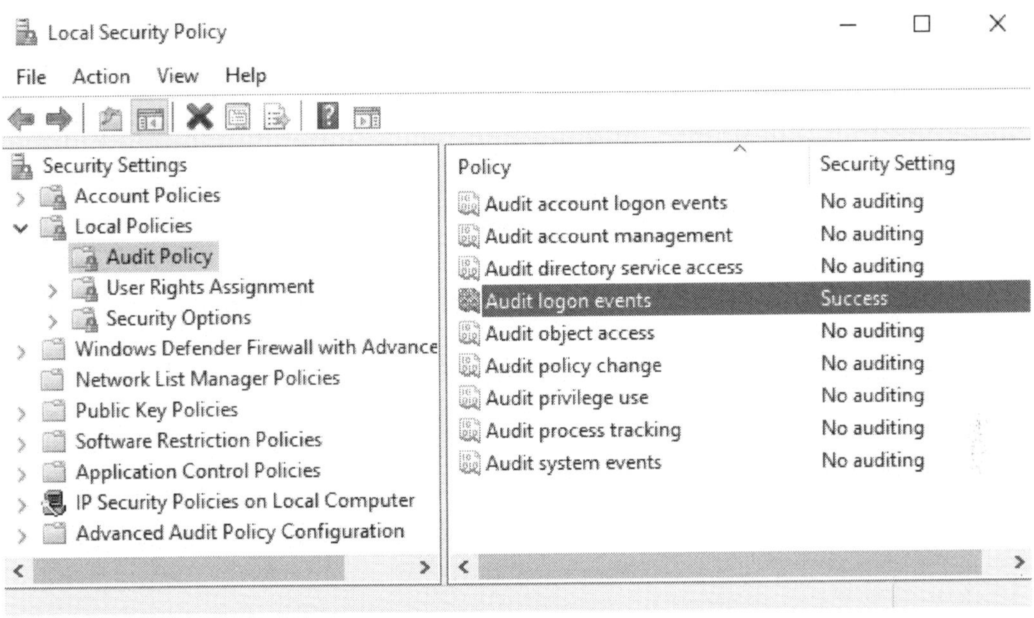

Figure 7.4 – Local Security Policy audit policy

In case there's a User-ID agent, check if it is able to pick up user mappings: it may take a while for any users to populate. When the agent starts, it will read the 50,000 latest event logs in an attempt to find logon events, but in lieu of older log events it needs to wait for new events to occur before it can pick up new mappings. Once new users are detected, they will start showing up in **Monitoring**, as illustrated in the following screenshot:

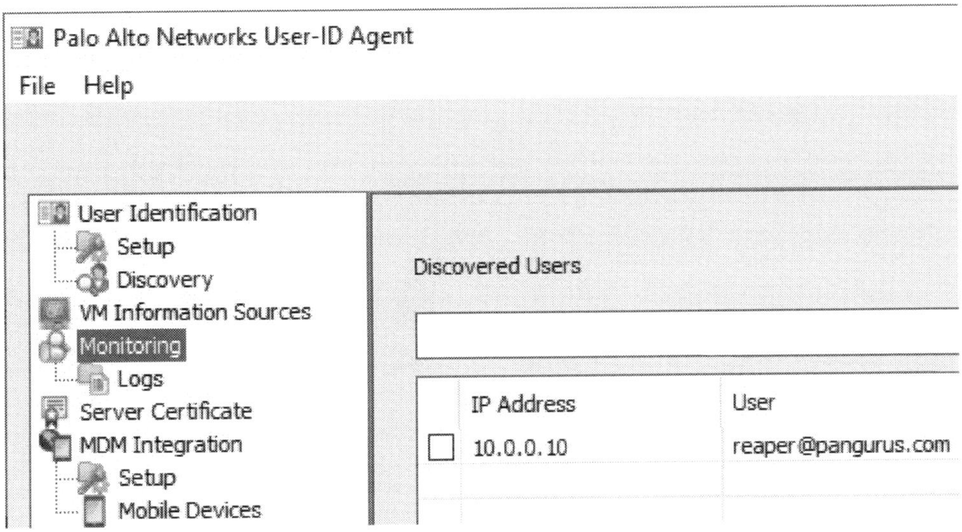

Figure 7.5 – Monitoring with a mapped user

If users are still not showing up, make sure **Enable User Identification** is enabled in **Network** > **Zones** > **<zone name>**.

Set the internal zones in a similar way to how they appear in the following screenshot:

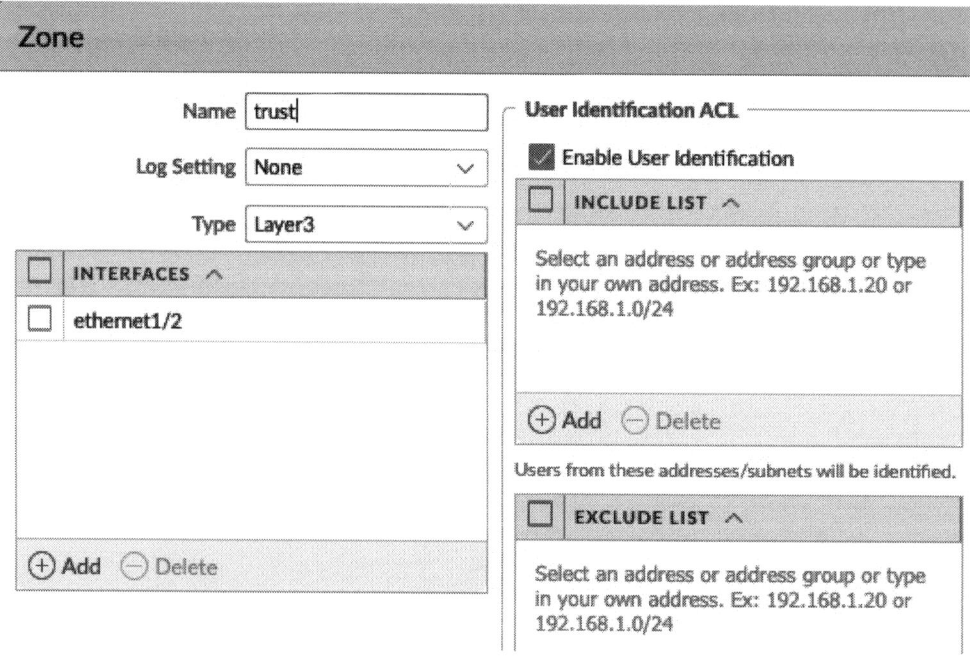

Figure 7.6 – User-ID enabled zone

> **Important note**
>
> Do *not* enable **User Identification** on **Untrust/outside** zones: the firewall will query the User-ID agent for each source IP it does not have a mapping for. Mapping an outside zone could cause a torrent of unresolvable requests. If User-IP mapping is needed on a zone where only a subset of the connected subnets has User-IP information, add these subnets to **INCLUDE LIST** or use **EXCLUDE LIST** to exclude some subnets from User-ID.

The individual zones can contain include and exclude lists, but the User-ID configuration also has **Include/Exclude Networks** options. As illustrated in the following screenshot, the agentless configuration can be found in **Device** > **User Identification** > **User Mapping** > **Include/Exclude Networks**. The list is evaluated top to bottom, so an exclude at the top may override all following subnets, or an exclude at the bottom may go ignored. Enter the subnets in the proper order, or use **Custom Include/Exclude Network Sequence** to customize the order of the subnets so that they can be evaluated properly:

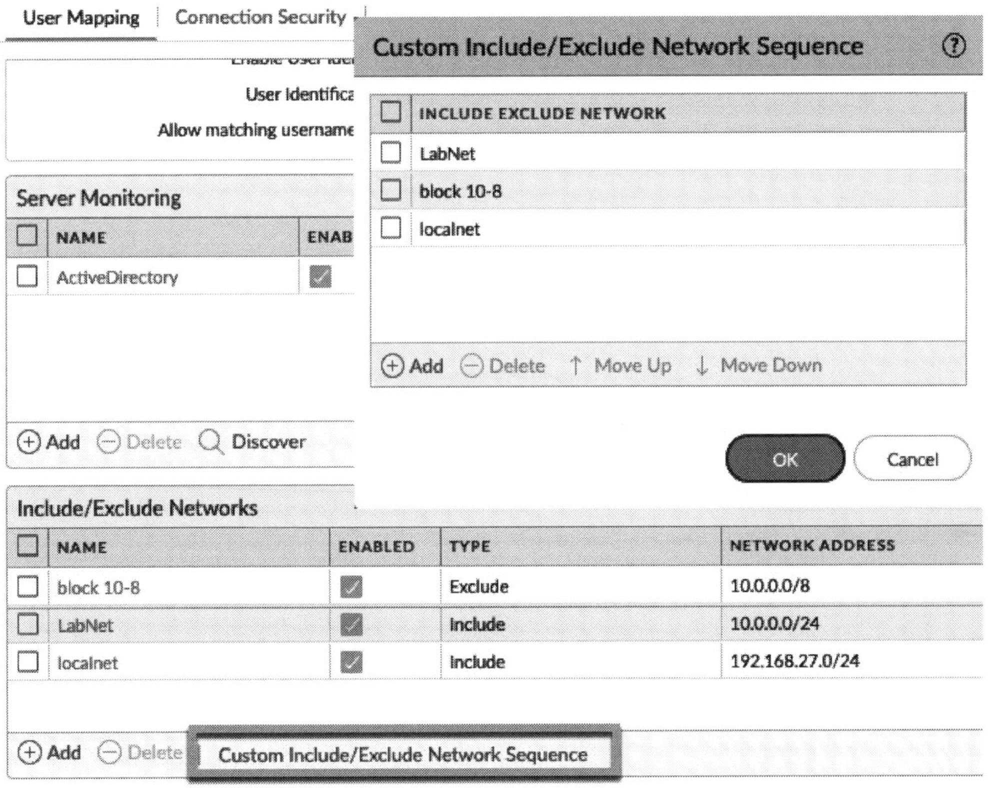

Figure 7.7 – Include/Exclude networks

The User-ID agent has these networks in the **Discovery** tab. As indicated in the following screenshot, sort the **Include** and **Exclude** networks by using the **Move Up** or **Move Down** button so that exclusions don't override inclusions:

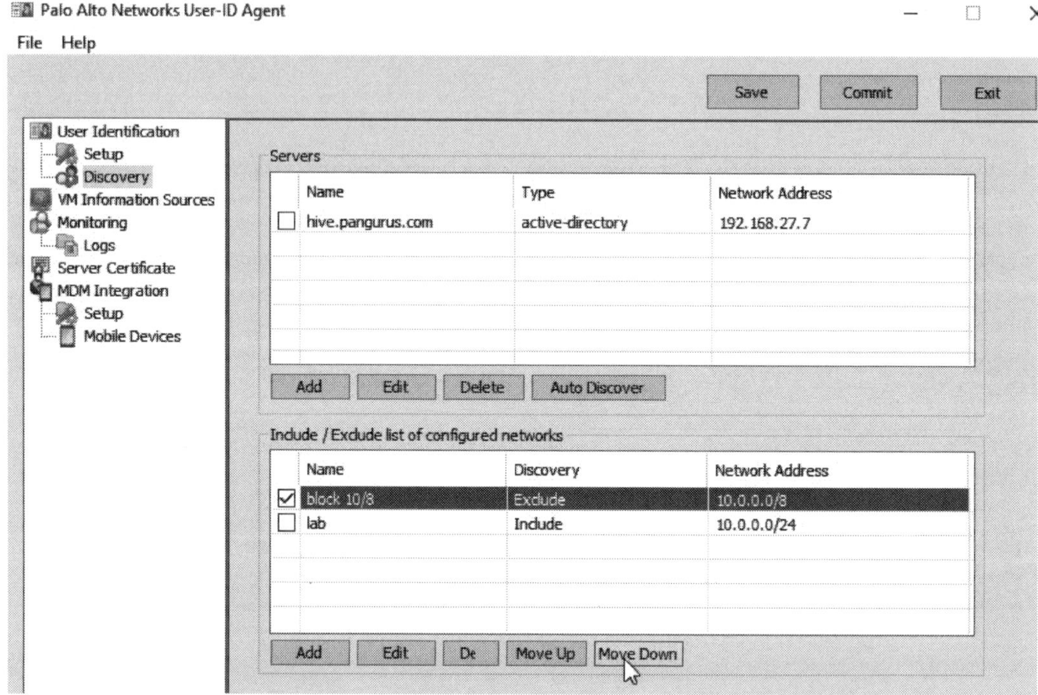

Figure 7.8 – User-ID agent Include/Exclude list of configured networks

If you followed these checks, the users should now start getting mapped.

Users are mapped briefly

Another common issue is users getting mapped but their mapping not consistently matching. First, determine whether the mapping is inconsistent because the username is being overwritten by a different user, the user's IP keeps changing, or the mapping is removed.

Users getting overwritten

If the username is overwritten by a different user, as illustrated next, the endpoint is being used to authenticate different users and the **User-ID agent** (UIA) is picking up these logon events in the **Active Directory event log**. There are a few reasons this could be expected, including the following:

- There are scripts being run with certain privileges that cause an authentication when they execute.
- The user is *actively* connecting to remote systems using different usernames to log on, such as an administrator or IT person connecting to different systems using **Remote Desktop Protocol** (**RDP**).
- Multiple users are connected to a machine running terminal services, as illustrated in the following code snippet:

```
reaper@LABFW> show user ip-user-mapping all
IP         Vsys  From  User
IdleTimeout(s) MaxTimeout(s)
--------- ----- ----- ---------------------- -----------
--- -------------
10.0.0.10 vsys1 UIA   pangurus\reaper         30389
30389
Total: 1 users
reaper@LABFW> show user ip-user-mapping all
IP         Vsys  From  User
IdleTimeout(s) MaxTimeout(s)
--------- ----- ----- ---------------------- -----------
--- -------------
10.0.0.10 vsys1 UIA   pangurus\paloalto       2694
30544
Total: 1 users
reaper@LABFW> show user ip-user-mapping all
IP         Vsys  From  User
IdleTimeout(s) MaxTimeout(s)
--------- ----- ----- ---------------------- -----------
--- -------------
10.0.0.10 vsys1 UIA   pangurus\administrator  2693
30543
Total: 1 users
```

For the first two reasons, this is expected behavior: the local machine is generating an authentication request toward the **Active Directory** sourced from the user's machine, so the User-ID agent will pick this up. If the username used for these authentications is a generic service account (`svc_logon-script`) or a specific admin account used for maintenance (`adm_userX`), these usernames can be added to an exclude list so that they are not picked up by the User-ID agent. To create an ignore list for the **User-ID agent**, a file needs to be created in `C:\Program Files (x86)\Palo Alto Networks\User-ID Agent`. The file must be named `ignore_user_list.txt` and can contain a list of all usernames that should be ignored. Each username must be placed on a new line. In most cases, the username can be added without the domain name, but multi-domain forests may require the domain be added as the `netbios` domain (`domain\user`).

> **Pay attention**
>
> When creating the `ignore_user_list.txt` file, all letters must be in lowercase. Disable **Hide extensions for known file types** in Windows Explorer - in place of 'also, pay close attention to hidden extensions in windows' as this could lead to a file being created with double `.txt` extension, which will cause the exclusions to fail. An asterisk (*) can be used as wildcard, but only as the last character of a username e.g. adm_*

For an agentless deployment on a firewall, the **Ignore User List** setting is part of the configuration and can be accessed via **Device** > **User Identification** > **User Mapping** > **Palo Alto Networks User-ID Agent Setup** > **Ignore User List**, where we can add one user per line, as shown in the following screenshot:

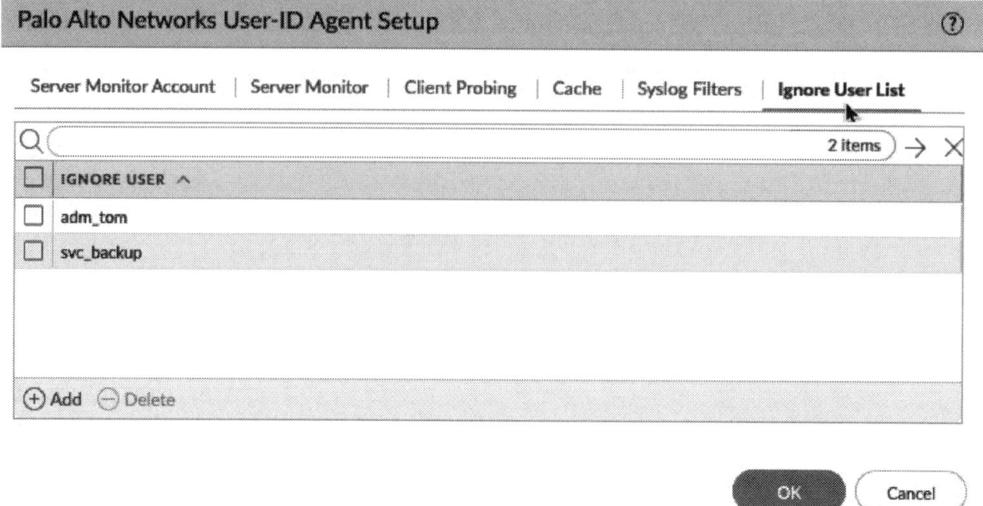

Figure 7.9 – Ignore User List

For the third reason (multiple users on the same system via terminal services), the system IP should be added to the exclusion list and the **Terminal Services Agent** needs to be installed on the host. This agent can be downloaded from `support.paloaltonetworks.com` and is able to host multiple users on the same source IP, using source ports as an identifying factor.

If the user is mapped correctly but the mapping is removed shortly thereafter, there may be several things causing this.

User mapping removed after a short time

There are a few mechanisms to ensure users don't stay mapped to an IP after they have left the network or shut down their system. These could also cause mappings to be removed before we want them to be.

The first mechanism is client probing. As illustrated in the following screenshot, both agent and agentless deployments have a probe. The agent configuration can leverage both **Windows Management Instrumentation** (**WMI**) and **Network Basic Input/Output System** (**NetBIOS**), while the agentless configuration can only perform WMI probes:

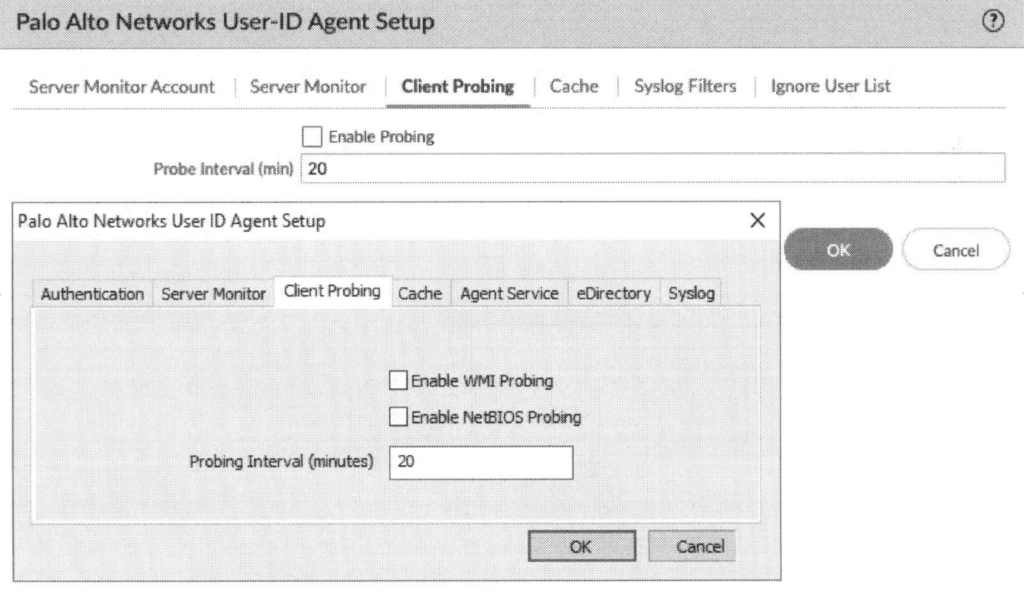

Figure 7.10 – Client Probing

The default value for probing is set to 20 minutes, which means that for any new mapping added, a probe is sent out every 20 minutes thereafter to verify if the user is still logged on to the system. In theory, this is a great mechanism to detect logged-off users and remove mappings to prevent other users snatching up a privileged IP address because it was in use by an administrator, but in practice it comes with some drawbacks. In a large and extended network, all these probes can be chatty and consume valuable resources: if the firewall receives a packet from an unmapped IP on a **User-ID enabled zone** and probing is enabled on the agent, the agent will send out a probe to perform the initial detection.

Many systems will not support NetBIOS, and WMI may be disabled or restricted by policy, which also then needs to be controlled. If this probe was not considered, it is likely many IP addresses will fail probing, and existing mappings will be removed after 20 minutes.

The second mechanism is the **Cache** setting, which appears in the same agent and agentless configuration. The default value is 45 minutes, which is a hard timeout after which the user mapping is removed if no new successful authentication event is registered in the **Active Directory event log**. If many authentication events happen throughout the day, these 45 minutes can be a valid *timeout* to remove users that appear to have left the network, but it can also lead to *false positives*: users that logged on in the morning and then no longer need to interact with **Active Directory** (a Kerberos ticket was granted for 9 hours; all tools are web-based, so there are no internal authentication events) will be removed after the **User Identification Timeout** expires and are blocked from accessing resources until a logon event occurs, as illustrated in the following screenshot:

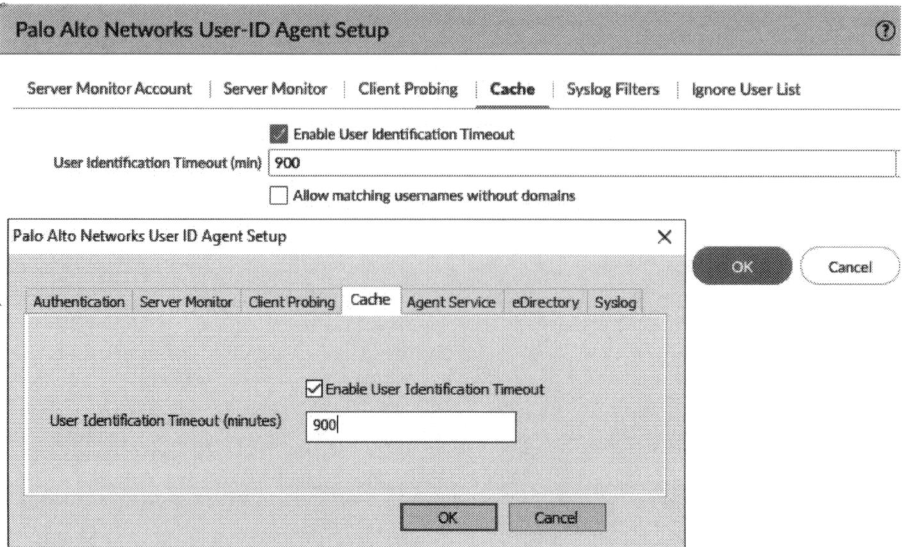

Figure 7.11 – User mapping cache

Sometimes, domains may not get normalized as expected.

Inconsistent domain in username

When a user-to-IP mapping is learned, the *user* part of the mapping will be collected with the associated user domain in NetBIOS format (`domain\username`). In some cases, the domain associated to a user may display the full **fully qualified domain name** (**FQDN**) of the domain or, in multidomain forests, some users may show up with incorrect subdomains associated to their user.

Because user information can come from many different sources, each source may also provide the username in a different format; some may actually provide the FQDN, while others provide the NetBIOS information. To normalize all usernames, the firewall retains a domain map with each known domain's FQDN and NetBIOS information so that it is able to rewrite any usernames detected with the FQDN to the proper NetBIOS configuration. This file is written to disk, so it survives reboots and upgrades, but if the organization goes through some changes, the data may also become incorrect. Have a look at the following code snippet:

```
reaper@LABFW> show user ip-user-mapping all

IP            Vsys   From  User                IdleTimeout(s)
MaxTimeout(s)
------------- ------ ----- ---------------- -------------
-------------
192.168.27.11  vsys1  AD   pan-gurus\reaper         53582
53582
192.168.27.115 vsys1  AD   pangurus\paloalto        51566
51566
192.168.27.13  vsys1  AD   pangurus.com\servitor  51920
51920
Total: 3 users
```

A common issue is that domain names are upgraded or changed over the course of time, or domains are merged with similar NetBIOS names, as illustrated in the following code snippet:

```
reaper@LABFW> debug user-id dump domain-map

lab.pangurus.com                                        : lab
 vsys1 dc=test,dc=pangurus,dc=com
lab.pan-gurus.com                                       : lab
 vsys1 dc=test,dc=pan-gurus,dc=com
```

These can be cleared out by clearing the domain map and *refreshing* the group mapping information, as follows:

```
reaper@LABFW> debug user-id clear domain-map

reaper@LABFW> debug user-id reset group-mapping all
group mapping 'PGmapping' in vsys1 is marked for reset.
```

A second common issue is for incorrect domains to show up when the domain map is empty. The domain map is populated by information gathered through the **Lightweight Directory Access Protocol** (**LDAP**) profile configured on the firewall. If there are no domain maps configured or the existing one is incorrect, the firewall will not be able to retrieve the domains from the primary **Domain Controller**. This will result in no normalization for received usernames, and is illustrated in the following code snippet:

```
reaper@LABFW> debug user-id dump domain-map

reaper@LABFW>
```

To resolve this issue, configure an LDAP server in **Device** > **Server Profiles** > **LDAP**, as shown next:

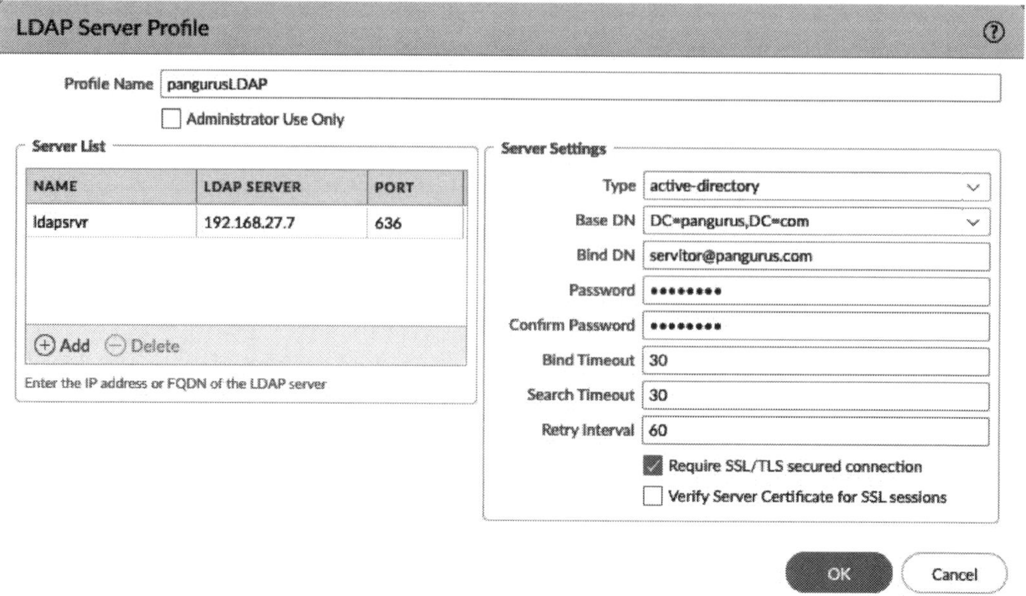

Figure 7.12 – Creating an LDAP profile

Next, create a new group mapping in **Device** > **User Identification** > **Group Mapping Settings**, as illustrated in the following screenshot:

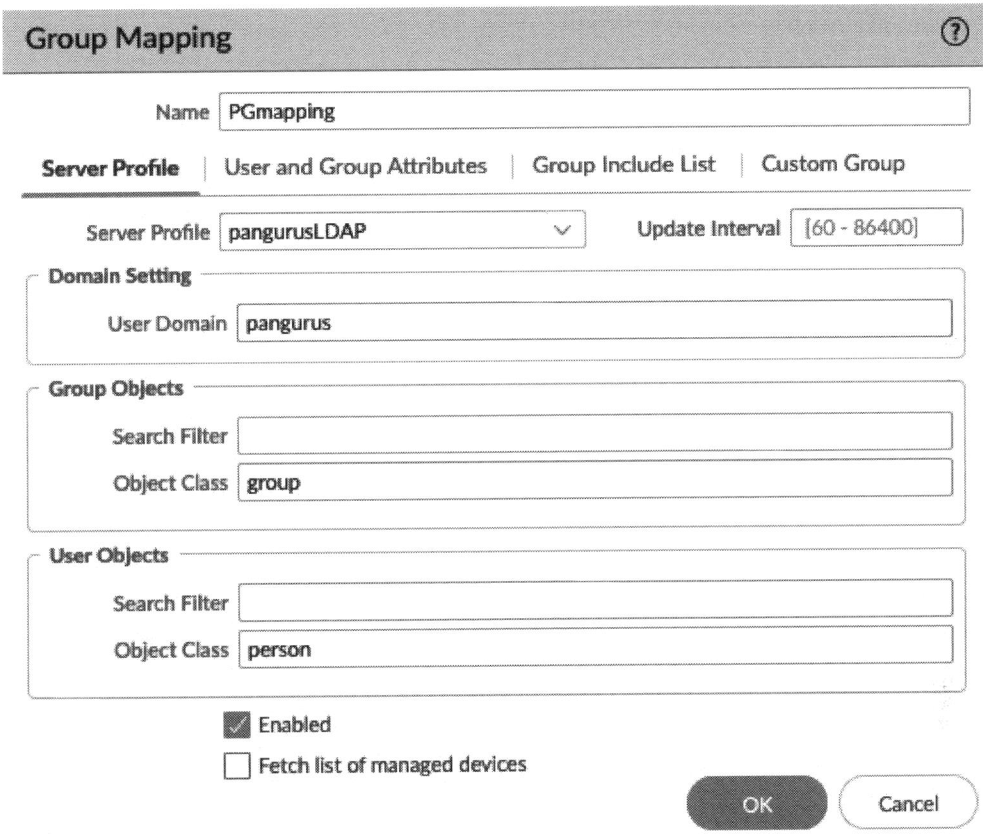

Figure 7.13 – Creating a group mapping

Commit the configuration and refresh the group mapping to make sure the information is fetched, as follows:

```
reaper@LABFW> debug user-id reset group-mapping all
group mapping 'PGmapping' in vsys1 is marked for reset.
```

Now, recheck the domain map. It should now look like this:

```
reaper@LABFW> debug user-id dump domain-map
pangurus.com                                        : pangurus
 vsys1 dc=pangurus,dc=com
```

Command-line interface (CLI) cheat sheet

To help you find the commands you need more quickly, here's a list of the most useful commands to troubleshoot User-ID issues.

To test basic connectivity, you have the following options:

- Ping a host from the management interface: `ping host x.x.x.x`.
- Ping a host from a data plane interface: `ping source a.a.a.a host x.x.x.x`.
- Trace the routing path to a host: `traceroute host x.x.x.x`.

For group mapping, you have the following options:

- **Refresh group mapping**, used to refresh group members: `debug user-id refresh group-mapping all|group-mapping-name <groupmapping profile>`.
- Forcibly **purge and refresh group** members: `debug user-id reset group-mapping all|<group mapping profile>`.
- **Display all** known user groups: `show user group list`.
- **Show all members** of a specific user group: `show user group name <group name>`.
- **Show the domain map**: `debug user-id dump domain-map`.
- **Clear the domain map**: `debug user-id clear domain-map`.
- Return more information about the **state of group mapping**: `show user group-mapping state all`.
- Information on the number of groups retrieved, the time since the last update, and the time until the next update: `show user group-mapping statistics`.
- Clear cached domain information if the mapped domain is changed: `delete user-group-cache`.

For IP user mapping, you have the following options:

- Show all/specific currently **known users**: `show user ip-user-mapping all|ip <IP>`.
- **Refresh all mappings** from a specific User-ID agent: `debug user-id refresh user-id agent <agent name>`.
- Refresh a **specific IP address**: `debug user-id refresh ip <IP>`.

- **Clear the data plane cache** of a mapped user. Add `type UIA|GP|AD` to only clear a specific set of user-IP mappings: `clear user-cache all|ip <IP>` (that is, `clear user-cache all type UIA`).
- **Clear the management plane cache** of a mapped user. Add `type UIA|GP|AD` to only clear a specific set of user-IP mappings: `clear user-cache-mp all|ip <IP>` (that is, `clear user-cache-mp ip x.x.x.x`).

For debugging, you have the following options:

- Review the **logs** of the `useridd` daemon for issues: `less mp-log useridd.log`.
- Set the **debug log level** for a specific **User-ID agent**: `debug user-id agent <UID agent name> on debug|dump|info`.
- Increase debug logging for **agentless** User-ID: `debug user-id set agent all`.
- Set the **global debug** log level: `debug user-id on debug`.
- Show the agentless **server monitoring state**: `show user server-monitor state all`.
- Show the User-ID agent's **connection state**: `show user user-id-agent state all`.
- Show the User-ID agent's **connection statistics**: `show user user-id-agent statistics`.
- Check if **clientless probing** is enabled: `debug user-id test probing`.

For power-user commands, you have the following options:

- Enable or disable if the firewall queries the User-ID agent if it receives a packet from an unmapped IP in a zone where User-ID is enabled (default on): `debug user-id query-unknown-ip off`.
- **Trigger** an agentless WMI **probe** manually: `debug user-id test probing`.

In the next section, we'll look at troubleshooting NAT.

Troubleshooting NAT

NAT is commonly applied when address space is running out or to hide internal address space. There are many ways to apply NAT, but this can bring about some challenges. In this section, we'll cover some useful commands and special use cases.

In my lab, I have set up the following NAT rules:

NAME	Original Packet						Translated Packet	
	SOURCE ZONE	DESTINATION ZONE	DESTINATION INTERFACE	SOURCE ADDRESS	DESTINATION ADDRESS	SERVICE	SOURCE TRANSLATION	DESTINATION TRANSLATION
hide-nat	trust lab	untrust	ethernet1/1	any	any	any	dynamic-ip-and-port ethernet1/1	none
inbound 1	*untrust*	*untrust*	*ethernet1/1*	*any*	*192.168.27.220*	*any*	*none*	*destination-translation* *address: 10.0.0.7*
inbound static NAT	untrust	untrust	ethernet1/1	any	198.51.100.1	any	none	destination-translation address: 10.0.0.7

Figure 7.14 – Lab NAT rules

The following command shows which NAT rules are active on the **data plane** and in which order they are installed. You will notice `inbound 1` is missing. This is because it is disabled, so it is not installed on the **data plane**:

```
reaper@LABFW> show running nat-policy

"hide-nat; index: 1" {
        nat-type ipv4;
        from [ trust lab ];
        source any;
        to untrust;
        to-interface ethernet1/1 ;
        destination any;
        service 0:any/any/any;
        translate-to "src: ethernet1/1 192.168.27.110(*)
(dynamic-ip-and-port) (pool idx: 1)";
        terminal no;
}

"inbound static NAT; index: 2" {
        nat-type ipv4;
        from untrust;
        source any;
        to untrust;
```

```
        to-interface ethernet1/1 ;
        destination 198.51.100.7;
        service 0:any/any/any;
        translate-to "dst: 10.0.0.7";
        terminal no;
}
```

From the preceding output, we can see there are two NAT rules currently active: `hide-nat` and `inbound static NAT`. `hide-nat` is an outbound rule that uses `dynamic-ip-and-port` to hide everything behind its `ethernet1/1` address, but there's a catch: next to the `192.168.27.110` IP address is an **asterisk** (`*`). This indicates the IP is **dynamic**, and the interface is set as a **Dynamic Host Configuration Protocol** (**DHCP**) client. As you can see in *Figure 7.14*, the **Source Translation** field does not have an IP assigned. This will tell the firewall to simply use the assigned IP address on the interface as the NAT source IP.

If an interface has multiple IP addresses assigned, leaving the **Source Translation** IP empty will result in the first IP in the list being used. If a different IP needs to be used, the IP must be selected from the **IP Address** dropdown. If all available IP addresses should be used, the **Address Type** field can be changed to **Translated Address** and all IPs can be added manually, as illustrated in the following screenshot:

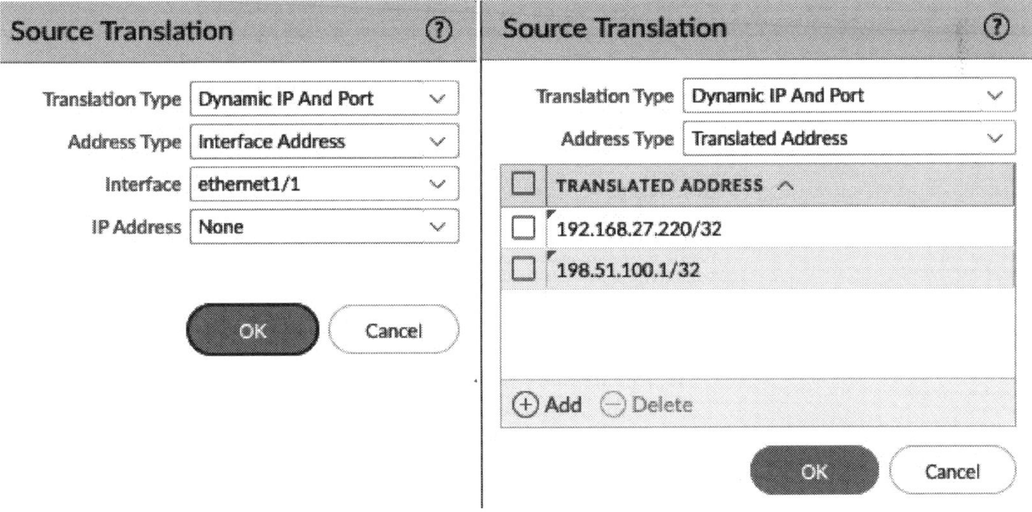

Figure 7.15 – Interface IP or address pools

If the interface is set up as a DHCP client, the NAT rule can still be configured with manually entered IP addresses. If the configured IP does not correspond with the dynamically assigned IP, outgoing sessions may fail. Check the assigned IP with one of the following commands:

```
reaper@LABFW> show dhcp client state ethernet1/1

Details:
  Interface: ethernet1/1
  State: Bound
  IP: 192.168.27.110
  Gateway: 192.168.27.1
  DHCP Server IP: 192.168.27.1
  DHCP Server ID: 192.168.27.1
  Primary DNS: 195.130.130.4
  Secondary DNS: 195.130.131.4
```

And check the interface itself, as shown here:

```
reaper@LABFW> show interface ethernet1/1

-----------------------------------------------------------------------------
------------
Name: ethernet1/1, ID: 16
Link status:
  Runtime link speed/duplex/state: 10000/full/up
  Configured link speed/duplex/state: auto/auto/auto
MAC address:
  Port MAC address 00:0c:29:ce:47:2c
Operation mode: layer3
Untagged sub-interface support: no
-----------------------------------------------------------------------------
----------------
Name: ethernet1/1, ID: 16
Operation mode: layer3
Virtual router VR1
Interface MTU 1500
```

```
Interface IP address (dynamic): 192.168.27.110/24
Interface management profile: ping
  ping: yes  telnet: no  ssh: no  http: no  https: no
  snmp: no  response-pages: no  userid-service: no
Service configured:
Zone: untrust, virtual system: vsys1
Adjust TCP MSS: no
Policing: no
```

One neat trick the firewall can perform is `Proxy-ARP`. This means IP addresses used in the NAT policy do not need to exist on any interface, and the firewall will still respond to **Address Resolution Protocol** (**ARP**) requests for these IPs.

In the output of the preceding command, `show interface ethernet1/1`, you will see that only IP address `192.168.27.110` is assigned to the interface, but an `inbound static NAT` NAT rule is set for destination IP `198.51.100.7`, as illustrated in the following code snippet:

```

"inbound static NAT; index: 2" {
        nat-type ipv4;
        from untrust;
        source any;
        to untrust;
        to-interface ethernet1/1 ;
        destination 198.51.100.7;
        service 0:any/any/any;
        translate-to "dst: 10.0.0.7";
        terminal no;
}
```

In the ARP table of a host connected to the outside, we can see the `198.51.100.7` IP is mapped to the **Media Access Control** address of `ethernet1/1`, `00:0c:29:ce:47:2c`, as shown here:

```
reaper@Comodore64:~$ ping 198.51.100.7
PING 198.51.100.7 (198.51.100.7) 56(84) bytes of data.
^X^C
--- 198.51.100.7 ping statistics ---
```

```
2 packets transmitted, 0 received, 100% packet loss, time
1030ms

reaper@Comodore64:~$ arp
Address                 HWtype  HWaddress           Flags Mask
Iface
192.168.27.110          ether   00:0c:29:ce:47:2c   C
eth0
192.168.27.1            ether   5c:35:3b:67:26:e0   C
eth0
198.51.100.7            ether   00:0c:29:ce:47:2c   C
eth0
```

This means multiple IP addresses from different subnets can exist on an interface without needing to have been configured on the interface itself, as adding it in a NAT rule will make it exist through `Proxy-ARP`. Some caveats to setting it up this way are shown here:

- IPs used only via NAT rules can't be selected in the configuration where there is a dropdown, such as `source NAT` bound to an interface.
- These IPs can't be used to respond to a system service such as `ping` through a management profile, or `GlobalProtect`, and others. So, add the IP to the data plane interface or onto a loopback interface if it needs to respond to a system service.
- This is a powerful feature but is prone to misconfiguration.

Loss of connectivity – proxy-ARP misconfiguration

Some perceived routing issues can be rooted in a NAT misconfiguration, where a NAT rule is causing ARP issues. Let's look at an example next.

If reports come in that connectivity to the internet is lost or very spotty, we can check if routing is set properly in `fib` (short for **forwarding information base**), which will tell us which routes are currently active. If multiple identical routes are configured with a different metric, `fib` will only list the route that is actually in use, as follows:

```
reaper@LABFW> show routing fib virtual-router VR1

total virtual-router shown :              1


```

```
---------------------------------------------------------
virtual-router name: VR1
interfaces:
   ethernet1/1 ethernet1/2 ethernet1/3


route table:
flags: u - up, h - host, g - gateway, e - ecmp, * - preferred
path

maximum of fib entries for device:                    5000
maximum of IPv4 fib entries for device:               5000
maximum of IPv6 fib entries for device:               5000
number of fib entries for device:                     7
maximum of fib entries for this fib:                  5000
number of fib entries for this fib:                   7
number of fib entries shown:                          7

id      destination           nexthop            flags
interface         mtu
-------------------------------------------------------------
-----------------
670     0.0.0.0/0             198.51.100.1       ug
ethernet1/1         1500
2       10.0.0.0/24           0.0.0.0            u
ethernet1/2         1500
1       10.0.0.254/32         0.0.0.0            uh
ethernet1/2         1500
4       10.10.10.0/24         0.0.0.0            u
ethernet1/3         1500
3       10.10.10.2/32         0.0.0.0            uh
ethernet1/3         1500
652     198.51.100.0/24       0.0.0.0            u
ethernet1/1         1500
651     198.51.100.254/32     0.0.0.0            uh
ethernet1/1         1500
-------------------------------------------------------------
-----------------
```

In the output, we can see `198.51.100.1` is the default route and the firewall has IP `198.51.100.254` assigned to its interface. So, the next thing we can do is ping the next hop IP, as follows:

```
reaper@LABFW> ping source 198.51.100.254 host 198.51.100.1
PING 198.51.100.1 (198.51.100.1) from 198.51.100.254 : 56(84)
bytes of data.
^C
--- 198.51.100.1 ping statistics ---
4 packets transmitted, 0 received, 100% packet loss, time
2999ms
```

We can then check if the hardware (ARP) address is known, which is not the case, as follows:

```
reaper@LABFW> show arp ethernet1/1

maximum of entries supported :        2500
default timeout:                      1800 seconds
total ARP entries in table :          0
total ARP entries shown :             0
status: s - static, c - complete, e - expiring, i - incomplete

interface         ip address        hw address          port
status   ttl
----------------------------------------------------------------
-----------------

reaper@LABFW>
```

The next step will be a physical inspection of the routing device to make sure it is still online and to try connecting to it from a different host in the network.

`ping` may behave strangely, as shown here:

```
reaper@Comodore64:~$ ping 198.51.100.1
PING 198.51.100.1 (198.51.100.1) 56(84) bytes of data.
64 bytes from 198.51.100.1: icmp_seq=1 ttl=64 time=23.8 ms
^C
--- 198.51.100.1 ping statistics ---
```

```
9 packets transmitted, 1 received, 88.8889% packet loss, time
8172ms
rtt min/avg/max/mdev = 23.798/23.798/23.798/0.000 ms
```

Upon closer inspection, the `arp` entries on the host may look similar to the table shown next, with all IP addresses in the subnet assigned to the same MAC address:

```
reaper@Comodore64:~$ arp
Address                  HWtype  HWaddress           Flags Mask
Iface
198.51.100.9             ether   00:0c:29:ce:47:2c   C
eth0
198.51.100.8             ether   00:0c:29:ce:47:2c   C
eth0
198.51.100.11            ether   00:0c:29:ce:47:2c   C
eth0
198.51.100.10            ether   00:0c:29:ce:47:2c   C
eth0
198.51.100.13            ether   00:0c:29:ce:47:2c   C
eth0
198.51.100.12            ether   00:0c:29:ce:47:2c   C
eth0
198.51.100.15            ether   00:0c:29:ce:47:2c   C
eth0
198.51.100.14            ether   00:0c:29:ce:47:2c   C
eth0
198.51.100.1             ether   00:0c:29:ce:47:2c   C
eth0
```

When we double-check the firewall interface, we can see it is the MAC address owned by the firewall that is now taking ownership of `198.51.100.1`, as illustrated in the following code snippet:

```
reaper@LABFW> show arp ethernet1/1

maximum of entries supported :      2500
default timeout:                    1800 seconds
total ARP entries in table :        0
total ARP entries shown :           0
```

```
status: s - static, c - complete, e - expiring, i - incomplete

interface          ip address        hw address          port
status   ttl
--------------------------------------------------------------------
-----------------

reaper@LABFW> show interface  ethernet1/1

--------------------------------------------------------------------
-----------------
Name: ethernet1/1, ID: 16
Link status:
  Runtime link speed/duplex/state: 10000/full/up
  Configured link speed/duplex/state: auto/auto/auto
MAC address:
  Port MAC address 00:0c:29:ce:47:2c
Operation mode: layer3
Untagged sub-interface support: no
--------------------------------------------------------------------
-----------------
Name: ethernet1/1, ID: 16
Operation mode: layer3
Virtual router VR1
Interface MTU 1500
Interface IP address: 198.51.100.254/24
Interface management profile: ping
  ping: yes  telnet: no  ssh: no  http: no  https: no
  snmp: no  response-pages: no  userid-service: no
Service configured:
Zone: untrust, virtual system: vsys1
Adjust TCP MSS: no
Policing: no
```

This behavior is caused by a misconfigured NAT rule that causes `Proxy-ARP` for the entire subnet instead of just a single IP.

As you can see in *Figure 7.16*, an administrator intended to create a NAT rule that translates `198.51.100.7` to `10.0.0.7` but added `subnetmask/24` to both the addresses. This causes the firewall to create an active NAT policy on the data plane for `198.51.100.0/25` to `10.0.0.0/24`, which causes the firewall to reply to every ARP request for the `198.51.100.0/24` subnet. The code can be seen here:

```
"inbound static NAT; index: 2" {
        nat-type ipv4;
        from any;
        source any;
        to untrust;
        to-interface  ;
        destination 198.51.100.0/24;
        service 0:any/any/any;
        translate-to "dst: 10.0.0.0-10.0.0.255";
        terminal no;
}
```

This is the rule as seen from the **graphical user interface** (**GUI**):

		Original Packet						Translated Packet	
	NAME	SOURCE ZONE	DESTINATION ZONE	DESTINATION INTERFACE	SOURCE ADDRESS	DESTINATION ADDRESS	SERVICE	SOURCE TRANSLATION	DESTINATION TRANSLATION
1	hide-nat	trust lab	untrust	ethernet1/1	any	any	any	dynamic-ip-and-port ethernet1/1	none
2	inbound static NAT	untrust	untrust	ethernet1/1	any	198.51.100.7/24	any	none	destination-translation address: 10.0.0.7/24

Figure 7.16 – Proxy-ARP subnet NAT rule

Troubleshooting destination NAT issues

The following scenario regularly causes connection issues, as NAT rules are not (yet) tweaked: a server is set in a **demilitarized zone** (**DMZ**) and a DNS record points to the public IP. Users are unable to reach the server by its FQDN but can reach it via the internal IP, as illustrated in the following diagram:

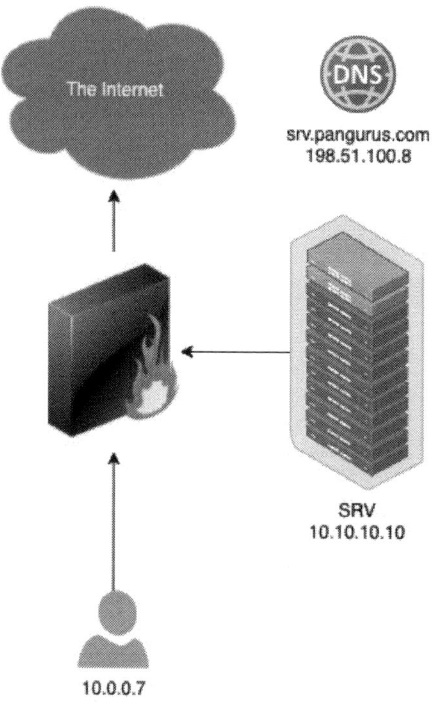

Figure 7.17 – Lab design

Depending on the way the NAT rules are sorted, different issues can arise. Just as with security rules, NAT rules are evaluated top to bottom, and the first positive hit will be applied.

Any given session can only have one NAT action applied to it, which we'll see in the following examples:

Example 1: The following NAT policy is applied on the firewall. The `hide-nat` rule is at the top when client `10.0.0.7` tries to connect to `198.51.100.8`:

```
reaper@LABFW> show running nat-policy

"hide-nat; index: 1" {
```

```
        nat-type ipv4;
        from [ trust lab ];
        source any;
        to untrust;
        to-interface ethernet1/1 ;
        destination any;
        service 0:any/any/any;
        translate-to "src: ethernet1/1 198.51.100.254 (dynamic-
ip-and-port) (pool idx: 4)";
        terminal no;
}

"labsrvr; index: 2" {
        nat-type ipv4;
        from untrust;
        source any;
        to untrust;
        to-interface ethernet1/1 ;
        destination 198.51.100.8;
        service 0:any/any/any;
        translate-to "dst: 10.10.10.10";
        terminal no;
}
```

The session is unsuccessful and the application remains undecided, as illustrated in the following code snippet:

```
reaper@LABFW> show session all filter source 10.0.0.7

--------------------------------------------------------------
-------------
ID   Application State Type Flag Src[Sport]/Zone/Proto
(translated IP[Port])
Vsys                                      Dst[Dport]/Zone
(translated IP[Port])
--------------------------------------------------------------
-------------
10600 undecided  ACTIVE FLOW NS  10.0.0.7[58431]/trust/6
```

```
(192.168.27.110[85478])
vsys1                              198.51.100.254[80]/untrust
(198.51.100.8[80])
```

Reviewing the session information will reveal that the `hide-nat` rule is hit, but the firewall will not apply the second NAT rule and the session will fail.

If we review the global counters, we see a **drop counter** for `flow_host_service_deny`, as illustrated in the following code snippet:

```
reaper@LABFW> show counter global filter delta yes packet-
filter yes

Global counters:
Elapsed time since last sampling: 7.157 seconds

name                    value rate severity category aspect
description
------------------------------------------------------------
----------------
session_allocated       5     0    info     session  resource
Sessions allocated
session_installed       5     0    info     session  resource
Sessions installed
session_discard         5     0    info     session  resource
Session set to discard by security policy check
flow_host_service_deny 5      0    drop     flow     mgmt
Device management session denied
flow_ip_cksm_sw_validation 5    0 info       flow     pktproc
Packets for which IP checksum validation was done in software
nat_dynamic_port_xlat        5    0 info       nat      resource
The total number of dynamic_ip_port NAT translate called
------------------------------------------------------------
----------------
Total counters shown: 6
------------------------------------------------------------
----------------
```

This is when the firewall receives a connection pointed at an IP address that is assigned to one of its interfaces and tries to establish a connection to a management service (such as **Secure Shell** (**SSH**), **HyperText Transfer Protocol** (**HTTP**), or **HTTP Secure** (**HTTPS**)), which is denied.

This phenomenon occurs because the outbound session is source-translated and forwarded. The forwarding stage points it back to an interface on the firewall for which it is not able to apply a NAT action. Because the NAT lookup is skipped, the firewall can only try to match the packet against a local management profile that does *not* exist, and the session is dropped.

`flow_host_service_deny` happens when the source NAT does not match the same IP address as the destination IP. In the previous example, the source NAT translated `10.0.0.7` to `198.51.100.254` and the destination IP was `198.51.100.8`. If both the source NAT and destination IP are identical, the firewall will drop the packet as a **Local Area Network Denial** (**LAND**) attack, as illustrated in the following code snippet:

```
reaper@LABFW> show counter global filter delta yes packet-
filter yes

Global counters:
Elapsed time since last sampling: 9.867 seconds

name                    value  rate severity  category  aspect
description
----------------------------------------------------------------
session_allocated           4     0  info      session   resource
Sessions allocated
session_freed               4     0  info      session   resource
Sessions freed
flow_policy_nat_land        4     0  drop      flow      session
Session setup: source NAT IP allocation result in LAND attack
nat_dynamic_port_xlat       4     0  info      nat       resource
The total number of dynamic_ip_port NAT translate called
nat_dynamic_port_release 8        0  info      nat       resource
The total number of dynamic_ip_port NAT release called
----------------------------------------------------------------
----------------
Total counters shown: 5
----------------------------------------------------------------
----------------
```

A **LAND attack** occurs when the firewall receives a packet that has the same source and destination IP.

While the ideal solution is to set an internal `DNS A` record that points internal clients to the private IP of the server, this may not always be possible. Accounting for the source and destination zone in a specific NAT rule, or as part of the inbound NAT rule by adding the trust zone, will resolve the previous issues. As illustrated in the NAT rules shown next, both `labsrvr-from-trust` and `labsrvr` are appropriate rules to allow connections from internal sources to an external IP for a DMZ resource. The rules **must** be placed above any generic outbound NAT rule:

```
reaper@LABFW> show running nat-policy

"labsrvr-from-trust; index: 1" {
        nat-type ipv4;
        from trust;
        source any;
        to untrust;
        to-interface ethernet1/1 ;
        destination 198.51.100.8;
        service 0:any/any/any;
        translate-to "dst: 10.10.10.10";
        terminal no;
}

"labsrvr; index: 2" {
        nat-type ipv4;
        from [ untrust trust ];
        source any;
        to untrust;
        to-interface ethernet1/1 ;
        destination 198.51.100.8;
        service 0:any/any/any;
        translate-to "dst: 10.10.10.10";
        terminal no;
}

"hide-nat; index: 3" {
```

```
        nat-type ipv4;
        from [ trust lab ];
        source any;
        to untrust;
        to-interface ethernet1/1 ;
        destination any;
        service 0:any/any/any;
        translate-to "src: ethernet1/1 198.51.100.8 (dynamic-
ip-and-port) (pool idx: 5)";
        terminal no;
}
```

If the server and client are in the same network, as illustrated next, this also introduces a connectivity issue if NAT is required to reach the server's public IP:

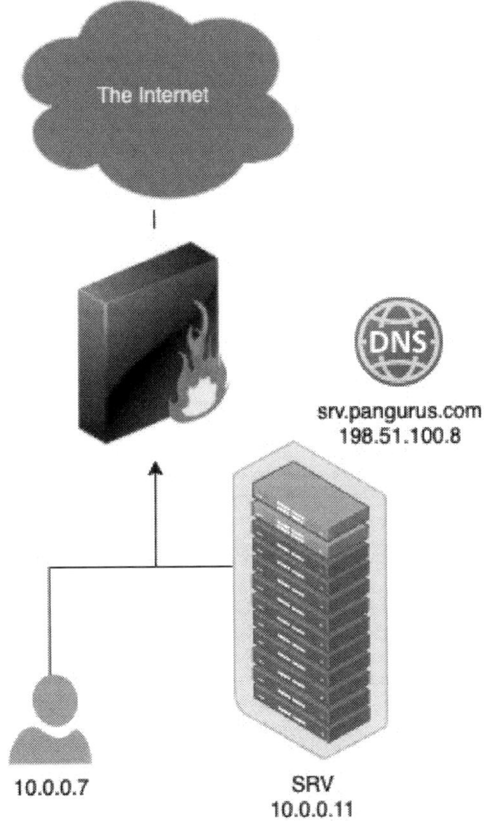

Figure 7.18 – Client and server in the same network

When the NAT rules are set up in a similar way to the previous example, destination NAT is applied to translate `198.51.100.8` to `10.0.0.11`, but the source address is not changed, as illustrated in the following code snippet:

```
reaper@LABFW> show running nat-policy

"labsrvr-from-trust; index: 1" {
        nat-type ipv4;
        from trust;
        source any;
        to untrust;
        to-interface ethernet1/1 ;
        destination 198.51.100.8;
        service 0:any/any/any;
        translate-to "dst: 10.0.0.11";
        terminal no;
}
```

Sessions will fail and the session output will show an `undecided` application, even though NAT is applied as expected, as illustrated in the following code snippet:

```
reaper@LABFW> show session all filter destination-port 80

------------------------------------------------------------
-------------
ID          Application    State   Type Flag  Src[Sport]/Zone/
Proto (translated IP[Port])
Vsys                                          Dst[Dport]/Zone
(translated IP[Port])
------------------------------------------------------------
-------------
12585        undecided        ACTIVE  FLOW  ND   10.0.0.7[53268]/
trust/6

(10.0.0.7[53268])
```

```
vsys1
198.51.100.8[80]/trust

(10.0.0.11[80])
12584        undecided      ACTIVE  FLOW  ND   10.0.0.7[53267]/
trust/6

(10.0.0.7[53267])
vsys1
198.51.100.8[80]/trust

(10.0.0.11[80])
```

The session output will look like the output shown in the following code snippet, where the `c2s` (client-to-server) packets have a count, but the `s2c` (server-to-client) packets and bytes are `0`:

```
reaper@LABFW> show session id 12585

Session            12585

        c2s flow:
                source:      10.0.0.7 [trust]
                dst:         198.51.100.8
                proto:       6
                sport:       53268            dport:      80
                state:       INIT             type:       FLOW
                src user:    unknown
                dst user:    unknown

        s2c flow:
                source:      10.0.0.11 [trust]
                dst:         10.0.0.7
                proto:       6
```

```
                sport:          80                      dport:          53268
                state:          INIT                    type:           FLOW
                src user:       unknown
                dst user:       unknown

        start time                                      : Tue Apr 27
00:05:35 2021
        timeout                                         : 5 sec
        total byte count(c2s)                           : 132
        total byte count(s2c)                           : 0
        layer7 packet count(c2s)                        : 2
        layer7 packet count(s2c)                        : 0
        vsys                                            : vsys1
        application                                     : incomplete
```

This is caused by a lack of source NAT. As you can see in *Figure 7.19*, the following happens:

1. The client will send out a **SYN packet** (where **SYN** stands for **synchronize**) to the public IP of the server via its default route: **the firewall**.
2. The firewall receives the packet and applies destination NAT, translating `198.51.100.8` to `10.0.0.11` and sending the **SYN packet** back out of the internal interface toward the server.
3. The server receives the SYN packet, but the source IP was not translated. Depending on the server, it will send a **SYN/ACK** packet (where **ACK** stands for **acknowledgment**) directly to the client, or send a **reset** (**RST**) packet because the packet was received from a different source.
4. The client will discard the **RST** packets as the source is the server private IP, for which the client has no active session. It will resend its original **SYN** packet as it has not received a valid **SYN/ACK** packet.

Eventually, the session times out, as illustrated in the following screenshot:

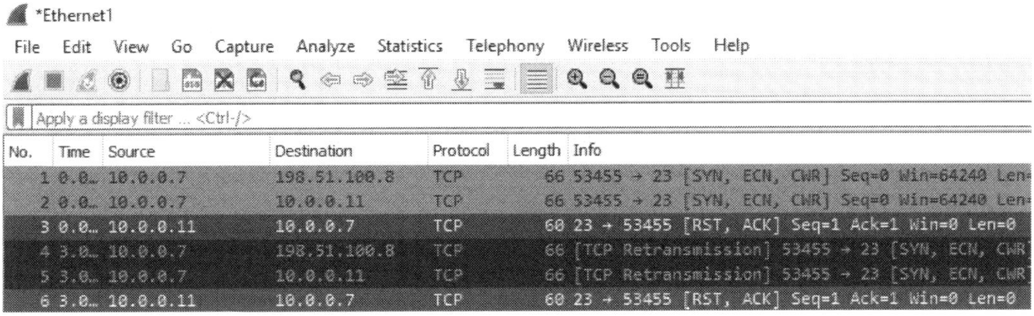

*Ethernet1

File Edit View Go Capture Analyze Statistics Telephony Wireless Tools Help

Apply a display filter ... <Ctrl-/>

No.	Time	Source	Destination	Protocol	Length	Info
1	0.0…	10.0.0.7	198.51.100.8	TCP	66	53455 → 23 [SYN, ECN, CWR] Seq=0 Win=64240 Len=
2	0.0…	10.0.0.7	10.0.0.11	TCP	66	53455 → 23 [SYN, ECN, CWR] Seq=0 Win=64240 Len=
3	0.0…	10.0.0.11	10.0.0.7	TCP	60	23 → 53455 [RST, ACK] Seq=1 Ack=1 Win=0 Len=0
4	3.0…	10.0.0.7	198.51.100.8	TCP	66	[TCP Retransmission] 53455 → 23 [SYN, ECN, CWR
5	3.0…	10.0.0.7	10.0.0.11	TCP	66	[TCP Retransmission] 53455 → 23 [SYN, ECN, CWR
6	3.0…	10.0.0.11	10.0.0.7	TCP	60	23 → 53455 [RST, ACK] Seq=1 Ack=1 Win=0 Len=0

Figure 7.19 – Asymmetric NAT flow

To correct this issue, source NAT needs to be applied as well. This causes the server to receive the SYN packet from the firewall IP. Replies go back to the firewall and are reverse NATed so that the client receives the SYN/ACK packet via the firewall from the public IP, as illustrated in *Figure 7.20*. The NAT policy will look like the one shown next:

```
reaper@LABFW> show running nat-policy

"labsrvr-from-trust; index: 1" {
        nat-type ipv4;
        from trust;
        source any;
        to untrust;
        to-interface ethernet1/1 ;
        destination 198.51.100.8;
        service 0:any/any/any;
        translate-to [ "src: ethernet1/2 10.0.0.254 (dynamic-ip-and-port) (pool idx: 2)" "dst: 10.0.0.11" ];
        terminal no;
}
```

This type of NAT is called **U-Turn** or **hairpin NAT** and is illustrated in the following diagram:

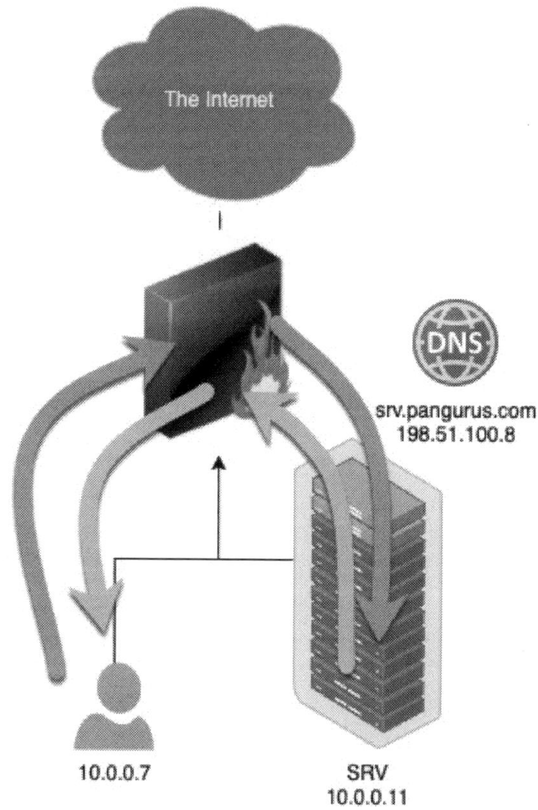

Figure 7.20 – U-Turn NAT

Outbound NAT can also cause a few challenges.

Troubleshooting source NAT

Due to the shortage of public `IPv4` addresses, most office locations will be assigned a much smaller public IP subnet by their **internet service provider** (**ISP**) than the actual number of connected devices on the internal network. To ensure all network-connected devices are able to connect out to the internet, **Hide NAT** or source NAT is applied to an outgoing connection. Source NAT masks internal IP addresses behind a single IP address or multiple public IP addresses.

There are three types of NAT that can accomplish these tasks, and each accomplishes a different task. These are listed as follows:

- **Static NAT** translates one internal IP address to one external IP address, and the same IP will always be used for the same source. Except for the source IP address, all other parameters in the original packet header, such as the source port, are unchanged.
- **Dynamic NAT** source addresses are translated behind the next available pool IP. As with static NAT, the source port is unchanged, but the pool IP may change for the same source IP. Dynamic NAT supports up to 32,000 concurrent connections per IP in the IP pool.

  The previous two types of NAT work well for small groups of internal devices, but due to the source port being reused post-NAT, conflicts may arise quickly where two different sessions try to claim the same resources. For large-scale source NAT, a third type is required, as follows:
- **Dynamic IP and Port** (**DIPP**) NAT: If multiple external IPs are available, DIPP will select an address based on a hash of the source IP, and consecutive connections will all be assigned the same IP. A random source port is assigned to all outbound connections post-NAT, which severely reduces potential conflicts. DIPP supports approximately 64,000 concurrent connections per source IP and, depending on the chassis or **virtual machine** (**VM**) size, x2, x4 or x8 oversubscription is supported, allowing even more concurrent connections.

  The command that appears in the next code block shows how the system's overall **DIPP memory pool** is doing.

  The `Dynamic IP/Port` NAT pool should not reach 100%. If the pool is getting depleted, additional IP addresses need to be added to the outbound NAT rules. You can see the code here:

```
reaper@LABFW> show running global-ippool

Idx  Type              From                          To
ToNum Ref. Cnt Mem Size Ratio Ready
---- --------------- ------------------------ ----------
----- ----- -------- -------- ----- ------
2    Dynamic IP/Port 0.0.0.0-255.255.255.255   10.0.0.254
1     0          20392      2 k0 /p1
```

```
5     Dynamic IP/Port 0.0.0.0-255.255.255.255
198.51.100.8     1     1            20392        2 k1 /p1

Usable NAT DIP/DIPP shared memory size: 34615700
Used NAT DIP/DIPP shared memory size: 40784(0.12%)
Dynamic IP NAT Pool: 0(0.00%)
Dynamic IP/Port NAT Pool: 2(0.12%)
```

Details for specific NAT rules, including the oversubscription rate, can be retrieved with the following command:

```
reaper@LABFW> show running nat-rule-ippool rule hide-nat

VSYS 1 Rule hide-nat:
Rule: hide-nat, Pool index: 5, memory usage: 20392
----------------------------------------
Oversubscription Ratio:                  2
Number of Allocates:                   941
Last Allocated Index:                58262
```

The available pool-per-NAT rule can be retrieved with the following command. The available column indicates the number of NAT sessions that are still available, accounting for the oversubscription ratio:

```
reaper@LABFW> show running ippool

VSYS 1 has 1 NAT rules, DIP and DIPP rules:
Rule                       Type            Used    Available
Mem Size Ratio
------------------------ --------------- ------- ----------
-------- -----
hide-nat                   Dynamic IP/Port 0       129024
20392    2
```

In the next and final section, we'll take a look at the BPA tool.

BPA tool

The BPA tool is a free tool made available to all customers and partners of **Palo Alto Networks** and can be run directly from the support portal at `https://support.paloaltonetworks.com`.

The BPA tool can ingest a **tech support file** (**TSF**), which contains the device configuration and device metrics, and perform an analysis against a database of best practices. The output can be used to further button down the configuration.

First, we will need to generate and collect a TSF. Go to **Device** > **Support** and click **Generate Tech Support File**, as illustrated in the following screenshot:

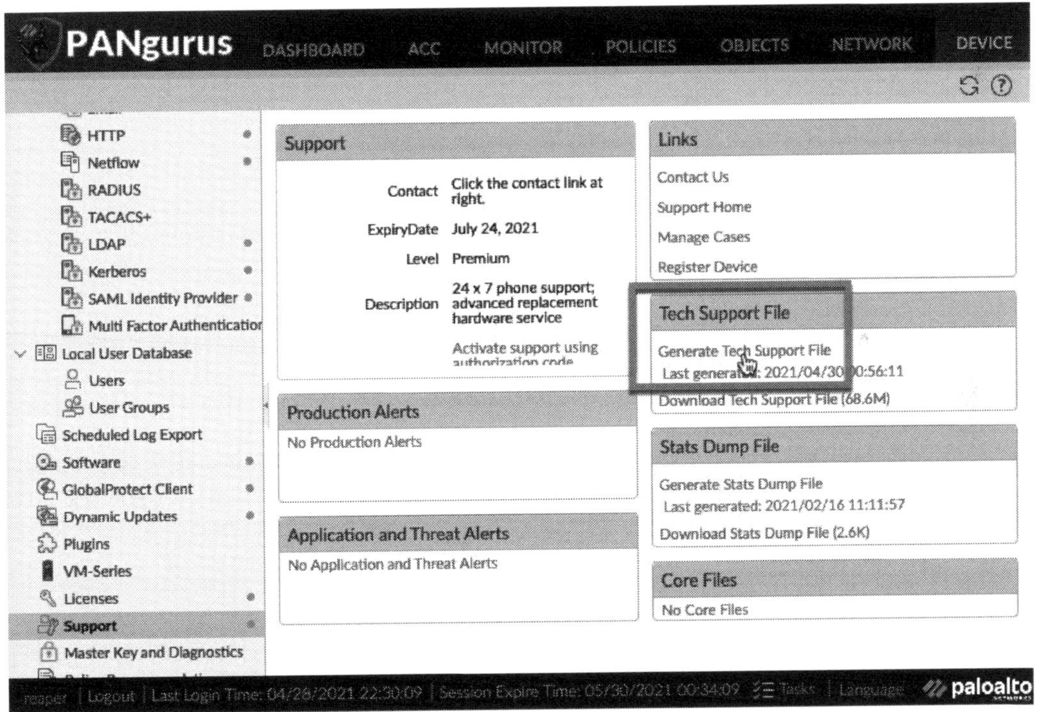

Figure 7.21 – Generating a TSF

> **Note**
> While the TSF is being generated, the web interface will be greyed out and can't be used by the admin that initiated the operation. Commit jobs, including automated content updates, are paused until the file is generated.

The file can also be exported via secure copy (`scp`) or **Trivial File Transfer Protocol** (`tftp`) via the CLI, as follows:

```
reaper@LABFW> scp export tech-support to
reaper@192.168.27.254:/tsf/
Group 'batch' suspend
Collecting command output...
configure
save config to techsupport-saved-currcfg.xml
exit
show admins all
show clock
show system software status
show jobs pending
show jobs processed
...
Finish generating tech support.
reaper@192.168.27.254's password:
PA_007051000120304_ts_100.4_20210501_0011.tar.gz
90%   61MB  60.6MB/s   00:00 ETA
reaper@LABFW>
```

When the TSF is collected, it can then be uploaded to the BPA tool.

> **Note**
>
> Sensitive data such as password hashes and certificate private keys are removed from the saved configuration files.

On the **Palo Alto Networks** support portal at `https://support.paloaltonetworks.com`, navigate to **Members** > **Manage Users** and make sure that the user account used to log in has the **BPA User** or **Super User** role, as illustrated in the following screenshot. This is required to be able to use the BPA tool, so if the account does not have at least one of the roles, reach out to the account superuser and request the role be added to your account:

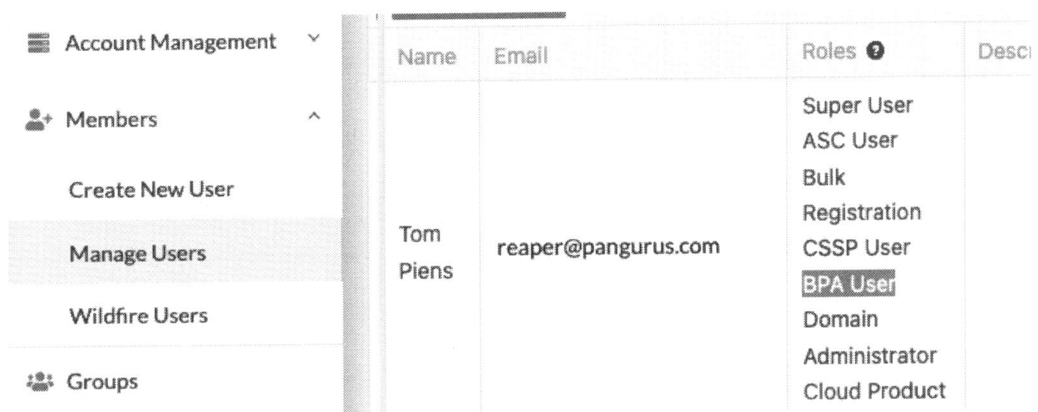

Figure 7.22 – Support portal user role

Once we have our accounts sorted, navigate to **Tools** > **Best Practice Assessment**.

If any BPAs have already been run, they will be listed on this page. Only the summary data is stored; the actual BPA file is only downloaded once when it is created, and it is not stored after that. To start a new BPA, click **Generate New BPA**, as illustrated in the following screenshot:

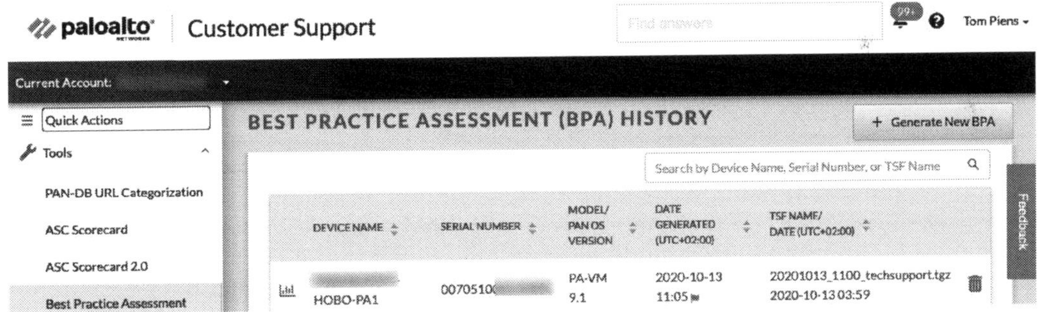

Figure 7.23 – BPA landing page

On the first page, we are prompted to upload the TSF. Once the file is uploaded, the configuration file is extracted and a list of zones is displayed. We can optionally indicate what certain zones represent by setting a classification, as illustrated in the following screenshot. This classification is used to customize recommendations in the report:

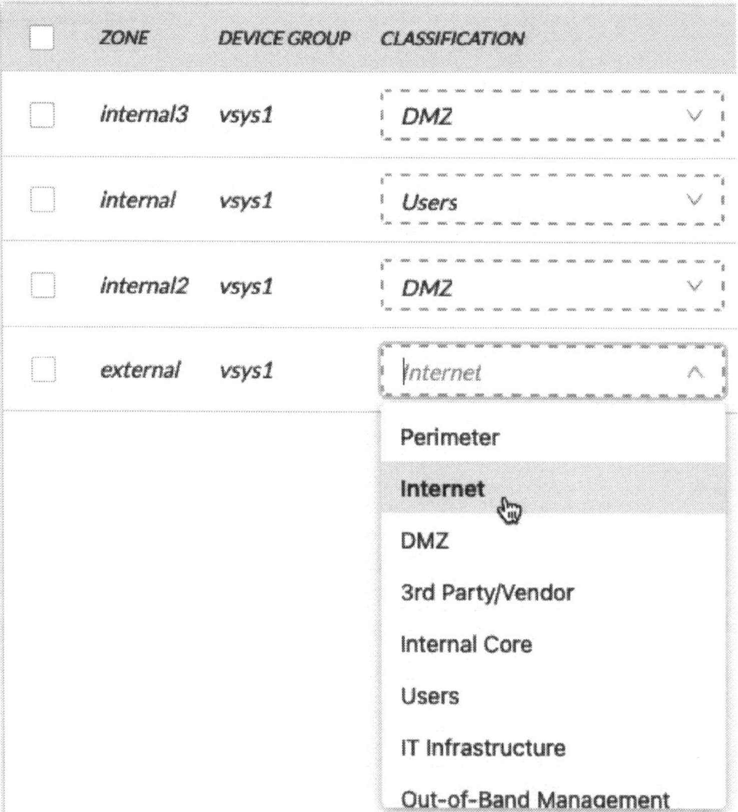

Figure 7.24 – Selecting zones in the BPA tool

Either set the classifications and click **Next** or click **Skip this step** if you do not wish to classify the zones. In the next screen, we can select an appropriate industry and then select **Generate & Download Report**, as illustrated in the following screenshot. Before starting the operation, make sure your browser is set to allow downloads from the support portal, as there will be an automatic download of the report bundle once the operation completes. If the download is blocked, the file is lost, and the BPA needs to be run again:

If you need to review or edit your Architecture Classifications, please go BACK now.

Otherwise, you are now ready to generate your Best Practice Assessment Report.

Click on "Generate & Download Report" button to view your summary and download the detailed report.

Your current industry is selected by default. To compare your BPA results against a particular industry, please make a selection from the drop down below.

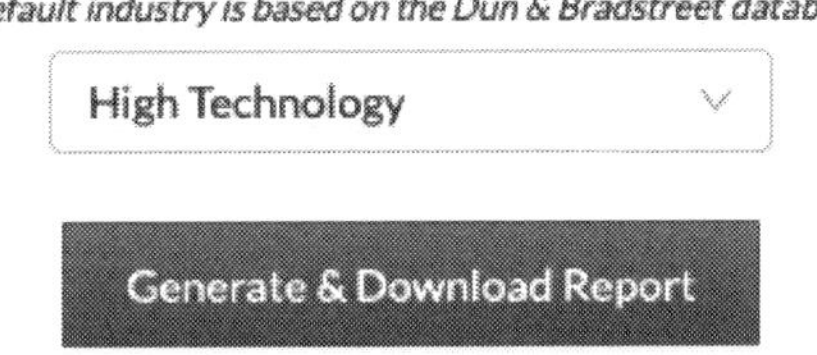

Figure 7.25 – Generating the BPA

After the report is generated, the portal will display summary information, such as overall feature adoption and security profile adoption rates compared to the industry average, as illustrated in the following screenshot:

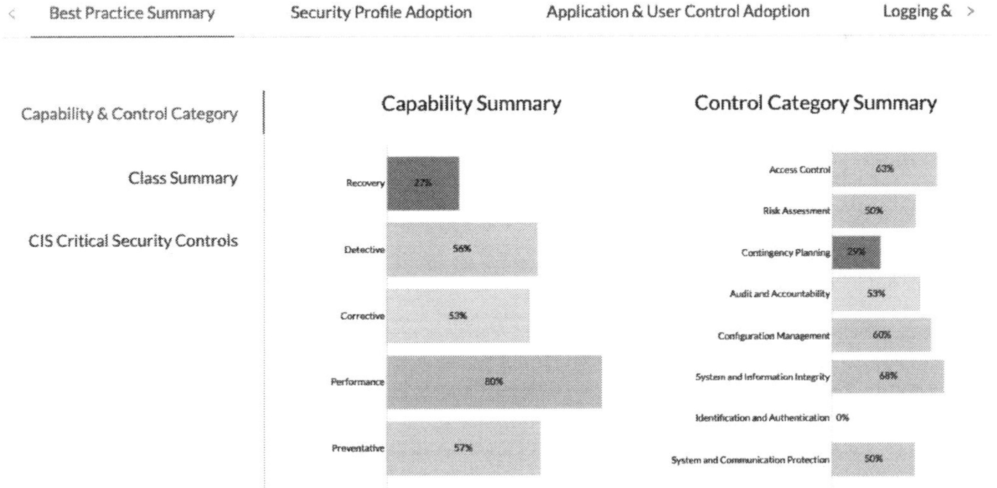

Figure 7.26 – BPA summary report

The actionable information is found in the downloaded ZIP file. There are three files, outlined as follows:

- The **BPA Executive Summary Portable Document Format** (**PDF**) file, which has the same information as the portal.
- The **Best Practices Checks** Excel file contains a spreadsheet of all the checks that require attention, sorted by the tabs in the firewall GUI, as illustrated in the following screenshot:

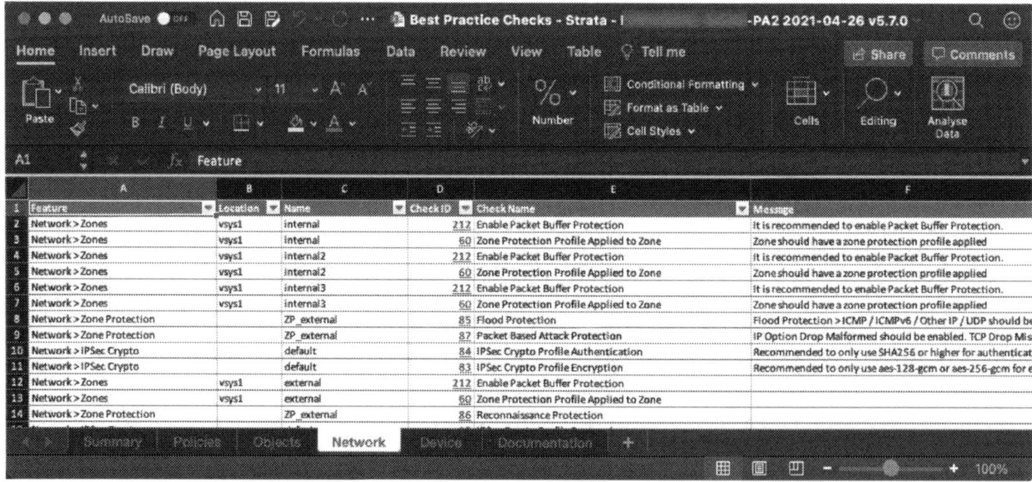

Figure 7.27 – Best Practice Checks

- The **Best Practice Assessment HyperText Markup Language** (**HTML**) file. The HTML file contains heatmaps of how well features are adopted, and the BPA and all the information needed to remedy any shortcomings or apply recommendations, as illustrated in the following screenshot:

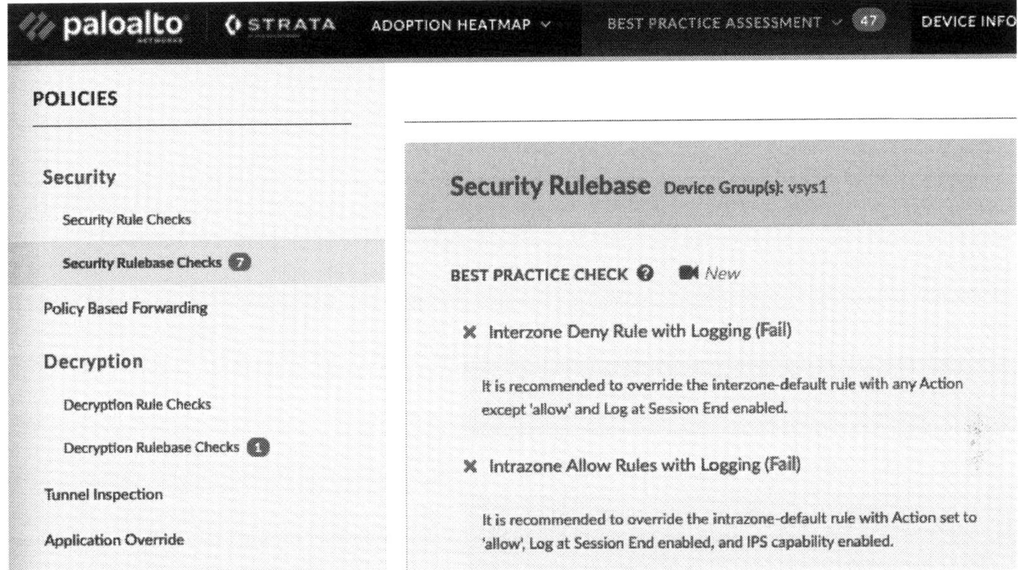

Figure 7.28 – Best Practice Assessment

Reviewing all the sections of the **Best Practice Assessment** file will help further tune the firewall configuration and find more areas where security can be tightened.

Summary

In this chapter, we learned how to troubleshoot different User-ID issues and the steps needed to verify which component or configuration might be causing an issue. We also reviewed some common NAT issues and how to quickly determine the next course of action. Lastly, the BPA tool will help you find the remaining configuration that can be geared up to improve the overall security posture of the firewall.

Other Books You May Enjoy

If you enjoyed this book, you may be interested in these other books by Packt:

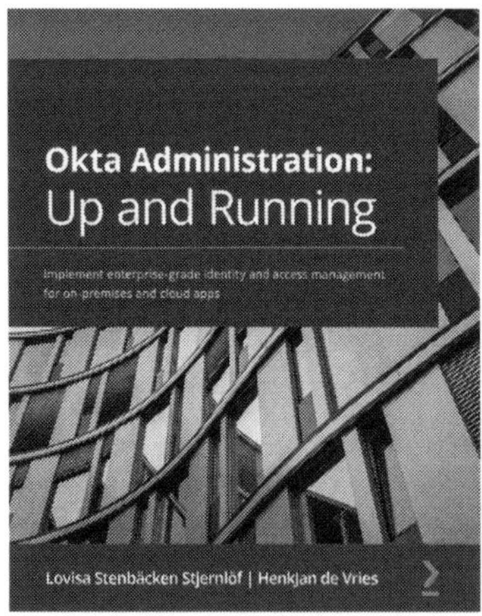

Okta Administration: Up and Running

Lovisa Stenbäcken Stjernlöf and HenkJan de Vries

ISBN: 978-1-80056-664-4

- Understand different types of users in Okta and how to place them in groups
- Set up SSO and MFA rules to secure your IT environment
- Get to grips with the basics of end-user functionality and customization
- Find out how provisioning and synchronization with applications work
- Explore API management, Access Gateway, and Advanced Server Access
- Become well-versed in the terminology used by IAM professionals

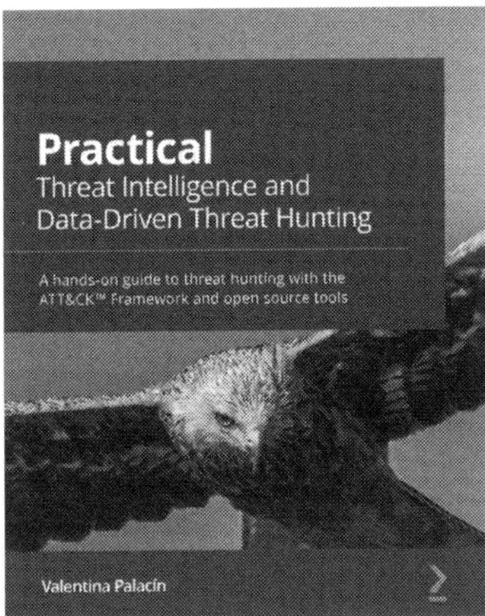

Practical Threat Intelligence and Data-Driven Threat Hunting

Valentina Palacín

ISBN: 978-1-83855-637-2

- Understand what CTI is, its key concepts, and how it is useful for preventing threats and protecting your organization
- Explore the different stages of the TH process
- Model the data collected and understand how to document the findings
- Simulate threat actor activity in a lab environment
- Use the information collected to detect breaches and validate the results of your queries
- Use documentation and strategies to communicate processes to senior management and the wider business

Packt is searching for authors like you

If you're interested in becoming an author for Packt, please visit `authors.packtpub.com` and apply today. We have worked with thousands of developers and tech professionals, just like you, to help them share their insight with the global tech community. You can make a general application, apply for a specific hot topic that we are recruiting an author for, or submit your own idea.

Leave a review - let other readers know what you think

Please share your thoughts on this book with others by leaving a review on the site that you bought it from. If you purchased the book from Amazon, please leave us an honest review on this book's Amazon page. This is vital so that other potential readers can see and use your unbiased opinion to make purchasing decisions, we can understand what our customers think about our products, and our authors can see your feedback on the title that they have worked with Packt to create. It will only take a few minutes of your time, but is valuable to other potential customers, our authors, and Packt. Thank you!

Index

T

U

V

W

Z

Printed in Poland
by Amazon Fulfillment
Poland Sp. z o.o., Wrocław

87361304R00190